RELATIONAL DATABASE THEORY

■ ■ ■ ■ ■ ■ ■ ■ ■ ■

PAOLO ATZENI
UNIVERSITY OF ROME

VALERIA De ANTONELLIS
UNIVERSITY OF MILAN

THE BENJAMIN/CUMMINGS PUBLISHING COMPANY, INC.

REDWOOD CITY, CALIFORNIA • MENLO PARK, CALIFORNIA

READING, MASSACHUSETTS • NEW YORK • DON MILLS, ONTARIO

WOKINGHAM, U.K. • AMSTERDAM • BONN • SYDNEY

SINGAPORE • TOKYO • MADRID • SAN JUAN

Sponsoring Editor: Dan Joraanstad
Production Coordinator: Alyssa Wolf
Cover Designer: Yvo Riezebos
Copyeditor: Nick Murray
Proofreader: Angela Santos

Library of Congress Cataloging-in-Publication Data

Atzeni, Paolo, 1957–
    Relational database theory / Paolo Atzeni, Valeria De Antonellis.
        p. cm.
    Includes bibliographical references and index.
    ISBN 0-8053-0249-2
1. Relational data bases. I. De Antonellis, Valeria, 1951–
II. Title.
QA76.9.D3A925 1992
005.75'6–dc20
                                                   92-30507
                                                       CIP

ISBN 0-8053-0249-2

1 2 3 4 5 6 7 8 9 10-HA-97 96 95 94 93 92

The Benjamin/Cummings Publishing Company, Inc.
390 Bridge Parkway
Redwood City, California 94065

Preface

This book presents a systematic treatment of the formal theory of the relational model of data, which is the foundation of current database management systems. It can be used as a text for a graduate course in database theory, or as an additional reference for an undergraduate course on data management. It will also be useful to researchers and professionals as a comprehensive introduction to the technical literature and its applications.

Relational database theory has been a popular subject of research for more than twenty years, since E. F. Codd published his seminal papers in the early 1970s. The subject is important for various reasons. First, results obtained in relational theory, for instance those on normal forms, are being used by practitioners in database design. Second, while many research problems have been solved, many remain open. New avenues continue to be explored, some of which have connections to current topics of investigation in other fields, such as logic programming and object-orientation. Third, the techniques used in relational database theory and explored in this book will serve any student in theoretical computer science well, as these tools can be usefully applied to various divisions of computer science.

This book presents a comprehensive treatment of the most important results in relational database theory. It is intended to serve three main purposes:

1. To present established research results in a clear way, comprehensible to both theoreticians and practitioners.

2. To introduce the reader to the relevant literature, simplifying the task by unifying notation and terminology, pointing at the most recent trends, and indicating open problems.

3. To help the reader develop skills in the proof of theorems by employing various techniques and methodologies.

Consequently, the theoretical development of the subject always involves precise notation and rigorous proofs. At the same time, theory is never discussed merely for its own sake; motivation is always present, along with practical applications of the results. Many examples and exercises are included to support the readers' exploration of the topic. Each chapter is followed by a bibliographic note that discusses the relevant literature, outlines the historical development of the topic, and points out the most important open problems. A comprehensive bibliography appears at the end of the volume.

While the book is self-contained, basic knowledge of database systems would be very useful. We recommend the use of *Fundamentals of Database Systems* by Elmasri and Navathe (The Benjamin/Cummings Publishhing Company, Inc. 1989) as a source for reference material. Similarly, knowledge of modern database design methodologies may be useful, as described in *Conceptual Database Design* by Batini, Ceri, and Navathe (The Benjamin/Cummings Publishhing Company, Inc. 1991). No specific mathematics is needed—the standard notions covered in introductory mathematics in computer science or engineering curricula are sufficient.

The book is composed of nine chapters. Chapter 1 contains the formal definition of the relational model of data, clarifying the differences between the traditional notion of relation and the notion of database relation, and previews the main topics to be dealt with in subsequent chapters. Chapters 2 through 5 deal with the most important topics in relational database theory. Chapter 2 presents a detailed treatment of query languages for the relational model, relational algebra, and various versions of relational calculus. The differences between relational calculus and first-order predicate calculus are shown, and the motivations for a tuple calculus and for versions with range declarations are discussed in depth. This chapter also covers the expressive power of these languages and their limitations.

Chapters 3 and 4 cover integrity constraints, with attention devoted mainly to functional dependencies. The implication problem is studied, first by means of inference rules, then by means of the chase procedure, and algorithms for the most important problems are shown. Multivalued, join, and inclusion dependencies are also considered. Chapter 5 deals with normal forms and decomposition of relational databases. A general framework for studying the problem is presented and motivated. Third normal form and Boyce-Codd normal are explored in depth, and design algorithms for them are presented. Other normal forms are briefly discussed.

Chapters 6 and 7 deal with the more specific topics of null values and the weak instance model, both of which have practical implications. Chapters 8 and 9 are devoted to the theoretical aspects of database systems currently under development—*next-generation database systems*. There is a great deal of significant material in this area, and the field is not yet mature enough to single out a few topics for in-depth study. For this reason, these chapters have a different style than the previous ones: rather than technical, detailed studies of the respective topics, they present tutorial introductions, with reference to the relevant literature. Chapter 8 presents extensions of the relational model considered in the systems under development. Chapter 9 describes the main features of the relationship between relational databases and first-order logic, with specific reference to deductive databases and to Datalog.

Acknowledgements

This project began as a three-person effort. Carlo Batini unfortunately had to withdraw, but his early contributions to the organization and to the drafts of some chapters are still evident. Moreover, he provided support, encouragement, and advice during the whole process.

Many people commented on draft versions, including David Embley, Richard Hull, Roger King, Dennis McLeod, Jeffrey Naughton, Riccardo Torlone, and Letizia Tanca. Many students in the database courses at Università di Roma "La Sapienza" also contributed. They include Giansalvatore Mecca, Andrea Giovannelli, Luca Menicocci, Alessandro Rossignoli, Vincenzo Sabatini, Elisabetta Spontoni, Elena Tabet, and Romano Zabini.

Paolo Atzeni would also like to thank the colleagues with whom he conducted research in database theory, particularly Stott Parker, Ed

Chan, Riccardo Torlone, Nicola Morfuni, and Cristina De Bernardis.

Many people from The Benjamin/Cummings Publishhing Company, Inc. supported the production of this book, including Alan Apt and Dan Joraanstad. Alyssa Wolf was an efficient production editor, and the copyediting by Nicholas Murray was extremely accurate.

Finally, Paolo Atzeni would like to thank his wife Gianna for her continuous support throughout the preparation of this book and his son Francesco, who provided inspiration during the final months of effort. Valeria De Antonellis would like to thank all the people that directly or indirectly contributed with their encouragement and support to the completion of this book.

Contents

Chapter 1

The Relational Model of Data

A *database* is an integrated collection of persistent data, representing the information of interest for the various programs that compose the computerized information system of an organization. A major feature of databases is that data are separated from the programs that use them: data are described autonomously, and programs make use of these descriptions. In this way, different programs may access and modify the same database and share common data, thus reducing inconsistencies and redundancies among the representations of the same data in different programs.

In order to manage databases, suitable software systems have been defined, called *database management systems (DBMSs)*, which provide a common and controlled means for accessing and modifying data, along with an integrated set of services, which include support for security, integrity, and reliability. A fundamental aspect of these systems is the data model used for the high-level (or *logical*) description of data. This model should be as independent as possible of the physical representation of data, in order to guarantee that modifications made to the physical representation do not involve modifications to the logical representation and, as a consequence, to the corresponding procedures. The separation between logical and physical aspects is often referred to as *data independence*.

The relational model of data was formulated by E. F. Codd [76] to respond to this requirement. Previous models, the hierarchical and network models, included explicit reference at the logical level to underlying physical features, such as pointers or links. Other important motivations for the relational model were, on the one hand, the desire for ease of use by nonspecialists (say, nonprogrammers) and for flexibility with respect to a wide variety of possible operations, especially queries, and, on the other hand, the availability of a formal definition to make the approach sound and precise. The relational model makes use of a single structure to organize data: a variant of the mathematical concept of n-ary relation. A database is composed of a collection of relations, and connections and relationships among data in different relations are represented just by the values of data, without any physical reference. The major reasons for the success of the relational model were the high degree of logical independence that was provided in this way and the fact that, as a complement to its mathematical definition, it allows a natural and expressive representation based on tables.

This chapter is aimed at presenting the relational model and at giving an overview of the main issues considered in the rest of the book. Specific theoretical development is deferred to subsequent chapters; here, attention is devoted to some of the problems and areas of study. Section 1.1 contains an introduction to the concept of relation in databases, showing and motivating the differences from the usual mathematical notion. Section 1.2 presents the formal definition of the relational model. Sections 1.3 and 1.4 extend and refine this definition by introducing, respectively, the notion of an integrity constraint, as a means for modeling specific aspects of the application, and some operators on relations, which form the basis for an algebra used to query databases. Section 1.5 discusses the notions of flat and nested relations, clarifying the kinds of relations usually considered in the relational model. Finally, Section 1.6 presents an introduction to normal forms, which constitute one of the most important topics in the theoretical study of databases.

1.1   Relations

The relational model successfully couples a precise mathematical definition with a useful representation based on tables. Let us begin with

book	BookCode	Author	Title	Price
	01	Dante	Inferno	20
	27	Joyce	Ulysses	30
	21	Tolstoy	War and Peace	27
	54	Greene	The Third Man	15

sale	Salesman	BookCode	Quantity
	Jones	21	80
	Smith	54	50
	Robinson	54	50
	Smith	21	100

Figure 1.1. The tabular representation of a database

the latter concept. A relational database is represented as a collection of tables. Each table is assigned a unique name in the database. A row in a table represents a relationship among sets of values. Column headings contain distinct names, and for each column there is a set of possible values, called the *domain*. Figure 1.1 shows the tabular representation of some information about books and salesmen for a publishing company. By observing the tables, we can say that each row is an ordered n-tuple of values $< d_1, d_2, \ldots, d_n >$ such that each value d_j is in the domain of the jth column, for $j = 1, 2, \ldots, n$, where n is the number of columns.

In mathematical set theory, given a sequence of sets D_1, D_2, $\ldots$, D_n, not necessarily distinct, a *relation* is a subset of the Cartesian product $D_1 \times D_2 \times \ldots \times D_n$. $D_1, D_2, \ldots, D_n$ are the *domains* of the relation; n is the *degree* of the relation. A relation is, therefore, a set of ordered n-tuples of the form $< d_1, d_2, \ldots, d_n >$ such that each value d_j is in the domain D_j, for $j = 1, 2, \ldots, n$. We can see a close correspondence with the tabular representation, the only difference being the absence of column names. The number of n-tuples in the relation is the *cardinality* of the relation. In general, if domains are infinite, the cardinality of a relation can also be infinite. Obviously, in real database applications, the cardinality of every relation is a finite number. In the following, unless otherwise stated, we will consider finite relations over infinite domains.

According to the given definition, we have the following:

1. A relation is a set of n-tuples; therefore (1) the ordering of n-tuples in the relation is immaterial and (2) the n-tuples are distinct.

2. Each n-tuple of the relation is an ordered list of values; that is, the ith value of each n-tuple is in the ith domain (and domains are not necessarily distinct). Therefore, the ordering of domains in the relation is significant.

> **Example 1.1** By means of a relation, we represent information about the school calendar for a university degree program. We call this relation *calendar*:
>
> $calendar \subseteq$ *string* × *string* × *date* × *date*
> $calendar = \{$ < Smith, Logic, 10-Jan-92, 30-May-92 >,
>   < Jones, Algebra, 20-Feb-92, 30-Jun-92 >,
>   < Robinson, Physics, 1-Sep-91, 20-Dec-91 > $\}$
>
> In the relation, the domain *date* has two distinct roles to indicate: respectively, the dates a course starts and ends. The only way to distinguish between them is the fact that they are respectively the third and fourth domains in the sequence. The same happens to the domain *string*.

As shown in Example 1.1, in order to understand the meaning of the relation correctly, one has to refer to domains by means of their position in the sequence. An alternative definition is usually adopted in order to avoid this shortcoming: it assigns *roles* to domains, for each occurrence of them in the sequence. Roles are referred to by means of symbolic names, called *attributes*, which closely correspond to the column names of the tabular representation. Formally, the association between attributes and domains is established by means of a function $dom : X \rightarrow D$, between the set of attributes $X = \{A_1, A_2, \ldots, A_n\}$ and the set of domains D. Then, a *tuple* over the set of attributes X is a function t that associates with each attribute $A_i \in X$ a value of the domain $dom(A_i)$; this value is indicated with the notation $t[A_i]$.

The notation can be extended to a set of attributes $Y \subseteq X$ and $t[Y]$ indicates the restriction of the function t to the attributes in Y.[1]

Example 1.2   Let us consider the data in Example 1.1. We can introduce the following attributes:

Professor	with *dom(Professor)*	= *string*
Course	with *dom(Course)*	= *string*
Beginning	with *dom(Beginning)*	= *date*
End	with *dom(End)*	= *date*

The tuple $<$ Smith, Logic, 10-Jan-92, 30-May-92 $>$ can be described by means of the function t such that $t[Professor]$ = Smith, $t[Course]$ = Logic, $t[Beginning]$ = 10-Jan-92, $t[End]$ = 30-May-92.

As suggested by the examples, a relation can be seen as the representation of the information currently available on the application of interest. Since it is possible that not all aspects of the application to be represented in the database are known, it is reasonable to admit that a relation contains values not specified at the moment. To take this into account, we can extend the domains of relations by adding the so-called *null value*, which represents the absence of information: it is indicated by the symbol $\perp$. In Chapters 2–5 we assume our relations to be free of nulls; we will deal with the problems of null values in Chapter 6.

Coming back to the tabular representation of relations, now we can properly state that a relation can be represented in a natural way by means of a table in which every row corresponds to a tuple, and every column contains values of an attribute of the relation (see Figure 1.2). It is important to clarify that a relation is the formal description of a correspondence among elements of sets, whereas a table is only a possible representation of the relation itself. By observing a relation represented by means of a table, we can state the following:

---

[1] There is an incoherence in notation here: if A is an attribute, then $t[A]$ is a value; at the same time, if X is an attribute, then $t[X]$ is a tuple, that is, a function. Also, as we will see, singleton sets of attributes are often denoted by the name of the involved attribute; therefore, if $X = A$, then $t[A]$ is both a value and a tuple. This ambiguity is often irrelevant, and we will clarify the meaning of the notation in all significant cases.

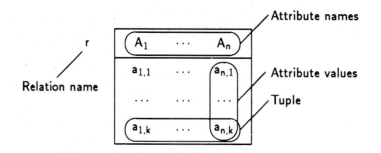

Figure 1.2. **Attributes, tuples, and values**

- The values of each column are homogeneous: the values of an attribute belong to the same domain (integers, strings, etc.).

- The rows are different with respect to one another: a relation is a set, and therefore it never contains identical tuples.

- The order of the columns is irrelevant, since they are always identified by name and not by position.

- The order of the rows is irrelevant, since they are identified by content and not by position.

1.2   Formal Definition of the Relational Model

A data model is a formal tool for describing information of interest for an application. There are two possible description levels:

1. The *intensional level*, involving the general properties of classes of values and classes of correspondences among them

2. The *extensional level*, involving the actual values and the correspondences between them

In the relational model the intensional level corresponds to the time invariant description of relations *(schemes)* and the extensional level to the contents of relations *(instances)* at a particular moment. Precise definitions follow.

1. *Relation scheme*: a name (*relation name*) together with a set of distinct attribute names. To indicate a relation scheme with name R and attributes $A_1, A_2, \ldots, A_n$, we write $R(A_1 A_2 \ldots A_n)$. We use names with capital letters to indicate relation schemes. *Database scheme*: a set of relation schemes with distinct relation names, denoted by **R**.

2. *Relation instance* (or simply *relation*), defined on a scheme $R(X)$: finite set r of tuples over X. Whenever possible, we use for relations the same names as the corresponding schemes, but with lowercase letters.
   Database instance (or simply *database*), on a database scheme $\mathbf{R} = \{R_1(X_1), R_2(X_2), \ldots, R_n(X_n)\}$: a set of relations $\{r_1, r_2, \ldots, r_n\}$, where each r_i is defined on the corresponding scheme R_i.[2]

   Example 1.3   Let us consider the information on books and salesmen in Figure 1.1. The database scheme contains two relation schemes:

   $$BOOK\ (BookCode, Author, Title, Price)$$
   $$SALE\ (Salesman, BookCode, Quantity)$$

   The relation instances shown in Figure 1.1 are

   $$book = \{t_1, t_2, t_3, t_4\}$$
   $$sale = \{t_5, t_6, t_7, t_8\}$$

   where $t_1[BookCode] = 01$, $t_1[Author] = $ Dante, $t_1[Title] = $ Inferno, $t_1[Price] = 20$, and so on.

For the sake of readability, we will usually represent relations by means of tables, adopting the formal notation only with respect to individual values. In the figures, to indicate that a set of relations forms a database instance, we will often include the various tables in a rectangle, as in Figure 1.3.

In many cases we will refer to abstract schemes and instances, using some notational standards that are common in the scientific literature of the field. Individual attributes will be denoted by capital

---

[2] More precisely (but with less clarity), a database could be defined as a mapping that associates a relation r on $R(X)$ with each relation scheme $R(X)$ in the database scheme.

book	BookCode	Author	Title	Price
	01	Dante	Inferno	20
	27	Joyce	Ulysses	30
	21	Tolstoy	War and Peace	27
	54	Greene	The Third Man	15

sale	Salesman	BookCode	Quantity
	Jones	21	80
	Smith	54	50
	Robinson	54	50
	Smith	21	100

Figure 1.3. A database instance

letters from the beginning of the alphabet, possibly with subscripts and primes $(A, B, \ldots, A_1, A', \ldots)$; sets of attributes will be denoted by letters from the end of the alphabet $X, X_1, X', Y, \ldots$, or by juxtaposition of the names of the involved attributes (e.g., $X = A_1 A_2 \ldots A_k$); also, the union of sets of attributes will be denoted by the juxtaposition of the names of the sets or of the single attributes (so, XA will stand for $X \cup \{A\}$). For relation names, we will use the capital letters R and S, again with subscripts and primes. For relation instances, we will use the same names as for the respective schemes, but in lower case (so, r_k will be a relation over the scheme with name R_k); sometimes (e.g., in the results of the algebraic operations; see Section 1.4), we may omit relation names, and write something like $r(X)$ to say that relation r is defined over the attributes X. Finally, database schemes will be denoted by boldface letters ($\mathbf{R}, \mathbf{R}_1$, etc.).

1.3   Integrity Constraints

We have stated that relations can be used to model available knowledge about an application of interest. In many cases, however, it is not true that *any* finite set of tuples can be an acceptable relation, from the viewpoint of its interpretation, even if the tuples have the

enrollment	Student	Student#	Age
	Smith	8456	20
	Jones	7689	250
	Robinson	7689	23

Figure 1.4. A relation with impossible values

right degree and the component values belong to the domains of the respective attributes.

> **Example 1.4**   Consider the relation in Figure 1.4, which refers to information about students in a university. Here, it is clearly unreasonable to have a student who is 250 years old; also, in all universities, the Student Number is a unique identifier for each student, and it is therefore impossible to have two students with the same value for the attribute *Student#*.

Therefore, modeling the application also means pointing out the properties that must be respected by the tuples in the database, so that they can give rise to correct interpretations. Hence, the concept of *integrity constraint* is introduced to model the properties that must be satisfied by all the instances of a relational scheme. We will deal with constraints extensively in Chapters 3 and 4. In this chapter we introduce two important classes of constraints: this section introduces the notion of a *key*; in Section 1.5, we define *functional dependencies*.

A subset K of the attributes of a relation r is a *key* of r if it has the following properties:

- *Unique identification:* r does not contain two distinct tuples t_1, t_2 that agree on all the attributes in K ($t_1[K] = t_2[K]$);

- *Minimality:* no proper subset of K enjoys the unique identification property.

A set K that enjoys the unique identification property is called a *superkey*, since it is a superset of a key, not necessarily proper; clearly, each key is also a superkey. Since relations are sets, no relation

students

SSN	LastName	BirthDate	Student#	Program
734-59-8589	Smith	5-Jun-1962	5497	Computer Sc.
834-04-6587	Jones	3-Apr-1970	8970	Mathematics
746-20-6775	White	30-Nov-1965	9999	Computer Sc.
580-74-3490	Black	28-Jul-1970	1020	Physics
853-34-0076	Smith	15-Jun-1961	4850	Chemistry

Figure 1.5. A relation with various keys

contains two identical tuples; thus, for each relation, the set of all its attributes is a superkey. Therefore, each relation has at least one key.

In this way, we have defined the notion of key with respect to instances of relations. The concept is even more important at the level of relation schemes. In fact, a key constitutes the assertion of a property that must be valid for all acceptable (with respect to the application of interest) instances of a relation scheme: it is an integrity constraint on the relation scheme.

Example 1.5   Suppose we want to handle data about students; for each of them, we are interested in Social Security Number (SSN), last name, date of birth, Student Number, and program. Therefore, we use a relation whose scheme has the name *STU-DENTS*, and the attributes *SSN, LastName, BirthDate, Student#, Program*. Clearly, since no pair of students has identical SSNs or Student Numbers, both *SSN* and *Student#* are superkeys for every acceptable relation over this scheme and are therefore considered as superkeys for the scheme itself. Also, if we assume that no pair of students with the same name was born on the same day, we have that the set of attributes {*LastName, BirthDate*} is also a superkey for the scheme. Also, all of them are minimal and there-fore are indeed keys. For the first two, the fact is trivial; as regards {*LastName, BirthDate*}, it follows from the fact that neither names nor birthdates are unique. An example relation over this scheme is shown in Figure 1.5. Note that in the figure, the attribute *Birth-Date* also allows a unique identification of the tuples in the relation; however, this is just coincidental, since it need not happen for all the relations over the scheme.

students

SSN	LastName	BirthDate	Student#	Program
⊥	Jones	⊥	⊥	Mathematics
7462075	White	30-Nov-1955	⊥	Computer Sc.

students

SSN	LastName	BirthDate	Student#	Program
⊥	Smith	05-Jun-1952	5497	Computer Sc.
7462075	Smith	⊥	⊥	Computer Sc.

Figure 1.6. Relations with null values for the keys

If null values are allowed, then the definition of unique identification is relaxed and refers only to tuples that have no null values on the involved set of attributes. Therefore, no restriction is imposed on the tuples that have null values in the key. This can lead to some undesirable situations.

> **Example 1.6**   Consider the scheme in Example 1.5 and the first relation in Figure 1.6. Here, the first tuple has null values on each key, and it is therefore impossible to identify it in any way.[3] If we want to add to the relation another tuple with *LastName* equal to Jones, we do not know whether it refers to the same student or to another one. A similar problem arises in the second relation in Figure 1.6: even if each tuple has a non-null value on at least one key, we do not know whether the two tuples refer to the same student or to two different students.

Example 1.6 suggests that some restrictions should be put on the possible appearance of null values in the keys. The easiest solution that allows unique identification of each tuple in the relation is the following: select one of the keys of the relation (call it the *primary key*), and require that each tuple be null-free on the attributes of the primary key. The existence of a null-free primary key is important

---

[3] As we said in Section 1.1, no order is defined among the tuples in a relation; however, for the sake of simplicity, we will often refer to tuples by means of their positions in the tabular representations.

students

SSN	LastName	BirthDate	Student#	Program
$\perp$	Jones	$\perp$	7432	Mathematics
$\perp$	Jones	$\perp$	4321	Computer Sc.
7462075	White	30-Nov-1955	9305	Computer Sc.

Figure 1.7. A relation with a (null-free) primary key

because it guarantees that all values in the database can be accessed: each value is uniquely identified by means of a relation name, a primary key value, and an attribute name. In most of this book, the notion of a primary key will not be relevant, since we will often assume relations to be null-free. Whenever it is necessary, we will indicate the primary key of a relation scheme by underlining the attributes that compose it.

> **Example 1.7**   In the *STUDENTS* relation scheme, it is reasonable to require that *Student#* be the primary key. Therefore, the relations in Figures 1.6 are not allowed, whereas the relation in Figure 1.7 is allowed (as well as the relation in Figure 1.5, which contains no null values).

Before concluding the section, we introduce a notion related to that of keys that has practical importance, even if it does not allow a formal treatment. A subset X of the attributes of a relation r_1 is a *foreign key* of r_1 if the values of the tuples of r_1 on X are values of the primary key of some other relation r_2. Foreign keys provide a means of relating tuples of distinct relations.

> **Example 1.8**   Consider the scheme of the database in Example 1.3. Primary keys of the relation schemes *BOOK* and *SALE* are, respectively, *BookCode* and {*Salesman, BookCode*}. In the *SALE* relation, *BookCode* is a foreign key since its values are values of the primary key of the *BOOK* relation. For a given value of *BookCode* in the *sale* relation, it is possible to consult the *book* relation to find information associated with that value.

1.4   Query Languages

As relational databases are used to represent information for applications of interest that must retrieve and modify relevant data, it follows that languages for queries and updates are integral components of the relational model. Updates can be seen as functions from the set of database states to itself, and queries as functions from the set of states to the space of relations over all possible schemes. Several issues are therefore common to the two families of languages. More attention has been devoted in the literature to query languages than to update languages. We will follow this trend by devoting Chapter 2 to query languages and just referring to updates in the References. In this section, we present a few operators, required in subsequent discussions, that are included in the family of operators of *relational algebra*, one of the fundamental query languages for relational databases. In order to allow for composition, all the operators produce relations as results.

Selection

The *selection* operator is a unary operator on relations, defined with respect to propositional formulas. Let r be a relation over the set of attributes X; a *propositional formula F* over X is defined recursively from atoms and connectives, as follows. *Atoms* over X have the form $A_1 \theta A_2$ or $A_1 \theta a$, where $A_1, A_2 \in X$, a is a constant, and θ is one of the comparison operators: $=, \neq, <, >, \leq, \geq$.[4] Every atom over X is a propositional formula over X; if F_1, F_2 are propositional formulas over X, then $\neg(F_1)$, $F_1 \wedge F_2$, $F_1 \vee F_2$ are formulas over X. Parentheses may be used as needed. Nothing else is a formula. A propositional formula over X can be seen as a function that associates a Boolean value with each tuple. An atom $A_1 \theta A_2$ ($A_1 \theta a$) has the value *true* over a tuple t if the comparison θ holds between the values $t[A_1]$ and $t[A_2]$ ($t[A_1]$ and a) and *false* otherwise. A formula $\neg(F_1)$ is *true* on t if and only if F_1 is false on t; $F_1 \wedge F_2$ is *true* on t if and only if both F_1 and

---

[4]The operators $<, >, \leq, \geq$ require that the involved domains be ordered, a reasonable assumption for all practical applications.

$\sigma_{\text{Quantity} > 70}(\text{sale})$

Salesman	BookCode	Quantity
Jones	21	80
Smith	21	100

Figure 1.8. A selection

F_2 are true on t; $F_1 \vee F_2$ is *true* on t if and only if at least one of F_1 and F_2 is true on t. Then, given a relation $r(X)$ and a propositional formula F over X, the *selection* of r with respect to F, denoted by $\sigma_F(r)$, is a relation over X again, containing the tuples of r that make F true:

$$\sigma_F(r) = \{t \in r \mid F(t) = true\}$$

Figure 1.8 shows an example of selection on the *sale* relation in Figure 1.1.

Projection

Given a relation $r(X)$ and a subset Y of X, the *projection* of r onto Y, denoted by $\pi_Y(r)$, is a relation on the attributes in Y consisting of the restriction of the tuples of r to the attributes in Y:

$$\pi_Y(r) = \{t[Y] \mid t \in r\}$$

Figure 1.9 shows an example of projection on the *sale* relation in Figure 1.1.

Projection is in some sense orthogonal to selection: the former considers all tuples of the operand[5] on a subset of the attributes, whereas the latter considers a subset of the tuples of the operand on all the attributes. Therefore, we also say that by means of projections

---

[5] However, the result of the operation need not contain as many tuples as the operand, since some of them may make identical contributions; as an example, the second and third tuples in the *sale* relation in Figure 1.1 have the same values on both *BookCode* and *Quantity*, and therefore contribute to the same tuple in the projection.

$\pi_{\text{BookCode, Quantity}}(\text{sale})$

BookCode	Quantity
21	80
54	50
21	100

Figure 1.9. A projection

we perform *vertical decompositions*, whereas by means of selections we perform *horizontal decompositions*.

Natural Join

Let $r_1(YX)$ and $r_2(XZ)$ be two relations, such that $YX \cap XZ = X$. The *natural join* of r_1 and r_2, denoted by $r_1 \bowtie r_2$, is a relation on YXZ consisting of all the tuples (on YXZ) resulting from concatenation of tuples in r_1 with tuples in r_2 that have identical values for the attributes X:

$$r_1 \bowtie r_2 = \{t \text{ over } YXZ \mid \text{ there exist } t_1 \in r_1, \ t_2 \in r_2 \text{ such that}$$
$$t[XY] = t_1[XY] \text{ and } t[XZ] = t_2[XZ]\}$$

We say that two tuples $t_1 \in r_1$, $t_2 \in r_2$ are *joinable* if they contribute to the join, and therefore $t_1[X] = t_2[X]$. If a tuple does not contribute to the join, then we say that it is *dangling*. If neither relation contains dangling tuples, we say that they have a *complete join* (or that they *join completely*).

> **Example 1.9**   The join of the relations *sale* and *book* in Figure 1.1 is shown in Figure 1.10. Clearly, the last tuple in the relation *book* is joinable with the second tuple in the relation *sale*; the first two tuples in the relation *book* are dangling.

Interestingly, the above definition is meaningful even if X is the empty set; that is, the two relations have no common attributes. In this case, for every $t_1 \in r_1$ and $t_2 \in r_2$, t_1 and t_2 are joinable, and therefore $r_1 \bowtie r_2$ contains a tuple for each such pair of tuples t_1 and t_2.

book ⋈ sale

BookCode	Author	Title	Price	Salesman	Qty
21	Tolstoy	War and Peace	27	Jones	80
54	Greene	The Third Man	15	Smith	50
54	Greene	The Third Man	15	Robinson	50
21	Tolstoy	War and Peace	27	Smith	100

Figure 1.10. A natural join

For this reason we say that if r_1 and r_2 have no common attributes, then their join is a *Cartesian product*. Note that the Cartesian product as we have defined it here differs from the Cartesian product in set theory: the reason is that we want the result to be a relation (see Exercise 1.7).

Two general comments are useful here. First, it follows from the definitions that a join is in some sense the inverse of a projection: the latter generates vertical decompositions, whereas the former generates vertical compositions. At the end of this section, after introducing the notion of *expression*, we will clarify the relationship between these two operators.

The second, more general point is that in the relational model, all the information is represented by means of values—there are neither explicit references nor pointers. As a consequence, relationships between two relations are represented by means of the presence of identical values in the two relations. The natural join is the fundamental operator that correlates data in different relations.

Expressions

Since all the operators produce relations as their results, it is possible to compose their applications (provided that the intermediate results respect the definitions of the operators applied to them) and thus obtain expressions with unrestricted depth. Using again the relations in Figure 1.1, the following is an example of an expression (its result

$$\pi_{\text{Salesman, Title}}(\text{book} \bowtie \sigma_{\text{Quantity} > 70}(\text{sale}))$$

Title	Salesman
War and Peace	Jones
War and Peace	Smith

Figure 1.11. The result of an expression

is shown in Figure 1.11):

$$\pi_{Salesman,Title}(book \bowtie \sigma_{Quantity>70}(sale))$$

As we said, relational algebra is a query language, that is, a language that allows us to express functions from the set of database states to the set of relations. Therefore, the operands in the expressions should be considered as variables, and we will indicate them by means of the names of the relation schemes (with capital letters). Therefore, given the database scheme in Example 1.3, if we want to represent a query, we write the expression above as

$$\pi_{Salesman,Title}(BOOK \bowtie \sigma_{Quantity>70}(SALE))$$

It is also reasonable to include in the expressions constant relations: relations whose value is fixed and that do not belong to the database state. Therefore, queries are formulated in relational algebra by means of expressions that involve both relation names (to denote variables) and constant relations. Given the relation c in Figure 1.12, the following expression could be used to produce a list of books in which each is considered expensive if it costs more than $20 and cheap otherwise:

$$\pi_{Title,Category}(\sigma_{(Price>20 \wedge Cat='expensive') \vee (Price \leq 20 \wedge Cat='cheap')}(BOOK \bowtie c))$$

Its result, with respect to the database in Figure 1.1, is also shown in Figure 1.12.

Other operators of the relational algebra as well as other languages with a more declarative basis will be presented and discussed in Chapter 2.

c	Category
	cheap
	expensive

Title	Category
Inferno	cheap
Ulysses	expensive
War and Peace	expensive
The Third Man	cheap

Figure 1.12. A constant relation and the result of an expression involving it

Expressions Involving Join and Projection

Join and projection are the most typical relational operators. A number of interesting properties may be stated about expressions that involve them.

First of all, the join operator is commutative and associative (see Exercise 1.6). In fact, for every r_1, r_2, r_3, it is the case that

- $r_1 \bowtie r_2 = r_2 \bowtie r_1$

- $(r_1 \bowtie r_2) \bowtie r_3 = r_1 \bowtie (r_2 \bowtie r_3)$

It is therefore possible to write sequences of joins without parentheses,

$$r_1 \bowtie r_2 \bowtie \ldots \bowtie r_m$$

denoted in short form by $\bowtie_{i=1}^{m} r_i$. In this way, the join can be considered as an n-ary operator for every $n \geq 1$. Given $r_1(X_1)$, $\ldots$, $r_n(X_n)$,

$$\bowtie_{i=1}^{m} r_i = \{t \text{ over } X_1 \ldots X_n \mid \text{there exist } t_1 \in r_1, \ldots, t_n \in r_n$$
$$\text{such that } t[X_i] = t_i[X_i], \text{ for } i = 1, 2, \ldots, n\}$$

The other properties we want to state clarify the intuitive fact that projection is a sort of inverse of join, and vice versa. We present an example first.

> **Example 1.10**   If we project the relation in Figure 1.10 over the attributes *Salesman*, *BookCode*, *Quantity*, then we obtain the original *sale* relation. On the other hand, if we project the same

relation over the attributes *BookCode, Author, Title, Price*, then we obtain a subset of the original *book* relation that does not contain the dangling tuples.

The next lemma shows that the cases in the example correspond to general properties.

LEMMA 1.1   Let $r_1(X_1)$, $r_2(X_2)$, $\ldots$, $r_m(X_m)$ be relations.

1. $\pi_{X_i}(\bowtie_{j=1}^m r_j) \subseteq r_i$, for $i = 1, 2, \ldots, m$.

2. $\pi_{X_i}(\bowtie_{j=1}^m r_j) = r_i$, for $i = 1, 2, \ldots, m$, if and only if $r_1, r_2, \ldots, r_m$ have a complete join.

3. $\pi_{X_i}(\bowtie_{k=1}^m (\pi_{X_k}(\bowtie_{j=1}^m r_j))) = \pi_{X_i}(\bowtie_{j=1}^m r_j)$, for $i = 1, 2, \ldots, m$.   □

Claim 1 in the lemma states that the operator that joins m relations and then projects the result over the schemes of the operands produces a set of m relations, each of which is contained in the corresponding operand. Claim 3 states that this operator is *idempotent*—if it is applied several times, then the result is the same as that of a single application.

Somehow dual results hold for expressions that perform projections and then rejoin the intermediate results.

LEMMA 1.2   Let $r(X)$ be a relation and $X_1, X_2, \ldots, X_m$ be sets of attributes whose union equals X.

1. $\bowtie_{j=1}^m (\pi_{X_j}(r)) \supseteq r$

2. $\bowtie_{k=1}^m (\pi_{X_k}(\bowtie_{j=1}^m (\pi_{X_j}(r)))) = \bowtie_{j=1}^m (\pi_{X_j}(r))$ □

There is also a dual notion to that of a complete join: r has a *lossless decomposition* with respect to $X_1, X_2, \ldots, X_m$ if $\bowtie_{j=1}^m (\pi_{X_j}(r)) = r$, that is, if r can be exactly reconstructed from its projections. Figures 1.13 and 1.14 respectively show a lossless and a nonlossless (or *lossy*) decomposition.

r	House	Area	Keeper	Head
	fence	West	Tom	White
	lair	East	Bob	White

$\pi_{\text{House, Keeper, Head}}(r)$

House	Keeper	Head
fence	Tom	White
lair	Bob	White

$\pi_{\text{House, Area}}(r)$

House	Area
fence	West
lair	East

$\pi_{\text{House, Keeper, Head}}(r) \bowtie \pi_{\text{House, Area}}(r)$

House	Area	Keeper	Head
fence	West	Tom	White
lair	East	Bob	White

Figure 1.13. A relation with a lossless decomposition

r	House	Area	Keeper	Head
	fence	West	Tom	White
	lair	East	Bob	White

$\pi_{\text{House, Keeper, Head}}(r)$

House	Keeper	Head
fence	Tom	White
lair	Bob	White

$\pi_{\text{Area, Head}}(r)$

Area	Head
West	White
East	White

$\pi_{\text{House, Keeper, Head}}(r) \bowtie \pi_{\text{Area, Head}}(r)$

House	Area	Keeper	Head
fence	West	Tom	White
lair	East	Bob	White
fence	East	Tom	White
lair	West	Bob	White

Figure 1.14. A lossy decomposition

students

Student#	Year	Courses Taken
0012	1985	{CS101, MA101}
0012	1986	{CS202, CS205, MA202}
0867	1985	{CS102, MA101}
0867	1986	{CS228}

Figure 1.15. A relation with a multivalued attribute

1.5   Flat and Nested Relations

In all the examples of relations we have seen so far, it has always been the case that the value of every attribute in every tuple is *atomic*, that is, unique and indivisible (in the database). Let us call *simple* an attribute whose domain contains only atomic values. There are two other kinds of attributes.

An attribute is *multivalued* if its possible values are sets (of values); in this case the domain is a set of subsets of a given set.

> **Example 1.11**   Given the relation scheme *STUDENTS (Student#, Year, CoursesTaken)*, if we want to have, for each student and each year, a tuple with the list (or set) of the courses taken (see the example in Figure 1.15), then *CoursesTaken* is a multivalued attribute, and its domain is the powerset of the set of all courses offered.

An attribute is *structured* if its possible values are tuples (of values); in this case, the domain is already a relation (and this is not illegal, since a relation is a set).

> **Example 1.12**   In the relation scheme *STUDENTS (Student#, Date, Exam)*, if we want to store both the course code and the grade obtained by the student for each exam, then *Exam* is a structured attribute; its domain is the Cartesian product of the set of the codes of the courses and the set of possible grades. A relation over this scheme is shown in Figure 1.16.

Domains may even have more complex structures, built up from repeated set and tuple constructions.

students	Student#	Date	Exam
	0012	20-Jan-1990	<CS101,C>
	0012	14-May-1990	<C102,B>
	3413	28-May-1987	<MA101,A>

Figure 1.16. A relation with a structured attribute

students	Student#	Program	Exams		
			Date	Course	Grade
	0012	CS	20-Feb-1985	CS101	C
			12-Jun-1985	CS102	B
			21-Jun-1985	MA101	C
			31-Jan-1986	CS201	B
	3413	EE	23-Feb-1985	MA101	A
			25-Jun-1985	CS101	B
			30-Jan-1986	MA201	B

Figure 1.17. A relation with a multivalued and structured attribute

Example 1.13   In the relation scheme *STUDENTS (Student#, Program, Exams)*, where the domain of *Exam* is the powerset of the Cartesian product of the set of possible dates, the set of the codes of the courses, and the set of possible grades, then *Exams* is a multivalued and structured attribute. Its values are sets of tuples (that is, relations); therefore, it is possible to give names to the components, say, *Date, Course, Grade*. A relation over this scheme is shown in Figure 1.17, where we use a slightly different convention to indicate the levels of structure.

A relation scheme $R(X)$ is in *first normal form (1NF)*, or *flat*, if every attribute in X is simple. Otherwise, it is *nested*.

In the relational model, only relations in 1NF are considered, in order to provide a simple and uniform way of representing data. Consider, for example, the representation in table form of a relation: if

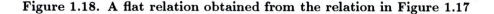

students	Student#	Program	Date	Course	Grade
	0012	CS	20-Feb-1985	CS101	C
	0012	CS	12-Jun-1985	CS102	B
	0012	CS	21-Jun-1985	MA101	C
	0012	CS	31-Jan-1986	CS201	B
	3413	EE	23-Feb-1985	MA101	A
	3413	EE	25-Jun-1985	CS101	B
	3413	EE	30-Jan-1986	MA201	B

Figure 1.18. A flat relation obtained from the relation in Figure 1.17

the values appearing in the table are atomic, the manipulation operations (insertions, modifications, deletions) are performed easily, and
the query operations give as a result tuples whose elements can be
interpreted immediately. It can be shown that every nested relation
can be transformed into a flat relation that is somehow equivalent to
it. To avoid the need for introducing more concepts and notation, we
limit ourselves to an example.

> **Example 1.14**   If in the relation scheme *STUDENTS (Student#,
> Program, Exams)* in Example 1.13 the multivalued, structured at-
> tribute *Exams* is replaced by three simple attributes, *Date, Course,
> Grade*, then we obtain a flat relation scheme. A relation corre-
> sponding to the one in Figure 1.17 is shown in Figure 1.18.

In most of this book we refer to flat relations. In Chapter 8, we
consider extensions and variations of the relational model that include
nested relations and other nonflat structures. Thoughout Chapters 1–
7, the term *relation* will mean "flat relation."

1.6   Relations in Boyce-Codd Normal Form

Let us consider a database scheme referring to the animals in a zoo,
containing the relation scheme *ZOO (Kind, InventoryNo, Area, House,
Cage, Keeper, Head)*. The park is divided into areas; in each area

Redundancy

location	Kind	Inventory#	Area	House	Cage	Keeper	Head
	giraffe	01	West	fence	1	Tom	White
	giraffe	02	West	fence	2	Tom	White
	lion	01	South	lair	3	Bob	Green
	bear	01	East	cave	6	Sam	Smith
	bear	02	East	cave	9	Sam	Smith
	zebra	01	West	fence	8	Tom	White

Figure 1.19. A single-relation database for the zoo application

there is a set of houses, and all the animals of a given kind live in the same house (for example, the Rustic house is designated for the elephants, the Fence house for the giraffes and the zebras, and so on). Every house contains a set of cages in which each specific animal lives. Each house has a unique keeper and each area has a unique head keeper. Every animal is identified by its kind (such as giraffe, lion, elephant) and by an inventory number (unique within the kind, but not in general), and has a unique location; therefore, {*Kind, InventoryNo*} is the only key of the relation scheme. A relation over the *ZOO* scheme is shown in Figure 1.19.

It is clear that the relation in Figure 1.19 (like most relations over this scheme) presents a lot of *redundancy*:

- The house designated for a kind of animal and its keeper are repeated for all the animals of that kind.

- The area in which an house is located and its head keeper are repeated for all the animals that live in that house.

Other problems arise with respect to the update operations that we can perform on relations over the scheme *ZOO*. The first, called *update anomaly*, is related to redundancy: if the house of one kind of animal changes, then all the tuples containing instances of the animals of that kind must be updated. Similarly, multiple updates arise from a change of the keeper of an house or from a change of the head keeper of an area.

The second and third problems are called *insertion* and *deletion anomaly*, respectively, and are related to the fact that we cannot keep track of the house of a kind if there is no animal of that kind[6] (and similarly for the area and keeper of a house and for the head keeper of an area). More precisely we say that there are

- *insertion anomalies*, because it is not possible to insert the house of a kind if the inventory number of an animal of that kind is not known, and

- *deletion anomalies*, because the elimination of all the individuals of one kind of animal leads to the loss of information on the house of that particular kind.

More generally, the occurrence of anomalies is due to the presence, in a single relation, of different concepts (in the example, the location of the kinds of animals, the location of specific animals, general information about houses and areas) which are also of individual interest. The study of problems related to the elimination of anomalies leads to the definition of *normal forms* for relation schemes, which are expressed in terms of integrity constraints that formalize properties of the application (e.g., "each house has a unique keeper"). The fundamental normal forms refer to a constraint called *functional dependency* (abbreviated as *FD*). Given two attributes A and B of a relation, we say that B *functionally depends* on A if and only if to every value of A in r there corresponds only one value of B in r. Symbolically we write $A \rightarrow B$. The notion of dependency can be extended to sets of attributes. Given two sets of attributes X and Y of a relation r, we say that Y functionally depends on X in r if for every (sub)tuple of value x for the attributes X in r, a single tuple of value y corresponds in r for the attributes Y. Formally, $r(U)$ *satisfies* $X \rightarrow Y$ (or, equivalently, $X \rightarrow Y$ *holds* in r), with $XY \subseteq U$, when for every pair of tuples $t_1, t_2 \in r$, if $t_1[X] = t_2[X]$, then $t_1[Y] = t_2[Y]$.

---

[6]The problems would arise even by using null values, since *Kind* and *Inventory#* form the only (and so primary) key of the relation scheme and therefore do not allow null values.

The above definition refers to instances of relations, but an FD corresponds to an integrity constraint on the relation scheme; thus, it constitutes the assertion of a property that must be valid for all possible instances of a relation scheme. Several normal forms based on FDs can be defined; here we introduce only one of them.

A relation scheme $R(U)$, with some keys and some FDs, is in *Boyce-Codd normal form (BCNF)* if for every dependency $X \rightarrow Y$ (where Y is not a subset of X), the set of attributes X contains a key for $R(U)$ (i.e., it is a superkey).

This definition requires that no attribute can depend on any set of attributes that is not a superkey. Essentially (the formal definition will be presented in Chapter 5), this means that all functional dependencies can be described by means of keys. This fact is particularly important from the practical point of view because all existing DBMSs implement the enforcement of keys, but not the enforcement of functional dependencies.

In the relation scheme *ZOO* above, because of the properties of the application ("all the animals of a given kind stay in the same house," etc.), we can identify the following functional dependencies:

$$Kind, Inventory\# \rightarrow Cage, House \qquad Kind \rightarrow House$$
$$House \rightarrow Keeper, Area \qquad\qquad Area \rightarrow Head$$

where neither *Kind*, nor *House*, nor *Area* is a superkey for the scheme. Therefore, *ZOO* is not a BCNF scheme. Let us consider, instead, the following set of relation schemes:

$$ANIMALS(\underline{Kind, Inventory\#}, Cage)$$
$$KINDS(\underline{Kind}, House)$$
$$HOUSES(\underline{House}, Area, Keeper)$$
$$AREAS(\underline{Area}, Head)$$

where the corresponding relations are obtained by means of projections from the *zoo* relation, as in Figure 1.20. We say that the database scheme containing these four relation schemes is a *decomposition* of the database scheme with the single *ZOO* relation scheme. It is easy to verify that the anomalies previously illustrated do not arise any

animals	Kind	Inventory#	Cage
	giraffe	01	1
	giraffe	02	2
	lion	01	3
	bear	01	6
	bear	02	9
	zebra	01	8

kinds	Kind	House
	giraffe	fence
	lion	lair
	bear	cave
	zebra	fence

houses	House	Area	Keeper
	fence	West	Tom
	lair	South	Bob
	cave	East	Sam

areas	Area	Head
	West	White
	South	Green
	East	Smith

Figure 1.20. A decomposed database for the zoo application

more. Note, in fact, the correspondence between a keeper and the house to which he is designated: it is possible to insert this information in the *houses* relation. The relationship between a house and the area in which it is located is maintained independently of the presence of animals in that house. Finally, changes of a keeper of a house or of a head keeper of an area can occur without causing updating anomalies.

The formalization and application of the concept of BCNF (as well as of other normal forms) require a deeper study of the properties of keys and functional dependencies. This is developed in Chapter 5, on the basis of the results shown in Chapters 3 and 4 for integrity constraints. Here we give an idea of the basic problems related to replacing an unnormalized scheme with a normalized one.

The example of normalization shown above suggests that during the design of a relational database scheme, we may need to decompose unsatisfactory relation schemes into smaller schemes that respect a given normal form. Consider the relation scheme ZOO above and its decomposition into four normalized schemes. The corresponding relations are obtained by projections onto the respective attributes. In order to answer some queries on the database, we still need the original relation. For example, if we want to know the head keeper of the area in which a certain animal is located, then we need to reconstruct the *zoo* relation; this can be done by means of a composition of natural joins:

$$animals \bowtie kinds \bowtie houses \bowtie areas$$

followed by a projection on the attributes *Kind, Head*:

$$\pi_{Kind,Head} \, (animals \bowtie kinds \bowtie houses \bowtie areas)$$

Note that in this case the join of the four relations always reconstructs the original *zoo* relation: the original scheme has a lossless decomposition with respect to the decomposed schemes. It is fundamental that when replacing a scheme with its projections, we should be able to reconstruct the original relations from the projections. As we know, this is not always the case.

> **Example 1.15**   If we have the relation scheme
>
> $$R(\underline{House},Area,Keeper,Head)$$
>
> with the same dependencies as above and, realizing that it is not in BCNF, we decompose it into the relation schemes
>
> $$HOUSES(\underline{House},Keeper,Head)$$
> $$AREAS(\underline{Area},Head),$$
>
> we obtain a BCNF database scheme; however, the reconstruction of the generic relation *r* does not work as in the previous example. The motivation is that the involved relation does not have a lossless decomposition with respect to the decomposed relation schemes: we have seen an example in Figure 1.14.

Exercises

1.1 Consider the courses offered at a university. Courses have to be taken according to a specific sequence; that is, each course has an associated set (possibly empty) of other courses as its prerequisites. Given a domain for courses (say, integers for Course Numbers), define a relation scheme to represent the above information, and show a possible instance in table form.

1.2 Define a database scheme to organize the information about the cars used by a company, according to the following specifications. The company owns cars and also rents cars. For each car, we are interested in plate number, maker, model, and year. For owned cars, we are interested in price and date of purchase, and in all expenses for maintenance, with date and cost. For rented cars, we are interested in the owner and in the individual rental agreements, with initial and final dates and cost.

1.3 Define a database scheme for an application concerning the employment history of people, according to the following details:
- For each person there is interest in name, date and place of birth, and employers (companies), with initial and final dates of each employment period.
- Name and city are relevant for each company.

1.4 Suppose we want to represent the composition of a product in terms of parts. The product structure can be seen as a tree where, at each level, you can find a set of composed and/or simple parts. The leaves of the tree are only simple parts. Given that simple parts have an identifying code and other relevant information such as cost and weight, define a database scheme to represent the above information. Show the tabular representation of one of its instances.

1.5 Find the minimum and maximum cardinality of the join of n relations, in terms of the cardinalities of the operands.

1.6 Prove that the join operator is commutative and associative.

1.7 Discuss the difference between the usual definition of Cartesian product in set theory and the definition of Cartesian product in relational algebra.

1.8 A unary operator f is *monotone* if $r_1 \subseteq r_2$ implies $f(r_1) \subseteq f(r_2)$ for every r_1 and r_2. Prove that selection and projection are monotone. Extend the definition of monotonicity to n-ary operators, and prove that the join operator is monotone.

1.9 Find the keys for the relation schemes defined in Exercises 1.1–1.4.

1.10 Consider the following database scheme:

$COURSES(Course\#, Title, Instructor)$

$EXAMS(Course\#, Student\#, Date, Grade)$

$STUDENTS(Student\#, LastName, FirstName, Address, Age)$

Write expressions involving projections, selections, and joins that retrieve the following:

- The exams passed by John Smith, with course titles and grades.
- The instructors that have given at least an A to a teenage student.

1.11 Consider the following database scheme:

$PERSONS(Name, Age, Sex)$

$FATHERHOOD(Father, Child)$

$MOTHERHOOD(Mother, Child)$

Write an expression that retrieves the parents of all the persons for whom both parents are known to the database.

1.12 Prove Lemma 1.1.

1.13 Prove Lemma 1.2.

1.14 Define nested relation schemes for the applications in Exercises 1.2 and 1.3.

1.15 Represent with a BCNF database scheme the following information. A student may attend several courses (and a course is attended by several students). For each course, several books are adopted (and a book can be adopted by several courses). We are interested in the code, name, address, and attended courses for each student. For each course, we want to know the code, title, adopted books, and enrolled students. For each book, we want to know the code, title, and adopting courses.

1.16 Consider the relation scheme $STUDENT(S\#, C\#, Grade, S\text{-}Name, Sex, Age, C\text{-}Name)$, where S# and C# are the code numbers of a student and of a course, respectively. Identify appropriate functional dependencies. Define the corresponding BCNF database scheme.

1.17 Consider the relation scheme *STUDENT(S#, S-Name, Lab#, Lab-Name, Computer#, Computer-Name)*, with the following functional dependencies:

$$S\# \rightarrow S\text{-}Name \qquad\qquad S\# \rightarrow Lab\#$$
$$S\# \rightarrow Lab\text{-}Name \qquad\qquad S\# \rightarrow Computer$$
$$Lab\# \rightarrow Lab\text{-}Name \qquad\qquad Lab\# \rightarrow Computer$$
$$Lab\text{-}Name \rightarrow Lab\# \qquad\qquad Computer\# \rightarrow Computer\text{-}Name$$
$$Computer\# \rightarrow Lab\#$$

Analyze anomalies, and transform the scheme into BCNF.

1.18 Prove that for every $r(X)$ and every $X_1 X_2 = X$, it is the case that $(\pi_{X_1}(r) \bowtie \pi_{X_2}(r)) \supseteq r$; generalize the result to the n-ary case (for every $X_1 X_2 \ldots X_k = X$, $\bowtie_{i=1}^{k} (\pi_{X_i}(r)) \supseteq r$).

Comments and References

The relational model was defined by Codd [76], with the declared objective of data independence, in order to overcome the limitations of the existing models: hierarchical and network. The same paper discusses first normal form, keys, and the basic operators for relational algebra.

Various textbooks exist on database systems, presenting and discussing the three models. See Date [85,87], ElMasri and Navathe [95], Korth and Silberschatz [144], Ullman [212,217]. Various database management systems adopting the relational model have been produced since 1980 (that is, more than ten years after the definition of the abstract model); there are books devoted to specific systems (Date [86,88], Stonebraker [203]). A number of relational systems running on microcomputers have recently became available; Korth and Silberschatz [144], ElMasri and Navathe [95], and Valduriez and Gardarin [219] indicate some of them, giving additional references.

The various topics introduced in Sections 1.3–1.6 are the subjects of subsequent chapters, which include specific references.

Chapter 2

Relational Query Languages

Section 1.4 described the major role played by query languages in the theory and practice of relational databases. This chapter is devoted to a careful analysis of the main languages proposed in formal frameworks. Some knowledge of the languages used in commercial systems, such as SQL, Quel, and QBE, may be useful, but is not essential. The chapter is organized as follows. In Section 2.1 we give a few general definitions. In Section 2.2 we introduce the operators that complete the presentation of relational algebra begun in Section 1.4; relational algebra is the major representative of the class of *procedural* languages, whose expressions describe, step by step, the computation required to compute the result. Section 2.3 describes the expressive power of relational algebra by characterizing its capacity for extracting information from a given database instance. In Section 2.4 we introduce a class of languages with different characteristics: they are based on first-order predicate calculus, and allow the formulation of queries by specifying the properties of the result (and are therefore called *declarative*). The subsequent sections analyze various languages of this class. In Section 2.5 we present *domain relational calculus*. In Section 2.6 we explain a weakness of such a language and consider a modified version that removes this weakness. Then, in Section 2.7, we study the expressive power of calculus-based languages, which turns out to be the same as that of relational algebra, and leads to a notion of *completeness* of languages. In Section 2.8, on the basis of usability considerations, we present yet another language, *tuple relational calculus*, which is actually the basis for Quel and SQL (although these languages also inherit algebraic features). Finally, in Section 2.9, we discuss the limitations of the expressive power of relational languages, by showing significant queries that cannot be specified by means of these languages.

2.1 Basic Notions

Throughout this chapter we assume a countably infinite set of attributes U_∞, and we assume that all the attributes have the same domain D, which may be finite or infinite. The first assumption allows us to introduce new attributes whenever needed; obviously, all relations (operands or results) have finite schemes, but it is convenient that there be no bound on their dimensions. The second assumption may appear limiting, as it is reasonable to have different domains for the various attributes; however, for the results we are going to discuss, the distinction would only overload notation and presentation, whilst the results would not change.

We indicate with $\mathcal{U}$ the set of all relations over every finite subset of U_∞. Given a database scheme $\mathbf{R}$, and using $I(\mathbf{R})$ to indicate the set of all its instances, a *query Q* is a partial recursive function: $Q : I(\mathbf{R}) \to \mathcal{U}$. Given $\mathbf{r} \in I(\mathbf{R})$, we say that $Q(\mathbf{r})$ is the *result* of Q on $\mathbf{r}$. In most cases, for each query Q, there is a set of attributes X such that the result of Q, if defined, is always a relation over X. If we indicate with $\mathcal{X}$ the set of all the relations on X, then Q becomes a function from $I(\mathbf{R})$ to $\mathcal{X}$.

Queries are formulated in the various languages by means of *expressions*: each language has its own syntax, characterizing the legal expressions, and semantics, giving the value $E(\mathbf{r})$ (defined or undefined) of each legal expression E for each database instance $\mathbf{r}$. Therefore, expressions define functions, and so we say that an expression E *represents* a query Q if the function defined by E is indeed Q. It should be noted that, even if queries are defined with respect to a given database scheme, it is often possible to define the expressions of the languages with a looser reference to the scheme: for example, a relational algebra expression may refer to any database scheme that involves at least the relation schemes that are mentioned, each of which has at least the mentioned attributes.

Two expressions E_1 and E_2 (belonging to the same language or to two different languages) are *equivalent with respect to* a database scheme $\mathbf{R}$ (in symbols $E_1 \equiv_\mathbf{R} E_2$) if they represent the same query, that is, if $E_1(\mathbf{r}) = E_2(\mathbf{r})$ for every instance $\mathbf{r} \in I(\mathbf{R})$. In most cases, the reference to the database scheme may be loosened: E_1 and E_2 are *equivalent* ($E_1 \equiv E_2$) if they are defined for the same set of database schemes and equivalent with respect to each of them.

Given two query languages L_1 and L_2, we say that L_1 is *at least as expressive as* L_2 if for every expression E_2 of L_2 there is an expression E_1 of L_1 such that $E_1 \equiv E_2$. L_1 and L_2 are *equally expressive* or *equivalent* if each is at least as expressive as the other.

2.2   Relational Algebra

A language is said to be *procedural* if its expressions describe, step by step, the computation of the result from the database instance. Relational algebra, whose basics we have seen in Section 1.4, is a procedural language. The expressions are composed of suitable operators that have relations as operands, and the result is constructed by applying the operators according to the order stated by the composition.

The collection of operators includes (variations of) the classical operators on sets (union, intersection, difference), and some specific operators on database relations (projection, selection, renaming, join).

Relations are defined as sets of tuples, and therefore it is meaningful to apply the set-theoretic operators to them. However, in order to build complex expressions whose operators are defined on relations, we must ensure that the result of each operation is also a relation, that is, a set of tuples defined on a fixed set of attributes (and not a set of tuples defined on sets of attributes that vary from one tuple to another). Therefore, we define the *union, intersection,* and *difference* operators in the same way as for generic sets, but with the restriction that the involved operands are defined on the same set of attributes.[1]

The specific operators on relations include *selection, projection, natural join*, already defined in Chapter 1, and *renaming*, plus a few more operators, which, however, are redundant because they can be defined by means of the others.

Renaming is a unary operator, and owes its name to the fact that, intuitively, it changes the names of the attributes, leaving the body of the operand unchanged. Formally, given a relation r on the attributes X and an injective function f defined on X (which therefore, assigns a [new] name to each attribute) the renaming of r with respect to f is denoted and defined as follows:

$$\rho_f(r) = \{t \mid \text{ there exists } t' \in r \text{ s.t. } t'[A] = t[f(A)], \text{ for all } A \in X\}$$

To reduce overloading of notation, the function f will usually be represented as $f(A_1), \ldots, f(A_k) \leftarrow A_1, \ldots, A_k$, where $A_1, \ldots, A_k$ is the list of the attributes in X on which f is not the identity (that is, the attributes whose names are changed).

The renaming operator overcomes the rigidity of those operators (such as natural join and the set-theoretic ones) that rely heavily upon attribute names: after a suitable renaming, union, intersection, and difference can be performed on any pair of relations of the same degree; similarly, joins may be performed on a subset or a superset of the common attributes of two relations.

> **Example 2.1** Let us consider a database scheme referring to a royal dynasty, involving four relation schemes, each with a single key:
>
> REIGNS (Sovereign, From, To)
> PERSONS (Name, Sex, Birth, Death)
> FATHERHOOD (Father, Child)
> MOTHERHOOD (Mother, Child)

---

[1]Other authors propose a looser restriction, requiring the operands to have only the same degree; then the attributes in the result are either undefined, or coincide with those of the first operand. The present approach guarantees uniformity and symmetry, and it does not limit the expressive power, due to the introduction of the renaming operator.

persons

Name	Sex	Birth	Death
James I	M	1566	1625
Elizabeth	F	1590	1662
Charles I	M	1600	1649
Charles II	M	1630	1685
Mary	F	1631	1659
James II	M	1633	1701
Henrietta A.	F	1640	1670
Mary II	F	1662	1694
Anne	F	1665	1714
James F.E.	M	1686	1766

reigns

Sovereign	From	To
James I	1603	1625
Charles I	1625	1648
Charles II	1660	1685
James II	1685	1688
Mary II	1688	1694
Anne	1702	1714

fatherhood

Father	Child
Lord Darnley	James I
James I	Elizabeth
James I	Charles I
Charles I	Charles II
Charles I	Mary
Charles I	James II
Charles I	Henrietta A.
James II	Mary II
James II	Anne
James II	James F.E.

motherhood

Mother	Child
Mary Stuart	James I
Anne of Denmark	Elizabeth
Anne of Denmark	Charles I
Henrietta Maria	Charles II
Henrietta Maria	Mary
Henrietta Maria	James II
Henrietta Maria	Henrietta A.
Anne Hyde	Mary II
Anne Hyde	Anne
Mary of Modena	James F.E.

Figure 2.1. The Stuart database

REIGNS stores the names of the sovereigns of the family, with the beginning and ending dates of the reign; *PERSONS* stores data about the main members of the family; the last two relations store the parental relationships. This scheme is used throughout the chapter for many examples; to save space, we will abbreviate relation names and attribute names as necessary in unambiguous ways. A database on this scheme, which refers to the Stuart dynasty of Great Britain, is shown in Figure 2.1.

An expression producing the union of the relations *fatherhood* and *motherhood* (representing therefore a parental relationship), must involve some preliminary renaming, for instance in the following way:

$$\rho_{Parent \leftarrow Father}(F) \cup \rho_{Parent \leftarrow Mother}(M) \qquad (2.1)$$

Two examples of renaming used in combination with natural join follow. The first computes the pair of parents of each sovereign, and the second computes information about the sovereigns who reigned until their death.

$$R \bowtie \rho_{Sovn \leftarrow Child}(F) \bowtie \rho_{Sovn \leftarrow Child}(M) \qquad (2.2)$$

$$\rho_{Name, Death \leftarrow Sovn, To}(R) \bowtie P \qquad (2.3)$$

The results of applying these expressions to the database in Figure 2.1 are shown in Figures 2.2.

There is another operator usually included in relational algebra, the theta-join (with its specialization, equi-join), which is in fact redundant because it can be expressed by means of the operators we have already seen. However, it is important to mention it for two reasons. First, it sometimes allows a more synthetic or more expressive specification for some queries. Second, it is often mentioned in the literature, and it is useful to be familiar with it. Given two relations $r_1(X_1)$, $r_2(X_2)$ with disjoint sets of attributes, a *theta-join* is denoted by $r_1 \bowtie_{A_1 \theta A_2} r_2$, where $A_1 \in X_1$, $A_2 \in X_2$, and θ is a comparison operator. Its result is a relation on the set of attributes $X_1 X_2$ to which a tuple t belongs if it is a combination of a tuple t_1 of r_1 and a tuple t_2 of r_2 such that the value $t_1[A_1]$ stands in relation θ with the value $t_2[A_2]$. Clearly, the result of theta-join $r_1 \bowtie_{A_1 \theta A_2} r_2$ can be obtained as a natural join (a Cartesian product, in fact) followed by a selection: $\sigma_{A_1 \theta A_2}(r_1 \bowtie r_2)$. A theta-join whose comparison operator is the equality is also called an *equi-join*. A generalization of the theta-join operator allows complex formulas, as in the selection operator: $r_1 \bowtie_F r_2$ is equivalent to $\sigma_F(r_1 \bowtie r_2)$.

Example 2.2   A theta-join on the dynasty database could be used to compute the members of the family who were alive when each sovereign got the throne:

Expression (2.1)

Parent	Child
Lord Darnley	James I
James I	Elizabeth
James I	Charles I
Charles I	Charles II
Charles I	Mary
Charles I	James II
Charles I	Henrietta A.
James II	Mary II
James II	Anne
James II	James F.E.
Mary Stuart	James I
Anne of Denmark	Elizabeth
Anne of Denmark	Charles I
Henrietta Maria	Charles II
Henrietta Maria	Mary
Henrietta Maria	James II
Henrietta Maria	Henrietta A.
Anne Hyde	Mary II
Anne Hyde	Anne
Mary of Modena	James F.E.

Expression (2.1)

Name	Sex	Birth	From	Death
James I	M	1566	1603	1625
Charles II	M	1633	1660	1685
Mary II	F	1662	1688	1694
Anne	F	1665	1702	1714

Expression (2.1)

Sovereign	From	To	Father	Mother
James I	1603	1625	Lord Darnley	Mary Stuart
Charles I	1625	1648	James I	Anne of Denmark
Charles II	1660	1685	Charles I	Henrietta Maria
James II	1685	1688	Charles I	Henrietta Maria
Mary II	1688	1694	James II	Anne Hyde
Anne	1702	1714	James II	Anne Hyde

Figure 2.2. The results of expression (2.1), (2.2), and (2.3) over the Stuart database

Sovereign	From	To	Name	Sex	Birth	Death
James I	1603	1625	James I	M	1566	1625
James I	1603	1625	Elizabeth	F	1590	1662
James I	1603	1625	Charles I	M	1600	1649
Charles I	1625	1648	Charles I	M	1600	1649
Charles II	1660	1685	Charles II	M	1630	1685
Charles II	1660	1685	James II	M	1633	1701
Charles II	1660	1685	Henrietta A.	F	1640	1670
James II	1685	1688	James II	M	1633	1701
James II	1685	1688	Mary II	F	1662	1694
James II	1685	1688	Anne	F	1665	1714
Mary II	1688	1694	Mary II	F	1662	1694
Mary II	1688	1694	Anne	F	1665	1714
Anne	1702	1714	Anne	F	1665	1714

Figure 2.3. The result of a theta-join

$$REIGNS \bowtie_{(Birth < From) \wedge (Death > From)} PERSONS \qquad (2.4)$$

Clearly, this expression is equivalent to a Cartesian product followed by a selection:

$$\sigma_{(Birth < From) \wedge (Death > From)}(REIGNS \bowtie PERSONS) \qquad (2.5)$$

Its result over the Stuart database is shown in Figure 2.3.

In relational algebra, queries are formulated by means of expressions involving the algebraic operators whose operands are relation schemes and constant relations.

Example 2.3   The expression (with relation names abbreviated)

$$\pi_{Sovn, Child}(R \bowtie (\rho_{Sovn \leftarrow Father}(F) \cup \rho_{Sovn \leftarrow Mother}(M))) \qquad (2.6)$$

computes the children (known to the database) of the sovereigns of the family. If k denotes the constant relation in Figure 2.4, then the expression

k	Sex	Title
	M	King
	F	Queen

Figure 2.4. A constant relation

Sovereign	Child
James I	Elizabeth
James I	Charles I
Charles I	Charles II
Charles I	Mary
Charles I	James II
Charles I	Henrietta A.
James II	Mary II
James II	Anne
James II	James F.E.

Title	Name
King	James I
King	Charles I
King	Charles II
King	James II
Queen	Mary II
Queen	Anne

Name	Sex	Birth	From	To	Death
Charles I	M	1600	1625	1648	1649
James II	M	1633	1685	1688	1701

Figure 2.5. The results of expressions (2.6), (2.7), and (2.8) over the Stuart database

$$\pi_{Name,\,Title}\big(k \bowtie \rho_{Name \leftarrow Sovereign}(REIGNS) \bowtie PERSONS\big) \qquad (2.7)$$

produces a set of pairs formed by attaching to the name of each sovereign of the family the title King or Queen, depending on the sex. Finally, the expression

$$\pi_{Name,To,Death}\big(\sigma_{Death > To}(\rho_{Name \leftarrow Sovereign}(R))\big) \bowtie P \qquad (2.8)$$

retrieves information about the sovereigns that abdicated or were dethroned. The results of these expressions for the Stuart database are shown in Figure 2.5. Figure 2.6 shows another database, which refers to the Tudor dynasty, and the results of expressions (2.6), (2.7), and (2.8) over it.

reigns

Sovereign	From	To
Henry VII	1485	1509
Henry VIII	1509	1547
Edward VI	1547	1553
Mary I	1553	1558
Elizabeth I	1558	1603

persons

Name	Sex	Birth	Death
Henry VII	M	1447	1509
Arthur	M	1480	1502
Margaret	F	1484	1541
Henry VIII	M	1491	1547
Mary	F	1495	1533
Mary I	F	1516	1558
Elizabeth I	F	1533	1603
Edward VI	M	1537	1553

fatherhood

Father	Child
Edmund Tudor	Henry VII
Henry VII	Arthur
Henry VII	Margaret
Henry VII	Henry VIII
Henry VII	Mary
Henry VIII	Edward VI
Henry VIII	Mary I
Henry VIII	Elizabeth I

motherhood

Mother	Child
Margaret Beaufort	Henry VII
Elizabeth York	Arthur
Elizabeth York	Margaret
Elizabeth York	Henry VIII
Elizabeth York	Mary
Jane Seymour	Edward VI
Catherine	Mary I
Anne Boleyn	Elizabeth I

Sovereign	Child
Henry VII	Arthur
Henry VII	Margaret
Henry VII	Henry VIII
Henry VII	Mary
Henry VIII	Edward VI
Henry VIII	Mary I
Henry VIII	Elizabeth I

Title	Name
King	Henry VII
King	Henry VIII
King	Edward VI
Queen	Mary I
Queen	Elizabeth I

Name	Sex	Birth	From	To	Death

Figure 2.6. The Tudor database and the results of expressions (2.6), (2.7), and (2.8) over it

2.3   The Expressive Power of Relational Algebra

A reasonable question to ask at this point is the following: Is relational algebra powerful enough to express all queries of interest? We will try to answer this question later in the chapter; in this section, we characterize the relations that, given a database instance, we can obtain as a result of relational algebra expressions. It will turn out that all the relations that are meaningful can be generated, thus confirming the significance of relational algebra as a query language. A comment, which will be expanded in Section 2.7, is needed here: in this context, we characterize what we can extract from a given database instance; we are *not* characterizing the queries that can be expressed in relational algebra.

In order to simplify the discussion, we assume that no ordering is defined on the common domain D of all the attributes. Therefore, selections involve only equality and inequality comparisons.

A first characteristic of relational algebra operators is that they cannot create values: a value appears in the result of an expression only if it appears in some operand. Given a database instance $\mathbf{r} = \{r_1, \ldots, r_n\}$, the *active domain* of $\mathbf{r}$ is the subset $D_{\mathbf{r}}$ of the domain D containing values that appear in $\mathbf{r}$ as values for some tuple of some relation. The result of an expression over the instance $\mathbf{r}$ contains only values from the active domain and values from the constant relations, if any. For the sake of simplicity, in the rest of this section we consider only expressions that do not involve constant relations. On the other hand, the renaming operator can introduce new attribute names; the only requirement is that the names must be distinct within each relation. Summarizing, the relations that can be generated by means of relational expressions involving only relations from a database instance $\mathbf{r}$ may have any scheme and may contain only values that come from $D_{\mathbf{r}}$.

It turns out that each of these relations may be obtained by means of careful use of selections. Consider, for example, the relations r_0 and r_1 in Figure 2.7. Relation r_1 can be obtained from r_0 by means of the following expression:

$$\sigma_{(D='CS')\wedge((E='Smith'\wedge S='White')\vee(E='Jones'\wedge S='Grey'))}(r_0) \qquad (2.9)$$

r_0	Employee	Dept	Secretary
	Smith	CS	White
	Jones	CS	White
	Smith	EE	White
	Jones	EE	White
	Smith	CS	Grey
	Jones	CS	Grey
	Smith	EE	Grey
	Jones	EE	Grey

r_1	Employee	Dept	Secretary
	Smith	CS	White
	Jones	CS	Grey

$$r_1 = \sigma_{(D='CS') \wedge ((E='Smith' \wedge S='White') \vee (E='Jones' \wedge S='Grey'))} (r_0)$$

Figure 2.7. A relation with undistinguishable values and a relation constructed value by value

The main characteristic of expression (2.9) is that it constructs its result value by value: all values are explicitly mentioned in the selection predicate. We will show later in the section that there is no conceptually different way of obtaining this result. The informal reason for this is that in the original relation, the values for each attribute cannot be distinguished from each other by means of the tuple to which they belong: each of them is related in the same way to the values for the other attributes. This can be formalized by saying that, for each attribute, the values are interchangeable: if we replace every occurrence of Smith with Jones, and vice versa, we obtain the same relation.

In other cases, the opposite extreme can arise; that is, all values can be distinguished from each other by means of their mutual relationships. For example, in the relation in Figure 2.8, which represents the succession relationship between the English kings of the Norman family, each value can be identified by means of its properties: William I did not succeed any other member of the family; William II was the direct successor of William I, and so on. Correspondingly, there are relational algebra expressions that can single out the individual values without mentioning them explicitly; two of them are shown in Figure 2.8.

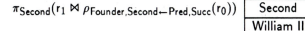

r_0	Predecessor	Successor
	William I	William II
	William II	Henry I
	Henry I	Stephen

$$r_1 = \rho_{\text{Founder} \leftarrow \text{Pred}}(\pi_{\text{Pred}}(r_0)) - \rho_{\text{Founder} \leftarrow \text{Succ}}(\pi_{\text{Succ}}(r_0))$$

Founder
William I

$$\pi_{\text{Second}}(r_1 \bowtie \rho_{\text{Founder,Second} \leftarrow \text{Pred,Succ}}(r_0))$$

Second
William II

Figure 2.8. A relation with distinguishable values

To summarize, a key issue is the distinguishability of the values in the database instance; we now show how it can be formalized.

A partial function $h : D \rightarrow D$ is an *automorphism* of a database instance **r** if

- it is a permutation of the active domain $D_{\mathbf{r}}$, and

- when we extend its definition to tuples, relations, and database instances, we obtain a function on instances that is the identity on **r**: $h(\mathbf{r}) = \mathbf{r}$.

In other words, an automorphism is a renaming of the values in the active domain that leaves the database instance invariant. With respect to the above discussion, a value can be considered as distinguishable in an instance if all the automorphisms of the instance are the identity on it. Two values are undistinguishable from each other if the function that (1) exchanges them, and (2) is the identity on the other values, is an automorphism.

> **Example 2.4** The only automorphism on relation r_0 in Figure 2.8 is the identity, which means that the values are really distinguishable from each other. In contrast, relation r_0 in Figure 2.7 has many automorphisms (in fact, eight) because, for each attribute, the two values in the active domain are interchangeable; as an example, the following is one of these automorphisms:

$h(r_1)$

Employee	Dept	Secretary
Jones	EE	White
Smith	EE	Grey

Figure 2.9. The result of an automorphism

$r_2 = h(r_2)$

Employee	Dept
Smith	CS
Jones	CS
Smith	EE
Jones	EE

Figure 2.10. A relation that is invariant by every automorphism of the relation r_1 in Figure 2.7

$h(\text{Jones}) = \text{Smith}$, $h(\text{Smith}) = \text{Jones}$, $h(\text{CS}) = \text{EE}$, $h(\text{EE}) = \text{CS}$, $h(\text{White}) = \text{White}$, $h(\text{Grey}) = \text{Grey}$.

Automorphisms have been defined by means of invariance of the database instance; it is interesting to see how they behave with respect to other relations.

> **Example 2.5**   The relation r_1 in Figure 2.7 is transformed by the automorphism h in Example 2.4 into the relation in Figure 2.9. On the other hand, the relation r_2 in Figure 2.10 is left unchanged by every automorphism.

In order to deal with selections that involve constants, we introduce two further notions. Let C be a subset of the active domain $D_{\mathbf{r}}$; a *C-fixed automorphism* is an automorphism that is the identity on C; a relational algebra expression *mentions (at most)* C if all constants appearing in the selection predicates belong to C.

We are now ready to state the main theorem of this section.

THEOREM 2.1 Let $\mathbf{r}$ be a database instance and C a subset of the active domain $D_{\mathbf{r}}$ of $\mathbf{r}$. A relation r can be obtained as the result of a relational algebra expression on $\mathbf{r}$ mentioning C if and only if r is invariant by every C-fixed automorphism of $\mathbf{r}$.   □

Before proving the theorem, we comment on its significance. Let us consider the case $C = \emptyset$ first: a relation can be obtained as the result of an expression that does not mention constants if and only if it is invariant by every automorphism of the database instance. If we consider the mutual relationships between values as the semantic content of the database instance, then the automorphisms represent the degree of "uncertainty" embedded in the instance, that is, the undetectable distinctions between values. The relations that are invariant by all the automorphisms preserve this uncertainty, whereas the others contain pieces of information that are not in the database instance. Therefore, the theorem could be informally rephrased as follows: *Relational algebra expressions can construct all relations that contain only information already in the database instance.* The idea can be extended to the general case: by using constants explicitly, an expression can obtain more information from the instance, distinguishing between values that would otherwise be undistinguishable. As an extreme, if an expression mentions all the values in a relation (as we did for relation r_1 in Figure 2.7), then it can construct it regardless of the automorphisms of the instance. In this case, where C_r is the set of values in r, the theorem would say that r can be obtained as the result of an expression mentioning C_r if and only if r is invariant by every C_r-fixed automorphism of r; but every C_r-fixed automorphism is the identity on r, and therefore r is trivially invariant by any such automorphism.

The proof of Theorem 2.1 needs some further notions. Let $D_\mathbf{r}$ contain d values $c_1, \ldots, c_d$ and for every $C \subset D_\mathbf{r}$, let the distinct C-fixed automorphisms of $\mathbf{r}$ be $h_1, \ldots, h_a$. Then the C-*fixed automorphism relation* r_C is a relation with d attributes $B_{c_1}, \ldots, B_{c_d}$, and a tuples, $t_1, \ldots, t_a$, with $t_i[B_{c_j}] = h_i(c_j)$; that is, each tuple describes, value by value, one of the automorphisms. For example, Figure 2.11 shows the $\{CS, EE\}$-fixed automorphism relation for relation r_0 in Figure 2.7.

LEMMA 2.1   For every $\mathbf{r}$ and $C \subseteq D_\mathbf{r}$, the C-fixed automorphism relation r_C can be obtained as the result of an algebraic expression whose operands are the relations in $\mathbf{r}$.

B_{Smith}	B_{Jones}	B_{CS}	B_{EE}	B_{Grey}	B_{White}
Smith	Jones	CS	EE	Grey	White
Jones	Smith	CS	EE	Grey	White
Smith	Jones	CS	EE	White	Grey
Jones	Smith	CS	EE	White	Grey

Figure 2.11. An automorphism relation

PROOF   We prove the claim assuming that **r** contains only one relation r_1; the extension is straightforward, apart from the need for heavier notation.

Let r_1 contain p tuples (namely, $t_1, \ldots, t_p$) and be defined on the attributes $A_1 \ldots A_q$. First of all, we build a relation that is essentially the Cartesian product of r_1 with itself p times; suitable renamings are needed, and if we assume that $C_1, C_2, \ldots, C_{p \times q}$ are distinct attribute names, the relation is as follows:

$$r_P = \rho_{C_1,\ldots,C_q \leftarrow A_1,\ldots,A_q}(r_1) \bowtie \ldots \bowtie \rho_{C_{(p-1) \times q+1},\ldots,C_{p \times q} \leftarrow A_1,\ldots,A_q}(r_1)$$

Now, consider a tuple $t \in r_P$ that is the juxtaposition of p distinct tuples: apart from the attribute names, it contains all the tuples in r_1; then, we transform r_P into another relation r_W by means of the following procedure, which explicitly refers to tuple t:

begin
    $r_W := r_P$;
    for $i := 1$ **to** $p \times q - 1$
    do   **for** $j := i + 1$ **to** $p \times q$
          do   **if** $t[C_i] = t[C_j]$
                 then $r_W := \sigma_{C_i = C_j}(r_W)$
                 else $r_W := \sigma_{C_i \neq C_j}(r_W)$
    end

Since all the selections are made on the basis of its values, the tuple t belongs to r_W. Also, since t contains all the tuples in r_1, it contains all the values in the active domain $D_\mathbf{r}$. For each value c_i, let C_{k_i} be the attribute (or one of them, if there are more) such that $t[C_{k_i}] = c_i$; then, we claim that

$$r_a = \rho_{B_{c_1},\ldots,B_{c_d} \leftarrow C_{k_1},\ldots,C_{k_d}} (\pi_{C_{k_1}\ldots C_{k_d}}(r_W))$$

is the $\emptyset$-fixed automorphism relation $r_\emptyset$. We prove this equality by showing containment in both directions.

1. $r_\emptyset \subseteq r_a$. Let $t_\emptyset$ be a tuple in $r_\emptyset$; by definition, it describes an automorphism h, such that $h(c_i) = t_\emptyset[B_{c_i}]$ for every $1 \leq i \leq d$. Since automorphisms transform tuples of r_1 into tuples of r_1, and t is the combination of tuples of r_1, it follows that the tuple $h(t)$ obtained by applying h to t elementwise is also a combination of tuples of r_1, and therefore belongs to r_P, which contains all such combinations. Also, automorphisms are bijections, and so preserve equalities and inequalities of values: thus, $h(t)$ has exactly the same pairwise equalities as t, and therefore it belongs to r_W. This part of the proof is then completed by noting that the tuple obtained by restricting $h(t)$ to $C_{k_1}, \ldots, C_{k_d}$ and then renaming the attributes to $B_{c_1}, \ldots, B_{c_d}$ is exactly $t_\emptyset$, which therefore belongs to r_a.

2. $r_a \subseteq r_\emptyset$. Let t_a be a generic tuple in r_a; we show that it belongs to $r_\emptyset$. Let t_1 be the tuple in r_a obtained from tuple t in r_W; by construction, $t_1[B_{c_i}] = c_i$ for every $1 \leq i \leq d$. Also, let h be the function on D_r such that $h(t_1) = t_a$; h is a bijection, since all the tuples in r_a have the same pairwise equalities. Then, let t_W be the tuple in r_W from which t_a originates: thus we have that $t_W = h(t)$, and so, since all tuples of r_W are obtained as juxtapositions of tuples of r_1, we have that h is an automorphism. Therefore $t_a = h(t_1)$ belongs to the automorphism relation $r_\emptyset$.

Then, for a given $C = \{c_{i_1}, \ldots, c_{i_C}\} \subseteq D_r$, the C-fixed automorphism relation r_C can be obtained by performing a selection on $r_\emptyset$ with the following condition:

$$(B_{c_{i_1}} = c_{i_1}) \wedge \ldots \wedge (B_{c_{i_C}} = c_{i_C}) \qquad \square$$

Example 2.6   Demonstrations of the procedure followed in the proof of Lemma 2.1 can be given only with very small examples. Two of them are shown in Figures 2.12 and 2.13, respectively.

r_P	C_1	C_2	C_3	C_4
	1	2	1	2
$t \rightarrow$	1	2	3	4
	3	4	1	2
	3	4	3	4

r_1	A_1	A_2
	1	2
	3	4

$$r_W = \sigma_{C_1 \neq C_2}(\sigma_{C_1 \neq C_3}(\sigma_{C_1 \neq C_4}(\sigma_{C_2 \neq C_3}(\sigma_{C_2 \neq C_4}(\sigma_{C_3 \neq C_4}(r_P))))))$$

C_1	C_2	C_3	C_4
1	2	3	4
3	4	1	2

$$r_\emptyset = \rho_{B_1 B_2 B_3 B_4 \leftarrow C_1 C_2 C_3 C_4}((r_W))$$

B_1	B_2	B_3	B_4
1	2	3	4
3	4	1	2

Figure 2.12. The construction of an automorphism relation

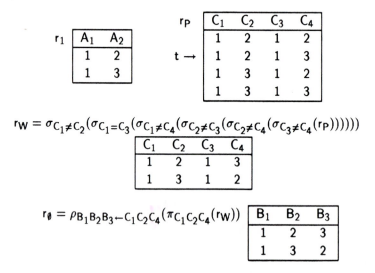

r_P	C_1	C_2	C_3	C_4
	1	2	1	2
$t \rightarrow$	1	2	1	3
	1	3	1	2
	1	3	1	3

r_1	A_1	A_2
	1	2
	1	3

$$r_W = \sigma_{C_1 \neq C_2}(\sigma_{C_1 = C_3}(\sigma_{C_1 \neq C_4}(\sigma_{C_2 \neq C_3}(\sigma_{C_2 \neq C_4}(\sigma_{C_3 \neq C_4}(r_P))))))$$

C_1	C_2	C_3	C_4
1	2	1	3
1	3	1	2

$$r_\emptyset = \rho_{B_1 B_2 B_3 \leftarrow C_1 C_2 C_4}(\pi_{C_1 C_2 C_4}(r_W))$$

B_1	B_2	B_3
1	2	3
1	3	2

Figure 2.13. The construction of another automorphism relation

We can finally prove Theorem 2.1.

PROOF OF THEOREM 2.1

Only if. Assume there is an expression E mentioning C that produces r; that is, $r = E(\mathbf{r})$. Without loss of generality (see Exercise 2.5), we may assume that E involves only unions, renamings, differences, Cartesian products, projections, and selections with only atomic conditions (of the form $A_1 = A_2$ or $A = c$, with $c \in C$). This part of the proof is completed by showing (by induction on the number of operators in E) that the result of E is invariant by every C-fixed automorphism of $\mathbf{r}$.

The basis (zero operators) is trivial: the expression is just a relation $r_i \in \mathbf{r}$, which is invariant by every automorphism of $\mathbf{r}$, since it is part of $\mathbf{r}$. For the induction, we assume that the operands of the outermost operator satisfy the claim (that is, they are invariant by every C-fixed automorphism of $\mathbf{r}$), and we show that the result also satisfies the claim. We distinguish various cases, depending on the outermost operator. In all cases we consider a C-fixed automorphism h of $\mathbf{r}$ and show that, for every $t \in E(\mathbf{r})$, $h(t)$ also belongs to $E(\mathbf{r})$.

- *Union:* $E = E_1 \cup E_2$. If $t \in E(\mathbf{r})$, then $t \in E_1(\mathbf{r})$ or $t \in E_2(\mathbf{r})$. By the induction hypothesis, we have in the first case $h(t) \in E_1(\mathbf{r})$ and in the second $h(t) \in E_2(\mathbf{r})$, and therefore in either case $h(t) \in E_1(\mathbf{r}) \cup E_2(\mathbf{r}) = E(\mathbf{r})$.

- For *renaming, projection,* and *Cartesian product,* we can argue in a similar way as for union.

- *Difference:* $E = E_1 - E_2$. By the induction hypothesis, $h(t)$ belongs to $E_1(\mathbf{r})$; therefore, to prove this step, we have to show that $h(t) \notin E_2(\mathbf{r})$. Assume, by way of contradiction, that $h(t) \in E_2(\mathbf{r})$. Since t does not belong to $E_2(\mathbf{r})$, which is finite, and h is a bijection on tuples, there would be a tuple $t' \in E_2(\mathbf{r})$ such that $h(t') \notin E_2$, against the induction hypothesis that $E_2(\mathbf{r})$ is invariant by the C-fixed automorphisms of $\mathbf{r}$.

- *Selection* with atomic conditions involving equality: (1) $E = \sigma_{A_1 = A_2}(E_1)$, or (2) $E = \sigma_{A=c}(E_1)$ (with $c \in C$). If t belongs to $E(\mathbf{r})$, then it also belongs to $E_1(\mathbf{r})$, and therefore, by the induction hypothesis, $h(t)$ also belongs to $E_1(\mathbf{r})$. Since $t \in E(\mathbf{r})$, by definition of selection, we have $t[A_1] = t[A_2]$ (in case (1)) or $t[A] = c$ (in case (2)). Then, since h is a C-fixed automorphism, we have $h(t)[A_1] = h(t)[A_2]$ (in case (1)) and $h(t)[A] = c$ (in case (2)); in both cases, it follows that $h(t) \in E(\mathbf{r})$.

If. Let r be a relation that is invariant by every C-fixed automorphism of the instance $\mathbf{r}$. Consider a tuple $t \in r$: since each tuple in the C-fixed automorphism relation r_C contains all the values in $\mathbf{r}$ (and so all the values in r, and so all the values in t), it is possible to obtain—by applying to r_C renamings, Cartesian products (if there are repeated values in t), and a projection—a relation r_t such that $t \in r_t$. By repeating the same construction for each $t \in r$, we can build a relation $r^* = \cup_{t \in r} r_t$. Since r is finite and, by Lemma 2.1, r_C can be obtained by means of a relational algebra expression mentioning C, we have that r^* can also be obtained as the result of an expression of that class.

To complete the proof, we show that $r^* = r$. Since, for every $t \in r$, t belongs to r_t, we have that $r \subseteq r^*$. With respect to the other direction, we have that, for every $t \in r$, the relation r_t follows directly from the C-fixed automorphism relation, and so, for each tuple t' in r_t, there is a C-fixed automorphism h such that $t' = h(t)$. Therefore (since r is invariant by every C-fixed automorphism), t' belongs to r; as a consequence, r_t is a subset of r for every $t \in r$, and so $r^* \subseteq r$. $\square$

> **Example 2.7**   The relation r_1 in Figure 2.7 can only be obtained by means of an expression mentioning at least one of {Smith, Jones}, one of {EE, CS}, and one of {White, Grey} (one member for each pair is sufficient because automorphisms are bijections, and therefore fixing one is sufficient to fix the other). If $C = \{\text{Smith}, \text{CS}, \text{White}\}$, then r_C (which contains one single tuple) can be obtained by means of a selection with the condition
>
> $$C_1 = \text{Smith} \ \wedge C_2 = \text{CS} \ \wedge C_3 = \text{White} \ \wedge$$
> $$C_4 \neq \text{Smith} \ \wedge C_5 \neq \text{CS} \ \wedge C_6 \neq \text{White}$$
>
> applied to
>
> $$\rho_{C_1 C_2 C_3 \leftarrow EDS}(r_0) \times \rho_{C_4 C_5 C_6 \leftarrow EDS}(r_0)$$

Then, by following the proof of the *if* part of Theorem 2.1, r_1 can be obtained as follows:

$$\rho_{EDS \leftarrow C_1 C_2 C_3}(\pi_{C_1 C_2 C_3}(r_C)) \cup \rho_{EDS \leftarrow C_4 C_2 C_6}(\pi_{C_4 C_2 C_6}(r_C))$$

As usual with general constructions, the proof of Theorem 2.1 generates an expression that is often complex, whereas there are much simpler expressions that would do the same job; for example, the relation r_2 in Figure 2.10, which is invariant by every automorphism of r_0, can be obtained by means of a single projection: $r_2 = \pi_{ED}(r_0)$.

2.4   Relational Calculus: Introduction

The term *relational calculus* is used to refer to a family of languages that are all based on first-order predicate calculus. The next few sections are devoted to some of these languages, which demonstrate the main features of the entire family. The main characteristic of these languages is that their expressions state the properties of the results without necessarily saying how the results should be computed. As mentioned in the introduction to this chapter, they are *declarative* languages, whereas relational algebra, whose expressions specify step by step how the result must be generated, is a *procedural* language.

The overall presentation does not assume a previous knowledge of predicate calculus. The rest of this section (which can be skipped without affecting comprehension of the subsequent sections) is directed to readers with some familiarity with predicate calculus and is intended to justify some of the technical choices.

With respect to a general first-order predicate calculus, all versions of relational calculus present a number of simplifications and modifications. First of all, first-order calculus usually involves predicate symbols (interpreted as relations over a given universe) and function symbols (interpreted as functions): in a database context, function symbols are not needed, and predicates are interpreted as database relations or as other standard relations (such as equality).

Second, formulas in first-order calculus may be distinguished in two classes: the *open* formulas (which contain free variables) and the *closed* formulas, or *sentences* (whose variables are all bound). Within a given interpretation, the latter have a fixed truth value, whereas the former have a truth value that depends on the values associated with the free variables. Since we want to use a calculus as a query language, that is, a language that defines functions from database instances to relations, we are not much interested in closed formulas, and we can consider that the meaning of an open formula is the set of tuples of elements of the universe that make the formula true.

Third, since our relations are defined differently than in set theory (that is, with respect to an unordered set of named attributes instead of an ordered set of domains), we need to use a notation that differs from that commonly used in first-order predicate calculus; this will not alter semantics.

In the next section we present a query language based in a straightforward way on predicate calculus; in the subsequent sections we will refine it, in order to take into account a number of issues that are meaningful in a relational database context.

2.5   Domain Relational Calculus

Expressions in domain relational calculus have the form

$$\{A_1 : x_1, \ldots, A_k : x_k \mid f\}$$

where f is a *formula*, $x_1, \ldots, x_k$ are *variables* appearing in f (these concepts will be defined below), and $A_1, \ldots, A_k$ are attributes. The list of pairs $A_1 : x_1, \ldots, A_k : x_k$ is called the *target list* of the formula, as it defines the structure of the result of the expression, which is a relation over $A_1 \ldots A_k$ containing tuples whose values $c_1, \ldots, c_k$, respectively substituted to $x_1, \ldots, x_k$, satisfy f.

> **Example 2.8**   In order to give a feeling of the features of the calculus, we present a number of expressions; the reader is invited to look at them now, and to consider them carefully during and after the detailed presentation of the language.
>
> The queries (1) retrieve names and birth dates of the female members of the family, (2) retrieve name, sex, and dates (birth, death, beginning and end of reign) of all the sovereigns of the family, (3) retrieve the names of the sovereigns whose fathers are known but not listed as members of the dynasty, and (4) retrieve the name and

Expression 2.10

Name	Birth
Elizabeth	1590
Mary	1631
Henrietta A.	1640
Mary II	1662
Anne	1665

Expression 2.11

Sovereign	Sex	Birth	From	To	Death
James I	M	1566	1603	1625	1625
Charles I	M	1600	1625	1648	1649
Charles II	M	1630	1660	1685	1685
James II	M	1633	1685	1688	1701
Mary II	F	1662	1688	1694	1694
Anne	F	1665	1702	1714	1714

Expression 2.12

Sovereign
James I

Expression 2.13

Sovereign	From	To
James I	1603	1625

Figure 2.14. Results of the expressions in Example 2.8

the dates of reign of the initiator of the dynasty can be formulated in domain relational calculus respectively as follows:

$$\{N : x_1, B : x_3 \mid$$
$$PERSONS(N : x_1, Sex : x_2, B : x_3, D : x_4) \wedge (x_2 =' F')\} \qquad (2.10)$$

$$\{Sovn : x_1, Sex : x_2, B : x_3, From : x_4, To : x_5, D : x_6 \mid$$
$$REIGNS(Sov : x_1, From : x_4, To : x_5)\wedge$$
$$PERSONS(N : x_1, Sex : x_2, B : x_3, D : x_6)\} \qquad (2.11)$$

$$\{Sovn : x_1 \mid REIGNS(Sovn : x_1, From : x_3, To : x_4)\wedge$$
$$FATHERHOOD(F : x_2, C : x_1)\wedge$$
$$\neg(\exists x_5(\exists x_6(\exists x_7(PERSONS(N : x_2, Sex : x_5, B : x_6, D : x_7)))))\} \qquad (2.12)$$

$$\{Sovn : x_1, From : x_2, To : x_3 \mid$$
$$REIGNS(Sovn : x_1, From : x_2, To : x_3) \wedge \forall x_4(\forall x_5(\forall x_6$$
$$(\neg REIGNS(Sovn : x_4, From : x_5, To : x_6) \vee (x_5 \geq x_2))))\} \qquad (2.13)$$

Their results, with respect to the Stuart database, are shown in Figure 2.14. These expressions confirm the declarative nature of the calculus: the scheme of the result is given in the target list, and tuples belong to the result if they satisfy the condition. At the same time, they demonstrate one of the drawbacks of this version of the language: its verbosity. Calculus expressions are often much longer than the equivalent algebraic expressions.

Let us now devote our attention to the precise definition of the calculus; we first give the syntax and then the semantics.

The symbols that may appear in a formula are *constants* (elements of the domain D); *variables* (elements of a countably infinite set V disjoint from the domain D); *relation names* and *attributes* (from the database scheme); *comparison operators* (the same as those allowed in the atomic conditions in the selection operator, namely, $=$, $\neq$, and, if the domain is ordered, $>$, $\geq$, $<$, $\leq$); the *logical connectives* $\wedge$ (called *and* or *conjunction*), $\vee$ (*or* or *disjunction*), $\neg$ (*not* or *negation*); the *existential* $\exists$ and *universal* $\forall$ quantifiers; and parentheses.

Atoms are the basic components of formulas; they have one of the following forms:

1. $R(A_1 : x_1, \ldots, A_p : x_p)$, where $R(A_1 \ldots A_p)$ is a relation scheme, and the x_i's are distinct variables. To simplify the notation, we will sometimes consider the attributes $A_1, \ldots, A_p$ as ordered, and therefore write the atom omitting them: $R(x_1, \ldots, x_p)$.[2]

2. $x \theta a$, where x is a variable, θ a comparison operator, and a either a constant or a variable.

Formulas are built recursively from atoms by means of connectives and quantifiers. For reasons that will become clear later, it is useful to distinguish occurrences of variables (note: occurrences of variables, and not just variables) in a (sub)formula in two categories, *free* and *bound*. The following rules define formulas completely (that is, nothing else is a formula) and also specify which occurrences of variables are free and which bound.

---

[2] It would be possible to define more general atoms of this form, allowing repetition of variables and constants in the place of variables; however, our limitation is only apparent, since the more general atoms can be simulated by means of conjunctions of atoms, as in item (1) above, and atoms with equalities.

1. Each atom is a formula; all occurrences of variables in atoms are free.

2. If f_1 and f_2 are formulas, then $(f_1) \wedge (f_2)$, $(f_1) \vee (f_2)$, and $\neg(f_1)$ are formulas (parentheses may be omitted when no ambiguity may arise); each occurrence of a variable in them is free (bound) if it is free (bound) in the subformula where it appears.

3. If f is a formula and x a variable, then $\exists x(f)$ and $\forall x(f)$ are formulas; the occurrences of x in f (if any) are bound in them; each occurrence of any other variable is free (bound) if it is free (bound) in f.

> **Example 2.9**   With respect to the dynasty database scheme, $x_4 = \text{F}$ and $PERSONS\ (Name : x_1,\ Sex : x_2,\ Birth : x_3,\ Death : x_4)$ are legal atoms; assuming that the attributes are ordered in the relation scheme $PERSONS$, we can write the second atom as $PERSONS\ (x_1,\ x_2,\ x_3,\ x_4)$. Examples of legal nonatomic formulas (with attribute names omitted) are the following:

$$\exists x_4(PERSONS(x_1, x_2, x_3, x_4) \wedge (x_2 = \text{F})) \tag{2.14}$$

$$\exists x_3(\exists x_4(PERSONS(x_1, x_2, x_3, x_4) \wedge (x_2 = \text{F}))) \tag{2.15}$$

$$\exists x_4(REIGNS(x_1, x_2, x_3) \wedge (\exists x_1(FATHERHOOD(x_4, x_1)))) \tag{2.16}$$

> In expression (2.14) all occurrences of variables are free except the occurrence of x_4; in (2.15) they are all free except the occurrences of x_3 and x_4; in (2.16) they are all free except the occurrences of x_4 and the occurrence of x_1 within the inner quantified formula.

Now we define the semantics of the domain relational calculus by giving the value of its generic expression with respect to a database instance $\mathbf{r} = \{r_1, \ldots, r_m\}$ over the scheme $\mathbf{R} = \{R_1(X_1), \ldots, R_m(X_m)\}$. In the same way as the syntax of expressions is based on formulas, which are recursively defined, the semantics of expressions is based on the recursive definition of the *value* of a formula, which is a truth value, depending on the values substituted for the free variables in it. We need a preliminary definition: a *substitution* is a total function

$s : V \to D$, which associates with each variable a constant.[3] Now, we recursively define the value of formulas on the various substitutions, following the recursive definition of a formula.

1. Atoms

   - The value of $R(A_1 : x_1, \ldots, A_p : x_p)$ for a substitution s is *true* if the relation r over R contains a tuple t such that $t[A_i] = s(x_i)$, for $1 \le i \le p$, and *false* otherwise.

   - $x_1 \theta a$. There are two cases; (1) if a is a variable x_2, then $x_1 \theta x_2$ is *true* for s if $s(x_1)$ stands in relation θ with $s(x_2)$ (for example, let θ be the equality: the atom $x_1 = x_2$ is *true* for s if $s(x_1)$ is equal to $s(x_2)$); (2) if a is a constant c, then $x_1 \theta c$ is *true* for s if $s(x_1)$ stands in relation θ with c.

2. The values of $(f_1) \wedge (f_2)$, $(f_1) \vee (f_2)$, $\neg(f_1)$ over a substitution s are defined according to the semantics of the Boolean connectives on the values of f_1 and f_2 on s.

3. The value of $\exists x(f)$ on a substitution s is *true* if there is a substitution s' on which f is *true* that differs from s at most on x; otherwise it is *false*. Symmetrically, the value of $\forall x(f)$ on a substitution s is *true* if f is *true* for every substitution s' that differs from s at most on x; otherwise it is *false*.

Finally, the value of a domain relational calculus expression

$$\{A_1 : x_1, \ldots, A_k : x_k \mid f\}$$

is a relation over the attributes $A_1, \ldots, A_k$ whose tuples are defined by the substitutions on which f is *true*:

$$\{t \mid \text{exists } s \text{ s.t. } f(s) = true \text{ and } t[A_i] = s(x_i), \text{ for } 1 \le i \le k\}$$

---

[3]It is only for technical reasons that substitutions are defined on all variables; from the practical point of view they are interesting only for the variables that appear in the formula under consideration. It turns out that two substitutions give the same value to a formula if they differ only on variables that do not appear in the formula.

Example 2.10   Consider again expression (2.13):

$$\{Sovn : x_1, From : x_2, To : x_3 \mid$$
$$REIGNS(Sovn : x_1, From : x_2, To : x_3) \wedge \forall x_4 (\forall x_5 (\forall x_6$$
$$(\neg REIGNS(Sovn : x_4, From : x_5, To : x_6) \vee (x_5 \geq x_2))))\}$$

In order to know its value, we have to find the value of its formula (through the values of the subformulas) on the various substitutions. The subformula

$$REIGNS(Sovn : x_4, From : x_5, To : x_6) \tag{2.17}$$

is *true* on a substitution s if and only if there is a tuple $t \in reigns$ such that $t[Sovn] = s(x_4)$, $t[From] = s(x_5)$, and $t[To] = s(x_6)$, regardless of the value of s on the other variables. Also, the subformula

$$(x_5 \geq x_2) \tag{2.18}$$

is *true* on s if the value of s on x_5 is greater than or equal to the value of s on x_2. Then the subformula

$$\neg REIGNS(Sovn : x_4, From : x_5, To : x_6) \tag{2.19}$$

is *true* on a substitution s if and only if (2.17) is *false* on s, and the subformula

$$(\neg REIGNS(Sovn : x_4, From : x_5, To : x_6)) \vee (x_5 \geq x_2) \tag{2.20}$$

is *true* on a substitution s if at least one of (2.18) and (2.19) is *true* on it. The quantified subformula

$$\forall x_6 (\neg REIGNS(Sovn : x_4, From : x_5, To : x_6) \vee (x_5 \geq x_2)) \tag{2.21}$$

is *true* on a substitution s if subformula (2.20) is *true* on all substitutions that differ from s at most on x_6. Reasoning as above for the other connectives and quantifiers in the formula, we can say that

$$REIGNS(Sovn : x_1, From : x_2, To : x_3) \wedge \forall x_4 (\forall x_5 (\forall x_6$$
$$(\neg REIGNS(Sovn : x_4, From : x_5, To : x_6) \vee (x_5 \geq x_2)))) \tag{2.22}$$

is *true* on a substitution s if there is a tuple $t \in reigns$ such that $s(x_1) = t[Sovn]$, $s(x_2) = t[From]$, $s(x_3) = t[To]$, and, for all substitutions that differ from s at most on x_4, x_5, and x_6, subformula (2.20) is *true*. With a little effort, we can see that the value of the expression is clearly what is requested, that is, data about the sovereign who started his reign not later than any other sovereign.

It is important to note that the value of a quantified formula $\exists x(f)$ or $\forall x(f)$ on a substitution s does not depend on the value of s on the bound variable x. By means of an inductive argument, this can be generalized: the value of a formula on s depends only on the values of s on the free variables in the formula (that is, if s and s' differ only on variables that do not appear free in a formula f, then f has the same value on s as on s'). On the basis of this and similar considerations, we can state the following lemma; we leave its proof as Exercise 2.9, and here we demonstrate the main issues by means of an example.

LEMMA 2.2   For every expression of the domain relational calculus, there is an equivalent expression such that the free variables in its formula are exactly the variables in the target list.   □

> **Example 2.11**   Expression (2.10), whose target list does not contain all the free variables, is equivalent to the following expression:
>
> $$\{N : x_1, B : x_3 \mid$$
> $$\exists x_2(\exists x_4(PERSONS(N : x_1, Sex : x_2, B : x_3, D : x_4) \wedge (x_2 = \text{F})))\} \quad (2.23)$$
>
> Any expression whose target list contains variables that do not appear free in the formula is not very meaningful; however, it is always possible to transform it by adding a dummy subformula with the missing variable; for example,
>
> $$\{A : x_1, Name : x_2 \mid \exists x_3(FATHERHOOD(Father : x_3, Child : x_2))\}$$
>
> can be transformed into
>
> $$\{A : x_1, Name : x_2 \mid$$
> $$(x_1 = x_1) \wedge \exists x_3(FATHERHOOD(Father : x_3, Child : x_2))\}$$

Therefore, whenever necessary, we may assume that the free variables appear in the target list and vice versa. Sometimes, as in expressions (2.10) and (2.23), the restricted version is less readable than the liberal one; however, the assumption simplifies some technical arguments. For similar reasons, it is convenient to assume that each formula has at least one free variable.[4]

Another simplification in the structure of formulas in domain relational calculus expressions can be obtained by considering the known equivalences existing between connectives and quantifiers: for every f_1 and f_2 and for every substitution, $f_1 \vee f_2$ has the same value as $\neg(\neg(f_1) \wedge \neg(f_2))$, and $\forall x(f_1)$ has the same value as $\neg(\exists x(\neg(f_1)))$. By formalizing these facts and embedding them in an inductive argument, we can prove the following lemma.

LEMMA 2.3   For every expression of the domain relational calculus, there is an equivalent expression whose formula involves negation, binary connectives of one form only (all conjunctions or all disjunctions), and quantifiers of one form (all existential or all universal).   □

> **Example 2.12**   Expression (2.13):
>
> $$\{Sovn : x_1, From : x_2, To : x_3 \ |$$
> $$REIGNS(Sovn : x_1, From : x_2, To : x_3) \wedge \forall x_4 (\forall x_5 (\forall x_6$$
> $$(\neg REIGNS(Sovn : x_4, From : x_5, To : x_6) \vee (x_5 \geq x_2))))\}$$
>
> can be transformed into an equivalent expression whose formula contains only conjunctions and existential quantifications, together with negations:
>
> $$\{Sovn : x_1, From : x_2, To : x_3 \ |$$
> $$REIGNS(Sovn : x_1, From : x_2, To : x_3) \wedge \neg \exists x_4 (\exists x_5 (\exists x_6$$
> $$(REIGNS(Sovn : x_4, From : x_5, To : x_6) \wedge \neg(x_5 \geq x_2))))\}$$

---

[4] Formulas that do not contain free variables have a truth value that does not depend on substitutions. Therefore, an expression whose formula does not contain free variables could be considered as a Boolean query: it is either *true* or *false* on an instance, without producing a set of tuples as a result.

2.6   Domain Independence

In this section and the next we will encounter a number of variants
of relational calculus, and we will denote them by acronyms. *DRC* is
the acronym for domain relational calculus, the language defined in
the previous section, and we will often abbreviate relational algebra
as *RA*. We will also use the terms *DRC expression* or *RA expression*,
and similar phrasing.

   DRC, as defined in the previous section, has some undesirable
properties.

> **Example 2.13**   Consider the following DRC expression, referring
> to our dynasty database scheme:
>
> $$\{Name\!:\!x_1 \mid \neg(\exists x_2(FATHERHOOD(Father\!:\!x_1, Child\!:\!x_2)))\} \qquad (2.24)$$
>
> The formula in expression (2.24) is *true* on a substitution s if there
> is no tuple t in *fatherhood* such that $t[Father] = s(x_1)$; that is, it is
> *true* on all the substitutions whose value on x_1 does not appear in
> the *Father* component of *fatherhood*. Since substitutions may map
> each variable to any domain value, the result of expression (2.24)
> is a relation on the attribute *Name*, with one tuple for each of the
> elements of the domain that does not appear as a *Father*-value in
> *fatherhood*.

   The expression in Example 2.13 has undesirable properties: it
depends not only on the values in the current database instance, but
also on the domain: if the domain changes, the result may change.
Also, if the domain is infinite, then the result is an infinite set of tuples,
and therefore it is not a relation. Thus, since queries were defined as
functions on the set of instances of a scheme, it follows that expression
(2.24) defines a different query for each different domain.

   We say that an expression is *domain-independent* if it represents
the same query regardless of the underlying domain. As the set of legal
instances may vary with the replacement of the domain, we formalize
the definition by saying that an expression E is domain-independent
if there is a query Q such that for every domain D, indicating with
$I_D(\mathbf{R})$ the set of instances of $\mathbf{R}$ with respect to D, expression E represents the restriction of Q to $I_D(\mathbf{R})$. A language is *domain-independent*

if all its expressions are domain-independent. Clearly, practical languages should be domain-independent; it is inconvenient to have to deal with results that vary with the underlying domain and may be infinite.

From Example 2.13, it follows that DRC is domain-dependent; we might be interested in considering the language formed by the DRC expressions that are domain-independent: let us call it the *domain-independent domain relational calculus (DI-DRC)*. Here we have a negative result expressed in the following theorem. Its proof is omitted and can be found in the literature [94,220].

THEOREM 2.2 The following problem is undecidable. Given a DRC expression, is it domain-independent?   □

Therefore, DI-DRC is not a recursive language; in contrast, it is easy to prove a positive result for relational algebra (Exercise 2.8).

THEOREM 2.3 Relational algebra is domain-independent.   □

Therefore, it also follows that DRC is strictly more powerful than relational algebra, because there are no RA expressions equivalent to the DRC expressions that are domain-dependent.

The rest of this section is devoted to the presentation of a language that is similar to DRC and has the same expressive power as DI-DRC.

We must first establish a few preliminaries. Let E be a DRC expression and $\mathbf{r}$ a database instance. Then the *active domain* of E and $\mathbf{r}$ is the union $D_{E,\mathbf{r}}$ of the *active domain* $D_{\mathbf{r}}$ of $\mathbf{r}$ (defined as the set of the domain values that appear in some tuple of some relation of $\mathbf{r}$) and the set of constants that appear in the formula f of the expressions.

Violation of domain independence is possible because variables may vary freely in domains; if variables were forced to vary in the active domain (or a subset thereof), then the problem would not arise. Therefore, the modified version of the calculus we propose, called *domain relational calculus with range declarations (DRC-RD)* requires, for each variable, a declaration of the subset of the active domain of relevance, by means of a set whose elements are constants and/or attributes of relations. For each variable, the declaration is done at the highest level for which it is meaningful: (1) globally, if it is free, and (2) together with its quantification, if it is bound. Before giving the precise definition of DRC-RD, we prove two results which establish the basis for the usefulness of the approach.

LEMMA 2.4   For every DRC expression E, there is a formula $d(x)$ with one free variable x that, for every database instance $\mathbf{r}$, is *true* on a substitution s if and only if the value of s on the free variable is an element of the active domain $D_{E,\mathbf{r}}$.

PROOF   Let $R_1(A_{1,1} \ldots A_{1,p_1})$, $\ldots$, $R_n(A_{n,1} \ldots A_{n,p_n})$ be the relation schemes in the database scheme of interest, and let $c_1, c_2, \ldots, c_q$ be the constants in E. Then for every attribute $A_{i,j}$ in relation scheme R_i, it is possible to define a formula $d_{i,j}$ with free variable x that, for every database instance, is *true* on substitution s if and only if $s(x)$ appears as a value for $A_{i,j}$ in the relation r_i; for example, for attribute $A_{1,1}$ (appearing in R_1) the formula $d_{1,1}$ is

$$\exists x_2(\ldots(\exists x_{p_1}(R_1(x, x_2, \ldots, x_{p_1})))\ldots)$$

Therefore, the formula $d_{\mathbf{R}}$ defined as the disjunction of the $d_{i,j}$'s is *true* on s if and only if $s(x)$ belongs to the active domain $D_{\mathbf{r}}$ of $\mathbf{r}$.
    Similarly, the formula d_E defined as

$$(x = c_1) \vee (x = c_2) \vee \ldots \vee (x = c_q)$$

is *true* on s if and only if $s(x)$ is one of the constants $c_1, c_2, \ldots, c_q$.
    It follows that the formula d defined as $d_{\mathbf{R}} \vee d_E$ satisfies the claim. $\square$

Note that the formula d in Lemma 2.4 does not depend on the database instance, but produces the active domain for every instance.

LEMMA 2.5   Let E be a domain-independent DRC expression, with free variables $x_1, \ldots, x_k$ and formula f, and let E' be the DRC expression with the same target list as E and formula $d(x_1) \wedge \ldots \wedge d(x_k) \wedge f'$, where f' is obtained by recursively substituting in f the quantified subformulas $\exists x(g)$ and $\forall x(g)$ by $\exists x(d(x) \wedge g)$ and $\forall x(\neg d(x) \vee g)$. Then, E and E' are equivalent.

PROOF   Since E is domain-independent by hypothesis, it is evident that E' is also domain-independent. Therefore, in order to show the equivalence of E and E', it suffices to show that, for each database instance $\mathbf{r}$, E and E' produce identical results if evaluated with respect to one domain. This domain may change from instance to instance, and it is therefore possible to choose, for each instance $\mathbf{r}$, the active domain of $\mathbf{r}$ and E (which, incidentally, is also the active domain of $\mathbf{r}$ and E'). Then, since the difference between E and E' is essentially in subformulas that force all variables to vary within the active domain, it follows that, for every instance, the respective results of the two expressions are equal, and therefore they are equivalent.   □

A direct consequence of Lemma 2.5 is that the result of a domain-independent DRC expression contains only values from the active domain of the expression and the instance.

Now we formally introduce the new version of the calculus. A *range component* either is a finite set of constants C or has the form $R[A]$, where $R(X)$ is a relation scheme, and A is an attribute in X. A *range declaration* is a finite, nonempty set of range components.

An *expression of the DRC with range declarations (DRC-RD)* is defined as an expression of the DRC, except that it contains a range declaration for each free variable in the associated formula and for each of its quantified subformulas. Syntactically, we write the declarations for the free variables in the target list as

$$\{A_1 : x_1(G_1), \ldots, A_k : x_k(G_k) \mid f\}$$

and those associated with the quantifiers as $\exists x(G)(f')$, $\forall x(G)(f')$. The semantics of queries in DRC-RD is defined as for general DRC expressions, except that in defining the value of each formula, substitutions are functions that associate with each variable a value of the corresponding range.

> **Example 2.14**   Consider again the dynastic database scheme, with relation and attribute names abbreviated with the respective initials. The query defined by expression (2.23) can be formulated in DRC-RD as
>
> $$\{N : x_1(P[N]), B : x_3(P[B]) \mid$$
> $$\exists x_2(P[S])(\exists x_4(P[D])(P(N:x_1, S:x_2, B:x_3, D:x_4) \wedge (x_2 = \text{F})))\}$$

THEOREM 2.4 DRC-RD is domain-independent and equivalent to DI-DRC.

PROOF   We prove equivalence of the two languages; then the domain-independence of DRC-RD will follow as a consequence. Equivalence is proved in two steps, by following the definition.

- *DRC-RD is at least as expressive as DI-DRC.* Let the database scheme contain n relation schemes,

$$R_1(A_{1,1}, \ldots, A_{1,p_1}), \ldots, R_n(A_{n,1}, \ldots, A_{n,p_n})$$

  Let E be a domain-independent DRC expression involving constants $c_1, c_2, \ldots, c_q$; then we may consider the expression E', equivalent to E, as defined and proved in Lemma 2.5.

  Let G be the range declaration corresponding to the active domain, which includes all the terms $R_i[A_{i,j}]$, for $1 \leq i \leq n$ and $1 \leq j \leq p_i$, and the set of constants $c_1, \ldots, c_q$, and nothing else. Then let E_d be the DRC-RD expression obtained from E by attaching to each variable the range G: it is straightforward (although a bit tedious) to show that E_d is equivalent to E', and so, by Lemma 2.5, also equivalent to E.

- *DI-DRC is at least as expressive as DRC-RD.* For every DRC-RD expression we can construct an equivalent DRC expression by transforming the range declarations into subformulas combined with the original formula in a similar way as in Lemma 2.5. As the two expressions are equivalent, the DRC expression is domain-independent and therefore belongs to DI-DRC.   □

  The transformation used in Theorem 2.4 is only technical, and in most cases it is possible to use much simpler range declarations.

> **Example 2.15**   If applied to expression (2.23), Theorem 2.4 produces the following DRC-RD expression:
>
> $$\{N : x_1(G), B : x_3(G) \mid$$
> $$\exists x_2(G)(\exists x_4(G)(P(N : x_1, S : x_2, B : x_3, D : x_4) \land (x_2 = \mathrm{F})))\}$$
>
> where G is the range declaration corresponding to the active domain:
>
> $$R[S], R[F], R[T], P[N], \ldots, M[C], \mathrm{F}$$
>
> However, there are much simpler DRC-RD expressions equivalent to expression (2.23), such as

$$\{N : x_1(P[N]), B : x_3(P[B]) \mid \exists x_2(P[S])(\exists x_4(P[D])$$
$$(P(N : x_1, S : x_2, B : x_3, D : x_4) \land (x_2 = F)))\} \qquad (2.25)$$

whose range declarations are elementary.

Most significant queries require only expressions with singleton range declarations. Notable exceptions are the queries that are formulated in relational algebra by using the union operator.

> **Example 2.16**   A query that retrieves the parental relationship from *FATHERHOOD* and *MOTHERHOOD*, formulated in algebra by means of expression (2.1), can be formulated in DRC-RD as follows:
>
> $$\{P : x_1(F[F], M[M]), C : x_2(F[C], M[C]) \mid$$
> $$M(M : x_1, C : x_2) \lor F(F : x_1, C : x_2)\}$$
>
> Since, for each attribute, the values originate from two different relations, the range declarations have to contain two elements each.

We conclude this section by discussing the possible use of DRC (or DRC-RD) as the basis for a query language in a real system. Calculus-based languages may be preferable to algebraic languages because of nonprocedurality (we will show in Section 2.7 that their expressive power is essentially the same); however, as we have seen in the various examples, DRC and, even more, DRC-RD expressions involve a lot of details and are often tedious to write, because for each relation involved in the query, the expression must usually contain a variable for each attribute, with the corresponding range declaration. These and other considerations motivate the definition of another language based on first-order predicate calculus, whose variables denote tuples instead of individual values, thus often reducing the verbosity of the expressions. As a matter of fact, the only practical language based on DRC, *Query-by-Example (QBE)* [235], uses a graphic interface that simplifies the specification of most of the details, especially in the most natural queries.

MEMBER	Name	Sex	Birth	Death
	P.x	'F'	P.y	z

Figure 2.15. A QBE-like expression

Example 2.17   Expression (2.25) would be formulated in QBE by means of the tabular notation in Figure 2.15. The *table skeleton* corresponding to a relation scheme is provided by the system upon request from the user, who may then insert the various elements; the $P.$ "operator" indicates which values contribute to the result. Note how range declarations and membership in relations are expressed easily by means of the graphic interface.

2.7   The Expressive Power of Relational Calculus

In this section we compare, in terms of their expressive power, the various versions of DRC with RA; we have already seen that general DRC allows expressions that are not domain-independent and therefore have no equivalent counterpart in relational algebra. It turns out that DI-DRC and DRC-RD are actually equivalent to RA.

The main equivalence can be proved by means of the following two lemmas.

LEMMA 2.6   For every DRC-RD expression E_c, there is an equivalent RA expression E_a. If all the ranges in E_c are relation attributes, then E_a does not involve constant relations.

PROOF   Without loss of generality, we assume by a variant of Lemma 2.3 for DRC-RD, that the formula f in E_c does not contain conjunctions or universal quantifiers, and, by a variant of Lemma 2.2, that the variable of each existential quantifier appears free in the corresponding subformula. The proof, by induction on the number of connectives and quantifiers in f, builds a relational algebra expression E whose result is a relation over a set of attributes that are named as the free variables in the formula $x_1, \ldots, x_p$; E is shown to be equivalent to the DRC-RD expression

$$\{x_1 : x_1, \ldots, x_p : x_p \mid f\}$$

The final RA expression equivalent to E_c is then obtained by means of a renaming. An important detail to be considered with respect to atoms is that variables may vary only within the defined ranges. For each variable x, there is an expression E_x that yields the corresponding range: it is the union of the renamings of the singleton projections and constant relations, corresponding to the elements in the respective range list.

Basis. The formula is atomic.

- $R(A_1 : x_1, \ldots, A_p : x_p)$; the RA expression

$$\rho_{x_1, \ldots, x_p \leftarrow A_1, \ldots, A_p}(R) \bowtie E_{x_1} \bowtie \ldots \bowtie E_{x_p}$$

  satisfies the claim. Note that the joins with the range expressions guarantee that the values come from the respective ranges.

- the RA expression is $\sigma_{x_1 \theta x_2}(E_{x_1} \bowtie E_{x_2})$, where the join is indeed a Cartesian product, if the atom has the form $x_1 \theta x_2$; it is $\sigma_{x \theta c}(E_x)$ if the atom has the form $x \theta c$.

Induction. By Lemma 2.3, it is sufficient to consider only negation, conjunction, and existential quantification.

- *negation:* $f = \neg(f_1)$. Let $x_1, \ldots, x_n$ be the free variables in f_1, and let E_{f_1} be the RA expression corresponding to f_1. By definition of negation, the tuples that satisfy f are those that do not satisfy f_1. Since we are only interested in tuples whose values come from the ranges of the various variables, the expression corresponding to f can be obtained by means of a difference involving the Cartesian product of the range expressions and the expression E_{f_1}:

$$(E_{x_1} \bowtie \ldots \bowtie E_{x_n}) - E_{f_1}$$

- *conjunction:* $f = f_1 \wedge f_2$. Let E_{f_1} and E_{f_2} be the expressions corresponding to the subformulas f_1 and f_2, respectively. Intuitively, the expression corresponding to f is the intersection of E_{f_1} and E_{f_2}; however, these two expressions need not be defined on the same set of attributes (as the formulas f_1 and f_2 need not have exactly the same free variables), and therefore we must be careful. Let V_1 and V_2 be the sets of free variables in f_1 and f_2 respectively, and $V_1 - V_2 = \{y_1, \ldots, y_h\}$, $V_2 - V_1 = \{z_1, \ldots, z_k\}$. In order to obtain compatible expressions, we extend E_{f_1} and E_{f_2} by means of Cartesian products: defining $E_1 = E_{f_1} \bowtie E_{y_1} \bowtie \ldots \bowtie E_{y_h}$ and $E_2 = E_{f_2} \bowtie E_{z_1} \bowtie \ldots \bowtie E_{z_k}$, it follows that the expression corresponding to f is the intersection of E_1 and E_2, which is indeed equivalent to $E_{f_1} \bowtie E_{f_2}$.

- *existential quantification:* $f = \exists x(f_1)$. We assumed that x appears free in f_1; let $x_1, \ldots, x_n$ be the other free variables in f_1 (and therefore the free variables in f), and let E_{f_1} be the expression corresponding to f_1. The expression for f is obtained by projecting x out of the expression for f_1: $E_f = \pi_{x_1 \ldots x_n}(E_{f_1})$.

This completes the induction. The RA expression corresponding to the DRC-RD expression $\{A_1 : x_1, \ldots, A_k : x_k \mid f\}$, where E_f is the RA expression for f, is obtained by a straightforward renaming:

$$\rho_{A_1, \ldots, A_k \leftarrow x_1, \ldots, x_k}(E_f)$$

The second part of the claim follows from the fact that we have used constant relations only in the subexpressions associated with ranges, and only to implement ranges involving constants. $\qquad\square$

As for other general transformations, the one suggested by Lemma 2.6 often produces a redundant expression.

> **Example 2.18**   Let us apply the procedure in Lemma 2.6 to the following DRC-RD expression, which represents the query that retrieves the names of the persons whose fathers are known to the database, but whose mothers are not:
>
> $$\{Name : x_1(F[C]) \mid$$
> $$\exists x_2(F[F])(F(F : x_2, C : x_1) \wedge \forall x_3(M[C])(\neg(x_3 = x_1)))\}$$

As a first step, we eliminate the universal quantifier (we also reduce a double negation):

$$\{Name : x_1(F[C]) \mid$$
$$\exists x_2(F[F])(F(F : x_2, C : x_1) \wedge \neg(\exists x_3(M[C])(x_3 = x_1)))\}$$

Then, indicating the expressions corresponding to the ranges as

$$E_{x_1} = \rho_{x_1 \leftarrow C}(\pi_C(F))$$
$$E_{x_2} = \rho_{x_2 \leftarrow F}(\pi_F(F))$$
$$E_{x_3} = \rho_{x_3 \leftarrow C}(\pi_C(M))$$

and repeatedly applying the procedure in the proof of the lemma, we obtain the following RA expression:

$$\rho_{Name \leftarrow x_1}\left(\pi_{x_1}(\rho_{x_2 x_1 \leftarrow FC}(F) \bowtie E_{x_1} \bowtie E_{x_2}) \bowtie \right.$$
$$\left.(E_{x_1} - \pi_{x_1}(\sigma_{x_3 = x_1}(E_{x_3} \bowtie E_{x_1})))\right)$$

A simpler, equivalent expression would be the following:

$$\rho_{Name \leftarrow C}(\pi_C(F) - \pi_C(M))$$

LEMMA 2.7   For every RA expression E_a, there is an equivalent DRC expression E_c, which is domain-independent.

PROOF   The second part of the claim is evident from the domain independence of relational algebra: if a DRC expression is equivalent to a relational algebra expression, then it is also domain-independent.

The main part of the proof is again by induction on the structure of the RA expression E_a, that is, on the number of operators. By Exercises 2.4 and 2.5, and by equivalences among operators, we may assume that the constant relations in E_a are defined over one attribute and contain exactly one tuple, that the intersection and theta-join operators do not appear, that all natural joins are indeed Cartesian products, that selections involve atomic conditions only, and that projections project out one attribute at the time.

Basis.   No operators; we have two subcases:

- *constant relation:* $E_a = \{t\}$, with $t[A] = c$; the DRC expression $E_c = \{A : x \mid x = c\}$ is equivalent to E_a.

- *relation from the database:* $E_a = R$, where the attributes of R are $A_1, \ldots, A_k$. Again, the translation is straightforward:

$$E_c = \{A_1 : x_1, \ldots, A_k : x_k \mid R(A_1 : x_1, \ldots, A_k : x_k)\}$$

Induction. We consider the various possibilities for the top-level operator, assuming that the translation is possible for the RA subexpression(s). For the unary operators, we assume that the subexpression E'_a is defined over $A_1 \ldots A_n$, and the DRC expression equivalent to it is

$$E'_c = \{A_1 : x_1, \ldots, A_n : x_n \mid \psi\}$$

- *projection:* $E_a = \pi_{A_1 \ldots A_{n-1}}(E'_a)$; that is, we assume that only attribute A_n is projected out. The DRC expression equivalent to E_a is

$$E_c = \{A_1 : x_1, \ldots, A_{n-1} : x_{n-1} \mid \exists x_n(\psi)\}$$

- *renaming:* $E_a = \rho_f(E'_a)$. Here only the target list has to be modified:

$$E_c = \{f(A_1) : x_1, \ldots, f(A_n) : x_n \mid \psi\}$$

- *selection:* $E_a = \sigma_{A_j \theta A_k}(E'_a)$ (the other case, with condition $A\theta c$, can be handled in a similar way); It suffices to transform the atomic condition by using the variables corresponding to the attributes, and to form a conjunction involving the atom thus obtained and the formula ψ:

$$E_c = \{A_1 : x_1, \ldots, A_n : x_n \mid \psi \wedge (x_j \theta x_k)\}$$

- *union:* $E_a = E'_a \cup E''_a$. By definition of union, E'_a and E''_a are defined on the same set of attributes, and therefore the same holds for the corresponding DRC expressions, which, however, need not have the same free variables:

$$E'_c = \{A_1 : x_1, \ldots, A_n : x_n \mid \psi'\}$$

$$E''_c = \{A_1 : y_1, \ldots, A_n : y_n \mid \psi''\}$$

Nevertheless, the variables can be renamed; if ψ''' is the formula obtained by renaming the free occurrences of $x_1, \ldots, x_n$ to

$y_1, \ldots, y_n$, respectively (some further renaming may be needed), then the DRC expression for E_a is

$$E_c = \{A_1 : x_1, \ldots, A_n : x_n \mid \psi' \vee \psi'''\}$$

- *difference:* similar to union, replacing the disjunction $\vee$ with the conjunction $\wedge$ preceded by a negation of the second subformula.

- *Cartesian product:* $E_a = E_a' \bowtie E_a''$. The two RA subexpressions generate results defined on disjoint sets of attributes, and we may assume that the corresponding DRC expressions have disjoint sets of free variables (otherwise we can rename them suitably):

$$E_c' = \{A_1 : x_1, \ldots, A_n : x_n \mid \psi'\}$$
$$E_c'' = \{B_1 : y_1, \ldots, B_n : y_n \mid \psi''\}$$

Then the DRC expression for E_a is obtained by putting together the two target lists and the two formulas:

$$E_c = \{A_1 : x_1, \ldots, A_n : x_n, B_1 : y_1, \ldots, B_n : y_n \mid \psi' \wedge \psi''\} \quad \square$$

Example 2.19　　Let us apply the procedure in the proof of Lemma 2.7 to the RA expression

$$\pi_{NT}(PERSONS \bowtie c)$$

where c is a constant relation defined on the attributes *Title* and *Sex* and contains two tuples t_1 and t_2, with $t_1[Title] = $ Mr., $t_1[Sex] = $ M, $t_2[Title] = $ Ms., $t_2[Sex] = $ F. We first transform the expression in order to have a Cartesian product instead of a natural join, projections that project out one attribute, and one-attribute, one-tuple constant relations:

$$\pi_{NT}(\pi_{NTS}(\pi_{NTSB}(\pi_{NTSBD}(\sigma_{S=E}($$
$$PERSONS \bowtie \rho_{E \leftarrow S}(((c_1 \bowtie c_2) \cup (c_3 \bowtie c_4)))))))))$$

where c_1 is a relation over the attribute *Title*, containing one tuple with value Mr., and c_2, c_3, c_4 are similarly defined for the respective values. By applying the transformation as in the proof of Lemma 2.7, we obtain the following DRC expression:

$$\{T : x_1, N : x_3 \mid \exists x_2(\exists x_4(\exists x_5(\exists x_6((x_4 = x_2) \wedge$$
$$PERSONS(N : x_3, S : x_4, B : x_5, D : x_6) \wedge$$
$$(((x_1 = \text{Mr.}) \wedge (x_2 = \text{M})) \vee ((x_1 = \text{Ms.}) \wedge (x_2 = \text{F})))))))\}$$

By Lemmas 2.6 and 2.7 and Theorem 2.4, we have the main result on the equivalence of algebraic and calculus-based languages.

THEOREM 2.5   The following languages are equivalent:

- Relational algebra
- Domain-independent domain relational calculus
- Domain relational calculus with range declarations   □

Theorem 2.5 states that two classes of languages, independently defined, have the same expressive power and therefore can implement the same set of queries; which means they are members of a *robust* class. This has led to a notion of completeness: a query language is *complete* if it is at least as expressive as relational algebra. An abstract characterization of completeness (therefore independent of any particular language chosen as yardstick) is that stated by Theorem 2.1. Limitations of the notion of completeness will be discussed in Section 2.9, the final section of this chapter.

2.8   Tuple Relational Calculus

As we said at the end of Section 2.6, DRC expressions are often inconvenient to write, mainly because of the number of variables needed; the situation is worsened in the version with range declarations because each of them requires a declaration. As a matter of fact, expressions would be easier to write and to read if they involved fewer variables; in this section, we present another version of the calculus, called *tuple relational calculus*, whose variables denote tuples and not individual domain elements. As shown in the next example, it is often the case that a smaller number of variables is required: in simple queries, one variable for each relation involved, plus possibly one for the result. As a price to be paid in exchange, a structure has to be associated with variables, to indicate the set of attributes on which the tuples they denote are defined;[5] in addition, comparisons require

---

[5] It should be noted that this does not mean to define a range for them, since the range requires a domain, not just a structure.

qualifications indicating the attributes involved. TRC has even more variants than DRC; the first we present is more useful for proving formal results, such as equivalence with DRC; then, we concentrate on the practical aspects. The general form of a TRC expression is

$$\{x(X) \mid f\}$$

where f is a formula, x is a *tuple variable*, the only free variable in f, and X is the set of attributes corresponding to x. The value of the expression is a relation over X consisting of all tuples that make f *true* when they are substituted for x.

Example 2.20   An expression that retrieves a relation of the database, which in DRC would require a variable per attribute, such as the following:

$$\{Sovn : x_1, From : x_2, To : x_3 \mid$$
$$REIGNS(Sovn : x_1, From : x_2, To : x_3)\}$$

can be written in TRC by using just one variable:

$$\{x(Sovn, From, To) \mid REIGNS(x)\}$$

Other TRC expressions are also simpler than their DRC counterparts; for example, the following is equivalent to expression (2.13):

$$\{x_1(Sovn, From, To) \mid REIGNS(x_1) \wedge$$
$$\forall x_2(Sovn, From, To)(\neg(REIGNS(x_2) \vee (x_2.From \geq x_1.From)))\} \quad (2.26)$$

Some others are as complex or even more so, because equalities have to be specified explicitly, rather than forced by means of equalities of variables, and because the tuple variable for the result is defined on a set of attributes that is not equal to any relation scheme. An expression equivalent to expression (2.11) is an example:

$$\{x_1(Sovn, Sex, B, From, To, D) \mid$$
$$\exists x_2(Sovn, From, To)(REIGNS(x_2) \wedge$$
$$(x_2.Sovn = x_1.Sovn) \wedge (x_2.From = x_1.From) \wedge (x_2.To = x_1.To) \wedge$$
$$\exists x_3(Name, Sex, B, D)(PERSONS(x_3) \wedge (x_3.Name = x_1.Sovn) \wedge$$
$$(x_3.Sex = x_1.Sex) \wedge (x_3.B = x_1.B) \wedge (x_3.D = x_1.D)))\} \quad (2.27)$$

The atoms of TRC differ from those of DRC only because of the different structure of the values denoted by the variables. Atoms of the first type are simplified, because only one variable appears in them, whereas atoms of the second type require a notation that allows a reference to the components of tuple variables, since usually we need comparison at the value level. Therefore, the atoms are as follows:

1. $R(x)$, where $R(X)$ is a relation scheme and x is a variable defined over X.

2. $x_1.A_1 \theta x_2.A_2$, $x_1.A_1 \theta c$, where x_1, x_2 are variables defined over X_1, X_2, respectively; A_1 belongs to X_1 and A_2 to X_2; c is a constant; and θ is a comparison operator, as in DRC.

Formulas are defined as in DRC, the only difference being that the syntax of quantifiers requires the specification of the structure of the bound variable. In this way, the structure is defined for every variable in an expression, since there is only one free variable, and its structure is declared in the target list.

The following theorem confirms that TRC and DRC have the same expressive power. Its proof is left as Exercise 2.17.

THEOREM 2.6 TRC and DRC are equivalent.   □

A direct consequence of Theorem 2.6 is that TRC is not domain-independent; it also implies that the domain-independent subset of DRC is equivalent to the domain-independent subset of TRC (DI-TRC), and therefore that the domain independence of TRC expressions is undecidable, and also that DI-TRC is equivalent to relational algebra.

COROLLARY 2.1 The following languages are equivalent:

- Relational algebra
- Domain-independent domain relational calculus
- Domain relational calculus with range declarations
- Domain-independent tuple relational calculus   □

As we did for DRC, it is reasonable at this point to look for a definition of a *TRC with range declarations (TRC-RD)*, with the same expressive power as DI-TRC, thus guaranteeing domain independence. The most natural way of defining ranges for tuple variables is to associate them with relations: each variable may vary within one relation. In this way ranges would also define the structures of the corresponding variables, and so this modification does not make the notation much heavier. Also, because ranges specify the membership of tuples in relations, atoms of the form $R(x)$ are not needed, at least in many cases. The first problem with this approach arises with respect to the target tuple, which need not have the same structure as any of the relation schemes. The solution to this problem is to define a *target list*, similar to the one we used in the domain calculus, but with elements that have the form $B : x.A$, where x is a tuple variable, A is an attribute of the relation over which it ranges, and B is the attribute for the result. If B is the same as A, we may omit it, in order to simplify the notation. We may also use shorthand sublists referring to the same variables: we may indicate $B_1 : x.A_1, \ldots, B_k : x.A_k$ by writing $B_1 \ldots B_k : x.A_1 \ldots A_k$. An even more concise form may be used if all the attributes of a variable appear in the target list and without renaming: we just write the name of the variable followed by a star $*$. Syntactically, we define ranges for bound variables as in DRC-RD, that is, at quantification time, and for free variables in a special section of the expression, called the *range list*, that precedes the formula.

Summarizing, expressions in TRC-RD conform to the following template:

$$\{\mathcal{T} \mid \mathcal{L} \mid f\}$$

where

- $\mathcal{T}$ is a target list with elements of the complete form $Y : x.Z$ (with x variable and Y and Z sequences of attributes of the same cardinality) or the simplified form $x.Z$ or $x.*$;

- $\mathcal{L}$ is a range list, whose elements have the form $x(R)$, where x is a variable and R a relation name

- f is a formula whose free variables are each present once and only once in the range list, whose atoms have the form $x.A\theta c$ or $x_1.A_1\theta x_2.A_2$, and which has ranges associated with the quantified variables.

Example 2.21   The query formulated by the TRC expression (2.26) can be expressed in TRC-RD as

$$\{x_1.* \mid x_1(REIGNS) \mid \forall x_2(REIGNS)(x_2.From \geq x_1.From)\}$$

and the query formulated by expression (2.27) as

$$\{x_1.*, x_2.(Sex, B, D) \mid x_1(REIGNS), x_2(PERSONS) \mid$$
$$x_1.Sovn = x_2.Name\} \qquad\qquad (2.28)$$

Expression (2.28) is clearly more readable than its counterpart (2.27). This situation is not coincidental; for many queries, including the most natural, the formulation by means of TRC-RD is simpler than with any other version of relational calculus. For this reason, SQL and Quel, the query languages used in the most popular relational DBMSs, are based on it: they do have a target list, as well as explicit or implicit range declarations, and formulas with no membership atoms.

However, this language is not as powerful as those we saw previously, because simple range declarations are not sufficient to implement queries whose results originate from different relations or involve values that do not appear in the database; for example, the usual union query expressed by the RA expression (2.1) cannot be formulated. We leave as Exercise 2.18 the possible extensions of TRC-RD that could make it equivalent to the other languages discussed in this chapter. Also, it is interesting to characterize the expressive power of TRC-RD; this is done by the next theorem, whose proof is also left to the reader.

THEOREM 2.7 TRC-RD is equivalent to an algebraic language that has all the RA operators except union and allows only relations from the database as operands.   □

Theorem 2.7 has a practical importance, as it explains why the SQL language, the most popular query language in relational DBMSs, has a "union" construct, despite being based on TRC. As a matter of fact, apart from extensions that are not relevant here, SQL is a TRC-RD with set-theoretic operators added.

2.9 Limitations of Relational Query Languages

We discussed at the end of Section 2.7 the notion of completeness of query languages, motivated by the equivalence of relational algebra and the various versions of relational calculus. Completeness has been assumed as a necessary requirement for the computational power of real query languages in database management systems; however, it was soon discovered that it was not sufficient, since more features are required to solve common practical problems.

The first point is that, strictly speaking, completeness refers to the *selective* power of a query language, rather than to its *computational* power: as we saw in Section 2.3, RA expressions (and thus calculus expressions) cannot create new values. Therefore, complete languages are not required to be able to express queries that involve computations on the actual values. The most natural forms of computation, which have been included in some form in query languages such as SQL and Quel, are the following:

- Value, or tuple-level computations, which can be defined by expressions (e.g., arithmetic or string expressions) on the values of each tuple of a relation (from the database or obtained as an intermediate result) in algebraic expressions, or by expressions on variables in calculus expressions. Examples would be queries calculating how long each sovereign of the family reigned or which sovereigns started their reigns before the age of eighteen. We invite the reader to devise extensions of relational algebra and of the various forms of calculus that could handle these queries.

- Computations that involve sets of tuples, such as counting their number or performing a sum or an average; these go under the name of *aggregate* computations.

Predecessor	Successor
William I	William II
William I	Henry I
William I	Stephen
William II	Henry I
William II	Stephen
Henry I	Stephen

r

Predecessor	Successor
William I	William II
William II	Henry I
Henry I	Stephen

Figure 2.16. The Norman succession and the result of expression (2.29) over it

Both classes of features can be introduced in calculus and algebra without much difficulty, and with the preservation of equivalence; therefore, we do not refer to them any more.

The second, and major, limitation of the notion of completeness is the existence of meaningful queries that complete languages need not be able to express, even if their results contain only database values and are invariant by every automorphism of the instance. The next example shows the most popular representative of this class of queries.

Example 2.22   The expression

$R \cup$

$\pi_{PredSucc}(\rho_{I_1 \leftarrow Succ}(R) \bowtie \rho_{I_1 \leftarrow Pred}(R)) \cup$

$\pi_{PredSucc}(\rho_{I_1 \leftarrow Succ}(R) \bowtie \rho_{I_1 I_2 \leftarrow PredSucc}(R) \bowtie \rho_{I_2 \leftarrow Pred}(R))$ (2.29)

computes the transitive succession relationship on the relation r in Figure 2.16, as shown there. However, expression (2.29) does not compute the transitive succession relationship for every given succession relationship; for example, given the relation r in Figure 2.17, it generates the relation shown in the same figure, which does not contain the tuple indicating that Elizabeth I was an indirect successor of Henry VII, as it should.

Predecessor	Successor
Henry VII	Henry VIII
Henry VII	Edward VI
Henry VII	Mary I
Henry VIII	Edward VI
Henry VIII	Mary I
Henry VIII	Elizabeth I
Edward VI	Mary I
Edward VI	Elizabeth I
Mary I	Elizabeth I

r	Predecessor	Successor
	Henry VII	Henry VIII
	Henry VIII	Edward VI
	Edward VI	Mary I
	Mary I	Elizabeth I

Figure 2.17. The Tudor succession and the result of expression (2.29) over it

Let us formalize a useful notion. The *transitive closure* of a (finite) binary relation $r(AB)$ is a relation $r^+(AB)$ that contains the tuples t such that for some $k > 0$, there exist k tuples $t_1, t_2, \ldots, t_k$ in r such that $t[A] = t_1[A]$, $t_i[B] = t_{i+1}[A]$, for every $1 \leq i \leq k - 1$, and $t_k[B] = t[B]$. We can now state and prove the following theorem, which refers to relational calculus, and because of the equivalence results, applies to all other relational languages.

THEOREM 2.8 The query that, for every binary relation, returns its transitive closure cannot be expressed in domain relational calculus.

PROOF   As we did in Section 2.3, we assume the domain to be unordered. Therefore, only equality or inequality comparisons appear in the expressions. We leave as an exercise the proof that this assumption does not cause a loss of generality.

We proceed by showing that for every relational calculus expression E, there is a binary relation whose transitive closure cannot be specified by E. For every $n > 0$, consider n distinct constants, and let r_n be the relation over $A_1 A_2$ with $n-1$ tuples $t_1, t_2, \ldots, t_{n-1}$ such that $t_i[A_1] = a_i$, and $t_i[A_2] = a_{i+1}$. We can see r_n as representing a graph with n nodes $a_1, \ldots, a_n$ and $n - 1$ edges $a_1 a_2, a_2 a_3, \ldots, a_{n-1} a_n$. In graph terminology, the transitive closure of r_n contains an edge $a_i a_j$ if and only if $i < j$.[6]

The major step in the proof is the fact that there exists $N > 0$ such that for every domain relational calculus expression E and for every $n > N$, the result $E(r_n)$ of E applied to r_n can be described by means of a propositional formula as follows.

- An *atom* has one of the following forms:

  - *equality atom*: $x = a$ or $x \neq a$, with x variable and a constant in $a_1, \ldots, a_n$; the meaning of atoms of these forms is the same as in domain relational calculus.

  - *distance atom*: $\mathbf{dist}(x, y) = k$ or $\mathbf{dist}(x, y) \neq k$, with x and y variables and k a non-negative integer. The atom $\mathbf{dist}(x, y) = k$ is *true* over a substitution s if $s(x) = a_i$, $s(y) = a_j$ and $j - i = k$. Essentially, in the graph framework, this atom states that the distance between the value of x and the value of y equals k. The converse is the case for $\mathbf{dist}(x, y) \neq k$.

  We say that the atoms involving $=$ are *positive* and those involving $\neq$ are *negative*.

- A *clause* is the conjunction of atoms.

- A *propositional formula in disjunctive normal form (DNF)* is the disjunction of clauses.

A DNF formula is shown in the example at the end of the proof.

We claim that every propositional formula (that is, with negations, conjunctions, and disjunctions) that includes atoms as above is equivalent to a DNF propositional formula. Reduction of propositional formulas to DNF is well known, producing a disjunction of clauses that are conjunctions of literals, each of which is in turn an atom or the negation of an atom. However, since for each atom we have the corresponding negated form, we can get rid of negations.

We can now state and prove the main lemma.

---

[6] Note that the domain is not ordered, and therefore no comparison exists among the values to implement $i < j$.

LEMMA 2.8   There exists $N > 0$ such that for every domain relational calculus expression E and for every $n > N$, the result $E(r_n)$ of E applied to r_n can be described by $\{x_1, \ldots, x_k \mid \psi\}$, where ψ is a DNF propositional formula.

PROOF   Consider the DRC expression $\{x_1, \ldots, x_k \mid f\}$, where we have omitted attribute names. We proceed by induction on the structure of f.

Basis. No connectives or quantifiers. That is, f is an atom. If it has the form $x = a$ or $x \neq a$, then it is allowed also in ψ. (We assume that only constants in a_1, ..., a_n appear in f). If the atom has the form $x = y$ (or $x \neq y$), then it can be replaced with $\mathbf{dist}(x, y) = 0$ (or $\mathbf{dist}(x, y) \neq 0$, respectively). Finally, if it has the form $R(x, y)$, then it can be replaced with $\mathbf{dist}(x, y) = 1$.

Induction. If the outermost structure involves negation, disjunction, or conjunction, then, by the induction hypothesis, all we have to do is reduce the formula to DNF, and this can be done by the claim above. Then the only significant cases involve quantifiers. Also, the universal quantifier can be reduced to the existential one—in fact, $\forall x(f)$ is equivalent to $\neg(\exists x(\neg f))$—and so it is sufficient to deal with the latter. Consider the expression $\{x_1, \ldots, x_e \mid \exists x(f)\}$. By the induction hypothesis, f can be replaced with the DNF formula $\psi = \psi_1 \vee \ldots \vee \psi_p$; therefore, what we need to do is to eliminate the quantifier from $\exists x(\psi_1 \vee \ldots \vee \psi_p)$. Then $\exists x(\psi_1 \vee \ldots \vee \psi_p)$ is equivalent to $\exists x(\psi_1) \vee \ldots \vee \exists x(\psi_p)$. We have already seen that disjunctions can be handled by reducing the formula to DNF, so it is sufficient to show how to eliminate the quantifier from $\exists x(\psi)$, where ψ is a clause. It is convenient to distinguish two cases.

1. The case in which ψ contains no positive atom involving x. In this case, we can replace $\exists x(\psi)$ with ψ', where ψ' is the clause that has the same atoms as ψ, except those involving x. Let us prove that there is an integer N such that $\{x_1, \ldots, x_e \mid \exists x(\psi)\}$ equals $\{x_1, \ldots, x_e \mid \psi'\}$, with respect to r_n, for all $n > N$. If a tuple satisfies $\exists x(\psi)$, then it satisfies all atoms that do not involve x, and so it satisfies ψ'. Conversely, if t satisfies ψ', then let N be the number of atoms in ψ involving x (all of them are negative). Then if $n > N$, there is at least a value a_h among $a_1, \ldots, a_n$ such

that ψ is true if a_h is substituted for x: essentially, each atom involving x forbids one value for x, and so N atoms cause N forbidden values—all the others are allowed.

2. The case in which ψ contains a positive atom α involving x. This atom forces x to assume a certain value or to have a fixed distance from some other variable. Then $\exists x(\psi)$ can be replaced with ψ', where ψ' contains the atoms of ψ that do not involve x and, for each atom involving x, one or more atoms, as follows:

   - If α has the form $x = a_i$, then (we refer only to positive atoms; the treatment of negative atoms is similar):
     - $\mathbf{dist}(x,y) = k$ becomes $y = a_{i+k}$ (which in turn becomes *false* if $i + k > n$; management of *true* and *false* atoms is discussed below);
     - $\mathbf{dist}(y,x) = k$ becomes $y = a_{i-k}$ (*false* if $i - k \leq 0$);
     - $x = a_j$ becomes *true* if $i = j$ and *false* if $i \neq j$.
   - If α has the form $\mathbf{dist}(x,y) = k$, then (considering again only positive atoms, and assuming that there is no atom of the form $x = a_i$, which could be treated as above):
     - $\mathbf{dist}(x,z) = h$ becomes $\mathbf{dist}(y,z) = h - k$ if $k \leq h$ and $\mathbf{dist}(z,y) = k - h$ if $k > h$;
     - $\mathbf{dist}(z,x) = h$ becomes $\mathbf{dist}(z,y) = k + h$.

   If α has the form $\mathbf{dist}(y,x) = k$, then the transformation is similar.

   Also, in the case where α has the form $\mathbf{dist}(x,y) = k$ (or the form $\mathbf{dist}(y,x) = k$), then $k - 1$ atoms $y \neq a_1, \ldots, y \neq a_{k-1}$ ($y \neq a_{n-k+1}, \ldots, y \neq a_n$, respectively) are added to the clause. Constant atoms are replaced with something that always has the same value: *false* is replaced with $\mathbf{dist}(x,x) \neq 0$, and *true* with $\mathbf{dist}(x,x) = 0$.   □

PROOF OF THEOREM 2.8 CONTINUED Now, assume that there is a DRC expression E that computes the transitive closure of binary relations. Then, if n is larger than the N in the claim of Lemma 2.8, we have that $E(R_n)$ can be expressed as $\{x_1, x_2 \mid \psi(x_1, x_2)\}$, where ψ

is a propositional formula. It is important to note that the formula ψ is essentially independent of n, except for the atoms $y \neq a_{n-k+1}$, ... $y \neq a_n$ added for the elimination of quantifiers. Moreover, the number of atoms in ψ is independent of n. Now, consider r_n with n greater than the maximum among

- N;

- the number of atoms in ψ;

- two plus the largest k appearing in a positive distance atom in ψ plus the largest p such that a_p appears in a positive equality atom;

- the minimum value such that there is a sequence of at least $k+2$ values a_p, ..., a_{p+k+1} such that none of them is involved in a negative equality atom in ψ, where k is the largest value in a negative distance atom in ψ.

We show that $E(r_n)$ is not equal to the transitive closure r_n^+ of r_n. We distinguish two cases.

1. Every clause of ψ has a positive atom. Each clause either forces one of the variables (x_1 or x_2) to be equal to a constant, or "fixes the distance" between x_1 and x_2. Now, let k be the largest integer appearing in a positive distance atom and p be the largest value such that a_p appears in a positive equality atom in ψ. Then a_{p+1} and a_{p+k+2} do not appear in any positive equality atom, and $k+1$ does not appear in any positive distance atom. Therefore, the pair a_{p+1}, a_{p+k+2}, which belongs to r_n^+ (note that $n \geq p+k+2$), does not belong to $E(r_n)$, because it does not satisfy any clause. Thus, $E(r_n) \neq r_n^+$.

2. Some clause ψ' of ψ has only negative atoms. Let a_p, a_{p+k+1} be two values that do not appear in negative equality atoms and such that k is the largest value in a negative distance atom in ψ. These values exist by the hypotheses above on n. Then the pair a_{p+k+1}, a_p satisfies ψ', since it does not violate any of the atoms in ψ' (which are all negative), and so it belongs to $E(r_n)$, whereas it does not belong to r_n^+. Again, this means that $E(r_n) \neq r_n^+$. $\square$

Example 2.23   Apart from some negative equality atoms (which, however, do not change the meaning), Lemma 2.8 generates for the expression

$$\{\, x_1, x_2 \quad | \quad R(x_1, x_2) \,\vee$$
$$\exists y_1(R(x_1, y_1) \wedge R(y_1, x_2)) \,\vee$$
$$\exists y_1(\exists y_2(R(x_1, y_1) \wedge R(y_1, y_2) \wedge R(y_2, x_2)))\,\}$$

which is equivalent to Expression (2.29) in Example 2.22, the following expression:

$$\{\, x_1, x_2 \mid \mathbf{dist}(x_1, x_2) = 1 \vee \mathbf{dist}(x_1, x_2) = 2 \vee \mathbf{dist}(x_1, x_2) = 3 \,\}$$

This confirms that relational calculus expressions can only specify a fixed number of distances in the transitive closures, and therefore cannot specify this operation for every binary relation.

At first, Theorem 2.8 may appear to contradict Theorem 2.1, because the result of a transitive closure is always invariant by every automorphism of the database instance. As we said at the end of Section 2.3, however, Theorem 2.1 refers to the queries over a *fixed* instance, and not to queries over *all* the instances of a scheme.

We can understand this matter better by means of a formalization that allows us to draw a corollary from Theorem 2.1. A query Q is *generic* if, for every database instance $\mathbf{r}$ and for every automorphism h of $\mathbf{r}$, it is the case that $h(Q(\mathbf{r})) = Q(\mathbf{r})$; that is, if Q preserves for every instance the automorphisms of the instance.

COROLLARY 2.2   For every database scheme, for every generic query Q, and for every database instance $\mathbf{r}$, there is a relational algebra expression such that the result of Q on $\mathbf{r}$ is equal to the value of E on $\mathbf{r}$: $Q(\mathbf{r}) = E(\mathbf{r})$.

PROOF   Let us consider a database scheme, a generic query Q, and a database instance $\mathbf{r}$. Because Q is generally partial, $Q(\mathbf{r})$ may be undefined; in this case it is sufficient to pick an RA expression whose value is undefined (e.g., referring to relation schemes not in the database scheme). Otherwise, since Q is generic, for every automorphism h of the instance $\mathbf{r}$, we have $h(Q(\mathbf{r})) = Q(\mathbf{r})$; that is, $Q(\mathbf{r})$ is invariant by every automorphism of **r**. By Theorem 2.1, there is an expression E whose value on **r** is equal to $Q(\mathbf{r})$. $\qquad\qquad\square$

Now, the fact is that for each binary relation, there is an RA expression that computes its transitive closure, since transitive closure is a generic function, but there is no RA expression that computes the transitive closure for *every* binary relation.

A more general notion of completeness may be defined by putting the emphasis not on the results of queries on a fixed instance, but on the queries themselves as functions: a query language L is *CH-complete* (from Chandra and Harel, who introduced the notion [69]) if for every database scheme and for every generic query Q, there is an L expression E such that for every database instance **r**, it is the case that $Q(\mathbf{r}) = E(\mathbf{r})$; here the expression E is the same for every instance **r**. The canonical example of a CH-complete language, QL, was also proposed by Chandra and Harel: informally, it includes relational algebra extended with an assignment statement (and so relation variables) and iteration with an emptiness test. As a matter of fact, the practical languages SQL and Quel are often used in existing systems *embedded* in a host language (any high-level programming language): the use of programming constructs leads to full computing power.

In Chapter 9 we will discuss languages based on first-order logic, which have more expressive power than relational algebra and calculus. They allow the specification of transitive closure.

Exercises

2.1 Show that the natural join of two relations with identical schemes is equal to their intersection.

2.2 Given two relations $r_1(X_1)$ and $r_2(X_2)$, with $X_2 \subset X_1$, the *division* $r_1 \div r_2$ is a relation over $X_1 - X_2$ containing the tuples t such that for each $t_2 \in r_2$ there is a tuple $t_1 \in r_1$ that is the combination of t and t_2 (that is, such that $t_1[X_2] = t_2$, and $t_1[X_1 - X_2] = t$). Show that

- division can be expressed in terms of other operators; and that

- division is a sort of inverse of the Cartesian product, by proving the following equality: $(r_1 \times r_2) \div r_2 = r_1$.

2.3 Consider a database scheme referring to a catalogue of books with personal data on the authors:

> *BOOKS (ISBN, Author, Title, Publisher, Year)*
> *COAUTHORS (ISBN, JointAuthor)*
> *PERSONS (Name, Birth, Residence)*
> *PUBLISHERS (Publisher, City),*

where *Author* indicates the senior author of each book, the others (if any) being stored in the *COAUTHORS* relation, and *Residence* is the city of residence of a person (assumed invariant).

Formulate the following queries in relational algebra:

- Find the books whose senior author lives in the city of the publisher.
- Find the joint authors who are younger than their senior authors, indicating also the title of the book and the year of publication.
- Find the pairs of people who published together more than one book, exchanging the roles of senior author and joint author.
- Find the authors who published a book before a coauthor of a subsequent book of theirs was born.

2.4 Show that every RA expression can be transformed to an equivalent expression whose constant relations are all defined on singleton schemes and contain only one tuple.

2.5 Show that every RA expression can be transformed to an equivalent expression such that selections have only atomic conditions, projections project out one attribute at a time, and the other operators involved are only union, renaming, difference, and Cartesian product.

2.6 Discuss the hypothesis that requires each formula and subformula to have at least one free variable; specifically, consider its implications for the semantics of expressions (the value of expressions on substitutions) and for the equivalence of DRC and relational algebra.

2.7 Formulate the queries in Exercise 2.3 in domain relational calculus.

2.8 Prove that the relational algebra is domain-independent (Theorem 2.3).

2.9 Prove Lemma 2.2.

2.10 Prove Lemma 2.3.

2.11 Prove Lemma 2.4.

2.12 Formulate the queries in Exercise 2.3 in domain relational calculus with range declarations.

2.13 On the basis of your knowledge of Query-by-Example, discuss why it can be considered as an implementation of DRC-RD. Find, to the extent possible, a method for the transformation of expressions between the two languages.

2.14 Discuss possible extensions of relational algebra that make it equivalent to DRC, thus allowing expressions that are not domain-independent.

2.15 Propose extensions of relational algebra and of the various forms of calculus that could handle queries involving numeric tuple-level computations, such as *How long did each sovereign of the family reign?* or *Which sovereigns started their reigns before reaching the age of eighteen?*

2.16 Formulate the queries in Exercise 2.3 in tuple relational calculus.

2.17 Give a complete proof of the equivalence of TRC and DRC (that is, prove Theorem 2.6).

2.18 Propose extensions to TRC-RD that would make it equivalent to the other languages discussed in the chapter.

2.19 Prove Theorem 2.7.

2.20 Prove that SQL is at least as expressive as relational algebra, and that it would be strictly less expressive if it had no union operator.

Comments and References

Most of the operators of relational algebra were presented by Codd [76] together with the presentation of the relational model. Various, slightly different presentations appear in the texts cited in Chapter 1 [87,95,144,212,217].

The study of the expressive power of relational algebra, as presented in Section 2.3, is due to Paredaens [178]; similar results for relational calculus were presented by Bancilhon [34].

Relational calculus is originally due to Codd [77,79], who presented a TRC (called ALPHA) with a form of range declarations. A detailed discussion of the various forms of relational calculus, showing the problems related to the transformation of a generic applied calculus into a query language, is in Pirotte [179], who also realized the distinction between domain and tuple calculus.

The notion of domain independence, known by other names in more general contexts [94], has evolved slowly in database theory. As soon as general definitions of DRC and TRC were given, the undesirability of expressions whose result could be the whole domain was detected, and notions of type or range were introduced [79,179]; however, the emphasis was on the impossibility (or at least the difficulty) of the effective computation of their results [162,212]. In formal contexts not using range declarations, two solutions were proposed: (1) restrict the language to a class of well-behaved expressions (*range-restricted* [174], *safe* [212], *evaluable* [92], *allowed* [209]); (2) interpret queries with respect to the active domain rather than the whole domain (*limited interpretation* [162]). Then the importance of *domain independence* as a semantic notion was recognized (introduced by Fagin [101] in the context of formulas describing integrity constraints); its undecidability was inferred from existing results [94,220]; and safety and the other properties above were understood as sufficient conditions for domain independence. Our approach in Section 2.6 follows this last pattern, except that the use of range declaration has the advantage of giving a formal justification to the properties of the languages actually used in existing systems.

The equivalence of algebraic and calculus-based languages was also shown by Codd [79]; other proofs were proposed by Ullman [212] and

Maier [162]. The equivalence induced Codd [79] to define the notion of completeness; by means of his language ALPHA, he also asserted the need for more than complete languages, providing tuple and aggregate functions. Completeness was then characterized by Paredaens [178] and Bancilhon [34]; Klug [143] extended the equivalence proof to an algebra and a calculus that both have aggregate functions. Aho and Ullman [16] proved that transitive closure cannot be expressed in relational algebra, which we have shown as Theorem 2.8. They proved it for relational algebra, whereas we have referred to the calculus, but the result is the same, since the two languages are equivalent. Chandra and Harel [71] introduced the notion of *computable queries* (what we called CH-completeness) and the CH-complete language QL. Related notions about generic queries were studied by Hull [123].

Chandra [70] presents an interesting survey of various issues related to query languages (including more powerful languages than those discussed in this chapter), describing hierarchies of languages based on expressive power, on complexity, and on programming primitives. His extensive bibliography includes references to papers published in the logic community that contain some of the results discussed here, proved earlier and in more general contexts.

As we said in Chapter 1, little attention was devoted for many years to update languages. It was believed that updates were usually specified by means of simple operations (the insertion of individual tuples, and the deletion and modification of sets of tuples that satisfy a condition) that could be reduced to algebraic operations. More recently, it has been argued that interesting issues may arise, and a new trend has developed. We have omitted this topic from the present book, but we point here to some references. An interesting survey on the major aspects was published by Abiteboul [1]. Important results are due to Abiteboul and Vianu [8,9,10,11,12].

Chapter 3

Dependency Theory: Part 1

In Chapter 1, we introduced integrity constraints as a tool for improving the description of the application of interest by means of a relational database. We also explained how constraints of specific forms (keys, functional dependencies) can be used to evaluate the quality of a database scheme and to suggest its decomposition. In the following chapters, we encounter other topics that involve integrity constraints. In fact, integrity constraints play a central role in relational database theory, and a deep study of their properties is therefore meaningful. This and the next chapter are entirely devoted to this task. This chapter presents an introduction to the topic and the fundamental results concerning functional dependencies. Chapter 4 presents more advanced material on functional dependencies and some results about other dependencies.

Section 3.1 establishes the framework with a formal introduction of the notion of *constraint*, with its main properties and definitions, including examples of specific classes of constraints (such as functional and inclusion dependencies), and the notion of *implication*. In Section 3.2 we present a first method for studying the implication problem of functional dependencies, based on formal systems of inference rules. Efficient algorithms based on this method are then presented in detail in Section 3.3. In Section 3.4 we study the relationship between keys and functional dependencies, and in Section 3.5 we analyze how sets of functional dependencies can be represented in a synthetic manner. In both these sections, we present some efficient algorithms and some negative complexity results.

3.1   Integrity Constraints: Basic Concepts

In formal terms, an *integrity constraint* γ on a database scheme $\mathbf{R}$ is a function that associates with each database $\mathbf{r}$ of $\mathbf{R}$ a Boolean value $\gamma(\mathbf{r})$. A database $\mathbf{r}$ of $\mathbf{R}$ *satisfies* γ if $\gamma(\mathbf{r}) = true$, and *violates* γ if $\gamma(\mathbf{r}) = false$. In the former case, we also say that γ *holds* in $\mathbf{r}$. Each constraint expresses a property that every acceptable database must satisfy. Therefore, it is common to associate with a database scheme $\mathbf{R}$ a set Γ of constraints, and to say that the *consistent* (or *legal*) databases of $\mathbf{R}$ are those that satisfy Γ (i.e., that satisfy all the constraints in Γ).

Constraints are grouped in *classes*. There is a notation to express the constraints in each class (the *syntax*) and a rule that defines the Boolean function associated with each constraint (the *semantics*). In most cases, the Boolean functions can be expressed by means of closed sentences of some first-order predicate calculus.

Integrity constraints and their classes can be divided into two main categories:

1. *Intrarelational constraints*, each of which involves one relation scheme

2. *Interrelational constraints*, which in general involve several relation schemes.

When dealing with intrarelational constraints, it is sometimes convenient to refer only to the involved relation, omitting any reference to the other relations, and even to the fact that there is a database involving other relations.

As we saw in Chapter 1, the most common constraint on relational databases (and usually one of the few to be actually implemented in existing systems) is the *key dependency*. Given a relation scheme $R(U)$, a *key dependency* is expressed as $key(K)$ (where $K \subseteq U$), and is satisfied by a relation r if r does not contain two distinct tuples, t_1 and t_2, with the same values on K ($t_1[K] = t_2[K]$). Thus the key dependency $key(K)$ is satisfied by a relation r if and only if K is a superkey for r, not necessarily minimal.

Together with key dependencies, the most studied class of intrarelational constraints is that of *functional dependencies* (hereinafter

zoo	Kind	Inventory#	Area	House	Cage	Keeper	Head
	giraffe	01	West	fence	1	Scott	White
	giraffe	02	West	fence	2	Scott	White
	lion	01	South	lair	3	Rogers	Green
	bear	01	East	cave	6	Grant	Smith
	bear	02	East	cave	9	Grant	Smith
	zebra	01	West	fence	8	Scott	White

Figure 3.1. A relation for Example 3.1

abbreviated FDs): given a relation scheme $R(U)$, an FD has the syntax $X \to Y$, where X and Y are nonempty subsets of U,[1] and are respectively called the *left-hand side (lhs)* and the *right-hand side (rhs)* of the FD. The associated predicate is

$$\forall t_1, t_2 \in r \ (\textit{if } t_1[X] = t_2[X], \textit{ then } t_1[Y] = t_2[Y])$$

It states that if a pair of tuples in r has the same values on the attributes in X, then it has the same values on the attributes in Y. Clearly, if $XY = U$, the FD $X \to Y$ on relation scheme $R(U)$ holds if and only if $key(X)$ holds. Therefore, we can say that key dependencies are a special case of FDs.

> **Example 3.1**   The relation in Figure 3.1, already shown in Chapter 1, satisfies the key dependency *key(Kind, Inventory#)* and the FD *House $\to$ Keeper*, and does not satisfy *key(Kind)* nor *House $\to$ Inventory#*.

Tuple constraints, which put restrictions on individual tuples, form another interesting class of intrarelational constraints. They are expressed by means of propositional formulas, with the same form as those we saw for the selection operator in Section 1.4. Many properties, meaningful from the application point of view, can be expressed by means of tuple constraints. The Boolean function associated with a tuple constraint can be expressed by means of a predicate with one

---

[1] Exercise 3.6 discusses the nonemptiness assumption.

payroll

Employee	Salary	Deductions	NetSalary
John	50000	10000	40000
Bob	65000	20000	45000
Mike	48000	9500	38500

Figure 3.2. A relation that satisfies the tuple constraint in Example 3.2

payroll

Employee	Salary	Deductions	NetSalary
John	50000	10000	40000
Bob	65000	20000	55000
Mike	48000	9500	38500

Figure 3.3. A relation that violates the tuple constraint in Example 3.2

universally quantified variable, representing the various tuples in the relation, which must satisfy the condition.

Example 3.2   If we want to define on the relation scheme

$$PAYROLL(Employee, Salary, Deductions, NetSalary)$$

the obvious constraint that for every employee, the net salary is positive and equals the (gross) salary minus the deductions, we can use the following tuple constraint:

$$(NetSalary = Salary - Deductions) \land (NetSalary > 0).$$

The associated predicate is the following:

$$\forall t \in payroll((t[NetSalary] = t[Salary] - t[Deductions]) \land (t[NetSalary] > 0)).$$

The relation in Figure 3.2 satisfies this constraint, whereas the relation in Figure 3.3 does not, because in the second tuple the net salary is not equal to the difference between gross salary and deductions.

The most interesting interrelational constraint is the *inclusion dependency*, used to express a containment relationship between projections of (possibly different) relations. For the sake of simplicity, we present here only a special case. Given a database scheme

r_1	Student	Course
	Bob	CS101
	Tom	CS101
	Mike	CS101
	Sean	CS201
	Luke	CS201

r_2	Course	Instructor
	CS101	Smith
	CS201	Jones
	CS224	Robinson

Figure 3.4. A database that satisfies the IND $R_2[Course] \supseteq R_1[Course]$

r_1	Student	Course
	Bob	CS101
	Tom	CS101
	Sean	CS201
	Luke	CS201

r_2	Course	Instructor
	CS101	Smith
	CS224	Robinson

Figure 3.5. A database that violates the IND $R_2[Course] \supseteq R_1[Course]$

$\mathbf{R} = \{R_1(X_1), \ldots, R_n(X_n)\}$, a *typed inclusion dependency* (IND) is expressed by the notation $R_i[Y] \supseteq R_j[Y]$, where $Y \subseteq X_i \cap X_j$. It is satisfied by a database $\mathbf{r} = \{r_1, \ldots, r_n\}$ of $\mathbf{R}$ if it is the case that $\pi_Y(r_i) \supseteq \pi_Y(r_j)$.

Example 3.3 In the databases over the scheme

$$\mathbf{R} = \{R_1(Student, Course), R_2(Course, Instructor)\}$$

which is used to represent the courses offered, their respective instructors, and the students taking them, it would be natural to require that a student can take a course only if it is offered. The IND $R_2[Course] \supseteq R_1[Course]$ expresses exactly this property. The database in Figure 3.4 satisfies this IND, whereas the database in Figure 3.5 does not.

Let us now turn to more general issues. Consider a generic database scheme $\mathbf{R}$ (or a generic relation scheme R, if we refer to intrarelational constraints only). Given a set of constraints Γ, it usually happens that if a database satisfies Γ, then it satisfies other constraints not in Γ. We say that Γ *implies* a constraint γ if γ holds in all the databases of $\mathbf{R}$ that satisfy Γ. As a special case, if Γ is the empty set of constraints and Γ implies γ, we say that γ is *trivial*, because it holds in every database of the given scheme (since every database satisfies the empty set of constraints).

> **Example 3.4**   Given the scheme in Example 3.2, every relation satisfies the constraint
>
> $$(NetSalary = Salary) \vee (NetSalary \neq Salary)$$
>
> which is therefore trivial. Also, every relation that satisfies the tuple constraint in Example 3.2 satisfies other tuple constraints, such as
>
> $$Salary = NetSalary + Deductions$$
> $$Salary > Deductions$$

The following fact will be used in subsequent proofs; its easy proof is left as an exercise.

FACT 3.1   A set of constraints Γ does not imply a constraint γ if and only if there is a database that satisfies Γ and does not satisfy γ. $\square$

Given a set Γ of constraints of a given class $\mathcal{C}$ defined on a scheme $\mathbf{R}$, the *closure* of Γ with respect to $\mathcal{C}$ is the set of constraints of the class $\mathcal{C}$ implied by Γ. It is indicated with $(\Gamma)_{\mathcal{C}}^{+}$. It must be noted that the notion of closure refers to a particular class of constraints: the closure $(\Gamma)_{\mathcal{C}_1}^{+}$ of Γ with respect to a class $\mathcal{C}_1$ may be different from the closure $(\Gamma)_{\mathcal{C}_2}^{+}$ of Γ with respect to another class $\mathcal{C}_2$. However, the class under consideration is often clear from the context, and therefore we will usually write Γ^{+} instead of $\Gamma_{\mathcal{C}}^{+}$. Interesting properties hold for closures of sets of constraints. They are stated in the next fact, whose proof is left as an exercise.

FACT 3.2   Let Γ and Γ_1 be sets of constraints. Then the following hold:

1. $\Gamma \subseteq \Gamma^{+}$. (Every set of constraints is contained in its own closure.)
2. $(\Gamma^{+})^{+} = \Gamma^{+}$. (The closure of the closure is the closure itself.)
3. If $\Gamma \subseteq \Gamma_1$ then $\Gamma^{+} \subseteq \Gamma_1^{+}$. (The closure operation is monotonic.)

4. It is not always the case that $\Gamma^+ \cup \Gamma_1^+ = (\Gamma \cup \Gamma_1)^+$. (The closure operation is not additive). □

A set of constraints is *closed with respect to implication* if it is equal to its closure: $\Gamma = \Gamma^+$.

As we said at the beginning of the chapter, integrity constraints are used to refine the description of the application of interest as far as possible. From this point of view, even the constraints that are not explicitly defined but are indeed implied should be considered as defined. Therefore, given a set Γ, what is important is its closure: two sets Γ_1 and Γ_2 are *equivalent* if they have identical closures; that is, $\Gamma_1^+ = \Gamma_2^+$. In this case we also say that Γ_1 is a *cover* of Γ_2 (and vice versa). It is obviously useful to have covers be as small as possible: a constraint γ is *redundant* in a set Γ if Γ and $\Gamma - \{\gamma\}$ are equivalent. A set Γ is *redundant* if there is a constraint γ that is redundant in Γ.

To see whether two sets of constraints Γ_1 and Γ_2 are equivalent, it is sufficient to check whether each constraint of Γ_1 is implied by Γ_2, and vice versa. Similarly, to verify that a set Γ of constraints is redundant, it is sufficient to confirm that there is a constraint $\gamma \in \Gamma$ such that $\Gamma - \{\gamma\}$ implies γ. As a consequence, both the equivalence and the redundancy tests can be reduced to the following problem, called the *implication problem*: Given Γ and γ, does Γ imply γ? This is therefore the fundamental problem in the study of constraints. As we will see, there are classes of constraints for which the implication problem can be solved efficiently, even in linear time, classes for which it can only be solved inefficiently, and classes for which it is undecidable.

An interesting method for the study of the implication problem is based on *inference rules*. Given a set Γ of constraints, inference rules generate a set that contains Γ and in general other constraints, called the set of constraints *derivable* from Γ by means of the rules. Precise definitions about inference rules will be given in the next section with the inference rules for FDs. Here we give the basic ideas. Since we want to use the inference rules to generate the constraints implied by any given set of a fixed class, we need rules that generate only constraints that are in $(\Gamma)_C^+$, for any given set Γ of the class C. A rule with this property is said to be *sound*. Moreover, in order to compute the closures, we need sets of rules that allow the derivation of all the constraints in the closure. A set of rules is *complete* for a given class $\mathcal{C}$ if it allows the derivation of $(\Gamma)_\mathcal{C}^+$ for every set Γ of constraints of $\mathcal{C}$.

> **Example 3.5**   The following is a sound inference rule: Given a relation scheme $R(X)$, for every $A_1, A_2, A_3 \in X$, from the FDs $A_1 \rightarrow A_2$ and $A_2 \rightarrow A_3$, derive the FD $A_1 \rightarrow A_3$. The rule is sound because the FD $A_1 \rightarrow A_3$ is implied by $A_1 \rightarrow A_2$ and $A_2 \rightarrow A_3$. This rule is a special case of the *transitivity* rule for FDs, which we will encounter in the next section, as we study rules for FDs.

Inference rules have been widely studied for various classes of constraints. They are interesting in their own right, because the existence of a simple sound and complete set of rules is often an elegant result, but they are important mainly because they allow a deep understanding of the implication problem: most of the algorithms for testing implication of constraints have completeness proofs that make use of the inference rules and of their completeness.

A second technique for the implication problem is based on the notion of *tableau* (intuitively, a relation whose values are not only constants, but also variables) and on the *chase* algorithm (a process that, given a tableau T and a set of constraints Γ, finds a tableau that is as similar to T as possible and satisfies Γ). Essentially, one tries to build a counterexample relation (according to Fact 3.1) with variables, and force it to satisfy all the dependencies; the given constraint is implied if and only if it holds in the resulting tableau. This method is interesting because it is (to a certain extent) parametric with respect to the class of constraint. We will discuss it in detail in Chapter 4.

3.2   Inference Rules for Functional Dependencies

In this section we present the inference rules for FDs and prove their correctness. We first prove some properties of FDs that follow from the definitions given in Section 3.1 and then show how they can be used as inference rules. We assume that all FDs are defined on a relation scheme $R(U)$. Therefore, all the sets of attributes mentioned are nonempty subsets of U.

LEMMA 3.1 An FD $X \rightarrow Y$ is trivial if and only if $X \supseteq Y$.

PROOF

If. Let $X \supseteq Y$. We show that $X \rightarrow Y$ is trivial, that is (following the definition), that $X \rightarrow Y$ holds in every database of R. Consider a pair of tuples $t_1, t_2 \in r$. If $t_1[X] = t_2[X]$, then $t_1[A] = t_2[A]$ for every $A \in X$. Then, since $Y \subseteq X$, $t_1[A] = t_2[A]$ for every $A \in Y$, which is equivalent to saying that $t_1[Y] = t_2[Y]$.

Only if. We proceed by showing that if $X \not\supseteq Y$, then $X \rightarrow Y$ is not trivial. Since $X \not\supseteq Y$, there is an attribute $A \in Y - X$. Let r be a relation containing two tuples t_1 and t_2 such that $t_1[X] = t_2[X]$ and $t_1[B] \neq t_2[B]$ for all the attributes $B \notin X$.[2] Relation r does not satisfy $X \rightarrow Y$, since $A \notin X$ and therefore $t_1[Y] \neq t_2[Y]$. □

LEMMA 3.2 If r satisfies $X \rightarrow Y$, and $Z \supseteq X$, $W \subseteq Y$, then r satisfies $Z \rightarrow W$.

PROOF Let r satisfy $X \rightarrow Y$; we show that it also satisfies $Z \rightarrow W$. Let t_1, t_2 be tuples in r such that $t_1[Z] = t_2[Z]$; we show that $t_1[W] = t_2[W]$. If $t_1[Z] = t_2[Z]$, then (since $Z \supseteq X$) $t_1[X] = t_2[X]$, and so (since r satisfies $X \rightarrow Y$) $t_1[Y] = t_2[Y]$; therefore (since $W \subseteq Y$) $t_1[W] = t_2[W]$. □

LEMMA 3.3 If r satisfies $X \rightarrow Y$ and $Z \rightarrow W$, with $Z \subseteq Y$, then r satisfies $X \rightarrow YW$.

PROOF Let r satisfy $X \rightarrow Y$ and $Z \rightarrow W$, and let $t_1, t_2 \in r$, with $t_1[X] = t_2[X]$. Since r satisfies $X \rightarrow Y$, it is the case that $t_1[Y] = t_2[Y]$, and (since $Z \subseteq Y$) $t_1[Z] = t_2[Z]$. Thus (since r satisfies $Z \rightarrow W$) $t_1[W] = t_2[W]$, and therefore $t_1[YW] = t_2[YW]$, which proves the claim, confirming that r satisfies $X \rightarrow YW$. □

These three lemmas give sufficient conditions for the implication of FDs. Their claims can be used as the basis for *sound inference rules*, that is, rules that, given a set F of FDs, generate FDs implied by F. Inference rules reduce implication to syntactic manipulation:

---

[2]Clearly, this requires that the domains have at least two elements each, a definitely reasonable assumption. Actually, we assume that domains are countably infinite, so that new values are available whenever they are needed.

constraints are derived by means of the rules, and this is simpler than proving each time, by means of arguments on tuples and values, that an FD is implied. An *inference rule* is a statement of the form[3]

$$\textbf{if } f_1, f_2, \ldots, f_k \textbf{ with } P, \textbf{ then } f_{k+1}$$

where f_i, for $i = 1, 2, \ldots, k + 1$, is an FD $X_i \rightarrow Y_i$,[4] and P is a decidable condition on $f_1, f_2, \ldots, f_{k+1}$. The FDs $f_1, f_2, ..., f_k$ are the *antecedents* of the rule, and f_{k+1} is the *consequence*. An example of an inference rule is the following:

$$\textbf{if } X_1 \rightarrow Y_1, \ X_2 \rightarrow Y_2 \textbf{ with } Y_1 = X_2 \wedge X_1 = X_3 \wedge Y_2 = Y_3,$$
$$\textbf{then } X_3 \rightarrow Y_3$$

In most cases, we will use shorthand for our rules, embedding part of the condition P in the sets of attributes involved. Thus, the above rule may be written as

$$\textbf{if } X_1 \rightarrow Y_1, \ Y_1 \rightarrow Y_2, \textbf{ then } X_1 \rightarrow Y_2$$

or, more readably, as

$$\textbf{if } X \rightarrow Y, \ Y \rightarrow Z, \textbf{ then } X \rightarrow Z$$

If a rule has no antecedents, it is called an *axiom (scheme)*;[5] we write axiom schemes as follows:

$$\textbf{if } \perp \textbf{ with } P, \textbf{ then } f$$

Inference rules are used in many fields other than relational database theory as tools for the syntactic manipulation of phrases that have some semantics. The notions of the *soundness* and *completeness* of a set of rules relate syntax to semantics. A rule such as

$$\textbf{if } f_1, f_2, \ldots, f_k \textbf{ with } P, \textbf{ then } f_{k+1}$$

---

[3] For the sake of clarity, we explicitly refer to FDs, but the concepts can be extended with little effort to any kind of constraint.

[4] To be more precise, $X_i \rightarrow Y_i$ is a *scheme* of FD, since it stands for any FD that, together with the others, satisfy the condition P.

[5] The terms *axiom* and *inference rule* are often used as synonyms in the relational literature, as opposed to their use in the area of formal systems, from which they originate.

is *sound* if, for every relation scheme $R(U)$ and for every $(k+1)$-tuple $f_1, f_2, \ldots, f_k, f_{k+1}$ of FDs on $R(U)$ that satisfy P, it is the case that the set of FDs $\{f_1, f_2, \ldots, f_k\}$ implies f_{k+1}.

An immediate consequence of Lemmas 3.1, 3.2, and 3.3 is the soundness of the following inference rules:[6]

FD1. *Reflexivity:* **if** $\perp$, **then** $X \rightarrow X$.

FD2. *Decomposition:* **if** $X \rightarrow YZ$, **then** $X \rightarrow Y$.

FD3. *(Extended) transitivity:* **if** $X \rightarrow YW$, $W \rightarrow Z$, **then** $X \rightarrow YWZ$.[7]

We now discuss how inference rules can be used to deduce the implication of FDs. First of all, we say that f_{k+1} *follows from* f_1, $f_2, \ldots, f_k$ *by an application of rule* $\mathcal{R}$,[8] if $f_1, f_2, \ldots, f_{k+1}$ satisfy the condition P associated with $\mathcal{R}$. For example, the FD $A \rightarrow BCD$ follows from $A \rightarrow BC$ and $BC \rightarrow CD$ by an application of the rule of transitivity (with $X = A, Y = \emptyset, W = BC, Z = CD$). Given a set F of FDs and a single FD f, a *derivation of f from F by means of a set $\mathcal{S}$ of rules* is a finite sequence of FDs such that (1) each FD in the sequence is in F or follows from previous FDs in the sequence by an application of one of the rules, and (2) f appears in the sequence (usually as the last element). If there is a derivation of f from F by means of $\mathcal{S}$, we say that f is *derivable from F by means of rules $\mathcal{S}$*. We will often omit the reference to the set of rules if it is understood from the context.

> **Example 3.6**   The following is a derivation of $AC \rightarrow DE$ from $F = \{BC \rightarrow DE, A \rightarrow B, AEG \rightarrow H\}$, by means of Rules FD1, FD2, and FD3:
>
>   1. $AC \rightarrow AC$ (by FD1)

---

[6]As a matter of fact, Lemmas 3.1, 3.2, and 3.3 imply the soundness of more general rules. As we will see, these rules form a complete set and reflect more naturally the derivation process, as performed by the implication algorithms.

[7]In the literature, it is common to find other sets of inference rules that include the rule of *transitivity*: **if** $X \rightarrow Y$, $Y \rightarrow Z$, **then** $X \rightarrow Z$.

[8]Here, k is equal to the number of antecedents in the inference: for the three rules shown, we have $k = 0$ for FD1, $k = 1$ for FD2, and $k = 2$ for FD3.

2. $A \rightarrow B$ (in F)
3. $AC \rightarrow ABC$ (from [1] and [2] by FD3)
4. $AC \rightarrow BC$ (from [3] by FD2)
5. $BC \rightarrow DE$ (in F)
6. $AC \rightarrow BCDE$ (from [4] and [5] by FD3)
7. $AC \rightarrow DE$ (from [6] by FD2)

The soundness of the individual rules guarantees that, by repeated applications of the rules, only rules implied by the given set can be produced. The formal proof of this claim, stated in the next lemma, should be carried out by induction on the length of the derivation (see Exercise 3.7).

LEMMA 3.4 If f is derivable from F by means of Rules FD1, FD2, FD3, then F implies f (i.e., $f \in F^+$).   □

Obviously, a set of sound rules is really meaningful if it enjoys also the converse property, that is, if all implied FDs are also derivable. A set of inference rules is said to be *complete* (with respect to the implication of FDs) if for every set F of FDs, f is derivable from F if $f \in F^+$. Therefore, a set of rules is sound and complete when for every F, f is derivable from F if and only if $f \in F^+$. It is important to stress that soundness and completeness are independent notions; we may have sound sets that are not complete (any set containing only two of the Rules FD1, FD2, FD3, is sound but not complete), and sets that are complete without being sound.

Example 3.7   The rule

$$\textbf{if } \bot, \textbf{ then } X \rightarrow Y$$

is complete because it allows the derivation of every FD, but not sound because, in general, it is not the case that all possible FDs are in F^+.

We devote the rest of this section to the proof that FD1, FD2, and FD3 form a complete set of rules for FDs. First of all, we present a lemma that states interesting properties of FDs. Its proof is left as an exercise.

LEMMA 3.5 Let F be a set of FDs.

 a. A relation satisfies $X \to Y$ if and only if it satisfies $X \to A$ for every $A \in Y$.

 b. $X \to Y$ is derivable from F by means of FD1, FD2, and FD3 if and only if $X \to A$ is derivable from F by means of FD1, FD2, and FD3 for every $A \in Y$.

 c. $X \to Y \in F^+$ if and only if $X \to A \in F^+$ for every $A \in Y$.   □

Note that for the time being, Claims *(b)* and *(c)* in Lemma 3.5 have distinct meanings: one refers to derivation and the other to implication. When we will have proved the completeness of the rules, they will imply each other. An immediate consequence of Lemma 3.5*(c)* is the fact that for every set of FDs, there is an equivalent set containing only FDs with singletons on the rhs. Therefore, considering sets of FDs, we may assume without loss of generality that all the FDs have singletons on the rhs.

Given a set F of FDs and a set of attributes X, let $\mathcal{Y}$ be the following set of sets of attributes:

$$\mathcal{Y} = \{Y \mid X \to Y \text{ is derivable from } F \text{ by means of FD1 and FD3}\}$$

Also, let $X^+ = \cup_{Y \in \mathcal{Y}} Y$. The set X^+ is called the *closure of X with respect to F*.[9] This is a fundamental notion in the theory of FDs. The following lemma states its basic properties.

LEMMA 3.6

 a. $X \to X^+$ is derivable from F by means of Rules FD1 and FD3.

 b. If $Y \subseteq X^+$, then $X \to Y$ is derivable from F by means of Rules FD1, FD2, and FD3.

 c. If $A \in X^+$, then $X \to A$ is derivable from F by means of Rules FD1, FD2, and FD3.

---

[9]The notation is clearly incomplete, since it does not contain any reference to F. Again, it is usually understood from the context.

PROOF

a. Let $X \to Y_1, X \to Y_2, \ldots, X \to Y_k$ be all the FDs derivable from F by means of FD1 and FD3. Note that one of the Y_i's must be equal to X, since $X \to X$ is derivable by FD1. Therefore, $X \to Y_1 Y_2 \ldots Y_k$ can be obtained by means of a derivation that contains first all the derivations for the k FDs above, and then, for $i = 1, 2, \ldots, k$, applies FD3 to $X \to XY_1 \ldots Y_{i-1}$ and $X \to Y_i$ to generate $X \to XY_1 Y_2 \ldots Y_i$. Since $XY_1 \ldots Y_k = Y_1 \ldots Y_k$, the last step generates $X \to Y_1 \ldots Y_k$.

b. By part *(a)*, we have that $X \to X^+$ is derivable. Then, since $Y \subseteq X^+$, $X \to Y$ follows from $X \to X^+$ by FD2.

c. Same as *(b)*.   □

Then, we can immediately prove the following properties, which justify the name *closure* given to X^+: (1) X^+ contains X as a subset (not necessarily proper), and (2) X^+ is equal to its own closure $(X^+)^+$; also, (3) X^+ is the smallest set that satisfies (1) and (2).

> **Example 3.8**   Given the set of FDs F in Example 3.6, by exhaustive application of the rules, we can discover that the sets Y such that $AC \to Y$ is derivable from F by means of FD1 and FD3 are AC, B, ABC, $ABCDE$, and therefore $(AC)^+ = ABCDE$.

The most important property of X^+, which we will use in the proof of the completeness of FD1, FD2, and FD3, is stated in the next lemma.

LEMMA 3.7 If $X \to A \in F^+$, then $A \in X^+$.

PROOF   We proceed by showing that if $A \notin X^+$, then $X \to A \notin F^+$. On the basis of Fact 3.1, it will be sufficient to show a relation that satisfies F and does not satisfy $X \to A$. We claim that a suitable counterexample relation is a relation r containing exactly two tuples, t_1 and t_2, such that $t_1[B] = t_2[B]$ if and only if $B \in X^+$.

r does not satisfy $X \to A$. Self-evident, since $A \notin X^+$.

r satisfies F. We show that if $f \in F$, then r satisfies f. Let $f = W \rightarrow$
$Z \in F$. If $t_1[W] \neq t_2[W]$, then f is trivially satisfied. Otherwise,
by construction of r, $W \subseteq X^+$. Thus, since (by Lemma 3.6)
$X \rightarrow X^+$ is derivable by means of FD1 and FD3, we have that
$X \rightarrow ZX^+$ is also derivable by means of FD1 and FD3 (it follows
by FD3 from $X \rightarrow X^+$ and $W \rightarrow Z$). But, by definition, X^+
contains all the sets Y such that $X \rightarrow Y$ is derivable, and so it
must be the case that $Z \subseteq X^+$. Therefore $t_1[Z] = t_2[Z]$, and so
$W \rightarrow Z$ is satisfied. $\square$

By Lemmas 3.6 and 3.7, it follows that

- X^+ contains an attribute A if and only if $X \rightarrow A \in F^+$, and

- X^+ contains an attribute A if and only if $X \rightarrow A$ is derivable
  from F by means of FD1, FD2, FD3.

We are now ready to prove the main result of this section.

THEOREM 3.1   The set of inference rules {FD1, FD2, FD3} is sound
and complete with respect to the implication of FDs.

PROOF   Lemma 3.4 confirms soundness. With respect to completeness, we have to show that, given any set F of FDs, if $f \in F^+$, then f
is derivable from F by means of the rules. If $X \rightarrow Y \in F^+$, then, by
Lemma 3.5*(c)*, $X \rightarrow A \in F^+$ for every $A \in Y$. Then, by Lemma 3.7,
A is in X^+ for every $A \in Y$, and so $Y \subseteq X^+$. Thus, by Lemma 3.6*(b)*,
$X \rightarrow Y$ is derivable. $\square$

3.3   The Implication Problem for Functional Dependencies

The existence of a sound and complete set of inference rules for FDs
guarantees the decidability of the implication problem: given $R(U)$
and F, we can exhaustively apply the inference rules to generate F^+,
which can be used to test which FDs are implied by F and which are
not. This method is not practical, however, because F^+ often has a
cardinality that is exponential with respect to the cardinality of F.

For example, given the relation scheme $R(AB)$ and $F = \{A \rightarrow B\}$, the closure F^+ contains seven FDs (we leave the specification of the list to the reader). It should be noted that five of these seven FDs are trivial; in fact, the number of trivial FDs over a scheme $R(U)$ is always exponential in the cardinality $|U|$ of U (Exercise 3.13). Therefore, the cardinality of F^+ is always exponential in the cardinality of U.[10] However, we are seldom interested in all the FDs in F^+: in order to test whether $X \rightarrow Y \in F^+$ it is sufficient, by Lemmas 3.5 and 3.7, to compute X^+ and to test whether $Y \subseteq X^+$. As we will see shortly, this can be done very efficiently.

In order to perform what we have just described, we need an algorithm that computes the closure of X with respect to F for any given X and F. It relies on the following lemmas.

LEMMA 3.8 There is a derivation of $X \rightarrow X^+$ that, besides the FDs in F, involves only FDs with X as the lhs, the first being $X \rightarrow X$, and the others following by applications of FD3.

PROOF By Lemma 3.7, we know that there is a derivation σ of $X \rightarrow X^+$ from F that involves only applications of FD1 and FD3. Without loss of generality, we may assume that σ is nonredundant,[11] and contains (1) at the beginning, m FDs from F; then (2) $X \rightarrow X$ (assumed not in F); and then (3) n FDs generated by means of Rules FD1 and FD3. Therefore, the length of σ is $l = m + 1 + n$.

Claim. For every $1 \leq j \leq n$ there is a derivation σ' of $X \rightarrow X^+$, identical to σ in the first $l - j$ steps, and such that for every $k > l - j$, the FD derived in the kth step has a lhs equal to X.

The lemma follows from this claim for $j = n$.

Proof of Claim. We proceed by induction on j. The basis ($j = 1$) is trivial, since $X \rightarrow X^+$ is derived in the last step. Assume now that the FD f_k derived in the kth step, with $m + 1 < k < l$, is the last one with a lhs Y other than X. We transform σ into another derivation that (1) produces $X \rightarrow X^+$ in the last step, (2) coincides with σ in

---

[10] Note that the cardinality of F^+ need not be exponential in the cardinality of F; if the cardinality of F is already exponential in the cardinality of U, then the cardinality of F^+ can even be linear in the cardinality of F.

[11] A derivation is *nonredundant* if (1) every derived FD is subsequently used, (2) no FD is derived twice, and (3) no FD in F is derived.

the first $k-1$ steps, and (3) produces FDs with their lhs equal to X in all the steps that follow the $(k-1)$th.

If the rule used in the kth step is FD1, then $f_k = Y \to Y$. Since the derivation is nonredundant, f_k is used in a subsequent step h, involving FD3. By the inductive hypothesis, since $Y \neq X$, f_k cannot be used as the first antecedent; if it is used as the second antecedent, we have that $f_h = X \to YZ$ follows from $f_j = X \to Z$ (with $j < k$) and $Y \to Y$, with $Y \subseteq Z$. Then $YZ = Z$, and so $f_h = f_k$, with $h \neq k$, against the hypothesis of nonredundancy.

Therefore the rule used in the kth step must be FD3. Let $Y \to VWZ$ be generated from $Y \to VW$ and $W \to Z$. Again, $Y \to VWZ$ is used in a subsequent step as the second antecedent in an application of FD3: $X \to TYVWZ$ is generated from $X \to TY$ and $Y \to VWZ$. Then we can obtain the same effect if we drop the step producing $Y \to VWZ$ and derive $X \to TYVWZ$ in two steps, the first generating $X \to TYVW$ from $X \to TY$ and $Y \to VW$, and the second generating $X \to TYVWZ$ from $X \to TYVW$ and $W \to Z$.

Now we have completed the induction: (1) the derivation produces $X \to X^+$ (since all the steps generating FDs with X as their lhs have not been modified); (2) it is identical to the original one in the first $k-1$ steps; and (3) all the FDs generated in the steps after the $(k-1)$th have X as their lhs. □

Example 3.9   Let $F = \{BC \to DE, A \to B, AEG \to H\}$ as in Example 3.6. As we saw, $AC^+ = ABCDE$. A possible derivation of $AC \to ABCDE$ from F is the following:

1. $ABC \to ABC$ (by FD1)
2. $BC \to DE$ (in F)
3. $ABC \to ABCDE$ (from [1] and [2] by FD3)
4. $A \to B$ (in F)
5. $AC \to AC$ (by FD1)
6. $AC \to ABC$ (from [5] and [4], by FD3)
7. $AC \to ABCDE$ (from [6] and [3], by FD3)

Following Lemma 3.8, we can transform the derivation as follows:

1. $BC \to DE$ (in F)
2. $A \to B$ (in F)
3. $AC \to AC$ (by FD1)
4. $AC \to ABC$ (from [3] and [2], by FD3)
5. $AC \to ABCDE$ (from [4] and [1], by FD3)

```
Algorithm 3.1
input    a set of attributes X and
         a set of FDs F = {V₁ → W₁, . . . , Vₖ → Wₖ}
output  a set of attributes XPLUS
var WORK : set of attributes
    {The simple variables are not declared}
begin
   WORK := X
   repeat
      CLOSED := true
      for i := 1 to k
      do if (Vᵢ ⊆ WORK) and (Wᵢ ⊄ WORK)
         then begin
                   CLOSED := false
                   WORK := WORK ∪ Wᵢ
               end
   until CLOSED
   XPLUS := WORK
end
```

Figure 3.6. An algorithm for computing the closure of a set of attributes

We can now present a first version of the algorithm; its correctness is proved by the next theorem.

ALGORITHM 3.1   See Figure 3.6.   ☐

Example 3.10   Let us run Algorithm 3.1 to compute the closure of AC with respect to the set of FDs F in Example 3.6. The variable WORK is initialized to AC. During each iteration of the **repeat** loop, all the FDs in F are examined in the given order; therefore, during the first iteration, the **then** clause is entered only for the FD $A \to B$, and therefore B is added to WORK, which assumes the value ABC; similarly, the second iteration uses only $BC \to DE$, adding DE to WORK. Finally, when the loop is repeated for the third time, no FD satisfies the condition in the **if**; thus, no attribute is added to WORK, and CLOSED is left set to *true*: this causes the loop to be exited and $ABCDE$ to be returned as the value of XPLUS.

THEOREM 3.2   For every X and F, Algorithm 3.1 returns the closure of X with respect to F.

PROOF   First of all, the algorithm terminates: the body of the **repeat** loop is executed only if at least one new attribute has been added to XPLUS in the previous iteration; since the number of attributes mentioned in F is finite, the loop is abandoned after a finite number of iterations.

With respect to correctness, we prove that for every X and F, it is the case that at the end of the execution of the algorithm, XPLUS $= X^+$.

XPLUS $\subseteq X^+$.   We proceed by induction on the number of times the value of WORK is modified. We prove that the value of WORK after the jth modification (let us indicate this value with X_j) is indeed a subset of X^+. The basis ($j = 0$) holds because $X_0 = X \subseteq X^+$. Now assume that $X_{j-1} \subseteq X^+$, and let $V_{i_j} \to W_{i_j}$ be the FD involved in the jth step ($j > 0$); clearly, $V_{i_j} \subseteq X_j$, and $X_j = X_{j-1}W_{i_j}$. Then, by the induction hypothesis, $X_{j-1} \subseteq X^+$, and so $X \to X_{j-1} \in F^+$. Then $X \to X_{j-1}W_i$ is in F^+, since it is derivable by FD3 from $X \to X_{j-1}$ and $V_{i_j} \to W_{i_j}$. Then, by Lemmas 3.5 and 3.7, $X_j = X_{j-1}W_{i_j} \subseteq X^+$.

XPLUS $\supseteq X^+$.   By Lemma 3.8, there is derivation of $X \to X^+$ from F that generates only FDs with their lhs equal to X: $X \to X_0$, $X \to X_1$, ..., $X \to X_n$; for $1 \le j \le n$, $X \to X_j$ is derived from $X \to X_{j-1}$ and some $V_{i_j} \to W_{i_j}$, with $V_{i_j} \subseteq X_{j-1}$, and $X_j = X_{j-1}W_{i_j}$. Therefore, $X = X_0 \subset X_1 \subset \ldots \subset X_n = X^+$. We prove, by induction on j, that XPLUS $\supseteq X_j$. The basis is self-evident, since WORK is initialized to X. As regards the induction step, assume that XPLUS $\supseteq X_{j-1}$. Therefore, at some point during the execution of the algorithm, the condition WORK $\supseteq X_{j-1}$ is satisfied. Then, the first time that the **if** statement is executed for $V_{i_j} \to W_{i_j}$, after this event, the **then** clause is executed, and so W_j is added to WORK. Therefore WORK $\supseteq X_{j-1}W_j = X_j$, and so XPLUS $\supseteq X_j$. $\square$

Let us analyze the time complexity of Algorithm 3.1. Let $|F|$ be the number of FDs in F and $|U|$ be the number of attributes involved.

The **for** loop is executed $|F|$ times for each execution of the **repeat** loop. The **repeat** loop is executed as long as new attributes are added to WORK: in the worst case it can be executed $|U| - 1$ times. Therefore, the algorithm requires $O(|F| \times |U|)$ time.

Algorithm 3.1 is simple, but not very smart, since it repeatedly checks all FDs, even if they have already been used. Let us see how a better algorithm can be conceived. The basic idea is to simulate the derivation of $X \to X^+$ mentioned in Lemma 3.8; each FD in F is considered only once when it can be used, that is, when its lhs is contained in $WORK$. This can be done by associating with each FD $V_i \to W_i$ a counter that stores the number of attributes in V_i that are not contained in the current value of WORK. When the counter becomes 0, the FD can be applied, and W_i is added to WORK. Then, when an attribute A is added to WORK, the algorithm decreases the value of the counter for each FD whose lhs contains A. This last operation can be performed efficiently only if there is a structure that guarantees access to the involved counters: therefore, for each attribute A a list is kept that contains a reference to the FDs whose lhs contain A. We can now show the algorithm.

ALGORITHM 3.2   See Figure 3.7.   □

Let us define the *size* $\|F\|$ of a set of FDs $F = \{V_1 \to W_1, \ldots, V_k \to W_k\}$ as the sum of the cardinalities of the involved sets of attributes, $\sum_{i=1}^{k}(|V_i| + |W_i|)$. That is, the size of F is the space required to write F.

THEOREM 3.3   For every X and F, Algorithm 3.2 returns the closure of X with respect to F, in time $O(\|F\|)$.

PROOF   Termination and correctness can be proved as in the proof of Theorem 3.2 by noting that this is essentially an efficient implementation of Algorithm 3.1.

With respect to complexity, we consider first the initialization of lists, and the main loop. The initialization must be preceded by a reading of the input, which requires $O(\|F\|)$ time. In the initialization, the crucial operation is the **add**, which is executed once for each attribute in each lhs: globally, $\sum_{i=1}^{k}(|V_k|)$ times. In the main loop, the crucial

Algorithm 3.2
input   a set of attributes X and
          a set of FDs $F = \{f_1 = V_1 \rightarrow W_1, \ldots, f_k = V_k \rightarrow W_k\}$
          {the attributes in F and X are $A_1 A_2 \ldots A_m$}
output a set of attributes *XPLUS*
var CTR : **array** $[f_1 .. f_k]$ **of integer**
     LST : **array** $[A_1 .. A_m]$ **of list of integer**
     {The simple variables are not declared}
begin
  for $j := 1$ **to** m **do** LST $[A_j]$:= emptylist
  for $i := 1$ **to** k **do begin**
              CTR $[f_i]$:= $|V_i|$
                for each $A_h \in V_i$ **do** add i to LST$[A_h]$
           end
  WORK := X
  XPROCD := emptyset
  repeat
     select A_j from WORK - XPROCD
     XPROCD := XPROCD $\cup$ $\{A_j\}$
     for each $i \in$ LST$[A_j]$
     do begin
            CTR $[f_i]$:= CTR $[f_i]$ - 1
            if CTR $[f_i]$ = 0 **then** WORK := WORK $\cup$ W_i
       end
  until WORK = XPROCD
  XPLUS := WORK
end

Figure 3.7. A more efficient algorithm for computing the closure of a set of attributes

point is the pair of statements within the **for** loop: the assignment involving CTR$[f_i]$ is executed at most $|V_i|$ times for each f_i, whereas the assignment in the **then** clause is executed once for each FD, but requires time $|W_i|$. Therefore, the main loop requires time $O(\|F\|)$.

    Since the most expensive phase requires time $O(\|F\|)$, the time complexity of the Algorithm 3.2 is $O(\|F\|)$.   ☐

      Example 3.11   Let us execute Algorithm 3.2 on AC and F, as we did in Example 3.10 for Algorithm 3.1. The arrays CTR and LST have three and seven components, respectively, which are initialized as follows, assuming that $f_1 = BC \rightarrow DE$, $f_2 = A \rightarrow B$, and $f_3 = AEG \rightarrow H$: $\text{CTR}[f_1] = 2$, $\text{CTR}[f_2] = 1$, $\text{CTR}[f_3] = 3$, $\text{LST}[A] = <2, 3>$, $\text{LST}[B] = <1>$, $\text{LST}[C] = <1>$, $\text{LST}[D] = <>$, $\text{LST}[E] = <3>$, $\text{LST}[G] = <3>$, $\text{LST}[H] = <>$. WORK is initialized to AC. During the first iteration, A is selected from WORK $-$ XPROCD;[12] thus, $\text{CTR}[f_2]$ and $\text{CTR}[f_3]$ are decreased by 1, and since $\text{CTR}[f_2]$ becomes 0, the rhs of f_2 (i.e. B) is added to WORK. Then in the second iteration B is selected, $\text{CTR}[f_1]$ is decreased, but no attribute is added to WORK. In the third iteration, C is selected, $\text{CTR}[f_1]$ is decreased and becomes 0, and so D and E are added to WORK. Then in the next two iterations, D and E are added to XPROCD, but no counter becomes 0; therefore, the loop is exited, and XPLUS is set to $ABCDE$.

3.4   Keys and Functional Dependencies

We have already seen in Chapter 1 that the notion of a key is fundamental in the design of relational databases. Section 3.1 presented its formal definition as an integrity constraint and its relationship with the notion of FD.

Since keys play an important role in the design theory of relational databases, it is important to be able to solve, as efficiently as possible, some problems related to them, which assume that a set F of FDs over a relation scheme $R(U)$ is given.

The first problem is to check whether a given set of attributes X is a key for $R(U)$ with respect to F. It can be solved by just following the definition: X is a superkey if $X^+ = U$, and it is a key if it is also the case that for no $A \in X$, $(X - A)^+ = U$. The whole process requires $|X| + 1$ executions of Algorithm 3.2, and therefore we can say that it is possible to test whether a set X is a key in time $O(|X| \times ||F||)$.

The second problem is that of *finding* keys; however, since a relation scheme may have several keys, there may be different problems: (1) find a key; (2) find all the keys; (3) find the key with the smallest number of attributes; (4) check whether there is a unique key.

---

[12] We assume that attributes are selected in lexicographic order.

Algorithm 3.3
input a relation scheme $R(U)$, with $U = A_1 A_2 \dots A_n$ and
a set of FDs F over it
output a set of attributes K
begin
  KWRK $:= U$
  for $i := 1$ **to** n
  do if (KWRK $- \{A_i\})^+ = U$
    then KWRK $:=$ KWRK $- \{A_i\}$
  $K :=$ KWRK
end

Figure 3.8. An algorithm for finding a key of a relation scheme

The problem of finding one key, regardless of its size, can be easily solved by considering that U is always a superkey, and therefore a key can be obtained by repeatedly eliminating attributes from it as long as the property of superkey is maintained; the result is a key, since it is a superkey and none of its proper subsets is also a superkey. We have therefore justified the correctness of the following algorithm, which can be run in time $O(|U| \times ||F||)$.

ALGORITHM 3.3 See Figure 3.8. □

It is important to note that the output of Algorithm 3.3 depends on the order in which the attributes are considered, that is, on the order assumed for the attributes in U.

> **Example 3.12**   Let $U = ABCDE$, $F = \{AB \rightarrow C, AC \rightarrow B, D \rightarrow E\}$. If Algorithm 3.3 considers C before B, then it produces as output ABD; otherwise, it produces ACD.

The next theorem characterizes the relation schemes that have only one key.

THEOREM 3.4 Given $R(U)$ and $F = \{X_1 \rightarrow Y_1, \dots, X_p \rightarrow Y_p\}$, the relation scheme R has a unique key if and only if $U - Z_1 \dots Z_p$ is a superkey, where $Z_i = Y_i - X_i$, for every $1 \leq i \leq p$.

PROOF   If there is a unique key K, then it is contained in every superkey, and so in their intersection. For every $1 \leq i \leq p$, $U - Z_i$ is clearly a superkey, and so $K \subseteq \cap_{i=1}^{p}(U - Z_i) = U - Z_1 \ldots Z_p$. Therefore $U - Z_1 \ldots Z_p$ is a superkey.

If $K = U - Z_1 \ldots Z_p$ is a superkey, then we show that it is contained in all superkeys and is therefore the only key. Assume, by way of contradiction, that there exist a superkey L and an attribute $A \in K - L$. Then if we compute L^+ by means of Algorithm 3.1, there is no FD that can add A to the closure, since A does not belong to any rhs of FD (except when it also belongs to the lhs). Therefore $A \notin L^+$, and so $L^+ \neq U$, against the hypothesis that L is a superkey.   □

In most practical cases, the condition in Theorem 3.4 is satisfied; however, in general it is not, and this causes some relevant problems to have, in the general cases, only inefficient solutions. For example, consider the problem of finding the key with the minimum number of attributes; clearly, a scheme may have exponentially many keys, and so the order in which the attributes are considered becomes crucial, and there is no way to guess in an efficient manner which is the best order. As a matter of fact, the next theorem shows that it is unlikely that this problem has an efficient solution.[13]

THEOREM 3.5   Given a relation scheme, a set of FDs, and an integer k, it is NP-complete to find a superkey with cardinality k or smaller.

PROOF   Membership in NP can be easily shown, since it can be checked in polynomial-time whether a given set of attributes with cardinality $j \leq k$ is a superkey. We show that the *vertex cover problem*, one of the basic NP-complete problems, can be reduced in polynomial-time to this problem.

> *Vertex cover problem:* Given a graph $G = (V, E)$ and an integer k, find a vertex cover of cardinality k or smaller, where a *vertex cover* is a set of vertices $W \subseteq V$ such that

---

[13] We assume the knowledge of the notion of *NP-completeness* and of the basic techniques to prove that a problem is NP-complete [112]. However, Theorem 3.5 and the other results in this text that involve NP-completeness can be skipped without prejudice.

for every edge $\{i, j\} \in E$ at least one of i and j belongs to the set W.

Given a graph $G = (V, E)$ with n vertices in V, consider (1) the relation scheme $R(U)$, where U contains one attribute A_i for each vertex in V and one attribute $B_{i,j}$ for each edge $\{i, j\} \in E$; (2) the set F of FDs containing the FD $Z \rightarrow A_1 \ldots A_n$, where $Z = \{B_{i,j} \mid \{i, j\} \in E\}$, and two FDs $A_i \rightarrow B_{i,j}$, $A_j \rightarrow B_{i,j}$, for each edge $\{i, j\} \in E$.

Claim.   A set $W = \{h_1, \ldots, h_k\} \subseteq V$ is a vertex cover for the graph G if and only if the set of attributes $X = A_{h_1} \ldots A_{h_k}$ is a superkey for $R(U)$.

Proof of claim

Only if.   If $W = \{h_1, \ldots, h_k\}$ is a vertex cover, then for every edge $\{i, j\} \in E$, at least one of i and j is in W; therefore, for each $B_{i,j}$, at least one of the attributes A_i, A_j is in X. Therefore, $X^+ \supseteq Z$, and so (since $Z \rightarrow U \in F$), $X^+ = U$.

If.   Let $X = A_{h_1} \ldots A_{h_k}$ be a superkey; therefore, if we execute the closure algorithm (Algorithm 3.2) on X and F, all attributes in U are included in X^+; if $X = A_1 \ldots A_n$, then $W = V$, and therefore W is a vertex cover. Otherwise, consider an attribute $A_p \in U - XZ$. By construction of F, Algorithm 3.2 can include A_p in X^+ only if $Z \subseteq X^+$. Therefore, for each $\{i, j\} \in E$, $B_{i,j} \in X^+$, and so at least one of A_i and A_j must be in X (otherwise $B_{i,j}$ would not be included in X^+, since $A_i \rightarrow B_{i,j}$ and $A_j \rightarrow B_{i,j}$ are the only FDs with $B_{i,j}$ in the rhs). Thus, by construction of X, at least one of i and j is in W, for every $\{i, j\} \in E$; that is, W is a vertex cover for G. $\square$

3.5   Covers of Functional Dependencies

We have already said that in most cases a set of constraints can be replaced by any set equivalent to it, that is, by any of its covers. Therefore, it may be useful to know how to find covers as small as possible, for two reasons:

1. To reduce the time required to test whether a database satisfies the constraints

2. To reduce the time required to run Algorithm 3.1, or other algorithms that have a time complexity that depends on the size of the set of constraints

Various desirable conditions can be defined on sets of FDs, and therefore on the covers of given sets. Minimality can be defined with respect to the *cardinality* of the set (that is, the number of FDs in it) or with respect to the *size* (that is, the total number of attribute symbols that appear in the FDs). We said in Section 3.1 that a set of constraints F is *nonredundant* if no proper subset G of F is equivalent to F. A set F of FDs is *minimum* if there is no G equivalent to F with fewer FDs; F is *optimum* if there is no G equivalent to F with smaller size. A set of FDs G is a *nonredundant (minimum, optimum) cover* of F, if it is equivalent to F and it is *nonredundant (minimum, optimum)*. It is easy to show that a minimum cover is also nonredundant. An optimum cover is minimum, but this requires some discussion (and will be shown as Lemma 3.14 later). The reverse implications can be shown to be false by means of counterexamples.

> **Example 3.13**   The set $F_1 = \{AB \to C, C \to A, C \to B, ABD \to E\}$ is nonredundant, but not minimum, because $F_2 = \{AB \to C, C \to AB, ABD \to E\}$ is equivalent to it and contains fewer FDs; F_2 could be proved to be minimum, but it is not optimum, because $F_3 = \{AB \to C, C \to AB, CD \to E\}$ is equivalent to it and has a smaller size.

Since we know how to solve the implication problem in $O(\|F\|)$ time it is clear that we obtain a nonredundant cover in $O(|F| \times \|F\|)$ time by repeatedly eliminating redundant FDs.

With respect to minimum covers, we need a longer discussion. Let us say that two sets of attributes X and Y are *equivalent* with respect to the given set of FDs if $X^+ = Y^+$, and that X is *(strictly) weaker* than Y if X^+ is a proper subset of Y^+. By Lemma 3.5, we can merge the various FDs with the same lhs into a single FD, obtaining an equivalent set of FDs; therefore, any minimum set of FDs contains as many FDs as different lhs's. Also, if a set F is minimum, then the set $\{X \to X^+ \mid X \to Y \in F\}$ is also minimum; therefore, in the following discussion on minimum covers, we will sometimes assume that all FDs have the form $X \to X^+$. If F satisfies this property, we say that it is *attribute-closed*.

We need a few lemmas. The proof of the first one is left as Exercise 3.14.

LEMMA 3.9 If $Y \to W$ is used in a nonredundant derivation of $X \to V$ from F, then $Y^+ \subseteq X^+$.   □

LEMMA 3.10 If F and G are equivalent and nonredundant, then for every FD $X \to V \in F$, there is an FD $Y \to W \in G$ such that X and Y are equivalent.

PROOF Let F and G be distinct and equivalent. If $f = X \to V \in F$, then $f \in G^+$, and so there is a derivation of f from G. Let G' be a minimal subset of G used in the derivation. Since F is not redundant, $G' \nsubseteq F$; also, there is at least an FD $g = Y \to W \in G'$ such that every derivation of g from F involves f (otherwise, we could find a derivation of f from the FDs in $F - \{f\}$, against the hypothesis of nonredundancy). Then, by Lemma 3.9, it follows that $X^+ = Y^+$. □

Lemma 3.10 implies that all the nonredundant covers contain the same number of nonequivalent lhs's. Therefore, minimum covers have a minimum number of lhs's in each equivalence class.

Given F and two sets of attributes X, Y, we say that X *directly determines* Y with respect to F (in symbols, $X \dashrightarrow_F Y$) if $X \to Y$ is derivable from a subset of F that contains only FDs with their lhs weaker than X. The next lemma shows that the definition of direct determination does not depend on the cover chosen for F.

LEMMA 3.11 If $X \dashrightarrow_F Y$, then $X \dashrightarrow_G Y$ for every G equivalent to F.

PROOF Let G be equivalent to F, and $X \dashrightarrow_F Y$. By definition, $X \to Y$ can be derived from a subset F' of F whose elements have the lhs weaker than X. Thus, since G is equivalent to F, each FD $V \to W \in F'$ is derivable from a subset $G_{V \to W}$ of G that, by Lemma 3.9, involves only FDs $Z \to T$ such that $Z^+ \subseteq V^+ \subset X^+$. The union of these sets, $G' = \cup_{f \in F'} G_f$, (1) is a subset of G, (2) includes only FDs with their lhs weaker than X, and (3) contains $X \to Y$ in its closure: therefore, $X \overset{\cdot}{\to}_G Y$. □

As a consequence of Lemma 3.11, we can now omit the reference to the cover in the notation for direct determination: $X \overset{\cdot}{\to} Y$.

LEMMA 3.12 If F and G are attribute-closed, nonredundant, and equivalent, then for every $X \to X^+ \in F$, there is an FD $Y \to Y^+ \in G$ such that $X^+ = Y^+$, and $X \overset{\cdot}{\to} Y$.

PROOF   Let $X \to X^+ \in F$; if it is also in G, then we are done, since $X \overset{\cdot}{\to} X$, trivially. Otherwise, let Y be a lhs in G equivalent to X, such that for any other equivalent lhs Z of G, there is no derivation of $X \to Z$ from G that is shorter than the shortest derivation of $X \to Y$ from G. We claim that this derivation does not involve any FD $V \to V^+$ such that $V^+ = X^+$, and therefore $X \overset{\cdot}{\to} Y$. If there were such an FD, then the derivation of $X \to V$ from G would be shorter than the derivation of $X \to Y$, thus generating a contradiction.   □

LEMMA 3.13 An attribute-closed set of FDs F is minimum if and only if there is no pair of distinct, equivalent lhs's X_1, X_2 for which it is the case that $X_1 \overset{\cdot}{\to} X_2$.

PROOF
If.   Assume that F is not minimum, and let G be a minimum cover of F. Since the number of equivalence classes of lhs's in F and G is the same, there must be a class with more members in F than in G. Let $Y_1, \ldots, Y_p$, and $Z_1, \ldots, Z_q$ be the elements of the class, in F and G respectively, with $p > q$. By Lemma 3.12, for every Y_i, there is a Z_j such that $Y_i \overset{\cdot}{\to} Z_j$. Now, since there are more Y_i's than Z_j's, there is a set Z_j such that for two distinct Y_i, Y_k, it is the case that $Y_i \overset{\cdot}{\to} Z_j$, and $Y_k \overset{\cdot}{\to} Z_j$. Then, since (again by Lemma 3.12) for every Z_j there is a Y_h such that $Z_j \overset{\cdot}{\to} Y_h$, and h cannot equal both i and k (which are distinct), it is the case that $h \neq i$. Thus, $Y_i \overset{\cdot}{\to} Y_h$, or $h \neq k$, and so $Y_k \overset{\cdot}{\to} Y_h$ (transitivity of direct determination can be proved by juxtaposing the respective derivations).
Only if.   If F contains two FDs $X_1 \to Y$, $X_2 \to Y$ such that $X_1^+ = X_2^+ = Y$, and $X_1 \overset{\cdot}{\to} X_2$, then $X_1 \to X_2$ can be derived from a subset F' of F that contains only FDs with their lhs weaker than X_1. Therefore,

---

Algorithm 3.4
input   a set of FDs $F = \{X_i \rightarrow Y_i \mid i = 1, 2, \ldots, n\}$
output a set of FDs G
begin
    $G := \{X_i \rightarrow X_i^+ \mid i = 1, 2, \ldots, n\}$
    for $i := 1$ **to** n
    do if $X_i \rightarrow X_i^+$ is redundant in G
       then $G := G - \{X_i \rightarrow X_i^+\}$
end

Figure 3.9. An algorithm for computing a minimum cover

$X_1 \rightarrow Y$ can be derived from $F' \cup \{X_2 \rightarrow Y\}$. Thus, F is equivalent to $F - \{X_1 \rightarrow Y\}$, which contains fewer FDs than F.   □

THEOREM 3.6 An attribute-closed set of FDs F is minimum if and only if it is not redundant.

PROOF   The *only if* part follows from the definitions, as we saw above. The *if* part follows from Lemma 3.13: if F is not minimum, then it contains a pair of equivalent lhs's X_1, X_2 such that $X_1 \dot\rightarrow X_2$. Since all FDs are attribute-closed, this means that $X_1 \rightarrow X_1^+$ is redundant in F.   □

Theorem 3.6 guarantees the correctness of the following algorithm to compute the minimum cover of a set of FDs, which can clearly be run in $O(|F| \times ||F||)$.

ALGORITHM 3.4 See Figure 3.9.   □

Example 3.14   Let the following attributes be abbreviated with the respective initials *Employee#, Name, LastName, Category, Salary, Department, AmountOfTime, Manager, Project*. Let F contain the following FDs:

$E \rightarrow NS$
$NL \rightarrow EMD$
$EN \rightarrow LCD$
$C \rightarrow S$

$$D \rightarrow M$$
$$M \rightarrow D$$
$$EPD \rightarrow AE$$
$$NLCP \rightarrow A$$

If Algorithm 3.4 is applied to this set of FDs, then a set G containing the following FDs is produced in the first step:

$$E \rightarrow ENLCSDM$$
$$NL \rightarrow ENLCSDM$$
$$EN \rightarrow ENLCSDM$$
$$C \rightarrow CS$$
$$D \rightarrow DM$$
$$M \rightarrow DM$$
$$EPD \rightarrow APENLCSDM$$
$$NLCP \rightarrow APENLCSDM$$

Then, in the subsequent **for** loop, the FDs with the lhs EN and one of the last two (with lhs's EPD and $NCLP$) are eliminated because of redundancy. Thus, the following is a minimum cover for the given set of FDs:

$$E \rightarrow ENLCSDM$$
$$NL \rightarrow ENLCSDM$$
$$C \rightarrow CS$$
$$D \rightarrow DM$$
$$M \rightarrow DM$$
$$EPD \rightarrow APENLCSDM$$

Let us now devote our attention to optimum covers. Here, as we said, the size of the FDs (the number of attributes) is minimum, with no reference to the number of FDs; however, it turns out that any optimum set of FDs is also minimum.

LEMMA 3.14   If a set F of FDs is optimum, then it is minimum.

PROOF   If F is not minimum, then we can transform it into an equivalent set as suggested by the *if* part of Lemma 3.13, thus obtaining a set of FDs with smaller size ($X_1 \rightarrow Y_1$, $X_2 \rightarrow Y_2$, are replaced by $X_2 \rightarrow Y_1 Y_2$).   □

Unfortunately, with respect to optimum covers, we have a negative complexity result.

THEOREM 3.7   The problem of finding a cover for a set of FDs with a size not greater than a given k is NP-complete.

PROOF   The problem is in NP because, given a set of FDs F, we can check in polynomial-time whether a set G is a cover for F and has a size not greater than k.

To prove that the problem is NP-hard, we proceed by showing that if there were a polynomial-time algorithm for this problem, then there would be a polynomial-time algorithm for the minimum key problem, which we have already shown to be NP-complete (Theorem 3.5).

Let F be a set of FDs over a relation scheme $R(U)$. Also, let A and B be two attributes not in U, and let $F' = F \cup \{AU \rightarrow B\}$ be a set of FDs over a relation scheme $R(UAB)$.

Claim.   Every optimum cover G' of F' contains exactly one FD involving B, $KA \rightarrow YB$, where K is a minimum key for $R(U)$.

Proof of claim.   Let G' be an optimum cover for F'. Clearly, it contains at least an FD whose rhs contains B; otherwise, since $B \notin U$, G' would not imply $AU \rightarrow B$. Now, if G' contains an FD of the form $X \rightarrow BY$, then X must contain A (since all nontrivial FDs in F'^+ have B in their rhs only if they have A in their lhs), and must also contain a superkey K' of $R(U)$ (otherwise other FDs, not in F'^+, would be implied). Since $B \notin X$, it is the case that $X = AK'$, with K' superkey of $R(U)$ (otherwise, again, other FDs, not in F'^+, would be implied). Then, if there were more than one FD involving B, they could at least be reduced (since all of them have a lhs containing A and a key of $R(U)$), thus contradicting the hypothesis that G' is optimum. Now, let $AK' \rightarrow B$ be the unique FD with B in the rhs: if there is a key K smaller than K', then we could obtain a cover with smaller size, by replacing $AK' \rightarrow B$ with $AK \rightarrow B$. This completes the proof of the claim.

On the basis of the claim, if we had a polynomial-time algorithm for the optimum cover problem, then we would have a polynomial-time algorithm for the minimum key problem, thus contradicting its NP-completeness (unless P = NP).   □

Since the optimum cover problem is intractable, it is meaningful to see whether minimum covers are the best we can achieve. In fact, we can find special forms of minimum covers, still computable in polynomial-time, that have in general a smaller size than those computed by Algorithm 3.4 or enjoy other desirable properties. We give some definitions.

- A minimum set F of FDs is *L-minimum* if for no FD $X \to Y \in F$ is it the case that F is equivalent to $F - \{X \to Y\} \cup \{Z \to Y\}$, for a proper subset Z of X.[14]

- An L-minimum set F of FDs is *LR-minimum* if there is no FD $X \to Y \in F$ for which F is equivalent to $F - \{X \to Y\} \cup \{X \to W\}$, for a proper subset W of Y.

- An LR-minimum set F of FDs is *circular* if for every equivalence class $\mathcal{Y}$ of lhs's in F there is an ordering $Y_0, Y_1, \ldots, Y_k$ for the elements of $\mathcal{Y}$ such that F contains the FDs $Y_0 \to ZW_1, Y_1 \to W_2$, $\ldots, Y_{k-1} \to W_k, Y_k \to W_0$, where $W_h \subseteq Y_h$ for $h = 0, 1, \ldots, k$.

Let discuss these definitions. L-minimum and LR-minimum covers are motivated by the reduction of size. Circularity requires a structure among the FDs that gives a better readability: in a circular LR-minimum set of FDs, for each equivalence class of lhs's $\{Y_0, Y_1, \ldots, Y_k\}$, there is at most one FD whose rhs contains attributes not in $Y_0 Y_1 \ldots Y_k$.

It is self-evident that for any set of FDs there are equivalent sets that satisfy the above notions. Also, each of the notions is stronger than those that precede it. The next example shows that the ordering is proper.

> **Example 3.15**   The set $\{A \to B, B \to A, ABC \to D\}$ is minimum but not L-minimum, since it is equivalent to $\{A \to B, B \to A, AC \to D\}$.
>
> The set $\{A \to BC, B \to C\}$ is L-minimum but not LR-minimum, since it is equivalent to $\{A \to B, B \to C\}$.
>
> The set $\{A \to BC, B \to AD\}$ is LR-minimum but not circular, since A and B are equivalent lhs's, and the corresponding rhs's contain C and D, respectively. An equivalent circular LR-minimum set is $\{A \to BCD, B \to A\}$.
>
> It is also interesting that the set $\{A \to B, B \to A, AC \to BD, BD \to AC\}$ is L-minimum but not circular, because it is not

---

[14]The attributes in $X - Z$ are called *extraneous*.

Algorithm 3.5
input   a set of FDs F
output a set of FDs G
begin
    compute (using Algorithm 3.4) a minimum cover G of F
    for each $X \to X^+ \in G$
    do if there exists a proper subset Y of X such that $Y^+ = X^+$
        then $G := G - \{X \to X^+\} \cup \{Y \to Y^+\}$
    for each equivalence class $\mathcal{Y}$ of lhs's in G
            (let $\mathcal{Y} = \{Y_0, Y_1, \ldots, Y_k\}$ and $Z = Y_0^+ - Y_0 Y_1 \ldots Y_k$)
    do $G := G - \{Y_0 \to Y_0^+, Y_1 \to Y_1^+, \ldots, Y_k \to Y_k^+\}$
        $\cup \{Y_0 \to ZY_1, Y_1 \to Y_2, \ldots, Y_k \to Y_0\}$
    for each $X \to Y \in G$
    do if $G - \{X \to Y\} \cup \{X \to W\}$ is equivalent to G,
        with W a proper subset of Y
        then $G := G - \{X \to Y\} \cup \{X \to W\}$
end

Figure 3.10. An algorithm for computing a circular LR-minimum cover

LR-minimum. An equivalent circular LR-minimum set is $\{A \to B, B \to A, AC \to D, BD \to C\}$.

The following algorithm computes circular LR-minimum covers.

ALGORITHM 3.5   See Figure 3.10.   □

Example 3.16   Algorithm 3.5 applied to the minimum cover generated in Example 3.14 produces the following circular cover:

$$E \to NLCD$$
$$NL \to E$$
$$C \to S$$
$$D \to M$$
$$M \to D$$
$$EP \to A$$

or the cover where the first two FDs are replaced with the following two:

$$E \to NL$$
$$NL \to ECD$$

Exercises

3.1 Define keys, FDs, and INDs for the database schemes for Exercises 1.2, 1.3, and 1.4.

3.2 Prove Fact 3.1.

3.3 Prove Fact 3.2.

3.4 Prove Lemma 3.5.

3.5 Prove that if two sets of constraints are equivalent, then a database satisfies one set if and only if it satisfies the other.

3.6 Would we increase the expressive power of FDs if we admitted FDs with an empty lhs and/or an empty rhs?

3.7 Give a formal proof for Lemma 3.4.

3.8 A set of inference rules $\mathcal{S}$ is *independent* if no proper subset $\mathcal{S}'$ of $\mathcal{S}$ allows, for every set of constraints, the derivation of all the constraints derivable by means of $\mathcal{S}$. Show that the set $\{\mathrm{FD1}, \mathrm{FD2}, \mathrm{FD3}\}$ is independent.

3.9 Prove or disprove soundness of the following inference rules for FDs:
- **if $\bot$ with $X \supset Y$, then $X \to Y$.**
- **if $\bot$ with $X \supseteq Y$, then $Y \to X$.**
- **if $\bot$ with $X \supseteq Y$, then $X \to Y$.**
- **if $X \to Y$ with $W \supset X$, then $W \to Y$.**
- **if $X \to Y$ with $(W \supset X) \land (Y \supset Z)$, then $W \to Z$.**

3.10 Find relationships among the various inference rules in the text and in Exercise 3.9. Also, find complete and independent sets of rules.

3.11 Let us say that a set of attributes Y is *closed* (with respect to a given set of FDs) if it equals its own closure Y^+. Prove that for every X, X^+ is the smallest closed set that contains X.

3.12 Find a sound and complete set of inference rules for tuple constraints. (If necessary, make assumptions on the domains of the attributes).

3.13 Prove that if $n = |U|$, the number of trivial FDs over $R(U)$ is $3^n - 2^n$.

3.14 Prove Lemma 3.9.

3.15 Given $F = \{E \to G, BGE \to DH, AB \to B, G \to DE\}$, verify whether F implies the following FDs: (1) $ABG \to E$; (2) $BG \to DBE$; (3) $E \to D$.

3.16 Given $F = \{EA \to GH, BGE \to DH, A \to B, G \to DE\}$, verify whether F implies the following FDs: (1) $AG \to EHD$; (2) $BG \to DBE$; (3) $AG \to DBE$.

3.17 Find a key for a relation scheme $R(ABCDEGHI)$ with the FDs

$$\{E \to G, BGE \to DH, AB \to B, G \to DE\}$$

and verify whether it is unique.

3.18 Find all the keys for a relation scheme $R(ABCDEGHI)$ with the FDs

$$\{EA \to GH, GE \to DH, A \to B, G \to DE\}$$

3.19 Find an LR-minimum cover for the following set of FDs, and discuss whether it can be optimum:

$$\{EA \to GH, GE \to DH, A \to B, G \to DE\}$$

3.20 Find an LR-minimum cover for the following set of FDs, and discuss whether it can be optimum:

$$\{A \to BC, BD \to AEH, AB \to DHI, I \to C, H \to E,$$
$$E \to H, AJH \to AK, BDIJ \to K\}$$

3.21 Find an LR-minimum cover for the following set of FDs, and discuss whether it is unique:

$$\{A \to BCAEH, AB \to DHI, I \to C, E \to H, AJE \to AK, AIJ \to K\}$$

3.22 Find circular LR-minimum covers for the sets of FDs in the previous exercises.

Comments and References

Integrity constraints have been studied in this chapter from an essentially theoretical point of view. Readers interested in more practical aspects may consult the following general references on database systems: Date [85,87], Korth and Silberschatz [144], ElMasri and Navathe [95], Ullman [212,217]. See also those concerning specific systems: Date [88,86], Chamberlin et al. [65], and Stonebraker [203].

Formalizations of constraints, implication, and inference rules as presented in Section 3.1 can be found in a paper by Beeri et al. [42]. Keys and FDs were first studied by Codd [76,78]. Tuple constraints have never been studied formally, essentially because there are not many deep properties to prove about them (see Exercise 3.12); however, they are implemented in existing systems. See, for example, Date [88, p.134-35]. Inclusion dependencies were tackled much later, initially by Casanova et al. [59,60]. This is surprising, since INDs have much more practical meaning than many other classes of constraints that have been deeply studied in the literature; the motivation for this delay probably arises from the fact that in the beginning only intrarelational constraints were studied, and multirelational databases (such as those obtained by decomposing a relation for the sake of normalization) were considered under the restricted universal relation instance assumption (see Beeri et al. [41], Kent [135], or Atzeni and Parker [30] for a discussion), which make some INDs meaningless.

Inference rules were the first technique used to study the implication of constraints; Armstrong [19] presented a set of sound and complete rules. Section 3.2 presented another set (equivalent to it; otherwise it would not be sound and complete), which helps in understanding the notion of closure of a set of attributes, and allows us to simplify the proof of correctness of the subsequent Algorithms 3.1 and 3.2, which were invented by Bernstein [49], and Beeri and Bernstein [40], respectively. Strange as it may seem, the existence of a sound and complete set of inference rules (*full axiomatization*) for a class of constraints was considered for some time to be more important than the decidability of the implication problem itself. Various classes of constraints were proposed, and their axiomatizability studied; it was discovered that some classes cannot have a *bounded* full axiomatization, that is, a full axiomatization where each rule is required to have a number of antecedents not greater than a fixed value, even if the implication problem is decidable (see Casanova et al. [60] for a general result, and Kanellakis et al. [133] for a specific result). On the other hand, there are classes of constraints for which there is a bounded full axiomatization (Beeri and Vardi [47], Sadri and Ullman [190]), yet the implication problem is undecidable (Vardi [221], Chandra et al. [72]). Therefore, the nonexistence of a bounded full axiomatization and the decidability (actually, even the complexity) of the implication problem need not be related. However, the existence of a simple full axiomatization is a nice result and, as we saw for FDs, can be useful in reasoning about algorithms for the implication problem.

The study of keys and their relationship with FDs is clearly important in order to characterize normal forms, as we saw in Section 6 of Chapter 1. Algorithm 3.3 for computing a key of a relation was proposed by Lucchesi and Osborne [159], who also proved the NP-completeness of a number of problems related to keys, including the minimum key problem (also studied by Lipski [154]), and the problem of determining whether an attribute is *prime*, that is, whether it belongs to at least one key.

The need for having sets of FDs as small as possible arose as soon as it was discovered that other important problems have a complexity that depends on the size of the input set of dependencies. The various forms of covers were studied by Bernstein [49], Beeri and Bernstein [40], Paredaens [177], and Maier [161,162]. It should be noted that there is no complete agreement in the literature about the terms used to denote the various types of covers. We have mainly followed the terminology of Maier [161], except for the notion of circular LR-minimum cover, which is a variant of the notion of "annular cover of compound FDs"[162].

Chapter 4

Dependency Theory: Part 2

In this Chapter we present advanced topics on integrity constraints that complete those discussed in Chapter 3. In Section 4.1, we present the notions of *tableau* and *chase*, which constitute a fundamental tool for proving results involving constraints. We give the main properties of tableaux and the chase algorithm, and show how they can be used as a second method for the solution of the implication problem for functional dependencies. In Section 4.2, we study the relationship between functional dependencies and the notion of lossless decomposition (introduced in Section 1.4). The main theorem is based on the use of the chase. The relationship between functional dependencies and decompositions motivates the extension of the notion of functional dependencies to a multirelational context, studied in Section 4.3. The main results are also based on the chase. In Section 4.4, we introduce other classes of constraints, *multivalued* and *join dependencies*, which are also related to lossless decompositions. We study the implication problem for multivalued dependencies (extensible to join dependencies) and for the joint class of functional and multivalued dependencies, by means of the chase. In Section 4.5, we study another important class of constraints that are highly meaningful from the practical point of view: *inclusion dependencies*. For these it is easier to use an approach based on inference rules, rather than the chase. In Section 4.6, motivated by the study of the joint class of functional and inclusion dependencies, we distinguish between two notions of implication, and discuss their relationship to the decidability of the implication problem itself.

131

T	Employee	Dept	Manager
	Bob	v_D	n_1
	John	v_D	Jones
	Mike	n_2	n_3
	v_E	EE	n_4
	Tom	EE	n_5

r	Employee	Dept	Manager
	Bob	CS	Jones
	John	CS	Jones
	Mike	Math	Smith
	Ed	EE	Robinson
	Tom	EE	Robinson

Figure 4.1. A tableau and a relation

4.1   Tableaux and the Chase

In this section we introduce a few notions that do not at first appear important in their own right, but which are fundamental in proving results. The basic notion will be that of *tableau*, which is defined as a relation, except that it may contain other symbols, called *variables*, beside values from the domains. A tableau may be seen as a relation with unknown variables, which *represents* a relation (or a subset thereof). The notion of *containment mapping* will be introduced to formalize this representation of relations by means of tableaux. Figure 4.1 shows a tableau and a relation obtained from it by replacing variables with constants. The final notion, the *chase*, is based on the following observation. If the relation represented by a tableau is known to satisfy some given constraints, then its variables cannot freely represent constants. For example, given the tableau in Figure 4.1, if the associated relations satisfy the FD *Dept → Manager*, then we can infer that variable n_1 must correspond to the constant "Jones" and that variables n_4 and n_5 must represent the same value. The *chase* is an algorithm that transforms tableaux on the basis of constraints. For example, if the tableau in Figure 4.1 were chased with respect to *Dept → Manager*, then the tableau in Figure 4.2 would be produced.

Let us now discuss these three notions. For reasons that will become clear in the following, the variables in tableaux are divided into two categories:

T'	Employee	Dept	Manager
	Bob	v_D	Jones
	John	v_D	Jones
	Mike	n_2	n_3
	v_E	EE	n_4
	Tom	EE	n_4

Figure 4.2. A chased tableau

1. *Distinguished variables (dv's)*, one for each attribute: If A is an attribute of interest, then v_A is the corresponding dv.

2. *Nondistinguished variables (ndv's)*: we assume that there are countably many of them: $n_1, n_2, \ldots, n_k, \ldots$

Given a set of attributes X, a *row* over X is a mapping that associates with each attribute $A \in X$ either (1) a value in dom(A) (a *constant*), or (2) the dv v_A, or (3) an ndv. Clearly, this is a generalization of the notion of *tuple*: a row with no variables is a tuple. We extend to rows the notations adopted to indicate values in tuples and subtuples ($t[A]$, etc.). A *tableau* T over a set of attributes X, sometimes denoted in the following by the notation $T(X)$, is a set of rows over X such that no ndv appears as a value for two distinct attributes.[1] The reader can verify that what we have shown in Figure 4.1 is indeed a tableau.

The notion of containment mapping also requires a preliminary concept. Among the various symbols that may appear as values for an attribute in a tableau, we define a partial order, indicated with $\preceq$, as follows:

- Constants are pairwise incomparable, and precede all variables: for every constant a and variable v, we have $a \preceq v$;

- All dv's precede all ndv's;

- Ndv's are totally ordered according to the order of their subscripts: $n_i \preceq n_j$ if and only if $i \leq j$.

We write $s_1 \prec s_2$ if $s_1 \preceq s_2$ and $s_1 \neq s_2$.

---

[1] In the literature, tableaux with this restriction are sometimes called *typed*.

Now, given two tableaux T_1 and T_2 over the same set of attributes X, a *containment mapping from T_1 to T_2* is a function ψ from symbols to symbols that satisfies the following conditions:

1. For every symbol s appearing in T_1, $\psi(s) \preceq s$.

2. If ψ is extended to rows and tableaux, then $\psi(T_1) \subseteq T_2$ (that is, for every row $t_1 \in T_1$, there is a row $t_2 \in T_2$ such that, for every $A \in X$, $\psi(t_1[A]) = t_2[A]$).

Let us expand the consequences of the condition $\psi(s) \preceq s$. A containment mapping ψ maps

- constants to themselves (therefore we also say that it is the identity on constants);

- each dv to itself or to a constant; and

- each ndv (1) to a constant, or (2) to the dv for the corresponding attribute, or (3) to an ndv with a lower subscript.

Recalling the intuitive notion of representation of relations by means of tableaux given before, we can say that a tableau T represents a (subset of) a relation r if there is a containment mapping from T to r. Given the tableau T and the relation r in Figure 4.1, a function ψ that is the identity on constants and is defined as follows on variables:

$$\psi(v_D) = \text{CS} \qquad \psi(v_E) = \text{Ed} \qquad \psi(n_1) = \text{Jones}$$
$$\psi(n_2) = \text{Math} \qquad \psi(n_3) = \text{Smith} \qquad \psi(n_4) = \text{Robinson}$$
$$\psi(n_5) = \text{Robinson},$$

is a containment mapping from T to r. Similarly, if a function maps n_1 to Jones, n_5 to n_4, and is the identity on all the other symbols in the tableau T in Figure 4.1, then it is a containment mapping from T to the tableau T' in Figure 4.2.

The notion of containment mapping is transitive: given tableaux T_1, T_2, T_3, if there is a containment mapping from T_1 to T_2 and a containment mapping from T_2 to T_3, then there is a containment mapping from T_1 to T_3 (Exercise 4.1).

Let us define satisfaction of FDs for tableaux in the same way as for relations, just referring to rows rather than tuples: a tableau T

```
Algorithm 4.1
input a tableau T and a set of FDs F with singleton rhs's
output a tableau CHASE_F(T)
begin
    T' := T ;
    while there are t_1, t_2 ∈ T' and X → A ∈ F
            such that t_1[X] = t_2[X] and t_1[A] ≺ t_2[A]
    do change all the occurrences of the value t_2[A] in T' to t_1[A] ;
    CHASE_F(T) := T'
end
```

Figure 4.3. The chase algorithm for FDs

satisfies an FD $X \to Y$ if for every pair of rows t_1 and t_2 in T such that $t_1[X] = t_2[X]$, it is the case that $t_1[Y] = t_2[Y]$.

We are now ready to introduce a first version of the *chase* algorithm, explicitly referring to FDs. Later in the chapter we will extend the algorithm to handle other classes of constraints. The algorithm receives as input a tableau T and a set of FDs F, with the aim of transforming T into a tableau that satisfies F. We will often say that *T is chased with respect to F*, or, when F is irrelevant or understood, *the chase is applied to T*.

ALGORITHM 4.1   See Figure 4.3.   □

The individual executions of the inner statement are called *steps* of the chase (or *chase steps*), and if the FD f and the tuples t_1, t_2 are involved in a step, we say that there is an *application* of f (to t_1, t_2). Note that when the value of a row $t \in T$ for an attribute A is modified from v to w in a step of the chase, then all the occurrences of v in the tableau are changed to w; therefore, without referring explicitly to the involved rows, we can say that *a step changes v to w*, and that *a sequence of steps changes v_1 to w_1, v_2 to w_2*, and so on. We say that a sequence of steps *identifies v_1 and v_2*, if it changes both to a common value w, or if it changes v_1 to v_2 or v_2 to v_1.

> **Example 4.1**   Let us chase the tableau T in Figure 4.1 with respect to $F = \{E \to D, D \to M\}$. It is possible to apply $D \to M$

T'	Employee	Dept	Manager
	Bob	n_4	Smith
	Bob	EE	Jones

Figure 4.4. A tableau for Example 4.2

to the first and second rows, thus changing n_1 to "Jones," and then to the fourth and fifth rows, changing n_5 to n_4. No further applications are possible, and therefore the algorithm exits the loop and terminates, producing the tableau in Figure 4.2. The sequence of steps has identified n_1 and "Jones," and n_4 and n_5.

Algorithm 4.1 always terminates if applied to a finite tableau. The number of symbols in a finite tableau is finite, and the value of each row for each attribute can be modified only a finite number of times (because for each symbol v, there is a finite set of symbols that precede v); therefore, the inner statement can be executed only a finite number of times.

If applied to some tableaux, the chase detects violations of FDs, but cannot modify the involved values, because they are incomparable.

Example 4.2   Let us consider the tableau T in Figure 4.4 and chase it with respect to $F = \{E \rightarrow D, D \rightarrow M\}$. It is possible to apply $E \rightarrow D$ and change v_D to "EE." The two rows then agree on D and disagree on M, but their M-values are incomparable, and therefore are not modified. The resulting tableau, which is indeed a relation, violates F.

It is therefore useful to distinguish violations of FDs in tableaux as belonging to one of two categories. Given an FD $X \rightarrow A$, two rows that agree on X and disagree on A cause one of the following violations:

1. A *soft violation* of $X \rightarrow A$ if their A-values are comparable

2. A *hard violation* of $X \rightarrow A$ if their A-values are incomparable

It follows from the definitions that $CHASE_F(T)$ cannot contain soft violations; therefore, if it violates F, then it must contain one or more hard violations.

Employee	Dept	Manager
Bob	v_D	n_1
John	v_D	Jones
Bob	EE	Robinson

Figure 4.5. A tableau for Example 4.3

Employee	Dept	Manager
Bob	EE	Jones
John	EE	Jones
Bob	EE	Robinson

Employee	Dept	Manager
Bob	EE	Robinson
John	EE	Jones
Bob	EE	Robinson

Figure 4.6. Two chased tableaux for Example 4.3

Also, in some cases, the algorithm is nondeterministic, because of the freedom in the choice of the FD and the choice of the rows in the predicate of the **while** loop and, therefore, in the modification performed.

> **Example 4.3**   Let us consider the tableau in Figure 4.5 and chase it with respect to $F = \{E \rightarrow D, D \rightarrow M\}$. It is possible to apply $E \rightarrow D$ to the first and third rows, thus changing v_D to "EE," in both the first and second rows (note that the inner statement in the algorithm says that the value must be changed in all its occurrences). Then, $D \rightarrow M$ can be applied either to the first and second rows, or to the first and third rows. In the first case n_1 is changed to "Jones," in the second to "Robinson." That is, either of the tableaux in Figure 4.6 can be obtained as a result. In both cases, the resulting tableau violates $D \rightarrow M$, and no further FD can be applied.

The behavior demonstrated in Example 4.3 could jeopardize the practical applicability of of Algorithm 4.1. Fortunately, it arises only in limited situations: nondeterminism always appears together with hard violations of FDs, as in Example 4.3. We devote our attention to the formalization of this claim, as follows: If one execution of the chase with T and F produces a tableau that satisfies F, then every execution of the chase produces the same tableau, and if one execution produces a tableau that violates F, then every execution produces a tableau that violates F (but not necessarily the same tableau).

We need a few definitions and lemmas. Consider a set F of FDs. Two values v and w are *directly equatable* in T with respect to F if T contains two rows t_1 and t_2, such that for some FD $X \to A \in F$, it is the case that $t_1[X] = t_2[X]$, $t_1[A] = v$, and $t_2[A] = w$. That is, if two values are directly equatable, then either they are equal or they are involved in a soft or hard violation. We say that v and w are *equatable* in T with respect to F if

1. they are directly equatable in T (with respect to F), or

2. there is a value u such that both pairs (u, v), (u, w) are equatable in T, or

3. T contains two rows t_1, t_2, such that $t_1[A] = v$, $t_2[A] = w$, and for some FD $X \to A$, for every $B \in X$, values $t_1[B]$ and $t_2[B]$ are equatable in T.

It follows from the definition that, for every tableau $T(U)$, for every attribute $A \in U$, equatability is an equivalence relation on the A-values in T. Also, chase steps preserve equatability; that is, if v and w are equatable in T, and a sequence of chase steps transforms T into T', changing v to v' and w to w', then v' and w' are equatable in T'. Moreover, if two values are equatable in T', then they appear in and are equatable in T. Finally, if two values are identified by a sequence of chase steps applied to T, then they are equatable in T.

LEMMA 4.1 Let T be a tableau and F a set of FDs. If two values are equatable in T with respect to F but not equal, then T contains a violation (hard or soft) of F.

PROOF   Following the definition, let us assign to each pair of equatable symbols (v, w) a degree of equatability $deg(v, w)$, according to the three cases in the definition, respectively:

1. $deg(v, w) = 1$;

2. $deg(v, w) = deg(u, v) + deg(v, w)$;

3. $deg(v, w) = 1 + \sum_{B \in X} deg(t_1[B], t_2[B])$

Now consider the pair of distinct equatable symbols (v, w) with smallest degree d. Let us distinguish again the three cases: (1) v and w are directly equatable and not equal: the claim is immediate; (2) there is a symbol u such that (u, v) and (u, w) are equatable with a degree smaller than $deg(v, w)$; therefore $u = v$, $u = w$, and so $v = w$, a contradiction—this case never arises; (3) there are two rows t_1 and t_2, such that $t_1[A] = v$, $t_2[A] = w$, and for some FD $X \to A$, for every $B \in X$, the values $t_1[B]$ and $t_2[B]$ are equatable in T, with degree smaller than $deg(v, w)$. Therefore, we have that $t_1[X] = t_2[X]$, and so t_1 and t_2 violate $X \to A$. $\qquad\square$

THEOREM 4.1 Let T be a tableau and F a set of FDs. Consider the executions of Algorithm 4.1 with input T and F.

(1) If one execution generates a tableau that violates F, then every execution generates a tableau that violates F.

(2) If one execution generates a tableau that satisfies F, then every execution generates the same tableau.

PROOF Equatability is an equivalence relation, and therefore, for every attribute A, we can partition the symbols appearing as A-values into equivalence classes. We show that (1) every execution of Algorithm 4.1 produces a tableau that does not satisfy F if and only if there is an equivalence class that contains two incomparable symbols (i.e. two distinct constants); and (2) if an execution produces a tableau that satisfies F, then it identifies every symbol with the minimum symbol of its equivalence class. Clearly, (1) and (2) suffice to prove the claim.

1. *Only if.* If a and b are distinct constants, then they are incomparable. If they cause a hard violation in $CHASE_F(T)$, then they are incomparable and equatable in $CHASE_F(T)$, and so in T. Therefore, they belong to the same equivalence class.

   If. Consider an equivalence class that contains two distinct constants a and b. Since a and b are equatable in T and cannot be identified, then by preservation of equatability, they remain equatable in $CHASE_F(T)$ for every execution of Algorithm 4.1. Then by Lemma 4.1, $CHASE_F(T)$ violates F, and since it cannot contain soft violations, it contains a hard violation.

2. If $CHASE_F(T)$ satisfies F, then it does not contain any pair of distinct equatable symbols. Therefore, each symbol in T has been identified with another symbol also in T, belonging to the same equivalence class (if two symbols are identified, then they are equatable in the original tableau); also, for each equivalence class, all the symbols have been identified with the same value. The symbols in each equivalence class are all comparable (otherwise, by Part 1 of this lemma, $CHASE_F(T)$ would violate F), and therefore there exists a minimum. Then, since the internal step would never change a symbol to a symbol not preceding it in the ordering, all the symbols in each class are identified to the minimum of the class.   □

Theorem 4.1 is fundamental in confirming the usefulness of the chase: If the result of the chase satisfies the dependencies, then it is unique.

We devote our attention now to the connections between the chase and containment mappings. First of all, note that, for every T and F, there is a containment mapping from T and $CHASE_F(T)$: it is the function ψ that maps every symbol v appearing in T, to the symbol v' to which it is changed by the chase. Also, since containment mappings enjoy the transitive property, we have that if for some T_1, T_2, and F, there is a containment mapping from $CHASE_F(T_1)$ to T_2, then there is a containment mapping from T_1 to T_2. The following lemma presents another important property of the chase, which will be used in the subsequent discussion.

LEMMA 4.2 Let T and T' be tableaux and F be a set of FDs. If there is a containment mapping ψ from T to T', and T' satisfies F, then ψ is also a containment mapping from $CHASE_F(T)$ to T', and $CHASE_F(T)$ satisfies F.

PROOF   Let T_0, T_1, ..., T_k, with $T = T_0$ and $T_k = CHASE_F(T)$, be the tableaux successively generated during the execution of Algorithm 4.1. For every $1 \leq i \leq k$, we show that (1) there is a mapping from T_i to T', and (2) T_i does not contain any hard violation of F.

1. We proceed by induction on i. The basis holds trivially. Assume that there is a mapping from T_{i-1} to T', and let the ith

step change some value v to w as the result of applying an FD $X \to A$ to rows t_1, t_2 (clearly, $t_1[A] = v$, $t_2[A] = w$). Now let $t_1' = \psi(t_1)$ and $t_2' = \psi(t_2)$; by definition of containment mapping, $t_1', t_2' \in T'$, and $t_1'[X] = t_2'[X]$. Then, since T' satisfies F, we have that $t_1'[A] = t_2'[A]$, and so $\psi(v) = \psi(w)$. Therefore, since the only difference between T_{i-1} and T_i is that all occurrences of v are replaced by occurrences of w, it is the case that ψ is also a containment mapping from T_i to T'.

2. Assume, by way of contradiction, that T contains a pair of rows t_1 and t_2 such that $t_1[A]$ and $t_2[A]$ are distinct constants and $t_1[X] = t_2[X]$. Let $t_1' = \psi(t_1)$ and $t_2' = \psi(t_2)$. Then, by definition of containment mapping, we have $t_1'[X] = t_2'[X]$ and

$$t_1'[A] = t_1[A] \neq t_2[A] = t_2'[A]$$

against the hypothesis that T' satisfies F.   □

The chase is a useful tool for deciding the implication of constraints, as shown by the next theorem with respect to FDs. Given an FD $f = X \to Y$, the *tableau for f*, indicated with T_f, is a tableau with two rows, both with dv's on X, and distinct ndv's on $U - X$;[2] therefore, the two rows agree on X and disagree on all other attributes.

THEOREM 4.2 Let F be a set of FDs, and $f = X \to Y$, both defined on a relation scheme $R(U)$. Also, let T_f be the tableau for f. Then, F implies f if and only if the two rows in $CHASE_F(T_f)$ coincide on all the attributes in Y.

PROOF   Let us note that since T_f does not contain constants, the chased tableau $CHASE_F(T_f)$ satisfies F, for every F and f.

If.   Asssume that the two rows in $CHASE_F(T_f)$ coincide on Y. Let $r(U)$ satisfy F, and t_1, t_2 be tuples in r such that $t_1[X] = t_2[X]$; we claim that $t_1[Y] = t_2[Y]$, thus confirming that r satisfies f. Let ψ be the function that maps the two rows of T_f to t_1 and t_2, respectively; ψ is thus a containment mapping from T_f to $\{t_1, t_2\}$, since it is a

---

[2] Here and in the following, we will use the term *distinct ndv* to refer to an ndv that does not appear elsewhere in the tableau. This is always possible, since we have an infinite number of ndv's.

$T_{AC \to DE}$	A	B	C	D	E	G	H
	v_A	n_1	v_C	n_2	n_3	n_4	n_5
	v_A	n_6	v_C	n_7	n_8	n_9	n_{10}

$CHASE_F(T_{AC \to DE})$	A	B	C	D	E	G	H
	v_A	n_1	v_C	n_2	n_3	n_4	n_5
	v_A	n_1	v_C	n_2	n_3	n_9	n_{10}

Figure 4.7. Testing the implication of FDs with the chase

function on symbols (the two rows coincide on X and $t_1[X] = t_2[X]$) and maps variables to constants. Therefore, by Lemma 4.2 (since r satisfies F and so does $\{t_1, t_2\} \subseteq r$), it follows that ψ is also a containment mapping from $CHASE_F(T_f)$ to $\{t_1, t_2\}$. Then, since the two rows in $CHASE_F(T_f)$ coincide on Y, by definition of containment mapping, we have that $t_1[Y] = t_2[Y]$.

Only if. If the two rows in $CHASE_F(T_f)$ do not coincide on Y, any two-tuple relation r obtained from $CHASE_F(T_f)$ by mapping each variable to a distinct constant violates f, whereas it satisfies F, since $CHASE_F(T_f)$ satisfies F.   □

A consequence of Theorem 4.2 is that the two rows of the chased tableau $CHASE_F(T_{X \to Y})$ agree on an attribute A if and only if $A \in X^+$.

> **Example 4.4**   Let us use Theorem 4.2 to verify that the set of FDs $F = \{BC \to DE, A \to B, AEG \to H\}$ implies the FD $AC \to DE$ (as we saw in Example 3.6). The tableau $T_{AC \to DE}$ and the chased tableau are shown in Figure 4.7 and confirm the implication. The same tableaux can be used to prove that F does not imply $AC \to G$.

The method suggested in Theorem 4.2 for deciding the implication of FDs is based on the following intuitive idea: Given F and f, (1) build T_f, which can be seen as the most general tableau that violates f, and (2) transform T_f into a tableau that satisfies F. If the resulting tableau violates f, then a counterexample is obtained, and so there is no implication. Otherwise, we know that in order to satisfy F, a tableau (and therefore a relation) must satisfy f—this is the definition of implication.

Theorem 4.2 provides us with the possibility of deciding the implication of FDs independently of inference rules: we could have omitted Section 3.2, and still have been able to prove all the main results on FDs, including the correctness of Algorithms 3.1 and 3.2.

4.2 FDs and Lossless Decompositions

As we saw in Chapter 1, the property of lossless decomposition is very important in relational theory: design methods, aimed at producing normalized schemes, decompose relations by means of the projection operator. The relations $\pi_{X_1}(r), \ldots, \pi_{X_k}(r)$ obtained in this way "represent" the initial relation r if the latter can be obtained by means of a join of the projected relations, that is, if the original relation can be losslessly decomposed $(r = \bowtie_{i=1}^{n} (\pi_{X_i}(r)))$. Since FDs play a fundamental role with respect to normal forms, it is highly meaningful to study the relationship between FDs and lossless decomposition.

The next theorem characterizes the losslessness of *binary* decompositions of relation schemes. We omit its proof, since it will follow as a corollary from a more general result (Theorem 4.4), which we will prove independently.

THEOREM 4.3 Consider a relation scheme $R(U)$, a set of FDs F over attributes in U, and three subsets X, X_1, X_2 of U, with $X_1 X_2 = U$ and $X_1 \cap X_2 = X$. Then, all the relations over $R(U)$ have a lossless decomposition with respect to X_1, X_2 if and only if at least one of the FDs $X \rightarrow X_1$, $X \rightarrow X_2$ is in F^+. □

> **Example 4.5** Given the relation scheme *R(Employee, Department, Project, Manager)*, all the relations that satisfy the FDs $E \rightarrow D, D \rightarrow M$ have a lossless decomposition on EP, EDM, because $E \rightarrow DM$ is implied by the given FDs. An example relation that satisfies the FDs and therefore has a lossless decomposition is shown in Figure 4.8. On the other hand, it is not the case that all the relations can be losslessly decomposed on DP, EDM, since neither $D \rightarrow P$ nor $D \rightarrow EM$ is implied by the FDs; the same relation in Figure 4.8 is a counterexample.

Employee	Dept	Project	Manager
Jones	CS	K1	White
Jones	CS	AA	White
Smith	CS	BB	White
Lee	EE	K1	Black

Figure 4.8. A relation for Example 4.5

Employee	Dept	Project	Manager
Smith	CS	AA	White
Jones	CS	AA	White
Smith	CS	BB	White
Jones	CS	BB	White
Lee	EE	K1	Black

Figure 4.9. A relation with a lossless decomposition on EP, EDM

The condition in Theorem 4.3 is necessary and sufficient for *all* relations satisfying F to have a lossless decomposition. If we only consider individual relations, the condition is no longer necessary, as shown by the relation in Figure 4.9, which has a lossless decomposition on ED, DPM, and satisfies neither $D \to E$ nor $D \to PM$. Clearly, the sufficient condition still holds, as a consequence of Theorem 4.3.

COROLLARY 4.1 Let $R(U)$ and X, X_1, X_2 be as in Theorem 4.3. Then a relation over $R(U)$ has a lossless decomposition with respect to X_1, X_2 if it satisfies at least one of the FDs $X \to X_1$, $X \to X_2$. □

Let us now consider n-ary decompositions. As we saw in Section 1.4, the containment $r \subseteq \bowtie_{i=1}^{n} (\pi_{X_i}(r))$ always holds. Here, there is no synthetic characterization of lossless decomposition, as in the binary case; the simplest method requires the use of the chase algorithm.

THEOREM 4.4 Consider a relation scheme $R(U)$, a set of FDs F over attributes in U, and n subsets $X_1, X_2, \ldots, X_n$ of U, with $X_1 \ldots X_n =$

U. Let T be a tableau over U, with n rows, $s_1, s_2, \ldots, s_n$, where, for every $1 \leq i \leq n$, and for every $A \in U$, if $A \in X_i$, then $s_i[A]$ is equal to the dv v_A, and if $A \in U - X_i$, then $s_i[A]$ is a distinct ndv. Then all the relations over $R(U)$ that satisfy F have a lossless decomposition with respect to $X_1, X_2, \ldots, X_n$ if and only if the tableau $\text{CHASE}_F(T)$ contains a row entirely composed of dv's.

PROOF

If. Asssume that $\text{CHASE}_F(T)$ contains a row with only dv's. Let $r(U)$ satisfy F, and $t \in \bowtie_{i=1}^n (\pi_{X_i}(r))$. We claim that $t \in r$. This will complete this part of the proof, since it is always the case that $\bowtie_{i=1}^n (\pi_{X_i}(r)) \supseteq r$.

For every $1 \leq i \leq n$, let t_i be the tuple in $\pi_{X_i}(r)$ that contributes to t in the join, and t_i' the tuple in r from which it originates. Let ψ be the function that, for every $1 \leq i \leq n$ and for every $A \in U$, maps $s_i[A]$ to $t_i'[A]$. We have that ψ is a containment mapping from T to $\{t_1', t_2', \ldots, t_n'\}$, because if $s_i[A] = s_j[A]$ then $t_i'[A] = t_j'[A]$, and it is never the case that $s_i[A] = s_j[B]$, for $A \neq B$. Note that the dv's are mapped to the values in t, and therefore, if s is the row in $\text{CHASE}_F(T)$ entirely composed of dv's, we have that $\psi(s) = t$. Then, since $\{t_1', t_2', \ldots, t_n'\} \subseteq r$, and r satisfies F, it follows (by Lemma 4.2) that ψ is also a containment mapping from $\text{CHASE}_F(T)$ to $\{t_1', t_2', \ldots, t_n'\}$. Therefore, $\psi(s)$ also belongs to $\{t_1', t_2', \ldots, t_n'\}$. Thus, since $\psi(s) = t$, we have that $t \in \{t_1', t_2', \ldots, t_n'\} \subseteq r$, and so $t \in r$.

Only if. If $\text{CHASE}_F(T)$ does not contain a row with only dv's, any relation r obtained from T by mapping each variable to a distinct constant has a lossy decomposition with respect to $X_1, X_2, \ldots, X_n$: $\bowtie_{i=1}^n (\pi_{X_i}(r))$ contains the tuple whose values correspond to the dv's in T, which is not in r. At the same time, since T contains no constants, $\text{CHASE}_F(T)$ satisfies F, and so does r. $\square$

Example 4.6   Consider the relation scheme *R(Employee, Secretary, Project, Office)*, with the FDs $E \to P$, $S \to O$. By means of Theorem 4.4 we can show that every relation r that satisfies the FDs has a lossless decomposition on ES, EPO, SPO; the corresponding initial and chased tableaux are shown in Figure 4.10.

Again, as in the binary case, we have a necessary and sufficient condition for *all* relations satisfying F to have a lossless decomposition.

T	E	S	P	O
	v_E	v_S	n_1	n_2
	v_E	n_3	v_P	v_O
	n_4	v_S	v_P	v_O

$CHASE_F(T)$

E	S	P	O
v_E	v_S	v_P	v_O
v_E	n_3	v_P	v_O
n_4	v_S	v_P	v_O

Figure 4.10. Tableaux for Example 4.6

If we only consider individual relations, the condition is sufficient, but not necessary.

4.3   FDs as Interrelational Constraints

One of the major motivations for studying dependencies is their relationship with normalization and therefore with the decomposition of relations. When a relation (scheme) is decomposed, it is important to be able to enforce on the new database scheme the constraints defined on the original relation. This enforcement is not straightforward. Suppose that the constraints associated with a relation scheme $R(X)$ are a set of FDs F. If R is decomposed into a set of relation schemes $R_1(X_1)$, ..., $R_k(X_k)$, we would like to impose F as the set of constraints on R_1, ..., R_k. However, this is not trivial, because FDs are defined as intrarelational constraints, that is within individual relations, and cannot span over sets of relations. Therefore, there is a need for a definition of FD as an interrelational constraint: given a database scheme $\mathbf{R} = \{R_1(X_1), \ldots, R_k(X_k)\}$, when does one of its instances $\{r_1, \ldots, r_k\}$, satisfy an FD $Y \to Z$ such that $YZ \subseteq X_1 \ldots X_k$?

We argue for some desirable properties that the definition we are looking for should enjoy by discussing an example. Consider the database scheme

$$\mathbf{R} = \{R_1(EDM), R_2(DMA), R_3(EA)\}$$

obtained by decomposing a database scheme with one relation scheme $R_0(EDMA)$ (the attribute names are abbreviated and stand for *Employee, Department, Manager, Administrator*), and the FDs $F = \{E \to D, D \to M, M \to A\}$. Three database instances of $\mathbf{R}$ are

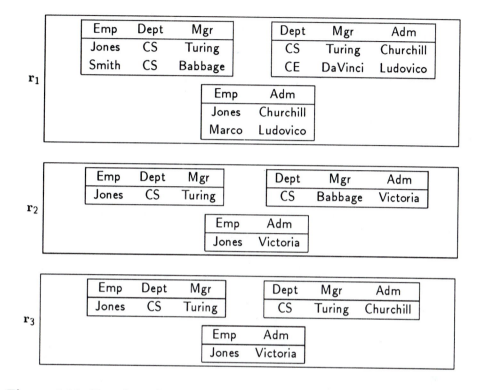

Figure 4.11. Database instances for the definition of interrelational FDs

shown in Figure 4.11. In database $\mathbf{r}_1$, the first relation violates the FD $D \to M$, which is in F and is embedded in its scheme (let us say that $Y \to Z$ is *embedded* in $R(X)$ if $YZ \subseteq X$); clearly, any reasonable definition should reject databases whose relations do not satisfy the embedded dependencies. Let us say that a database $\mathbf{r}$ of $\mathbf{R}$ *locally satisfies* a set F of FDs if each relation r in $\mathbf{r}$ satisfies the respective embedded FDs. This first requirement is not sufficient. Consider the database $\mathbf{r}_2$: every relation trivially satisfies the embedded dependencies, including $D \to M$; nevertheless, the relationship between departments and managers, as established by the first two relations taken together, is not functional, since CS is associated with Turing in the first, and with Babbage in the second. We would not expect our definition to classify this database as valid. Finally, consider the database $\mathbf{r}_3$; here neither of the above situations arise, yet,

there is something undesirable. By reasoning on the intuitive meaning of FDs (and on their implication properties within relations), we
have that each employee belongs to one department (by $E \to D$),
each department has one manager (by $D \to M$), and each manager
is related to one administrator (by $M \to A$). Therefore, each employee has some relationship with one administrator (as a matter of
fact, $E \to A \in F^+$). On the other hand, our database associates with
Smith two administrators: Victoria, directly, and Churchill, through
his department and manager. A reasonable definition of satisfaction
should require composition of functional relationships to behave naturally, thus ruling out databases such as r_3. This requirement can
be enforced by requiring the existence of a common "world" (that is,
a relation over all the attributes) where functions cannot be defined
independently of one another. Therefore, a suitable definition must
consider the various relations as containing a (possibly proper) subset
of the information globally expressed by our decomposed database;
the fragments in the various relations should not be contradictory.

These considerations can be formalized as follows. For the sake of
generality, they refer to a set of FDs rather than a single FD. Given a
database instance $\mathbf{r}$ of a database scheme $\mathbf{R} = \{R_1(X_1), \ldots, R_k(X_k)\}$,
a relation u over the set of attributes $X = X_1 \ldots X_k$ is a *containing
instance* for a database instance $\mathbf{r} = \{r_1, \ldots, r_k\}$ if its projections
over the relation schemes of $\mathbf{R}$ contain the respective relations in $\mathbf{r}$
(formally: $\pi_{X_i}(u) \supseteq r_i$, for $1 \leq i \leq n$). Given a set of dependencies
F, a database $\mathbf{r}$ *(globally) satisfies* F if there is a relation w that (1)
is a containing instance for $\mathbf{r}$, and (2) satisfies F. Such a relation w is
said to be a *weak instance* for $\mathbf{r}$ with respect to F. Since the definition
refers only to containment, and we assume the domains to be infinite,
if a database has a weak instance, then it has infinitely many finite
weak instances. It follows from the respective definitions that global
satisfaction implies local satisfaction, whereas the converse is not true,
as confirmed by the database instances in Figure 4.11.

> **Example 4.7**   The databases in Figure 4.11 do not satisfy F:
> no weak instance can be found for them. Instead, the database in
> Figure 4.12 satisfies F: a weak instance for it is shown in the same
> figure.

Emp	Dept	Mgr
Jones	CS	Turing
White	CS	Turing
Green	IE	Taylor

Dept	Mgr	Adm
CS	Turing	Churchill
CE	DaVinci	Ludovico
EE	Maxwell	Victoria

Emp	Adm
Jones	Churchill
Marco	Ludovico

Emp	Dept	Mgr	Adm
Jones	CS	Turing	Churchill
White	CS	Turing	Churchill
Black	CE	DaVinci	Ludovico
Marco	A	Vasari	Ludovico
Green	IE	Taylor	Roosevelt
Red	EE	Maxwell	Victoria

Figure 4.12. A database instance and one of its weak instances

The definition of *weak instance* is interesting, but not practical, since it does not say how weak instances can be computed. The concept can be made useful via the related notion of *representative instance*: For every database instance **r**, the representative instance is a tableau over U, defined as $CHASE_F(T_\mathbf{r})$, where $T_\mathbf{r}$ is the *state tableau* for **r**, formed by taking the union of all the relations in **r** extended to U by means of distinct ndv's.

> **Example 4.8**   The state tableaux for database $\mathbf{r}_3$ in Figure 4.11 and for the database in Figure 4.12 are shown in Figures 4.13 and 4.14, respectively, together with their representative instances. Note that both the database $\mathbf{r}_3$ in Figure 4.11 and its representative instance in Figure 4.13 violate F, and that both the database in Figure 4.12 and its representative instance in Figure 4.14 satisfy F.

The next theorem shows the fundamental relationship between weak instances and representative instances, confirming that the situation in Example 4.8 is not coincidental. We show two lemmas before

Emp	Dept	Mgr	Adm
Jones	CS	Turing	n_1
n_2	CS	Turing	Churchill
Jones	n_3	n_4	Victoria

Emp	Dept	Mgr	Adm
Jones	CS	Turing	Churchill
n_2	CS	Turing	Churchill
Jones	CS	Turing	Victoria

Figure 4.13. A state tableau with its representative instance

Emp	Dept	Mgr	Adm
Jones	CS	Turing	n_1
White	CS	Turing	n_2
Green	IE	Taylor	n_3
n_4	CS	Turing	Churchill
n_5	CE	DaVinci	Ludovico
n_6	EE	Maxwell	Victoria
Jones	n_7	n_8	Churchill
Marco	n_9	n_{10}	Ludovico

Emp	Dept	Mgr	Adm
Jones	CS	Turing	Churchill
White	CS	Turing	Churchill
Green	IE	Taylor	n_3
n_4	CS	Turing	Churchill
n_5	CE	DaVinci	Ludovico
n_6	EE	Maxwell	Victoria
Marco	n_9	n_{10}	Ludovico

Figure 4.14. Another state tableau with its representative instance

the theorem: the first one is in fact needed to prove the theorem, and the second is essentially its converse.

LEMMA 4.3   If a relation w over U is a weak instance for a database instance $\mathbf{r}$, then there is a containment mapping from the state tableau $T_{\mathbf{r}}$ to w.

PROOF   By definition of *state tableau*, for each relation $r_i \in \mathbf{r}$ and each tuple $t_0 \in r_i$, there is a row s in $T_{\mathbf{r}}$ such that (1) $t_0 = s[X_i]$ and (2) $s[A]$ is a distinct ndv for each attribute $A \in U - X_i$. By definition of *weak instance*, w is a containing instance. Therefore, for each t_0 as above there is (at least) a tuple $t \in w$ such that $t_0 = t[X_i]$. We can say that there is a function f that associates a tuple t in the weak instance with each t_0 in the database instance. Now, we can define a function ψ that is the identity on constants and is defined as follows on variables. Let v be a variable that appears as a value for $s[A]$, where s is the row in $T_{\mathbf{r}}$ that originates form a tuple t_0 in a relation in the database instance. By the argument above, there is a tuple $t \in w$ such that $t = f(t_0)$. Then $\psi(v)$ is defined as the constant that appears as the value of t on A. The definition is unambiguous, since each variable appears only once in $T_\mathbf{r}$. We claim that ψ is a containment mapping from $T_\mathbf{r}$ to w:

- For each x, we have that $\psi(x) \preceq x$, since constants are mapped to themselves, and variables are mapped to constants.

- For each row $s \in T_\mathbf{r}$, there is a tuple $t \in w$ such that, for every $A \in U$, $\psi(s[A]) = t[A]$. If t_0 is the tuple (in relation r_i in $\mathbf{r}$) from which s originates, then the tuple $t = f(t_0)$ satisfies the condition. In fact, $s[A]$ is a constant for every $A \in X_i$ and $t_0 = t[X_i]$. Also, for every $A \in U - X_i$, $s[A]$ is a variable, and so $\psi(s[A])$ is defined as $t[A]$.   □

LEMMA 4.4 Let w be a relation over the universe U and $\mathbf{r}$ a database instance. If

(a) there is a containment mapping from $T_\mathbf{r}$ to w, and

(b) w satisfies F,

then w is a weak instance for $\mathbf{r}$.

PROOF We have to show that if w satisfies conditions *(a)* and *(b)*, then it is a weak instance for $\mathbf{r}$; that is, it satisfies conditions (1) and (2) in the definition of global satisfaction. Since (2) is the same as *(b)*, it suffices to show that *(a)* implies (1). We show that for every relation $r_i \in \mathbf{r}$ and for every tuple $t_0 \in r_i$, there is a tuple $t \in w$ such that $t_0 = t[X_i]$, and so $t_0 \in \pi_{X_i}(w)$. By construction of $T_\mathbf{r}$, if $t_0 \in r_i$, there is a row $t' \in T_\mathbf{r}$ that is the extension of t_0 to U (that is $t_0 = t'[X_i]$). Then, since by condition *(a)* there is a containment mapping from $T_\mathbf{r}$ to w and (by definition) containment mappings map constants to themselves, w contains a tuple t such that $t[X_i] = t'[X_i]$. Therefore, $t_0 = t[X_i]$, and so $t_0 \in \pi_{X_i}(w)$.   □

THEOREM 4.5 A database instance $\mathbf{r}$ satisfies a set F of FDs if and only if the tableau $CHASE_F(T_\mathbf{r})$ satisfies F, where $T_\mathbf{r}$ is the state tableau for $\mathbf{r}$.

PROOF

If.   If we take the representative instance and replace all the variables with distinct constants, we obtain a relation that is a weak instance, since it satisfies F (because $CHASE_F(T_\mathbf{r})$ satisfies F) and it is a containing instance (by construction).

Only if.   Let w be a weak instance for $\mathbf{r}$ with respect to F, demonstrating that $\mathbf{r}$ satisfies F. By Lemma 4.3, there is a containment mapping ψ from $T_\mathbf{r}$ to w. Then, since w satisfies F, we have, by Lemma 4.2, that $CHASE_F(T_\mathbf{r})$ satisfies F.   □

It is clear from the definitions that local satisfaction is much easier to verify than global satisfaction: the latter requires the construction of the representative instance, whereas the former can consider individual relations separately. An interesting class of database schemes has been proposed and characterized for which the two notions of satisfaction coincide: a database scheme $\mathbf{R}$ with an associated set F of FDs is *independent* if every locally consistent instance of $\mathbf{R}$ is globally consistent. Efficient characterizations exist for independent schemes, in various contexts. The specific references are indicated in the Comments section at the end of the chapter.

4.4   Multivalued Dependencies

The concept of lossless decomposition (as noted in Section 4.2 and as we will see again in Chapter 5) is very important in relational theory, and it is therefore very important to be able to characterize it. The results in Section 4.2 confirm that it is not possible to give necessary and sufficient conditions based on FDs for the lossless decomposition of a single relation: there are relations that have a lossless decomposition without satisfying any FD (for example, the relation in Figure 4.15 does not satisfy any nontrivial FD and has a lossless decomposition on AB, BC, CD). Therefore, it is meaningful to introduce another constraint, called *join dependency (JD)* that is satisfied by a relation if and only if it has a lossless decomposition. Formally, given a relation scheme $R(U)$, a join dependency is denoted by $\bowtie [X_1, X_2, \ldots, X_n]$, where $X_1, X_2, \ldots, X_n$ are subsets of U such that $X_1 X_2 \ldots X_n = U$; a

A	B	C	D
a_1	b_1	c_1	d_1
a_1	b_1	c_1	d_2
a_1	b_1	c_2	d_2
a_1	b_2	c_2	d_2
a_2	b_2	c_2	d_2

Figure 4.15. A relation with a lossless decomposition on AB, BC, CD

r

A	B	C	D
a_1	b_1	c_1	d_1
a_1	b_1	c_1	d_2
a_2	b_1	c_2	d_2

$\pi_{AB}(r) \bowtie \pi_{BC}(r) \bowtie \pi_{CD}(r)$

A	B	C	D
a_1	b_1	c_1	d_1
a_1	b_1	c_1	d_2
a_1	b_1	c_2	d_2
a_2	b_1	c_1	d_1
a_2	b_1	c_1	d_2
a_2	b_1	c_2	d_2

Figure 4.16. A violation of the JD $\bowtie [AB, BC, CD]$

relation r satisfies $\bowtie [X_1, X_2, \ldots, X_n]$ if it is has a lossless decomposition on $X_1, X_2, \ldots, X_n$, that is, if $r = \bowtie_{i=1}^{n} \pi_{X_i}(r)$.

> **Example 4.9**   The relation in Figure 4.15 satisfies the JD $\bowtie$ $[AB, BC, CD]$, whereas the first relation in Figure 4.16 does not, because the join of its projections produces the second relation in that figure.

The most common case of decomposition is the binary one: a relation is decomposed into two parts. It corresponds to the binary JD: $\bowtie [X_1, X_2]$. As a matter of fact, binary JDs were considered (under the name of *multivalued dependencies*) well before the notion of a general JD was even conceived. In this text, we discuss essentially multivalued dependencies, beginning with a variation of their original definition, then showing their equivalence to binary JDs, and finally studying the implication problem. Implication will be studied by means of the chase, thus providing the basis for the extension to JDs and to other classes of constraints.

Given a relation scheme $R(U)$, a *multivalued dependency (MVD)* has the syntax $X \twoheadrightarrow Y$, where $X, Y \subseteq U$. Let $Z = U - XY$. A relation r *satisfies the MVD* $X \twoheadrightarrow Y$ if, for every pair of tuples $t_1, t_2 \in r$ such that $t_1[X] = t_2[X]$, there is a tuple $t \in r$ such that $t[XY] = t_1[XY]$ and $t[XZ] = t_2[XZ]$. Intuitively, we can say that the MVD $X \twoheadrightarrow Y$ requires that for every X-value in r, the associated Y-values are independent of the Z-values.

Since Y and Z can be interchanged in the definition without altering its meaning, we have that every relation $r(U)$ satisfies $X \twoheadrightarrow Y$ if and only if it satisfies $X \twoheadrightarrow Z$. (This is the *complementation* property of MVDs.)

> **Example 4.10**   Consider a relation scheme R over the attributes *F(amily)*, *C(hild)*, *P(et)*. A tuple in a relation over this scheme indicates that a child of a family plays with a pet belonging to the same family; names of children and pets are not unique. If it is the case that each child plays with all the pets belonging to its family, then all the relations over $R(FCP)$ satisfy the MVD $F \twoheadrightarrow C$: for every pair of tuples f_1, c_1, p_1, and f_1, c_2, p_2, there is also the tuple f_1, c_1, p_2, since it is the case that c_1, a member of the family f_1, plays also with pet p_2, which belongs to the same family. Consider the relations in Figure 4.17: the first one satisfies the MVD $F \twoheadrightarrow C$ whereas the second violates it (in order to satisfy $F \twoheadrightarrow C$, it should contain a tuple saying that in the Smith family, Tom plays with Jumbo). Note that they also satisfy and violate $F \twoheadrightarrow P$, respectively.

THEOREM 4.6   Let $r(U)$ be a relation and X_1, X_2, X be three subsets of U such that $X_1 X_2 = U$ and $X = X_1 \cap X_2$. Then r has a lossless decomposition with respect to X_1, X_2 if and only if r satisfies the MVD $X \twoheadrightarrow X_1$ (or, equivalently, the MVD $X \twoheadrightarrow X_2$).

PROOF

If.   Let r satisfy $X \twoheadrightarrow X_1$, and $t \in \pi_{X_1}(r) \bowtie \pi_{X_2}(r)$. We show that $t \in r$; again, this will complete this part of the proof, because it is always the case that $r \subseteq \pi_{X_1}(r) \bowtie \pi_{X_2}(r)$. By definition of the join and projection operators, there are tuples $t_1, t_2 \in r$ such that

Family	Child	Pet
Smith	Bob	Lessie
Smith	Tom	Lessie
Smith	Bob	Jumbo
Smith	Tom	Jumbo
Robinson	Jim	Fido
Jones	Tom	Felix
White	Tom	Felix

Family	Child	Pet
Smith	Bob	Lessie
Smith	Tom	Lessie
Smith	Bob	Jumbo

Figure 4.17. A relation that satisfies the MVD $F \twoheadrightarrow C$ and a relation that violates it

$t[X_1] = t_1[X_1]$, and $t[X_2] = t_2[X_2]$. Then by definition of MVD, since $X = X_1 \cap X_2$ and thus $t_1[X] = t_2[X]$, there is a tuple t in r such that $t'[X_1] = t_1[X_1]$ and $t'[X_2] = t_2[X_2]$. But this means that $t = t'$, and therefore $t \in r$.

Only if. Let $r = \pi_{X_1}(r) \bowtie \pi_{X_2}(r)$, and $t_1, t_2 \in r$ with $t_1[X] = t_2[X]$. We show that there is a tuple $t \in r$ such that $t[X_1] = t_1[X_1]$ and $t[X_2] = t_2[X_2]$, thus confirming that r satisfies $X \twoheadrightarrow X_1$. Let $t'_1 = t[X_1]$ and $t'_2 = t[X_2]$; therefore, $t'_1 \in \pi_{X_1}(r)$, and $t'_2 \in \pi_{X_2}(r)$. Then by definition of join, t is the tuple in $\pi_{X_1}(r) \bowtie \pi_{X_2}(r)$ originating from t'_1 and t'_2. Finally, since $r = \pi_{X_1}(r) \bowtie \pi_{X_2}(r)$, we can conclude that t belongs to r. □

The first relation in Figure 4.17 has a lossless decomposition on *FC*, *FP*, and the second one does not, thus confirming Theorem 4.6. It is worth noting that a relation has a lossless binary decomposition *if and only if* it satisfies an MVD; this is different from what happens for FDs, where only a sufficient condition can be given for individual relations (Corollary 4.1).

It is interesting to compare the definition of MVD with that of FD. An FD $X \to Y$ states a functional relationship between the X-values and the Y-values. The MVD $X \twoheadrightarrow Y$, instead, states that for each X-value x, the Y-values associated with x are independent of the Z-values associated with x; in other words, given x, there are a set of Y-values and a set of Z-values associated with it that appear in every possible combination. This argument justifies the name given to MVDs and suggests that each FD is a special case of the MVD on the same sets of attributes, as shown by the next theorem.

THEOREM 4.7   Let $R(U)$ be a relation scheme, with $XY \subset U$. If a relation r satisfies the FD $X \to Y$, then it also satisfies the MVD $X \twoheadrightarrow Y$.

PROOF   If r satisfies $X \to Y$, then, by Corollary 4.1, it has a lossless decomposition on XY, XZ (where $Z = U - XY$), and so, by Theorem 4.6, it satisfies $X \twoheadrightarrow Y$.   □

We leave as an exercise a proof of Theorem 4.7 that does not make use of the results on lossless decomposition (Exercise 4.4).

The converse of Theorem 4.7 does not hold, since a relation may satisfy $X \twoheadrightarrow Y$ and violate $X \to Y$. The relation in Figure 4.17 is such an example, as we have already seen. Therefore, we can say that the MVD is a strictly weaker constraint than the FD: for each set of MVDs M, there is a set of FDs F such that if a relation satisfies F, then it satisfies M. It would not be correct to say instead that MVDs generalize FDs, since it is not possible to express FDs by means of MVDs: Given a set of FDs F, it is not possible, in general, to find a set of MVDs M such that a relation satisfies F if and only if it satisfies M.

The implication problem for MVDs can be studied with the same techniques as the analogous problem for FDs: by means of inference rules or by means of the chase. We consider only the latter, omitting the treatment of inference rules, which is sketched in the exercises.

In order to use the chase to prove results on MVD implication, we have to extend the algorithm. Algorithm 4.1 "applies" FDs to the input tableau by following the definition of FD, which requires, for an FD $X \to A$, that if two rows agree on X, then they also agree on A. Therefore, the chase modifies values, *equating* them to one another. The definition of the MVD $X \twoheadrightarrow Y$ requires that if two rows agree on X, then there is a row (which may be one of the two or another one) defined in a suitable way; no condition is imposed on the original rows. Therefore, a variation of Algorithm 4.1 concerning

---

Algorithm 4.2
input a tableau T and a set M of MVDs
output a tableau $CHASE_M(T)$
begin
  $T' := T$;
  while there are $t_1, t_2 \in T'$ such that
        (1) $X \twoheadrightarrow Y \in M$ (with $Z = U - XY$),
        (2) $t_1[X] = t_2[X]$, and
        (3)   there is no $t \in T'$ with $t[XY] = t_1[XY]$ and $t[XZ] = t_2[XZ]$
  do add a row t to T' with $t[XY] = t_1[XY]$ and $t[XZ] = t_2[XZ]$;
  $CHASE_F(T) := T'$
end

Figure 4.18. The chase algorithm for MVDs

MVDs can be defined as follows, by having it *generate* new rows in case of violations of dependencies.

ALGORITHM 4.2 See Figure 4.18. $\square$

By examining Algorithm 4.2 and comparing it with Algorithm 4.1, we can observe a few things. First of all, Algorithm 4.2 adds a tuple for each violation: all violations of MVDs are *soft*, and therefore, given a tableau and a set of MVDs, it is always possible to add rows and obtain a consistent tableau. Second, for every set F of FDs, and for every tableau T, $CHASE_F(T)$ has no more rows than T; for every set M of MVDs, $CHASE_M(T)$ has at least as many rows as T. Third, and most important, there is a common structure in the two algorithms, which suggests the introduction of a parametrized algorithm. If a constraint is violated in a soft form, the algorithm performs an action, either equating values (for FDs) or generating a new row (for MVDs). Since each violation involves a constraint and some rows (two for FDs and MVDs; one or more for other constraints), we can define for each type of constraint a Boolean function that tests whether there is a k-tuple of rows involved in a soft violation of a given constraint and a procedure that specifies the actions to be performed in case of violation. Figure 4.19 shows the function *applicable* and the procedure

---

function *applicable* $(X \rightarrow A, < t_1, t_2 >, T)$: **boolean**
begin
   if $t_1[X] = t_2[X]$ and $t_1[A] \prec t_2[A]$
   then *applicable* := **true**
   else *applicable* := **false**
end

---

procedure *apply* $(X \rightarrow A, < t_1, t_2 >, T)$;
begin
   change all the occurrences of the value $t_2[A]$ in T to $t_1[A]$
end

---

function *applicable* $(X \twoheadrightarrow Y, < t_1, t_2 >, T)$: **boolean**
begin
   if $t_1[X] = t_2[X]$ and there is no $t \in T$ such that
     $t[XY] = t_1[XY]$ and $t[XZ] = t_2[XZ]$ (where $Z = U - XY$)
   then *applicable* := **true**
   else *applicable* := **false**
end

---

procedure *apply* $(X \twoheadrightarrow A, < t_1, t_2 >, T)$;
begin
   add a row t to T with $t[XY] = t_1[XY]$ and $t[XZ] = t_2[XZ]$
end

Figure 4.19. The function *applicable* and the procedure *apply* for functional and multivalued dependencies

---

Algorithm 4.3
input a tableau $T(U)$ and a set D of dependencies
output a tableau $CHASE_F(T)$
begin
   $T' := T$;
   while $t_1, t_2, \ldots, t_k \in T'$, $d \in D$, and *applicable* $(d, < t_1, t_2, \ldots, t_k >, T)$
   do *apply* $(d, < t_1, t_2, \ldots, t_k >, T)$
end

Figure 4.20. The generalized chase algorithm

apply for FDs and MVDs. Then, the following is the general chase algorithm.

ALGORITHM 4.3   See Figure 4.20.   □

In order to show the analogue of Theorem 4.2, we must first be sure that the result of chasing a tableau with respect to a set of MVDs is a unique tableau, regardless of the order of application of the steps. We leave as Exercise 4.7 the proof of a result similar to Theorem 4.1. Now let us define the tableau for an MVD $m = X \twoheadrightarrow Y$, over a relation scheme $R(U)$, with $Z = U - XY$. T_m is composed of two rows, with dv's on XY and XZ, respectively, and distinct ndv's elsewhere.

THEOREM 4.8   Let M be a set of MVDs and m be an MVD. Then, M implies m if and only if the tableau $CHASE_F(T_m)$ contains a row entirely composed of dv's.

PROOF   Left as an exercise (Exercise 4.8).   □

Having now studied various classes of constraints, there is a further issue we can consider. In Sections 3.2 and 3.3, we have studied the implication of FDs *alone*. In fact, we have shown how to answer the question, "Given a set of FDs F and an fd f, does F imply f?" Similarly, in this section, we have studied the implication problem for MVDs alone. It is interesting to see what happens if we consider sets of constraints containing *both* FDs and MVDs. The result is that the two classes of constraints do *interact*, in the sense that, given $D = F \cup M$ (where F is a set of FDs and M a set of MVDs), its closure D^+ is not just the union of the respective closures F^+ and M^+: it contains other FDs and MVDs.

> **Example 4.11**   Consider a relation scheme $R(ABCD)$, with $F = \{B \rightarrow C\}$ and $M = \{A \twoheadrightarrow B\}$. Then we can see that every relation that satisfies $F \cup M$ satisfies also $A \rightarrow C$ (which is not in F^+) and $B \twoheadrightarrow AD$ (which is not in M^+). Let us prove the claim for $A \rightarrow C$. Let $t_1, t_2 \in r$, where r satisfies $F \cup M$ and $t_1[A] = t_2[A]$; we show that $t_1[C] = t_2[C]$. Since r satisfies $A \twoheadrightarrow B$, it contains a tuple t such that (1) $t[AB] = t_1[AB]$, and (2) $t[ACD] = t_2[ACD]$. Therefore, by (1), $t[B] = t_1[B]$, and thus, since r satisfies $B \rightarrow C$, $t[C] = t_1[C]$. Then, by (2), we have $t[C] = t_2[C]$, and so $t_1[C] = t_2[C]$, as we had to prove.

Again, the implication problem for the *joint class* of FDs and MVDs can be studied both by means of inference rules and by means of the chase algorithm. In keeping with what we have done in the previous part of the section, we consider only the chase. As a matter of fact, the result we need is just a combination of Theorems 4.2 and 4.8, and relies upon the general version of the chase algorithm.

THEOREM 4.9   Let D be a set of FDs and MVDs.

1. D implies an FD $f = X \rightarrow Y$ if and only if, for every $A \in Y$, the chase of T_f with respect to D identifies the A-values of the two rows in T_f.

2. D implies an MVD m if and only if the tableau $CHASE_D(T_m)$ contains a row entirely composed of dv's.   □

> **Example 4.12**   Let us see how the chase would confirm the implications we have already seen in Example 4.11. Figure 4.21 shows the tableaux for dependencies $A \rightarrow C$ and $B \twoheadrightarrow AD$, and the tableaux obtained by chasing them with respect to $F \cup M$. The figure also shows the tableaux that confirm that the FD $AB \rightarrow D$ is not implied by $F \cup M$.

The extension to JDs of all the concepts presented for MVDs (chase algorithm, implication problem for the class, and for the joint class with FDs) is left to the reader (Exercises 4.14, 4.15).

$T_{A \to C}$

A	B	C	D
v_A	n_1	n_2	n_3
v_A	n_4	n_5	n_6

$\text{CHASE}_{F \cup M}(T_{A \to C})$

A	B	C	D
v_A	n_1	n_2	n_3
v_A	n_4	n_2	n_6
v_A	n_4	n_2	n_3
v_A	n_1	n_2	n_6

$T_{B \twoheadrightarrow AD}$

A	B	C	D
v_A	v_B	n_1	v_D
n_2	v_B	v_C	n_3

$\text{CHASE}_{F \cup M}(T_{B \twoheadrightarrow AD})$

A	B	C	D
v_A	v_B	v_C	v_D
n_2	v_B	v_C	n_3

$T_{AB \to D}$

A	B	C	D
v_A	v_B	n_1	n_2
v_A	v_B	n_3	n_4

$\text{CHASE}_{F \cup M}(T_{AB \to D})$

A	B	C	D
v_A	v_B	n_1	n_2
v_A	v_B	n_1	n_4

Figure 4.21. Tableaux for Example 4.12

4.5 Inclusion Dependencies

As we said in Section 3.1, inclusion dependencies are the most natural type of interrelational constraints. We discuss in this section the main properties of this class of constraints and its interaction with the class of functional dependencies.

In Section 3.1 we saw the definition of a restricted version of IND; let us now see the general one. Given a database scheme

$$\mathbf{R} = \{R_1(X_1), R_2(X_2), \ldots, R_n(X_n)\},$$

an *inclusion dependency* has the syntax $R_{i_1}[S_1] \supseteq R_{i_2}[S_2]$, where $1 \leq i_1, i_2 \leq n$, $S_1 =< A_{1,1}, \ldots, A_{1,p} >$ is a *sequence* of distinct attributes from X_{i_1}, and $S_2 =< A_{2,1}, \ldots, A_{2,p} >$ is a sequence of distinct attributes from X_{i_2} (note that the two sequences have the same length). A database instance $\mathbf{r}$ of $\mathbf{R}$ satisfies the IND above if for every tuple $t_2 \in R_{i_2}$, there is a tuple $t_1 \in R_{i_1}$ such that $t_1[A_{1,j}] = t_2[A_{2,j}]$, for $1 \leq j \leq p$. An equivalent definition can be given by using the renaming operator: $\mathbf{r}$ satisfies $R_{i_1}[S_1] \supseteq R_{i_2}[S_2]$ if $\pi_{S_1}(r_{i_1}) \supseteq \rho_{S_1 \leftarrow S_2}(\pi_{S_2}(r_{i_2}))$.

flights	Flight#	Origin	Dest'n		schedule	Flight#	Day
	AZ654	FCO	YYZ
	AZ655	YYZ	FCO
	AZ660	MPX	JFK
	AZ661	JFK	MPX

schedule

Flight#	Day
AZ660	Monday
AZ660	Friday
AZ654	Sunday
AZ655	Monday
AZ661	Tuesday
AZ661	Saturday

reservations

Flight#	Date	Day	Passenger
AZ654	June 26	Sunday	Smith
AZ654	June 19	Sunday	Jones
AZ655	June 27	Monday	White
AZ660	June 24	Friday	Lee
AZ661	July 2	Saturday	Black

Figure 4.22. A database instance for Example 4.13

Example 4.13   Consider a database scheme for an airline reservation system, with the following relation schemes:

$$FLIGHTS(Flight\#, Origin, Destination)$$
$$SCHEDULE(Flight\#, Day)$$
$$RESERVATIONS(Flight\#, Date, Day, Passenger)$$

Here, it could be reasonable to require that each flight has at least one return connection, that the schedule refers only to known flights, and that seats are reserved only for days on which the flight is offered. We can enforce these requirements with the following INDs:

$$d_1: FLIGHTS[Origin, Dest] \supseteq FLIGHTS[Dest, Origin]$$
$$d_2: SCHEDULE[Flight\#, Day] \supseteq RESERVATIONS[Flight\#, Day]$$
$$d_3: FLIGHTS[Flight\#] \supseteq SCHEDULE[Flight\#]$$

The database in Figure 4.22 satisfies the three INDs, whereas the database obtained from it by eliminating the last row in the *flights* relation would violate d_1 and d_3.

In the example, we have seen that the two sequences may coincide (as in d_2 and d_3) or not (as in d_1); in the former case, the IND is said to be *typed*. Also, the two relations involved in an IND need not be distinct (dependency d_1 in the example). Therefore, INDs are in general interrelational, but they can also be intrarelational; clearly, an intrarelational IND is nontrivial only if it is not typed.

We have seen in the preceding sections two methods for studying constraints and deriving algorithms for the implication problem: (1) inference rules, and (2) tableaux and the chase algorithm.

The chase algorithm can be extended to handle INDs, but it does not enjoy the same properties we saw for FDs or MVDs. Since INDs are interrelational, the chase for them should consider sets of tableaux, rather than individual tableaux; however, since the problems we want to show arise also for intrarelational INDs, let us consider the simpler case. With respect to FDs and MVDs, we can say that the *apply* procedure changes the tableau as little as possible: this allowed the parametrization of the chase with respect to the various classes of constraints. This strategy, with respect to INDs, would add a tuple for each violation, which is similar to what happens for MVDs. However, in this case, only some of the values of the new tuple are known: those in the attributes involved in the IND. Nothing is known about the others, and therefore the most reasonable choice is to use a distinct ndv for each of these attributes. Formalizing this argument, we obtain the *applicable* function and the *apply* procedure in Figure 4.23, which refer to a tableau T defined on a relation scheme $R(X)$.

Now, it is possible to show a result analogous to Theorem 4.9, provided that the process terminates (see Exercise 4.16). Unfortunately, as opposed to what we saw in the previous cases, here termination is not guaranteed, since new ndvs may be added at each step. Consider, for example, the first tableau in Figure 4.24, and chase it with respect to the IND $R[Child] \supseteq R[Parent]$. At each step, a new tuple is added, and it introduces a new violation, without ever reaching an end. Figure 4.24 also shows the tableaux obtained after the first two steps, which violate the IND. We leave as Exercise 4.17 the search for conditions sufficient for the termination of the chase for INDs.

As a matter of fact, a variation of the above *apply* procedure could be used that would obtain termination, and allow the test for the implication of INDs. However, the result cannot be generalized to a

---

function *applicable* $(R[A_{1,1}, \ldots, A_{1,p}] \supseteq R[A_{2,1}, \ldots, A_{2,p}], < t_2 >, T)$:

                                                     boolean ;

begin

    if there is no $t_1 \in T$ such that $t_1[A_{1,j}] = t_2[A_{2,j}]$, for $1 \leq j \leq p$

    then *applicable* := **true**

    else *applicable* := **false**

end

---

procedure *apply* $(R[A_{1,1}, \ldots, A_{1,p}] \supseteq R[A_{2,1}, \ldots, A_{2,p}], < t_2 >, T)$;

begin

    add a row t to T with

    $t[A_{1,j}] = t_2[A_{2,j}]$, for $1 \leq j \leq p$

    and $t[A]$ equal to a distinct ndv, for every $A \notin A_{1,1}, \ldots, A_{1,p}$

end

Figure 4.23. The function *applicable* and the procedure *apply* for INDs

Parent	Child
David	Salomon

Parent	Child
David	Salomon
n_1	David

Parent	Child
David	Salomon
n_1	David
n_2	n_1

Figure 4.24. A nonterminating chase

framework involving other constraints. Therefore, we study INDs by means of inference rules, using ideas from the chase only in the proof of the completeness theorem.

Proceeding as we did for FDs, we first present some sufficient conditions for the implication of INDs, then formalize them as inference rules, and finally show their completeness. The discussion below refers to a generic database scheme $\mathbf{R} = \{R_1(X_1), R_2(X_2), \ldots, R_n(X_n)\}$. The proofs of the following lemmas are left as exercises (4.18, 4.19, and 4.20).

LEMMA 4.5 An IND $R_{i_1}[S_1] \supseteq R_{i_2}[S_2]$ is trivial if and only if $i_1 = i_2$ and $S_1 = S_2$. $\qquad\square$

LEMMA 4.6 If a database **r** satisfies an IND

$$R_{i_1}[< A_{1,1}, \ldots, A_{1,p} >] \supseteq R_{i_2}[< A_{2,1}, \ldots, A_{2,p} >]$$

then it satisfies

$$R_{i_1}[< A_{1,j_1}, \ldots, A_{1,j_q} >] \supseteq R_{i_2}[< A_{2,j_1}, \ldots, A_{2,j_q} >]$$

for every sequence of distinct integers $j_1, \ldots, j_q$ from $\{1, 2, \ldots, q\}$. □

LEMMA 4.7 If a database **r** satisfies the INDs $R_{i_1}[S_1] \supseteq R_{i_2}[S_2]$ and $R_{i_2}[S_2] \supseteq R_{i_3}[S_3]$, then it satisfies the IND $R_{i_1}[S_1] \supseteq R_{i_3}[S_3]$. □

The above lemmas prove the correctness of the following inference rules.

IND1. *Reflexivity for INDs:* **if** $\perp$, **then** $R_i[S] \supseteq R_i[S]$.

IND2. *Projection and permutation:*
    if $R_{i_1}[< A_{1,1}, \ldots, A_{1,p} >] \supseteq R_{i_2}[< A_{2,1}, \ldots, A_{2,p} >]$
    with $j_1, \ldots, j_q$ is a sequence of distinct integers from $\{1, 2, \ldots, q\}$,
    then $R_{i_1}[< A_{1,j_1}, \ldots, A_{1,j_q} >] \supseteq R_{i_2}[< A_{2,j_1}, \ldots, A_{2,j_q} >]$.

IND3. *Transitivity for INDs:*
    if $R_{i_1}[S_1] \supseteq R_{i_2}[S_2]$, $R_{i_2}[S_2] \supseteq R_{i_3}[S_3]$, **then** $R_{i_1}[S_1] \supseteq R_{i_3}[S_3]$.

THEOREM 4.10 The rules IND1, IND2, IND3 are complete for the derivation of INDs.

PROOF We show that, given a set D of INDs and an IND $d = R_{i_1}[< A_{1,1}, \ldots, A_{1,p} >] \supseteq R_{i_0}[< A_{0,1}, \ldots, A_{0,p} >]$, if D implies d, then d is derivable from D by means of the rules.

Let D imply d. We build a database instance **r** by applying, to an initial database, a sort of chase procedure. The initial database has one tuple t_0 in r_{i_0}, and the other relation empty. Assuming that all the attributes have a common, countable domain, and representing it by means of the natural numbers, we define t as follows:

$$t_0[A_{0,j}] = j \quad \text{for } 1 \leq j \leq p$$
$$t_0[A] = 0 \quad \quad \text{for } A \notin A_{0,1} \ldots A_{0,p}$$

This initial database is modified by means of a chase algorithm that uses a variation of the subprograms shown in Figure 4.23. The *applicable* function is the generalization of the one in Figure 4.23 to the interrelational case. The *apply* procedure, besides the generalization, differs from the one in Figure 4.23 because it uses the value 0, instead of new ndvs for the attributes not involved in the IND under consideration. Clearly, since no new values are ever introduced, the algorithm terminates and generates a database that satisfies D, and therefore it satisfies d, since we assumed that D implies d. Thus, r_{i_1} contains a tuple t such that for every $1 \leq j \leq p$, $t[A_{1,j}] = j$. Now the theorem will follow by the following claim:

Claim. If a relation r_i contains a tuple t that, for every $1 \leq h \leq q$, has value $j_h > 0$ for the attribute A_{k_h}, then it is possible to derive from D, by means of rules IND1, IND2, IND3, the IND

$$R_i[< A_{k_1}, \ldots, A_{k_q} >] \supseteq R_{i_0}[< A_{0,j_1}, \ldots, A_{0,j_q} >]$$

We omit the details of the proof of the claim (leaving them as Exercise 4.21), noting that it can be carried out by induction on the number of steps in the chase needed to add the tuple t to r_i.   □

By reasoning in a way similar to the one used for FDs (Theorem 3.2), we could find a decision algorithm for the implication problem for INDs that, given a database scheme, a set of INDs I, a relation scheme R_{i_1}, and a sequence of attributes S_1 from X_{i_1}, finds all the schemes R_{j_1} and sequences S_2 such that I implies $R_{j_1}[S_2] \supseteq R_{i_1}[S_1]$ (Exercise 4.22). However, despite its similarity to Algorithm 3.1, this procedure cannot be implemented efficiently because it has to handle not just a set of attributes (as Algorithm 3.1 does) but a set of sequences of attributes. It has been shown that the general implication problem for INDs is PSPACE-complete [60], and therefore it does not have a polynomial-time algorithm, unless P=PSPACE. The problem becomes polynomial for restricted classes (1) if all the INDs are *typed*, that is, of the form $R_{i_1}[S] \supseteq R_{i_2}[S]$, where S contains attributes in $X_{i_1} \cap X_{i_2}$, or (2) if the length of the sequences of attributes in the INDs are *bounded*; that is, if there is an integer k such that for every IND, $R_{i_1}[S_1] \supseteq R_{i_2}[S_2]$, where $1 \leq i_1, i_2 \leq n$, and $S_1 = < A_{1,1}, \ldots, A_{1,p} >$ $S_2 = < A_{2,1}, \ldots, A_{2,p} >$, it is the case that $p \leq k$. In the special case

$k = 1$, the INDs are called *unary* (Exercises 4.23 and 4.24).

Now, as we did for MVDs, it would be reasonable to study the interaction of INDs with FDs. However, since problems we have never encountered before arise, we handle the subject from a more general (even if more superficial) point of view in the next section.

4.6 Unrestricted and Finite Implication and Their Decidability

In this final section of the chapter, we take a more general view of some problems on constraints, concluding the discussion set up in Section 3.1 with the basic definitions and properties. As a starting point, we consider the interaction of INDs with FDs. The results here are not as straightforward as for the joint class of FDs and MVDs.

Let us begin with an example. Note that, since FDs are intrarelational constraints, it is necessary to indicate the relation that each FD refers to; we will write $R : Y \to Z$ to indicate the FD $Y \to Z$ defined on relation scheme $R(X)$ (with $X \supseteq YZ$).

> **Example 4.14**   Let us consider a database scheme with just one relation over two attributes, $R(AB)$, and the set of constraints $D = \{R : A \to B, R[B] \supseteq R[A]\}$. We claim that if a relation r is finite and satisfies D, then it also satisfies the IND $R[A] \supseteq R[B]$. Since r satisfies $A \to B$, the number of distinct values appearing for the attribute A is not smaller than the number of distinct values for B. Then, since it satisfies $R[B] \supseteq R[A]$, the set of values for B contains (possibly not properly) the set of values for A. As a consequence of these two facts, the two sets of values are identical, and therefore r satisfies $R[A] \supseteq R[B]$. However, the claim above does not hold for infinite relations (that is, relations with an infinite number of tuples), because it is not possible in such a case to argue on the basis of the number of distinct values. As a matter of fact, the counterexample relation sketched in Figure 4.25 satisfies D and violates $R[A] \supseteq R[B]$, because the value 0 does not appear as a value for the attribute A.

Example 4.14 shows a set D of FDs and INDs and a dependency d such that D does not imply d, whereas, for every finite relation r, if r satisfies D, then it also satisfies d. This situation never arises

A	B
1	0
2	1
3	2
...	
n	n − 1
n + 1	n
...	

Figure 4.25. An infinite relation for Example 4.14

if the constraints under consideration are only FDs, MVDs, and JDs (Exercise 4.26). It is therefore meaningful to distinguish between two notions of implication:

1. *D unrestrictedly implies d* if d holds in every (finite or infinite) relation that satisfies D.

2. *D finitely implies d* if d holds in every finite relation that satisfies D.

Let us say that a class of constraints is *finitely controllable* if the two notions of implication coincide. Example 4.14 shows that the joint class of FDs and INDs is not finitely controllable. Finite controllability is strongly related to the decidability of the implication problems.

We now briefly consider a few issues about the two versions of implication. The discussion requires a knowledge of the basic notions of computability, such as recursive enumerability and decidability, and can be skipped without affecting comprehension of the subsequent chapters. We refer to general classes of dependencies, the only restriction being that they are expressible as first-order sentences.

LEMMA 4.8 Let C be a class of constraints and $D \subset C$. Then the set of the constraints of class C that are not finitely implied by D is recursively enumerable.

PROOF   We can enumerate finite database instances and constraints (in a diagonal manner) and output the constraints that do not hold in some database instance that satisfies D.   □

LEMMA 4.9   Let C be a class of constraints and $D \subset C$. Then the set of the constraints of class C that are unrestrictedly implied by D is recursively enumerable.

PROOF   Since the constraints under consideration are first-order sentences, the claim follows from the recursive enumerability of sentences in first-order predicate calculus.   □

THEOREM 4.11   If a class of constraints C is finitely controllable, then both implication problems are decidable.

PROOF   If the class is finitely controllable, then, by definition, the two implication problems coincide, and so both the set of implied constraints and the set of nonimplied constraints are recursively enumerable (by Lemmas 4.9 and 4.8, respectively), and thus both are decidable.   □

Note that Theorem 4.11 says that finite controllability is a sufficient condition for decidability. It is often the case that a class of constraints is not finitely controllable, and its implication problems are undecidable: the class of FDs and INDs is a notable example [73,172]. However, the condition is not necessary: for example, the class of FDs and unary INDs is not finitely controllable (as confirmed by Example 4.14, where only unary INDs are used), but its implication problems are both decidable [83]. To confirm part of this claim, we show a solution to the unrestricted implication problem for this class.

In order to simplify the discussion, we refer to intrarelational unary INDs, since Example 4.14 confirms that even this subclass is not finitely controllable.

LEMMA 4.10   Let $R(U)$ be a relation scheme and $D = F \cup I$, where F is a set of FDs, and I is a set of unary intrarelational INDs over R. Then the following hold:

1. An FD is implied by D if and only if it is implied by F.
2. An IND is implied by D if and only if it is implied by I.

PROOF

1. Let $f = X \to A$ be an FD that is not implied by F; we show a (possibly infinite) relation that satisfies D and violates f, thus

confirming that D does not imply f.

Consider a two-tuple relation with the tuples that agree on all the attributes in X^+ and disagree on all the others (and therefore on A): the typical counterexample relation that satisfies F and violates f. If we chase this relation with respect to I by numbering the violations of INDs in the order in which they arise and applying the INDs in the same order, we obtain a countably infinite relation that satisfies I. We claim that this relation also satisfies F. This follows from the fact that the original relation satisfies F, and the chase on unary INDs cannot introduce violations of FDs. (The tuples it adds have new values for all the attributes except one, for which it has a value that appears in the relation, but only for other attributes.)

2. Left as an exercise (4.27).   □

The next theorem is a direct consequence of the Lemma 4.10.

THEOREM 4.12 The unrestricted implication problem for FDs and unary INDs is decidable.   □

Exercises

4.1 Prove that given tableaux T_1, T_2, T_3, if there are containment mappings from T_1 to T_2 and from T_2 to T_3, then there is a containment mapping from T_1 to T_3.

4.2 Prove that equatability is an equivalence relation and is preserved by the chase. Also, prove that the chase identifies only equatable values.

4.3 Prove Theorem 4.3 directly (without making use of Theorem 4.4).

4.4 Prove, using only the definitions of FD and MVD, that if a relation satisfies an FD $X \to Y$, then it satisfies the MVD $X \twoheadrightarrow Y$.

4.5 Prove that it is not possible, in general, given a set of FDs F, to find a set of MVDs M such that a relation satisfies F if and only if it satisfies M.

4.6 Prove that for every tableau T and for every set of FDs F, $CHASE_F(T)$ has no more rows than T, whereas for every set M of MVDs, $CHASE_M(T)$ has at least as many rows as T.

4.7 Prove the analogue of Theorem 4.1 for MVDs. (Note that here the claim is easier, since the chase with respect to MVDs always generates a tableau that satisfies them).

4.8 Prove Theorem 4.8.

4.9 Characterize trivial MVDs.

4.10 Prove that the decomposition property (analogous to FD2) does not hold for MVDs. That is, show that a relation r may satisfy $X \twoheadrightarrow YZ$ and violate $X \twoheadrightarrow Y$.

4.11 Prove that $X \twoheadrightarrow Y$ and $X \twoheadrightarrow Z$ imply $X \twoheadrightarrow Y - Z$ (and so, due to the complementation, $X \twoheadrightarrow Y \cap Z$).

4.12 Prove that the analogue of Lemma 3.3 holds for MVDs.

4.13 We know that MVDs enjoy complementation, some form of decomposition (Exercise 4.11), and transitivity (Exercise 4.12). We also know a characterizion for trivial MVDs (Exercise 4.9). Build a set of inference rules from these properties, and show its completeness. (Hint: the crux of the proof is something that replaces the closure X^+ of a set of attributes with respect to a set of FDs; it cannot be a set of attributes, because MVDs do not enjoy full decomposition, but it is a set of sets of attributes, closed under intersection, by Exercise 4.11.)

4.14 Define the function *applicable* and the procedure *apply* for JDs, and prove the analogue of Theorem 4.8.

4.15 Study the implication problem for the joint class of FDs and JDs (that is, prove the analogue of Theorem 4.9).

4.16 Find a characterization for the implication of INDs based on the chase, under the assumption that the algorithm terminates.

4.17 Find sufficient conditions for the termination of the chase with respect to INDs.

4.18 Characterize trivial INDs (Lemma 4.5).

4.19 Prove Lemma 4.6.

4.20 Prove Lemma 4.7.

4.21 Prove the *Claim* in the proof of Theorem 4.10.

4.22 Write an algorithm that, given a database scheme, a set of INDs I, a relation scheme R_{i_1}, and a sequence of attributes S_1 from X_{i_1}, finds all the schemes R_{j_1} and sequences S_2 such that I implies $R_{j_1}[S_2] \supseteq R_{i_1}[S_1]$. Show that it would solve the implication problem for INDs.

4.23 Show how the general inference rules for INDs can be simplified if the INDs are required to be typed; then show an efficient algorithm for deciding implication.

4.24 Find a sound and complete set of inference rules for unary INDs, and a linear-time algorithm for the implication problem.

4.25 Find a set D of FDs and INDs, and an individual FD f such that D does not (unrestrictedly) imply f, and D finitely implies f.

4.26 Show that finite and unrestricted implication coincide for FDs, MVDs, and JDs.

4.27 Complete the proof of Lemma 4.10.

Comments and References

Tableaux and the chase are used in various contexts and with slightly different definitions in proving results involving constraints. Tableaux were introduced by Aho, Sagiv, and Ullman [14,15] to model some restricted forms of queries and characterize their equivalence. As a tool for studying the implication of constraints, they were proposed, together with the chase, by Aho, Beeri, and Ullman [13], who proved Theorem 4.4, which essentially characterizes whether a set of FDs implies a JD. More general applicability of these notions (including the main results of Section 4.1) was demonstrated by Maier et al. [164] with respect to FDs, MVDs, and JDs, and by Beeri and Vardi [48] with respect to other classes of dependencies. It should be noted that we presented a more general notion of tableau than in these two last papers, which includes constants besides variables, because it allows us to prove more general results. However, this has made things more complex in some cases. For example, in the context of Maier et al. [164] the chase always produces a tableau that satisfies the constraints, and therefore Theorem 4.1 can be expressed by saying that the result of the chase is unique (in this case a process like the chase is sometimes said to be *Finite-Church-Rosser*).

As already mentioned, Theorem 4.4 was proven by Aho, Beeri, and Ullman [13]; Theorem 4.3, which we have proven as a consequence of it, was proven independently (and earlier) by Rissanen [184].

Section 4.3 follows a paper by Honeyman [120]. Extensions of the concept to other dependencies were studied by Graham et al. [114]. The importance of the notion of independence was discovered by Sagiv [191,192], who also gave a characterization with respect to key dependencies. An algorithm for testing independence with respect to FDs was proposed by Graham and Yannakakis [115] and later refined by Ito et al. [128] and Sagiv [193].

Multivalued dependencies were proposed independently by Fagin [98], and by Zaniolo [232]. The implication problem was solved by means of inference rules by Beeri et al. [42], whereas our treatment based on the chase follows, as we said, the work by Maier et al. [164]. Join dependencies were proposed by Rissanen [183]. It should be noted that no bounded full axiomatization is known for JDs (but there is no proof of its nonexistence, just conjecture), whereas their implication problem is decidable. Also, there are bounded axiomatizations for classes that properly contain JDs (Sciore [199]), and this fact was a motivation for looking for wider classes of constraints. Constraints of these more general classes were given various names in the literature (Fagin [101], Yannakakis and Papadimitriou [231], Beeri and Vardi [47,48]). We do not cite them here; we only note that they can be divided into two main classes [47,48]: (1) *equality-generating dependencies*, which include FDs and have an *apply* procedure in the chase that always equates values in the rows; and (2) *tuple-generating dependencies*, which include JDs (and therefore MVDs) and have an *apply* procedure that always adds tuples.

Inclusion dependencies, with their axiomatization and solution of the implication problem, were studied by Casanova et al. [60], who also recognized some of the problems (distinction between the two implication problems, and nonexistence of a bounded full axiomatization) for the joint class of FDs and INDs. The undecidability of the implication problem for the joint class was proved by Mitchell [172] and Chandra and Vardi [73]. The decidable subproblems for FDs and unary INDs have been deeply investigated by Cosmadakis et al. [83].

Chapter 5

The Theory of Normalization

We have seen in Section 1.6 that Boyce-Codd normal form is a quality of relation schemes that it is useful to try to obtain. Other normal forms exist with similar motivations, possibly with reference to slightly different frameworks. In the design of a relational database, it is not easy to find immediately a scheme that enjoys a given normal form. Therefore, the design process of relational databases is often divided into two steps:

1. *Modeling*, whose goal is to analyze the application of interest and organize the structure of the relevant data in terms of a database scheme **R** containing one or more relation schemes. For the sake of simplicity, we may assume that **R** contains one relation scheme; the discussion extends in a natural way to the general case.

2. *Normalization*: The relation schemes that do not satisfy the target normal form are replaced by (sets of) normalized relation schemes; the new relation schemes are usually projections of the original ones, and should be capable of representing at least the same information.

The modeling phase is by no means trivial. However, it is beyond the scope of this book. The interested reader can consult specific references, such as the text by Batini, Ceri, and Navathe [38]. Also, it is important to note that current practical methodologies follow a different pattern, which does not use normalization theory as a tool, but was nevertheless influenced by its results. We briefly discuss this point at the end of the Comments and References section of this chapter.

Beside normalization, other phases exist in the design process in which we are interested in using decompositions, and also other more general transformations. For example, in the design of distributed databases, we may initially produce the global database scheme of the application and then split the scheme into a set of local schemes, each one containing relations to be located in a specific node. The splitting may result both in projections and in selections. In other cases, it may happen that the local schemes are already available and must be merged into a global scheme. In this case the involved operators are union and join.

This chapter is devoted to a deep study of normalization. As a preliminary step, we discuss the relationship between schemes involved in transformations. Section 5.1 contains a discussion of the problem on an intuitive basis. The concept is then formalized in Section 5.2, with specific reference to the transformations induced by projections (called vertical decompositions) and to FDs—the framework needed for normalization. Then Section 5.3 considers the basic normal forms for FDs, namely, Boyce-Codd normal form and third normal form. Section 5.4 discusses the algorithms for achieving these normal forms. Sections 5.5 and 5.6 deal with a second group of normal forms, which extend the power of normalization with respect to more general contexts, where other constraints than FDs can be defined.

5.1 Adequacy and Equivalence of Transformations

In order to use a scheme **S** instead of another scheme **R** in modeling an application, some relationship must exist between the information content of **R** and that of **S**. The following sections of this chapter contain a formal study of this relationship. Here we present the notion on an intuitive basis, as an introduction to the technical discussion. The relationship between the original scheme and the transformed one depends on the motivation for the transformation. There are two main cases, whose representatives are those mentioned above: distribution and normalization.

In the case of distribution, the local schemes, taken together (let **S** be their juxtaposition), must have the same capacity to represent information. We say that **S** should be an *equivalent representation* of **R**. This can be expressed by saying that, for each consistent instance **r** of **R**, there is a consistent instance **s** of **S** such that the data in **s** represent the same information as the data in **r**, and vice versa (that is, there is a one-to-one correspondence between the instances of **R** and the instances of **S**). The phrase *the data represent the same information as* could be formalized in various ways, referring to strategies that allow us to obtain **s** from **r** and **r** from **s**, or to transform queries on **r** into equivalent queries on **s**. However, because of the informality of the discussion here, we leave this notion informal for the moment. The correspondence between instances of **R** and instances of **S**, if defined also on instances that do not satisfy the constraints (as is often the case), should map inconsistent instances of **R** to inconsistent instances of **S**, and vice versa.

In the case of normalization, the above requirements are too strict because the decomposed schemes must have instances that do not correspond to instances of the original schemes—otherwise insertion and deletion anomalies would not be removed. This can be expressed by requiring a one-to-one correspondence between the consistent instances of **R** and a subset of the consistent instances of **S**. In this case, **S** is an *adequate representation* of **R**.

In the framework of normalization, where the correspondence maps the instances of **R** to instances of **S** obtained by means of projections (and sometimes selections), we also use the terms *adequate* and *equivalent decomposition*. In the rest of the chapter, we refer mainly to *adequacy* of decompositions, because equivalence is less relevant to the framework of normalization.

Several factors influence the existence and properties of adequate representation:

1. The classes of constraints and the notion of satisfaction

2. The target type of normal form, when normalization is the goal we want to achieve

3. The types of allowed transformations: projections, selections, or other types

With respect to Point 1, some of the results change depending on the classes of constraints. For example, there are properties that hold for FDs and not for MVDs. This will not be very significant in the sequel, because we refer mainly to FDs.

Concerning Point 2, several normal forms have been investigated, each of them focusing on certain formal aspects of what we mean by a "good" scheme. We will see that there is a trade-off between normal forms and adequacy of decompositions.

We discuss Point 3 by means of an example. Consider a scheme **R** containing the relation scheme

$$R\ (Employee\#, Category, TimePercentage, Salary)$$

with the constraints:

c_1: **if** $Category \leq 6$, **then** $TimePercentage \to Salary$

c_2: $Employee\# \to Category,\ TimePercentage,\ Salary$

Constraint c_1 requires that for every instance $\mathbf{r} = \{r\}$ of **R**, there is a functional dependency $TimePercentage \to Salary$ in the relation containing the set of tuples of r whose $Category$-value is not greater than 6. Constraint c_2 specifies that $Employee\#$ is a key of r. Figure 5.1 shows a consistent instance of **R**.

The relation scheme R is in Boyce-Codd Normal Form, since all the functional dependencies can be represented by means of keys. On the other hand, it presents anomalies typical of unnormalized schemes: it could be meaningful to represent the salary related to each time percentage for the categories 1–6; if no employee in these categories exists, this is impossible, unless we use null values for the primary key. The problem can be specialized to insertions, deletions, updates.

The anomalies are due to the existence of the FD $TimePercentage \to Salary$, which is "hidden" in the scheme: for each relation of the scheme, the FD does not hold in general in the whole relation, but only in a subset of it.

It is easy to find a scheme **S** that does not present the above anomalies, involving three relations,

r	Employee#	Category	TimePercentage	Salary
	001	1	40	3000
	002	1	40	3000
	003	5	50	3500
r	004	7	40	3700
	005	7	40	4000
	006	8	50	4500
	007	8	60	4700
	008	8	60	5000

Figure 5.1. An instance of the example scheme R.

$$R_1 \ (Employee\#, Category, TimePercentage, Salary)$$
$$R_2 \ (Employee\#, Category, TimePercentage)$$
$$R_3 \ (TimePercentage, Salary)$$

and with the following constraints, which are intuitively those "inherited" from the constraints of **R**:

d_1: $\quad Category > 6$, defined on r_1
d_2: $\quad Employee\# \rightarrow Category, TimePercentage, Salary$, defined on r_1
d_3: $\quad Category \leq 6$, defined on r_2
d_4: $\quad Employee\# \rightarrow Category, TimePercentage$, defined on r_2
d_5: $\quad TimePercentage \rightarrow Salary$, defined on r_2

The generic instance $\mathbf{s} = \{r_1, r_2, r_3\}$ of $\mathbf{S}$ is obtained from an instance $\mathbf{r} = \{r\}$ of $\mathbf{R}$ by means of the following transformation (attribute names are denoted by the respective initials):

$$r_1 \ = \ \sigma_{C>6}(r)$$
$$r_2 \ = \ \pi_{ECP}(\sigma_{C\leq6}(r))$$
$$r_3 \ = \ \pi_{PS}(\sigma_{C\leq6}(r))$$

The instance of **S** obtained from the instance of **R** in Figure 5.1 is shown in Figure 5.2. **S** is free of the anomalies presented by **R**. At the same time, it is indeed an adequate decomposition of **R**, according to the intuitive definition given above:

r_1	Employee#	Category	TimeP	Salary
	004	7	40	3700
	005	7	40	4000
	006	8	50	4500
	007	8	60	4700
	008	8	60	5000

s

r_2	Employee#	Category	TimeP
	001	1	40
	002	1	40
	003	5	50

r_3	TimeP	Salary
	40	3000
	50	3500

Figure 5.2. An instance of the decomposed scheme S

- Given an instance $\mathbf{r} = \{r\}$ of $\mathbf{R}$, $\mathbf{r}$ can always be reconstructed from the corresponding instance $\mathbf{s} = \{r_1, r_2, r_3\}$ by means of the following "inverse" transformation:

$$r = r_1 \cup (r_2 \bowtie r_3)$$

As a consequence, every query on $\mathbf{r}$ can be expressed on $\mathbf{s}$ by first performing the inverse transformation.

- Consistent instances of $\mathbf{R}$ correspond to consistent instances of $\mathbf{S}$, and inconsistent instances of $\mathbf{R}$ correspond to inconsistent instances of $\mathbf{S}$.

We said that $\mathbf{S}$ is an adequate representation of $\mathbf{R}$. It is not an equivalent representation, because there are instances of $\mathbf{S}$ that do not correspond to instances of $\mathbf{R}$: they are exactly the instances that guarantee the elimination of the insertion and deletion anomalies by allowing values for *TimePercentage* without a corresponding *Employee#*. If we want to enforce the property of equivalent decomposition, we have to impose the constraint that the projections of r_2 and r_3 on the attribute *TimePercentage* be equal. (This can be done by means of two inclusion dependencies).

Note that the transformation that generates the instances of $\mathbf{S}$ can be seen as the composition of two elementary transformations

r	Employee#	Category	TimePercentage	Salary
	001	1	40	3000
	002	1	40	3000
	003	5	50	3500
	004	7	40	3700
	005	7	40	4000
	006	8	50	4500
	007	8	60	4700
	008	8	60	5000

r_1	Employee#	Category	TimePercentage	Salary
	004	7	40	3700
	005	7	40	4000
	006	8	50	4500
	007	8	60	4700
	008	8	60	5000

$r_{2,3}$	Employee#	Category	TimePercentage	Salary
	001	1	40	3000
	002	1	40	3000
	003	5	50	3500

Figure 5.3. A horizontal decomposition

(see Figures 5.3 and 5.4), the first one performing a horizontal "cut,"
and the second one performing a vertical "cut." We will call *horizontal
decompositions* the transformations using the selection operator, and
vertical decompositions the transformations using the projection operator. Thus, in dealing in particular with decompositions, we may consider only vertical decompositions, horizontal plus vertical, or more
general ones. Since vertical decompositions are mostly investigated
in the literature, they will be the primary concern in the following
discussion.

$r_{2,3}$	Employee#	Category	TimeP	Salary
	001	1	40	3000
	002	1	40	3000
	003	5	50	3500

r_2	Employee#	Category	TimeP
	001	1	40
	002	1	40
	003	5	50

r_3	TimeP	Salary
	40	3000
	50	3500

Figure 5.4. A vertical decomposition

5.2   Adequacy of Vertical Decompositions

In this section we define and characterize the notion of adequate representation. The definition we are going to present formalizes the notion discussed in the previous section with respect to the one-to-one mapping between the consistent instances of R and a subset of the consistent instances of S. We start with a general, though not practical, definition, and then we adapt it to the specific framework of vertical decompositions. As we will see, the adaptation can be done in various ways.

Let R and S be two database schemes, with the respective sets of integrity constraints, C_R and C_S. Also, let $I(R)$ and $I(S)$ be the sets of all their instances (regardless of constraints), and $L(R)$ and $L(S)$ the sets of consistent instances (that is, the instances that satisfy the respective constraints—see Section 3.1).

A *transformation from R to S* is a function $h : I(R) \to I(S)$. Let $H(S)$ be the set of instances of S obtained by applying h to elements of $L(R)$. We say that S is an *adequate representation* of R if there is a transformation h from R to S such that h is a bijection from $L(R)$ onto $H(S) \cap L(S)$.

Then we say that the scheme S is an *equivalent representation* of R if S is an adequate representation of R and R is an adequate representation of S.

The definition of *adequate representation* is very general with respect to the mappings and the consistent sets of instances: nothing is said about the function h and its inverse, which are needed in order to make the definition effective, and nothing is said about the sets of constraints that determine the consistent instances. In order to have a more practical definition, we present its adaptation to the framework of vertical decompositions.

We consider a database scheme $\mathbf{R} = \{R(U)\}$ and a "decomposed scheme" $\mathbf{S} = \{R_1(U_1), \ldots, R_n(U_n)\}$. Then, instead of considering general transformations, we restrict our attention to the "natural" one:

- For every $\mathbf{r} = \{r\} \in I(\mathbf{R})$, the transformation h maps $\mathbf{r}$ to an instance $\mathbf{s} = \{r_1, \ldots, r_n\}$ of $\mathbf{S}$, where $r_i = \pi_{U_i}(r)$, for $1 \leq i \leq n$. In what follows this function will be indicated with $\pi_{\mathbf{S}}$. Similarly, $\bowtie_{\mathbf{S}}$ will be used for the function that maps each instance $\mathbf{s} = \{r_1, \ldots, r_n\} \in I(\mathbf{S})$ to an instance in $I(\mathbf{R})$ whose relation is the join of the relations in $\mathbf{s}$: $\bowtie_{\mathbf{S}}(\mathbf{s}) = \{r\}$, where $r = \bowtie_{i=1}^{n}(r_i)$.

In this framework, $H(\mathbf{S})$ is the set of the instances of $\mathbf{S}$ that can be obtained by means of projections from (not necessarily consistent) instances of $\mathbf{R}$:

$$H(\mathbf{S}) = \{\mathbf{s} \mid \exists \mathbf{r} \in I(\mathbf{R}) : \mathbf{s} = \pi_{\mathbf{S}}(\mathbf{r})\}$$

Various reasonable definitions of the adequacy of vertical decompositions can be given; in order to distinguish between them we will prefix the word *adequate* (or *adequacy*) with Greek letters. Also, we will omit the explicit reference to the fact that we consider only vertical decompositions.

The first definition derives immediately from the above notion of adequate representation: $\mathbf{S}$ is an α-*adequate decomposition* of $\mathbf{R}$ if $\pi_{\mathbf{S}}$ is a bijection from $L(\mathbf{R})$ onto $L(\mathbf{S}) \cap H(\mathbf{S})$. A simple example shows that in some cases this definition is not satisfactory.

> **Example 5.1**   Let $\mathbf{R} = \{R_0(ABC)\}$, with $C_{\mathbf{R}} = \{A \twoheadrightarrow B\}$, and $\mathbf{S} = \{R_1(AB), R_2(AC)\}$, with $C_{\mathbf{S}} = \{\}$. We claim that $\mathbf{S}$ is an α-adequate decomposition of $\mathbf{R}$. We show that $\pi_{\mathbf{S}}$ is a bijection by showing that it is surjective and injective.

1. The transformation $\pi_{\mathbf{S}}$ is injective. Let $\mathbf{r}_1, \mathbf{r}_2 \in L(\mathbf{R})$ (that is, $\mathbf{r}_1$ and $\mathbf{r}_2$ are consistent instances of $\mathbf{R}$), $\mathbf{s}_1 = \pi_{\mathbf{S}}(\mathbf{r}_1)$, and $\mathbf{s}_2 = \pi_{\mathbf{S}}(\mathbf{r}_2)$, and assume $\mathbf{s}_1 = \mathbf{s}_2$. The MVD $A \twoheadrightarrow B$ guarantees lossless decomposition into AB, AC for all the instances in $L(\mathbf{R})$. Thus, $\mathbf{r}_1 = \bowtie_{\mathbf{S}} (\pi_{\mathbf{S}}(\mathbf{r}_1))$, and $\mathbf{r}_2 = \bowtie_{\mathbf{S}} (\pi_{\mathbf{S}}(\mathbf{r}_2))$, and so $\mathbf{r}_1 = \mathbf{r}_2$.

2. The transformation $\pi_{\mathbf{S}}$ is surjective onto $H(\mathbf{S}) \cap L(\mathbf{S})$, which coincides with $H(\mathbf{S})$, since $C_{\mathbf{S}}$ is empty. Let $\mathbf{s} \in H(\mathbf{S})$. By definition of $H(\mathbf{S})$, there is $\mathbf{r} \in I(\mathbf{S})$ such that $\mathbf{s} = \pi_{\mathbf{S}}(\mathbf{r})$. In fact $\mathbf{r}$ need not belong to $L(\mathbf{S})$, but we have that $\mathbf{r}' = \bowtie_{\mathbf{S}} (\pi_{\mathbf{S}}(\mathbf{r}))$ belongs to $L(\mathbf{S})$ (since it has a lossless decomposition, by Lemma 1.2), and by Lemma 1.1, $\pi_{\mathbf{S}}(\mathbf{r}') = \pi_{\mathbf{S}}(\mathbf{r}) = \mathbf{s}$. Thus, $\mathbf{s}$ is in the image of $\pi_{\mathbf{S}}$.

Despite the fact that $\mathbf{S}$ is an α-adequate decomposition of $\mathbf{R}$, the relationship between the two schemes presents some undesirable aspects: any instance $\mathbf{r} \in I(\mathbf{R}) - L(\mathbf{R})$ (this set is clearly not empty) is mapped by $\pi_{\mathbf{S}}$ into an instance in $L(\mathbf{S})$, and this is not completely desirable.

By means of Example 5.1, we can make the point that α-adequacy does not express the requirement that the constraints $C_{\mathbf{S}}$ associated with $\mathbf{S}$ must "represent" the constraints $C_{\mathbf{R}}$ associated with $\mathbf{R}$: in fact, the scheme $\mathbf{S}$ in the example has an empty set of constraints.

This aspect is taken into account by the second definition: $\mathbf{S}$ is a *β-adequate decomposition* of $\mathbf{R}$ if $\mathbf{S}$ is an α-adequate decomposition of $\mathbf{R}$ and $\pi_{\mathbf{S}}$ maps instances in $I(\mathbf{R}) - L(\mathbf{R})$ to instances in $H(\mathbf{S}) - L(\mathbf{S})$. In plain words, β-adequacy requires $\pi_{\mathbf{S}}$ to map inconsistent instances to inconsistent instances.

> **Example 5.2**   Let $\mathbf{R}$ and $\mathbf{S}$ be as in Example 5.1. The instances in Figure 5.5 show that $\mathbf{S}$ is not a β-adequate representation of $\mathbf{R}$: $\mathbf{r}$ belongs to $I(\mathbf{R}) - L(\mathbf{R})$ because $\mathbf{r}$ violates the MVD, whereas $\pi_{\mathbf{S}}(\mathbf{r}) \in L(\mathbf{S})$, because it trivially satisfies the empty set of constraints.

A general characterization of β-adequacy can be given by means of two other general notions, namely *lossless decomposition* and *constraint representation*.

The notion of lossless decomposition of database schemes is based on the notion of lossless decomposition of relations, introduced in Section 1.4 and studied in Sections 4.2 and 4.4: $\mathbf{S}$ is a *lossless decomposition* of $\mathbf{R}$ if, for every consistent instance $\mathbf{r} = \{r\} \in L(\mathbf{R})$, the

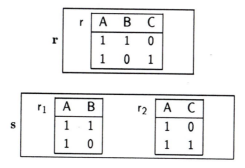

Figure 5.5. A decomposition for Example 5.2

relation $r(U)$ has a lossless decomposition with respect to $U_1, \ldots, U_n$; that is, $\mathbf{r} = \Join_{\mathbf{S}} (\pi_{\mathbf{S}}(\mathbf{r}))$.

The set of constraints $C_{\mathbf{S}}$ *represents the constraints* $C_{\mathbf{R}}$ of $\mathbf{R}$ if it is the case that for every $\mathbf{r} \in I(\mathbf{R})$, $\pi_{\mathbf{S}}(\mathbf{r}) \in L(\mathbf{S})$ if and only if $\mathbf{r} \in L(\mathbf{R})$.

THEOREM 5.1 $\mathbf{S}$ is a β-adequate vertical decomposition of $\mathbf{R}$ if and only if $C_{\mathbf{S}}$ represents $C_{\mathbf{R}}$ and $\mathbf{S}$ is a lossless decomposition of $\mathbf{R}$.

PROOF

If. We assume lossless decomposition and constraint representation and prove that $\mathbf{S}$ is a β-adequate decomposition of $\mathbf{R}$. We follow the definition.

1. The function $\pi_{\mathbf{S}}$ is a bijection from $L(\mathbf{R})$ to $L(\mathbf{S}) \cap H(\mathbf{S})$. In order to prove this claim, it suffices to prove three subclaims:

   a. For every $\mathbf{r} \in L(\mathbf{R})$, $\pi_{\mathbf{S}}(\mathbf{r})$ belongs to $L(\mathbf{S}) \cap H(\mathbf{S})$. By the *if* part of constraint representation, since $\mathbf{r} \in L(\mathbf{R})$, we have $\pi_{\mathbf{S}}(\mathbf{r}) \in L(\mathbf{S})$. Then $\pi_{\mathbf{S}}(\mathbf{r}) \in H(\mathbf{S})$ by definition of $H(\mathbf{S})$.

   b. The function $\pi_{\mathbf{S}}$ is injective. Let $\mathbf{r}, \mathbf{r}' \in L(\mathbf{R})$, with $\pi_{\mathbf{S}}(\mathbf{r}) = \pi_{\mathbf{S}}(\mathbf{r}')$. Then, by lossless decomposition, $\mathbf{r} = \Join_{\mathbf{S}} (\pi_{\mathbf{S}}(\mathbf{r}))$, and $\mathbf{r}' = \Join_{\mathbf{S}} (\pi_{\mathbf{S}}(\mathbf{r}'))$; therefore, $\mathbf{r} = \mathbf{r}'$.

   c. The function $\pi_{\mathbf{S}}$ is surjective. We show that if $\mathbf{s} \in L(\mathbf{S}) \cap H(\mathbf{S})$, then there is $\mathbf{r} \in L(\mathbf{R})$ such that $\pi_{\mathbf{S}}(\mathbf{r}) = \mathbf{s}$. If $\mathbf{s} \in L(\mathbf{S}) \cap H(\mathbf{S})$, then $\mathbf{s} \in H(\mathbf{S})$, and so there is $\mathbf{r} \in I(\mathbf{R})$ such that $\pi_\mathbf{S}(\mathbf{r}) = \mathbf{s}$. Therefore, $\mathbf{s}$ also belongs to $L(\mathbf{S})$, and so $\pi_\mathbf{S}(\mathbf{r}) = \mathbf{s} \in L(\mathbf{S})$. Then, by the *only if* part of constraint representation, $\mathbf{r} \in L(\mathbf{R})$.

2. The function $\pi_\mathbf{S}$ is a mapping from $I(\mathbf{R}) - L(\mathbf{R})$ to $H(\mathbf{S}) - L(\mathbf{S})$. If $\mathbf{r} \in I(\mathbf{R})$, then, by definition of $H(\mathbf{S})$, $\pi_\mathbf{S}(\mathbf{r}) \in H(\mathbf{S})$. Also, since $\mathbf{r} \notin L(\mathbf{R})$, by the *only if* part of constraint representation, we have $\pi_\mathbf{S}(\mathbf{r}) \notin L(\mathbf{S})$; therefore, $\pi_\mathbf{S}(\mathbf{r}) \in H(\mathbf{S}) - L(\mathbf{S})$.

Only if. Assume that $\mathbf{S}$ is a β-adequate decomposition of $\mathbf{R}$. We prove the two claims separately.

- $C_\mathbf{S}$ represents $C_\mathbf{R}$. We prove the two directions in turn:

   - If $\pi_\mathbf{S}(\mathbf{r}) \in L(\mathbf{S})$, then $\mathbf{r} \in L(\mathbf{R})$. Assume, by way of contradiction, that $\pi_\mathbf{S}(\mathbf{r}) \in L(\mathbf{S})$, and $\mathbf{r} \notin L(\mathbf{R})$. Then $\mathbf{r} \in I(\mathbf{R}) - L(\mathbf{R})$, and so, by the second condition in the definition of β-adequacy, $\pi_\mathbf{S}(\mathbf{r}) \in H(\mathbf{S}) - L(\mathbf{S})$.

   - If $\mathbf{r} \in L(\mathbf{R})$, then $\pi_\mathbf{S}(\mathbf{r}) \in L(\mathbf{S})$. This is part of the definition of α-adequacy.

- $\mathbf{S}$ is a lossless decomposition of $\mathbf{R}$. Following the definition, we prove that for every $\mathbf{r} \in L(\mathbf{R})$, it is the case that $\bowtie_\mathbf{S} (\pi_\mathbf{S}(\mathbf{r})) = \mathbf{r}$. If $\mathbf{r}' = \bowtie_\mathbf{S} (\pi_\mathbf{S}(\mathbf{r}))$, then, by Lemma 1.2, we have $\pi_\mathbf{S}(\mathbf{r}') = \pi_\mathbf{S}(\mathbf{r})$. Since $\mathbf{r} \in L(\mathbf{R})$, we have $\pi_\mathbf{S}(\mathbf{r}) \in L(\mathbf{S})$ (by α-adequacy), and so $\pi_\mathbf{S}(\mathbf{r}') \in L(\mathbf{S})$. Then, since we have already proved that $C_\mathbf{S}$ represents $C_\mathbf{R}$, $\mathbf{r}' \in L(\mathbf{R})$. Finally, since $\pi_\mathbf{S}$ is an injective function from $L(\mathbf{R})$, and $\mathbf{r}, \mathbf{r}' \in L(\mathbf{R})$, and $\pi_\mathbf{S}(\mathbf{r}) = \pi_\mathbf{S}(\mathbf{r}')$, we have $\mathbf{r} = \mathbf{r}'$. Thus, $\mathbf{r} = \bowtie_\mathbf{S} (\pi_\mathbf{S}(\mathbf{r}))$.   □

Now we restrict our attention to the framework we are mainly interested in. We assume that all the constraints are FDs, and show interesting characterizations for both lossless decomposition and constraint representation. Also, we assume that $C_\mathbf{S}$ is composed of a set of sets of FDs, one for each relation scheme in $\mathbf{S}$. F_i is the set of FDs associated with $R_i(U_i)$. Clearly, if $X \to Y \in F_i$, then $XY \subseteq U_i$; that is, the FDs are *embedded* in the relation schemes. The set $L(\mathbf{S})$ contains the instances $\mathbf{s} = \{r_1, \ldots, r_n\}$ such that each r_i satisfies the corresponding FDs F_i. That is, we refer to *local satisfaction* of FDs.

We first characterize constraint representation.

LEMMA 5.1 Let $YZ \subseteq X \subseteq U$, and let r be a relation over a scheme $R(U)$. Then $\pi_X(r)$ satisfies $Y \to Z$ if and only if r satisfies $Y \to Z$.

PROOF   Left as Exercise 5.2.   □

THEOREM 5.2 Let $C_{\mathbf{R}} = F$ and $C_{\mathbf{S}} = \cup_{i=1}^n F_i$. Then $C_{\mathbf{R}}$ represents $C_{\mathbf{S}}$ if and only if $F^+ = (\cup_{i=1}^n F_i)^+$.

PROOF
If.   Assume $F^+ = (\cup_{i=1}^n F_i)^+$. We prove that $\pi_{\mathbf{S}}(\mathbf{r}) \in L(\mathbf{S})$ if and only if $\mathbf{r} \in L(\mathbf{R})$. We consider the two directions in turn.

- If $\mathbf{r} = \{r\} \in L(\mathbf{R})$, then $\pi_{\mathbf{S}}(\mathbf{r}) \in L(\mathbf{S})$. Assume by way of contradiction that $\mathbf{r} \in L(\mathbf{R})$, and $\pi_{\mathbf{S}}(\mathbf{r}) \notin L(\mathbf{S})$. Then there is a relation scheme R_i such that $\pi_{U_i}(r)$ violates some FD $Y \to Z \in F_i$. By Lemma 5.1, r violates $Y \to Z$; thus, since $F^+ = (\cup_{i=1}^n F_i)^+$, r does not satisfy F, and this is a contradiction of the assumption $\mathbf{r} \in L(\mathbf{R})$.

- If $\pi_{\mathbf{S}}(\mathbf{r}) \in L(\mathbf{S})$, then $\mathbf{r} \in L(\mathbf{R})$. Assume by way of contradiction that $\pi_{\mathbf{S}}(\mathbf{r}) \in L(\mathbf{S})$, and $\mathbf{r} \notin L(\mathbf{R})$. Then there is an FD $Y \to Z \in F$ that r does not satisfy. Since $F^+ = (\cup_{i=1}^n F_i)^+$, there is an FD $V \to W \in F_i$ for some relation scheme R_i that r does not satisfy. Then, by Lemma 5.1, $\pi_{U_i}(r)$ violates $V \to W$, and so $\pi_{\mathbf{S}}(\mathbf{r}) \notin L(\mathbf{S})$—a contradiction.

Only if.   We assume that $C_{\mathbf{S}}$ represents $C_{\mathbf{R}}$, and show that $F^+ = (\cup_{i=1}^n F_i)^+$. We prove that $F^+ \supseteq (\cup_{i=1}^n F_i)^+$ and omit the proof of the converse, which is very similar. Assume, by way of contradiction, that there are FDs in $(\cup_{i=1}^n F_i)^+ - F^+$. Therefore, there is a relation r that satisfies F and does not satisfy at least an FD in one of the components, say F_i. Then if $\mathbf{r} = \{r\}$, we have $\mathbf{r} \in L(\mathbf{R})$, and $\pi_{\mathbf{S}}(\mathbf{r}) \notin L(\mathbf{S})$ (because $\pi_{U_i}(r)$ violates F_i)—a contradiction.   □

With respect to lossless decomposition, we already know from the results in Section 4.2 an effective characterization of the property of lossless decomposition with respect to FDs. However, in the context we are considering, a more expressive characterization is possible.

LEMMA 5.2   If $C_{\mathbf{R}}$ is a set of FDs F, and $C_{\mathbf{S}}$ is a set of embedded FDs $F_1 \cup \ldots \cup F_n$ such that $F^+ = (\cup_{i=1}^n F_i)^+$, then $\mathbf{S}$ is a lossless decomposition of $\mathbf{R}$ if and only if there is a relation scheme $R_i(U_i)$ in $\mathbf{S}$ such that $U_i \to U \in F^+$.

PROOF   In both directions we consider the tableau with n rows that can be used, by Theorem 4.4, to verify whether the FDs in F guarantee lossless decomposition with respect to $U_1, \ldots, U_n$, and so verify that $\mathbf{S}$ is a lossless decomposition of $\mathbf{R}$.

If.   Assume that U_i is a key for U with respect to F. Since $(\cup_{i=1}^n F_i)$ is equivalent to F, the computation of the closure of U_i with respect to $(\cup_{i=1}^n F_i)$ produces U. Assuming FDs with singleton rhs's, we have that at each significant step, one attribute is added to the running closure. Now, by induction on the number of steps, it can be shown that if $V \to A \in F_i$ is used to add A, then the same FD can be used to promote the variable for A in the row originating from $R_i(U_i)$. We omit the details.

Only if.   We can follow a similar argument by showing that if the variable for an attribute A is promoted in the row originating from R_i, then $A \in U_i^+$. $\square$

We say that the relation scheme R_i in the claim of Lemma 5.2 *embeds a database key*. By Lemmas 5.1 and 5.2, we have the following interesting characterization of β-adequacy for the current context.

THEOREM 5.3   In the framework of embedded FDs, $\mathbf{S}$ is a β-adequate decomposition of $\mathbf{R}$ if and only if $F^+ = (\cup_{i=1}^n F_i)^+$ and there is a relation scheme $R_i(U_i)$ that embeds a database key. $\square$

Now we can show another interesting result: the fact that, in the framework of FDs we are considering, the distinction between the two notions of adequacy is indeed immaterial. (By means of Examples 5.1 and 5.2, we already know that they are not equivalent in general.)

THEOREM 5.4   If $C_{\mathbf{R}}$ is a set of FDs and $C_{\mathbf{S}}$ is a set of embedded FDs, then $\mathbf{S}$ is an α-adequate decomposition of $\mathbf{R}$ if and only if $\mathbf{S}$ is a β-adequate decomposition of $\mathbf{R}$.

PROOF   It suffices to show that in this framework, α-adequacy implies β-adequacy. We proceed by showing that α-adequacy implies constraint representation and lossless decomposition.

- Let us prove that α-adequacy implies constraint representation. Assume, by way of contradiction, that $\mathbf{S}$ is an α-adequate decomposition of $\mathbf{R}$ and that $C_{\mathbf{S}}$ does not represent $C_{\mathbf{R}}$. By Theorem 5.2, there are two possibilities, as follows.

  - There exists $f = Y \rightarrow A \in F^+ - (\cup_{i=1}^{n} F_i)^+$. Let r be a relation that satisfies $(\cup_{i=1}^{n} F_i)^+$ and does not satisfy f. Consider the relation r' containing only the two tuples of r that cause the violation. Clearly, r' satisfies $(\cup_{i=1}^{n} F_i)^+$ and does not satisfy f, and so $\mathbf{r}' = \{r'\} \notin L(\mathbf{R})$, and $\pi_{\mathbf{S}}(\mathbf{r}') \in L(\mathbf{S})$, since it is relationwise contained in $\pi_{\mathbf{S}}(\mathbf{r})$. Then, since $\pi_{\mathbf{S}}$ is a surjective mapping from $L(\mathbf{R})$ onto $L(\mathbf{S}) \cap H(\mathbf{S})$, there is an instance $\mathbf{r}'' = \{r''\} \in L(\mathbf{R})$ such that $\pi_{\mathbf{S}}(\mathbf{r}'') = \pi_{\mathbf{S}}(\mathbf{r}')$. Then, by construction, r'' has only one value for each of the attributes in Y and two values for A, and so it cannot satisfy $Y \rightarrow A$, which is a contradiction.

  - There exists $f \in (\cup_{i=1}^{n} F_i)^+ - F^+$. Thus, there exists $f' \in F_i$ for some relation scheme R_i such that $f' \notin F^+$. Let r be a relation that satisfies F and does not satisfy f'. Then, by Lemma 5.1, $\pi_{U_i}(r)$ does not satisfy f', and therefore $\mathbf{r} = \{r\} \in L(\mathbf{R})$, and $\pi_{\mathbf{S}}(\mathbf{r}) \notin L(\mathbf{S})$, which contradicts the assumption of α-adequacy.

- Let us prove that α-adequacy implies lossless decomposition. Let $\mathbf{r} \in L(\mathbf{R})$. By the first part of the proof, we know that constraint representation follows from α-adequacy, and so we have that $\pi_{\mathbf{S}}(\mathbf{r}) \in L(\mathbf{S})$, since $\mathbf{r} \in L(\mathbf{R})$, and also $\mathbf{r}' = \bowtie_{\mathbf{S}} (\pi_{\mathbf{S}}(\mathbf{r})) \in L(\mathbf{R})$, since $\pi_{\mathbf{S}}(\mathbf{r}') = \pi_{\mathbf{S}}(\mathbf{r}) \in L(\mathbf{S})$. Then, since both $\mathbf{r}$ and $\mathbf{r}'$ belong to $L(\mathbf{R})$, their images under $\pi_{\mathbf{S}}$ are identical, and since $\pi_{\mathbf{S}}$ is an injective mapping from $L(\mathbf{R})$, we have $\mathbf{r} = \mathbf{r}'$; that is $\mathbf{r} = \bowtie_{\mathbf{S}} (\pi_{\mathbf{S}}(\mathbf{r}))$. $\square$

The next example shows that, despite the positive results seen so far, the notion of β-adequacy is not completely satisfactory.

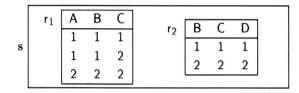

Figure 5.6. An instance for Example 5.3

Example 5.3   Let us consider the schemes $\mathbf{R} = \{R_0(ABCD)\}$,
with $C_{\mathbf{R}} = \{B \rightarrow CD\}$, and $\mathbf{S} = \{R_1(ABC), R_2(BCD)\}$, with
$C_{\mathbf{S}} = \{B \rightarrow CD(\text{on } R_2)\}$. $\mathbf{S}$ is a β-adequate representation of
$\mathbf{R}$, since lossless decomposition is satisfied (by Theorem 4.3, since
$BC \rightarrow BCD \in F^+$), and $F^+ = (F_1 \cup F_2)^+$ (because $F = F_1 \cup F_2$).
However, there are undesirable aspects in the relationship between
$\mathbf{R}$ and $\mathbf{S}$: consistent instances of $\mathbf{S}$ may involve relations r_1 that
violate $B \rightarrow C$ (see Figure 5.6). The violation cannot emerge in
the result of the reverse mapping $\bowtie_{\mathbf{S}}$ because r_2 satisfies $B \rightarrow C$,
and so the guilty tuples are filtered out.

On the basis of Example 5.3, we can say that β-adequacy does
not model satisfactorily the informal requirement that the decomposed scheme have the same capacity as the original scheme to reject
inconsistent instances. With reference to the specific framework of
FDs, the problem shown in Example 5.3 does not arise with the fol-
lowing notion of adequacy:[1] $\mathbf{S}$ is a γ-*adequate decomposition* of $\mathbf{R}$ if $\mathbf{S}$
is an α-adequate decomposition of $\mathbf{R}$ and, for every $i, j \in \{1, \ldots, n\}$,
if $X \rightarrow A \in F_i$ and $XA \subseteq U_j$, then $X \rightarrow A \in F_j$,

It follows from the definition that γ-adequacy implies β-adequacy
and that the converse does not hold in general, as the schemes in
Example 5.3 confirm. The converse holds if for every $X \rightarrow A \in F^+$,
there is at most one relation scheme $R_i(U_i)$ such that $XA \subseteq U_i$.

However, γ-adequacy does not avoid another problem, similar to
the one seen in Example 5.3.

---

[1]This definition explicitly refers to FDs; it is not known how a more general
version of it can be formulated. However, its importance will become apparent in
the following, because the stronger notion of δ-adequacy, though more interesting
in principle, is sometimes not practical.

r_1	A	B	C
	1	1	1
	2	2	2

r_2	B	C	D
	1	2	1
	2	1	1

s

Figure 5.7. An instance for Example 5.4

Example 5.4   Let **R** be as in Example 5.3 and $S = \{R_1(ABC),$ $R_2(BCD)\}$, with $C_S = \{B \to C(\text{on } R_1), B \to CD(\text{on } R_2)\}$. **S** is now a γ-adequate representation of **R**, since the FD $B \to C$ that is embedded in both relation schemes in **S** belongs to both F_1 and F_2. However, **S** would have consistent instances such as the one in Figure 5.7, where the D-values associated with the C-values in the two relations are not the same—a clearly undesirable situation.

Example 5.4 intuitively suggests that if an FD is embedded in more than one relation scheme, it has to be enforced in all of them, and with the same values. This is clearly related to the notion of *weak instance*, presented in Section 4.3. The final notion of adequacy that we present takes into account the fact that the problems in Examples 5.3 and 5.4 arise because the definition of β-adequacy refers only to the instances of **S** that can be obtained by means of mapping π_S from instances of **R**. That is, it refers to the elements of $H(S)$ and does not refer in any way to any element of $I(S) - H(S)$; specifically, it does not put any restriction on them. At the same time, however, it is apparent that the undesirable behavior of scheme **S** in Example 5.4 derives from the fact that no mutual restriction is imposed on the two relations. An interrelational constraint could probably help, but it could introduce other problems. A stronger definition of adequacy can be obtained by including reference to the instances in $I(S) - H(S)$, and putting on them the interrelational constraint of the existence of a weak instance. It is useful to introduce another subset of $I(S)$:

$$W(S) = \{\{r_1, \ldots, r_n\} \mid \exists \mathbf{r} = \{r\} \in L(\mathbf{R}) : r_i \subseteq \pi_{U_i}(r), \text{for } i = 1, \ldots, n\}$$

which is the set of the the instances of **S** that have a weak instance with respect to the constraints of **R**; clearly, $H(S) \subseteq W(S)$.

We are now ready for the final definition: $\mathbf{S}$ is a δ-*adequate decomposition* of $\mathbf{R}$ if $\mathbf{S}$ is a β-adequate decomposition of $\mathbf{R}$ and $W(\mathbf{S}) = L(\mathbf{S})$.

Again, δ-adequacy implies β-adequacy, and in the special case of FDs, it also implies γ-adequacy. The counterexample for the converse is the pair of database schemes in Example 5.4.

If the constraints are FDs, as above, δ-adequacy can be characterized by means of the notion of independence. We recall that a scheme $\mathbf{S} = \{R_1(U_1), \ldots, R_n(U_n)\}$, with a set of embedded FDs $F_1 \cup \ldots \cup F_n$, where F_i is defined on R_i, is independent if every instance $\mathbf{r} \in \mathbf{R}$ has a weak instance w with respect to $F_1 \cup \ldots \cup F_n$.

THEOREM 5.5 If $C_\mathbf{R}$ is a set of FDs and $C_\mathbf{S}$ is a set of embedded FDs, then $\mathbf{S}$ is a δ-adequate decomposition of $\mathbf{R}$ if and only if (1) $C_\mathbf{S}$ represents $C_\mathbf{R}$, (2) $\mathbf{S}$ is independent, and (3) $\mathbf{S}$ is a lossless decomposition of $\mathbf{R}$.

PROOF

If. Constraint representation and lossless decomposition imply β-adequacy. Therefore, it suffices to show that $L(\mathbf{S}) = W(\mathbf{S})$.

- $L(\mathbf{S}) \subseteq W(\mathbf{S})$. Let $\mathbf{s} \in L(\mathbf{S})$. By independence, $\mathbf{s}$ has a weak instance w with respect to $F_1 \cup \ldots \cup F_n$. By constraint representation, $(F_1 \cup \ldots \cup F_n)^+ = F^+$. Thus, w satisfies F, and so $\mathbf{r} = \{w\}$ is the instance in $\mathbf{R}$ whose existence confirms that $\mathbf{s} \in W(\mathbf{S})$.

- $W(\mathbf{S}) \subseteq L(\mathbf{S})$. Let $\mathbf{s} = \{r_1, \ldots, r_n\} \in W(\mathbf{S})$. There is a relation r that satisfies F such that, for every $i \in \{1, \ldots, n\}$, $\pi_{U_i}(r) \supseteq r_i$. By constraint representation, $(F_1 \cup \ldots \cup F_n)^+ = F^+$, and so r satisfies F_i. Thus, by Lemma 5.1, $\pi_{U_i}(r)$ and r_i also satisfy F_i, and therefore $\mathbf{s} \in L(\mathbf{S})$.

Only if. It suffices to show that δ-adequacy implies independence. Consider an instance $\mathbf{s} = \{r_1, \ldots, r_n\} \in L(\mathbf{S})$. By δ-adequacy, $\mathbf{s} \in W(\mathbf{S})$, and therefore there is an instance $\mathbf{r} = \{r\} \in L(\mathbf{R})$ such that $\pi_{U_i}(r) \supseteq r_i$. This means that r satisfies F, and by constraint representation (which we already know is implied by β-adequacy, which is in turn implied by δ-adequacy), r also satisfies $F_1 \cup \ldots F_n$. Therefore it is a weak instance for $\mathbf{s}$. □

5.3 Boyce-Codd Normal Form and Third Normal Form

Many normal forms have been defined in the literature with reference to various contexts, which may depend on the constraints and on the goals of normalization. In this section we consider the basic normal forms that arise in the decomposition process of schemes with FDs. In Section 5.5 we will present other normal forms.

In Section 1.6 we introduced the notion of Boyce-Codd normal form (BCNF) in a rather informal way. With the technical notions introduced in Chapter 3, we can reformulate the definition by saying that a relation scheme $R(U)$ with an associated set of FDs F (in order to simplify some of the arguments, we assume that all FDs in F have a singleton rhs) is in BCNF if for every nontrivial FD $X \rightarrow A \in F$, the set of attributes X is a superkey for R(U) (that is, $X \rightarrow U \in F^+$). Since the constraints associated with the relation scheme play a crucial role in the definition of BCNF (as well as in the definition of the other normal forms) it is better to make explicit reference to them; therefore, we will often write $[R, D]$, to indicate the relation scheme R with the associated constraints D. Also, most normal forms are defined on individual relation schemes; we will say that a database scheme is in a given normal form if all its relation schemes enjoy the normal form.

We show a few basic properties of BCNF. The first interesting fact is that it is very easy to check whether a relation scheme $[R(U), F]$ is in BCNF: it suffices to compute, for each FD $X \rightarrow A \in F$, the closure of the lhs X with respect to F by means of Algorithm 3.1. The scheme is in BCNF if and only if the closure equals U for every FD.

Another property is that if the given set of FDs is replaced by an equivalent one (that is, by one of its covers), then the new scheme is in BCNF if and only if the original one is in BCNF; therefore, we say that BCNF is *cover insensitive*. This result is a direct consequence of the following lemma.

LEMMA 5.3 The scheme $[R(U), F]$ is in BCNF if and only if for every nontrivial FD $X \rightarrow A \in F^+$, it is the case that X is a superkey.

PROOF   The *if* part is easy. With respect to the *only if* part, we show that if $X \rightarrow A \in F^+$ and $A \notin X$, then $X \rightarrow U \in F^+$. If $X \rightarrow A \in F^+$ and $A \notin X$, then $A \in X^+ - X$. Therefore if we apply the closure algorithm (Algorithm 3.1) to X and F, there is a nontrivial FD $Y \rightarrow A \in F$ that causes the inclusion of A in X^+. Specifically, at some point during the execution, $Y \subseteq$ XWORK, and $A \notin$ XWORK; therefore, we have that $Y \subseteq X^+$, and so $X \rightarrow Y \in F^+$. Then, since R is in BCNF and $Y \rightarrow A$ is not trivial and belongs to F, we have that Y is a superkey; that is, $Y \rightarrow U \in F^+$. Therefore, by transitivity, from $X \rightarrow Y \in F^+$ and $Y \rightarrow U \in F^+$ we have that $X \rightarrow U \in F^+$. □

THEOREM 5.6   Let G and F be equivalent sets of FDs over a set of attributes U. Then $[R(U), F]$ is in BCNF if and only if $[R(U), G]$ is in BCNF.   □

Lemma 5.3 justifies an extension of the definition of BCNF: Given a set of constraints D (which may include other constraints than FDs), a relation scheme $[R, D]$ is in BCNF if for every nontrivial FD $X \rightarrow A \in D^+$, it is the case that $X \rightarrow U \in D^+$. This new definition will turn out to be useful in the comparison of the various normal forms in different contexts.

We argued in Section 1.6 that BCNF is a natural property of relation schemes; therefore, a reasonable goal of decomposition would be, given a database scheme **R**, the achievement of a scheme **S** that (1) is a δ-adequate decomposition of **R** and (2) is in BCNF. Unfortunately, this is not possible in general, as can be confirmed by a simple counterexample. Consider a database scheme **R** with a single relation scheme

$$[R(Student\#, Professor, Course),\ F]$$

with

$$F = \{SC \rightarrow P, P \rightarrow C\}$$

The violation of BCNF is caused by the FD $P \rightarrow C$, whose lhs *Professor* is not a superkey. Consider a scheme **S** that is a δ-adequate (and so γ-adequate) decomposition of **R**: since γ-adequacy implies constraint representation, and every cover of F includes the FD $SC \rightarrow P$, which involves all the attributes, we have that **S** must include a relation scheme $[R_i(SCP), F_i]$. Then, since γ-adequacy requires that each FD in F embedded in R_i must also be in F_i, we have that $P \rightarrow C \in F_i$, and so $[R_i, F_i]$ is not in BCNF. As a matter of fact, a scheme **S** with the relation schemes

$$[R_1 \; (Student\#, Professor, Course), \; \{SC \rightarrow P\}]$$
$$[R_2 \; (Professor, Course), \; \{P \rightarrow C\}]$$

is a β-adequate decomposition of **R** and contains only BCNF relations. However, this just confirms the fact that β-adequacy is unsatisfactory: **S** contains a relation scheme that coincides with the one in **R**, plus another one. The fact that R_1 is in BCNF is only apparent, as any "correct" r_1 will also satisfy $P \rightarrow C$, with the same anomalies as in **R**. Moreover, it would be more difficult to check the instances of **S** for correctness, as interrelational operations are required.

These results are not surprising; the existence of adequate decompositions in BCNF depends on the structure of the functional dependencies defined on the scheme (i.e. from semantic properties of the application we want to model). The counterexample simply states that applications exist that cannot inherently be modeled by means of BCNF schemes.

As a matter of fact, many other normal forms have been defined in the literature, with different goals and with reference to different frameworks. BCNF is probably the "ideal" normal form in the context of vertical decompositions of database schemes whose constraints are FDs; however, we have just seen that in some cases it is too strict as a design goal. A weaker normal form for the same framework is based on the following notion: given a relation scheme $[R(U), F]$, an attribute $A \in U$ is *prime* if it belongs to at least one of the keys of R. Then $[R(U), F]$ is in *third normal form (3NF)* if for every nontrivial FD $X \rightarrow A \in F$ such that A is nonprime, it is the case that X is a superkey. It follows from the respective definitions that 3NF is indeed a strictly weaker property than BCNF; we state it as a lemma, for future reference.

LEMMA 5.4   If a relation scheme is in BCNF, then it is also in 3NF. $\square$

We leave as exercises the proofs of the analogues of Lemma 5.3 and Theorem 5.6.

LEMMA 5.5 The scheme $[R(U), F]$ is in 3NF if and only if for every nontrivial FD $X \to A \in F^+$ such that A is not prime, it is the case that X is a superkey. □

THEOREM 5.7 Let G and F be equivalent sets of FDs over a set of attributes U. Then the scheme $[R(U), F]$ is in 3NF if and only if the scheme $[R(U), G]$ is in 3NF. □

The relation scheme about professors, students, and courses shown earlier in this section proves that the converse of Lemma 5.4 does not hold: we have already seen that it is not in BCNF. At the same time, it is trivially in 3NF, because all its attributes are prime (both the pair *Professor, Student* and the pair *Course, Student* are keys). In fact, the differences between BCNF and 3NF are related to the multiplicity of keys; they disappear if there is only a key.

THEOREM 5.8 Let the relation scheme $[R, F]$ have only one key; then $[R, F]$ is in BCNF if and only if it is in 3NF.

PROOF It suffices to show the *if* part, as the *only if* part follows from Lemma 5.4. Therefore, assume that R is in 3NF and K is its only key. Consider the generic FD $X \to A \in F$; in order to complete the proof we show that X is a superkey or the FD is trivial (that is, $A \in X$). Now, it is convenient to distinguish whether A is prime or nonprime. If A is nonprime, then the thesis follows by definition of 3NF. If A is prime, then $(K - A) \cup X$ is also a superkey (since $K^+ \subseteq ((K - A) \cup X)^+$). Then, by definition of superkey, there is a key $K' \subseteq (K - A) \cup X$. Also, since we assumed that R has a single key, it must be the case that $K = K'$, and therefore, since $A \in K$, we have $A \in K'$. Thus, since $A \notin (K - A)$, we have that $A \in X$, and so $X \to A$ is a trivial FD. □

There is a negative result about 3NF: it is NP-complete to test whether a scheme is in 3NF. Its proof is omitted and can be found in the literature (Jou and Fischer [130]). In the next section we will see that this property does not jeopardize the usefulness of 3NF.

Finally, we show the equivalence of 3NF to another condition, which is in fact its original definition. It refers to the following notion: Given a relation scheme $R(U)$ with an associated set of FDs F, an attribute A is *transitively dependent* on a set of attributes W if there is a set of attributes Z such that $W \to Z, Z \to A \in F^+, Z \to W \notin F^+$, and $A \notin W$. By definition of a key, it follows that A is transitively dependent on a key K if there is a set Z such that Z is not a superkey and does not contain A, and the FD $Z \to A$ is in F^+.

LEMMA 5.6 $[R, F]$ is in 3NF if no nonprime attribute $A \in U$ is transitively dependent on any key K of R.

PROOF

If. We proceed by counterpositive. If R is not in 3NF, then there is a nontrivial FD $X \to A \in F$ such that X is not a superkey and A is nonprime. Now, consider a key K of R: by the observation above about transitive dependencies on keys, we have that A is transitively dependent on K, because X is not a superkey and $X \to A$ is nontrivial.

Only if. Again we proceed by counterpositive. Assume that an attribute A is transitively dependent on a key K; by the observation above, there is a set of attributes Z that does not contain A, is not a superkey, and is such that $Z \to A \in F^+$. Now consider the computation of the closure Z^+ of Z (by using Algorithm 3.1). Since $A \notin Z$ and $A \in Z^+$, there is a nontrivial FD $X \to A \in F$ with $X \subseteq Z^+$ that causes the inclusion of A in Z. Also, X is not a superkey (otherwise Z would also be a superkey, since $X \subseteq Z^+$), and so there is a nontrivial FD $X \to A$ such that A is nonprime and X is not a superkey. $\square$

5.4 Algorithms for Normalization

Two main techniques exist for the normalization of schemes through decomposition, *analysis* and *synthesis*.[2] Both of them assume as input to the design a unique relation scheme, and the set of dependencies

---

[2]In the literature, analysis is often called *decomposition* [97]. We decided to adopt the term *analysis* because it better contrasts with *synthesis* and because we use the term *decomposition* in a more general sense.

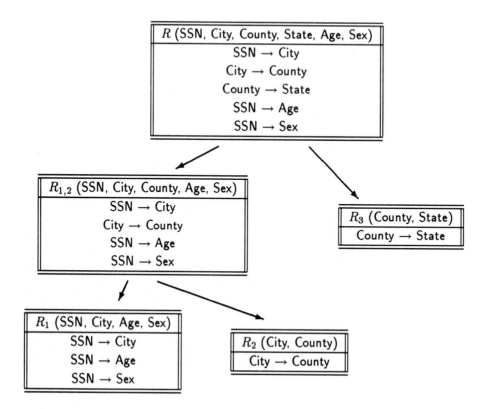

Figure 5.8. Decomposition by analysis

defined on it. The two techniques differ in the strategy they follow to obtain the normalized scheme. They are illustrated in Figures 5.8 and 5.9, with respect to the same example.

The analysis algorithms generate the normalized scheme by removing the cause for the lack of normalization. If a relation scheme does not satisfy the desired normal form because of a certain dependency, then it is decomposed into two or more relation schemes on the basis of that dependency. Each of the decomposed relation schemes inherits the relevant constraints. The process is iterated until all relations are normalized. Thus, at each step the overall scheme is changed into a new scheme with more relations.

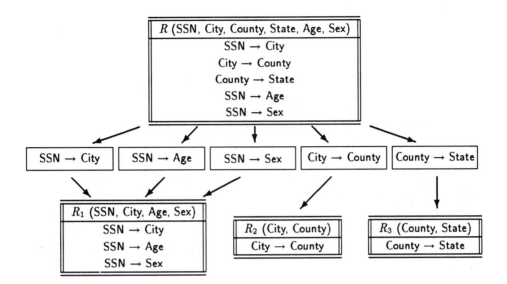

Figure 5.9. Decomposition by synthesis

There are two crucial points in any analysis algorithm. The first one is the test for satisfaction of the target normal form. We have seen that this may be expensive, for example in the highly significant case of 3NF. The second point is that most normal forms, including all those we have seen so far, refer to the individual relation schemes and to the constraints defined on each of them. Therefore, the decomposition step requires the computation of the constraints defined on each of the new relation schemes from the constraints defined on the old scheme. This problem may also be intractable because, in the general case, it could require the computation of the closure of the given set of dependencies.

Synthesis proceeds by considering the given dependencies, reducing them to a standard cover (for example, an LR-minimum cover if the dependencies are FDs), and partitioning them on the basis of a specific criterion. A relation scheme is then associated with each element of the partition, containing all the attributes that are involved in dependencies in the element. The partition is generated in such a

---

Algorithm 5.1
input   a set of attributes U and a set of FDs F
output a database scheme **S**
begin
1. Find G, minimum cover of F ;
2. Let **S** be the database scheme with one relation scheme
   $[R_i(X_iY_i), \{X_i \rightarrow Y_i\}]$ for each FD $X_i \rightarrow Y_i \in G$;
3. **if** there is no relation scheme $R_i(U_i) \in$ **S** such that $U_i \rightarrow U \in G^+$
   then add $[R_K(K), \{\}]$ to **S**, where $K \rightarrow U \in G^+$
4. **while S** contains a pair of distinct relation schemes
           $[R'(Z'), F']$ and $[R''(Z''), F'']$ with $Z' = Z''$
   do drop the two schemes from **S** and add $[R'(Z'), F' \cup F'']$
end

Figure 5.10. Algorithm 5.1: Synthesis of BCNF β-adequate decompositions

way that the corresponding relation schemes satisfy the desired normal form. Thus, the final scheme is synthesized without generating intermediate schemes.

Let us now consider the specific problem of the normalization of a database scheme **R** with a single relation scheme $R(U)$ whose constraints are FDs. The decomposed scheme **S** should enjoy a *target* normal form and be an adequate decomposition of **R**, according to a *target* notion of adequacy. Now, if the target normal form is BCNF, we have already seen that we have to limit our ambitions to β-adequacy. The way we handled the counterexample on professors, students, and courses in Section 5.3 suggests an algorithm for finding a BCNF scheme that is a β-adequate decomposition of **R**: **S** has one relation scheme for each FD in (a cover of) F, and the corresponding set of FDs contains only that FD, regardless of any other FD embedded in it. With a few improvements, we obtain the following algorithm.

ALGORITHM 5.1   See Figure 5.10.   □

The proof of correctness of the algorithm is left as an exercise. We also note that an algorithm with just steps (1)–(3) would already

r_1	Town	Basin	Nation
	Kiev	Dniepr	USSR
	Irkutsk	Ienissei	USSR
	Rome	Tiber	Italy

s

r_2	Nation	Continent
	USSR	Europe
	Italy	Europe
	India	Asia

r_3	Basin	Continent
	Tiber	Europe
	Donau	Europe
	Ienissei	Asia

Figure 5.11. A counterexample instance for a nonindependent scheme

produce a BCNF β-adequate decomposition of the original scheme:
step (4) possibly reduces the number of relation schemes, preserving
BCNF.

Since BCNF can be considered too strong as a target normal form,
we limit our objective to 3NF—this was in fact the motivation we gave
for its definition. Unfortunately, there are again examples of schemes
for which there is no 3NF δ-adequate decomposition. Consider a
database scheme **R** referring to towns, nations, basins of rivers, and
continents; we have one relation scheme $R(TNBC)$, with the func-
tional dependencies $T \rightarrow NB$, $N \rightarrow C$, $B \rightarrow C$. In a 3NF scheme
whose constraints represent the given set, there must be a relation
scheme over NC, and one over BC; it is then clear that there are
only two possibilities:

- Four relation schemes: $R_1(TN)$, $R_2(TB)$, $R_3(NC)$, $R_4(BC)$

- Three relation schemes: $R_1(TNB)$, $R_3(NC)$, $R_4(BC)$

In either case, the resulting database scheme is not independent, and
so it is not a δ-adequate representation of **R**. Figure 5.11 shows a
locally consistent instance of the scheme with three relations that is
not globally consistent.

Therefore, the best we can hope to obtain is an algorithm for a γ-
adequate decomposition in 3NF. Because of the complexity of testing
for 3NF, the desired algorithm is based on a synthesis approach.

Algorithm 5.2
input   a database scheme $\mathbf{R} = \{[R(U), F]\}$
output a database scheme $\mathbf{S}$
begin
1. Find G, circular LR-minimum cover of F
2. For each equivalence class $\mathcal{Y}$ of lhs's in G,
   let $\mathbf{S}$ contain one relation scheme $[R_i(U_i), F_i]$ with
   $U_i = \cup_{X \in \mathcal{Y}, X \to Y \in G} XY$ and
   $F_i = \{V \to A \mid V \to W \in G, A \in W, VA \subseteq U_i\}$
3. **if** there is no relation scheme $R_i(U_i) \in \mathbf{S}$ such that $U_i \to U \in G^+$
   then add $[R_K(K), \{\}]$ to $\mathbf{S}$, where $K \to U \in G^+$
end

Figure 5.12. Algorithm 5.2: Synthesis of 3NF γ-adequate decompositions

ALGORITHM 5.2   See Figure 5.12.   □

Before proving the correctness of Algorithm 5.2, let us briefly discuss it. Steps (1) and (2) implement the core of the synthesis approach. Finally, step (3), which essentially requires the computation of a key of $[R, U]$, and so can be implemented by means of Algorithm 3.3, guarantees that the final scheme is a lossless decomposition of the initial one. Let us demonstrate the process by means of an example.

Example 5.5   Let $U = ENLCSDAMPK$. Then consider the scheme $\mathbf{R} = \{[R(U), F]\}$, where F contains the following FDs:

$E \to NS$ $NL \to EMD$ $EN \to LCD$
$C \to S$ $D \to M$ $M \to D$
$EPD \to AE$ $NLCP \to A$

Note that attribute K does not appear in any FD. Let us apply Algorithm 5.2 to normalize $\mathbf{R}$, which is not in 3NF. A circular LR-minimum cover G for F (as computed in Example 3.14) contains the following FDs:

$E \to NLCD$ $NL \to E$ $C \to S$
$D \to M$ $M \to D$ $EP \to A$

Step (2) constructs the first version of $\mathbf{S}$, with four relation schemes:

$$[R_1(ENLCD), \{E \to N, E \to L, E \to C, E \to D, NL \to E\}]$$
$$[R_2(CS), \{C \to S\}]$$
$$[R_3(DM), \{D \to M, M \to D\}]$$
$$[R_4(EPA), \{EP \to A\}]$$

Finally, since no relation scheme contains a key for the original relation scheme (since the attribute K does not appear in any of them), step (3) adds a relation scheme $[R_0(EPK), \{\}]$.

THEOREM 5.9 For every database scheme **R**, the output **S** of Algorithm 5.2 is in 3NF and is a γ-adequate decomposition of **R**.

PROOF

- **S** is a γ-adequate decomposition of **R**.

  - Constraint representation is guaranteed by the fact that G is a cover of F, and every FD in G is included in some F_i.

  - Step (3) guarantees lossless decomposition, by Lemma 5.2.

  - The specific condition for γ-adequacy, namely, if $X \to A \in F_i$ and $XA \subseteq U_j$, then $X \to A \in F_j$, follows from the construction of the F_i's in step (2). The relation scheme possibly added in step (3) cannot introduce any violation because K is a key, and it cannot embed dependencies, otherwise it would be redundant.

- **S** is in 3NF. Let $V \to A \in F_i$, and assume by way of contradiction that V does not contain a key for R_i and that A is not prime in R_i. Consider the lhs's $Y_0, Y_1, \ldots, Y_k$ that form the equivalence class that has generated R_i. Since G is L-minimum, it follows that each of them is a key for R_i. Now, if the corresponding FDs are $Y_0 \to ZW_1$, $Y_1 \to W_2$, $\ldots$, $Y_k \to W_0$ (with $W_j \subseteq Y_j$, for $i = 0, 1, \ldots, k$), the attributes of R_i are $Y_0 Y_1 \ldots Y_k Z$. Since A is not prime, we have that $A \in Z$. We claim that $G' = G - \{Y_0 \to ZY_1\} \cup \{Y_0 \to (Z - A)Y_1\}$ is equivalent to G, which contradicts the fact that G is a circular LR-minimum cover. It suffices to show that $Y_0 \to A$ is implied by G'. Since $V \to A$ is nontrivial, we have $A \notin V$, and so $V \subseteq Y_0 Y_1 \ldots Y_k (Z - A)$. As a consequence, $Y_0 \to V$ is implied by G'; but $V \to A$ belongs to F_i, and so there is $V \to W \in G$ with $A \in W$. As a consequence, $V \to W$ is also in G'. By transitivity and decomposition, $Y_0 \rightarrow A$ is therefore implied by G'.   □

It should be noted that Algorithm 5.2 may produce different results, depending on the circular LR-minimum cover (which need not be unique, as we know from Section 3.5) chosen in step (1) and on the choice of the key. Moreover, Algorithm 5.2 may output schemes that are somehow redundant.

Example 5.6   If $\mathbf{R} = [R(ABC), \{AB \rightarrow C, C \rightarrow B\}]$, then the algorithm would produce a database scheme with two relation schemes:

$$[R_1(ABC), \{AB \rightarrow C, C \rightarrow B\}]$$
$$[R_2(BC), \{C \rightarrow B\}]$$

despite the fact that the original scheme is already in 3NF. Similarly, if $\mathbf{R} = [R(ABCD), \{AB \rightarrow C, C \rightarrow BD\}]$, then the algorithm produces a database scheme with two relation schemes:

$$[R_1(ABC), \{AB \rightarrow C, C \rightarrow B\}]$$
$$[R_2(BCD), \{C \rightarrow BD\}]$$

whereas a much more elegant scheme would embed $C \rightarrow B$ in only one relation scheme:

$$[R_1(ABC), \{AB \rightarrow C, C \rightarrow B\}]$$
$$[R_2(CD), \{C \rightarrow D\}]$$

The algorithm could be improved, in the direction suggested by the example, by adding the following two steps between step (2) and step (3):

2a. **while** there are relation schemes $R_i(U_i), R_j(U_j) \in \mathbf{S}$ and
         an FD $V \rightarrow A$ in both F_i and F_j such that
         A does not belong to any lhs in F_j
    do eliminate A from U_j and all FDs that involve A from F_j
2b. **while** there are relation schemes $R_i(U_i), R_j(U_j) \in \mathbf{S}$
         such that $U_j \subseteq U_i$
    do eliminate R_j from $\mathbf{S}$

5.5   Further Normal Forms and Decompositions

As we anticipated in Section 5.3, more normal forms can be defined besides 3NF and BCNF, if other classes of constraints are defined. The most important are *fourth normal form* and *projection-join normal form* (also called *fifth normal form*), which refer to MVDs and JDs (possibly together with FDs), respectively. Their definitions are as follows.

Given a set of attributes U and a set D of FDs and MVDs defined over attributes in U, a relation scheme $[R(U), D]$ is in *fourth normal form (4NF)* if, for every nontrivial MVD $X \twoheadrightarrow Y \in D^+$, the set of attributes X is a superkey for R(X) (that is, $X \to U \in D^+$). The motivation behind 4NF is essentially the same we saw in Section 1.6 for BCNF: keys are easier to check than nonkey FDs and than other constraints. Also, normalized schemes separate pieces of information, in the sense that a single relation embodies only one piece of information in each tuple.

> **Example 5.7**   Consider the database scheme **R** containing the single relation scheme
>
> $$R \ (Model, Version, Driver)$$
>
> with the MVDs *Model $\twoheadrightarrow$ Version* and *Model $\twoheadrightarrow$ Driver*. The constraints correspond to a reasonable application: a tuple $< m, v, d >$ indicates that driver d is authorized to drive cars with model m and version v; the constraints require that if a driver is authorized to drive cars of a model, then the authorization extends to all versions of the model. The scheme is in BCNF (since there are no nontrivial FDs), but presents anomalies related to the MVDs: essentially, the point is that each tuple embodies two distinct pieces of information, namely models with their versions and models with authorized drivers. As an example, consider the relation r and the tuple t in Figure 5.13; if we want to insert t in r, in order to maintain the MVDs, we have to add also tuples t_1, t_2, t_3, and t_4. The scheme **S** with two relation schemes:
>
> $$[R_1(Model, Version), \{\}]$$
> $$[R_2(Model, Driver), \{\}]$$
>
> separates the two concepts and is in 4NF; it is also an α-adequate decomposition of **R**. Figure 5.14 shows the instance of **S** and the

r	Model	Version	Driver
	Fiat Uno	55	Smith
	Fiat Uno	D	Smith
	Fiat Uno	55	Brown
	Fiat Uno	D	Brown
	VW Golf	D	Smith

t	Fiat Uno	Turbo	Jones

	Model	Version	Driver
t_1	Fiat Uno	Turbo	Brown
t_2	Fiat Uno	Turbo	Smith
t_3	Fiat Uno	55	Jones
t_4	Fiat Uno	D	Jones

Figure 5.13. A relation for Example 5.7

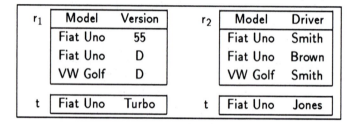

r_1	Model	Version
	Fiat Uno	55
	Fiat Uno	D
	VW Golf	D

t	Fiat Uno	Turbo

r_2	Model	Driver
	Fiat Uno	Smith
	Fiat Uno	Brown
	VW Golf	Smith

t	Fiat Uno	Jones

Figure 5.14. A decomposed instance for Example 5.7

insertion corresponding to those in Figure 5.13, demonstrating that the insertion does not involve anomalies.

The schemes in Example 5.7 (which are isomorphic to those in Example 5.1) also show that, if the constraints include MVDs, then, in general, we may only obtain decomposed schemes that are α-adequate decompositions of the initial one.

By Lemma 5.3 and the basic properties of FDs and MVDs, we have the following result (which would not hold if the definition of 4NF considered only the MVDs in D, ignoring those in $D^+ - D$, which include the MVDs implied by the FDs).

r	Agent	Product	Company
	Jones	screw	KKK
	Jones	bolt	KKK
	White	nail	KKK
	Black	nail	KKK
	Black	nail	ZZZ
	Smith	hammer	AAA
	Smith	drill	BBB
	Green	drill	AAA
	Smith	hammer	BBB

Figure 5.15. A relation for Example 5.8

THEOREM 5.10   If a relation scheme is in 4NF, then it is in BCNF. □

A further normal form, with the same goals, can be defined if the constraints include also join dependencies. A relation scheme $[R(U), D]$, where D is a set of FDs and JDs, is in *projection-join normal form (PJNF)*, or *fifth normal form (5NF)*, if every JD $j \in D^+$ is implied by the set of key dependencies $\{K \to U \mid K \to U \in D^+\}$.

Example 5.8   Consider the scheme $\mathbf{R} = [R(APC), \{j\}]$, where the attribute names are abbreviations for *Agent, Product, Company*, and j is the JD $\bowtie [AP, PC, AC]$. The dependency requires that if an agent a sells a product p, company c produces p, and a sells products of c, then a sells p as produced by c. At the same time, since there are no FDs, an agent may sell more products, even produced by different companies; each company produces more products; and so on. Similarly, there are no MVDs: for example, an agent may sell one product of a company, and not sell another one. Figure 5.15 shows a relation that satisfies j and does not satisfy any nontrivial FD or MVD. The first five tuples contain violations of all possible nontrivial FDs and MVDs, and the other four tuples show the typical pattern for JDs: if the last tuple were not in the relation, then the JD would be violated, because of the three tuples that precede it. Thus, j does not imply any nontrivial MVD, and therefore the relation scheme is in 4NF, whereas it is not in PJNF, since the only key contains all the attributes.
In this case, the "natural" decomposition would be a scheme **S** with

three relation schemes, one for each pair of attributes, and without dependencies. Again, we would have an α-adequate decomposition of **R**. The intuitive reason for the decomposition would be the orthogonality of the three binary pieces of information: each of the three could be available independently of the others.

THEOREM 5.11   If a relation scheme is in PJNF, then it is in 4NF. □

It is important to note that for JDs that are not equivalent to sets of MVDs, the decomposition in PJNF is inherently n-ary: there is no way to produce the decomposition as a sequence of lossless binary decompositions. This is in contrast with what happens for FDs, where, even when using the synthesis approach, a binary decomposition strategy, although computationally inconvenient, could be devised.

We conclude this discussion by noting that all the constraints (and corresponding normal forms) we have considered so far induce vertical decompositions. On the other hand, if we consider FDs or other constraints that, as happens in the example discussed towards the end of Section 5.1, hold in a subset of a relation, we have that anomalies possibly arise only in that subset, and in general not in the whole relation. As a matter of fact, the scheme **R** defined there is in BCNF, because its FDs follow from a key. A normal form (violated by **R**) that takes into account its anomalies can be defined as follows: A relation scheme $[R, D]$ is in *(3,3) normal form* if the following condition holds:

- For every selection condition P, it is the case that a nontrivial FD $X \rightarrow A$ holds in $\sigma_P(r)$ for every consistent instance r of R if and only if X is a superkey of R.

It can be easily shown that (3,3)NF implies BCNF.

5.6   Domain-Key Normal Form: The Ultimate Normal Form

The notion of anomaly we have given in Chapter 1 is intuitive; we now investigate how it can be made more precise. A formal definition of anomaly can be provided by means of a set of primitive properties that the scheme should satisfy. We define as anomaly any situation such that for any instance of the scheme, an update exists that does not violate any primitive property, and at the same time violates some other constraint defined on the scheme. In other words, this means that some integrity constraint is defined in the scheme that cannot be deduced from primitive properties.

In this section, we consider a generic database scheme $[R(U), C]$, where C is a set of static constraints without any restriction except that (as we have always assumed, at least implicitly), they are *coherent*; that is, there exist relations that satisfy them. Also, we make explicit reference to the domains of the attributes; as we did in Section 1.1, we indicate with $dom(A)$ the domain of each attribute $A \in U$. Note that, in some cases, the domains may interact with the constraints. For example, if a domain is empty, only the empty relation may be consistent, and so all FDs, MVDs, and many other constraints that hold in the empty relation hold therefore in every consistent relation, and are in some sense implied by the structure of the domains. Similarly, if the domain of an attribute A contains only one element, then all FDs $X \rightarrow A$, for every $X \subseteq U$, hold in every consistent relation. Therefore, we can say that the domains play a role that is similar to that of constraints; in the rest of this section, we assume that their definitions are indeed constraints (called *domain constraints*): given $[R(U), C]$, C contains, for every $A \in U$ the constraint $dom(A) = D_A$, where D_A is the set of consistent values for A. As a matter of fact, in the previous chapters we assumed the domains to be infinite exactly because infinite domains do not interact with any of the specific constraints we considered (FDs, MVDs, JDs, INDs, etc.). The next two lemmas formalize this claim.

LEMMA 5.7   Let $R(U)$ be a relation scheme, D a set of FDs and MVDs, and I a set of domain constraints. If for every attribute $A \in U$, the domain constraint allows at least two distinct values, then for every FD or MVD d on U, d is implied by $D \cup I$ if and only if d is implied by D.

PROOF   The *if* part is easy. We prove the *only if* part only for FDs, leaving as an exercise its extension to MVDs. Consider a set of FDs F and a set of domain constraints I, and assume that $F \cup I$ implies the FD f and F does not imply f; therefore, there is a relation r

that satisfies F and violates f and I. Let t_1, t_2 be the two tuples of r that cause the violation of f, and consider the two-tuple relation r_0 that contains them. Clearly, we have that $r_0 \subseteq r$ and r_0 satisfies F and violates f; it must also violate I (otherwise, since $F \cup I$ implies f, it would satisfy f). Now let r_0' be the relation obtained by replacing each illegal value (that is, each value that does not satisfy the domain constraints) in r_0 with a legal value, with the condition that identical (distinct) illegal values are replaced with identical (distinct) legal values: that is, there is an isomorphism between r_0 and r_0'. Note that the substitution is always possible, because r_0 contains only two tuples, and so at most two values for each attribute $A \in U$, and by hypothesis, there are at least two legal values for A. Because of the isomorphism, r_0' satisfies f if and only if r_0 satisfies f. Since we assumed that r_0 violates f, we also have that r_0' violates f. But this is a contradiction, because r_0' satisfies F (since it is a subset of r, which satisfies F) and I (since it does not contain illegal values), and we assumed that $F \cup I$ implies f.   □

With respect to JDs, the analogue of Lemma 5.7 requires a stronger hypothesis, because the counterexamples for JDs may contain as many tuples as elements in the JDs. The proof is left as an exercise.

LEMMA 5.8   Let $R(U)$ be a relation scheme, D a set of key dependencies, and I a set of domain constraints. If j is a JD with n components, $\bowtie [X_1, \ldots, X_n]$, and for every attribute $A \in U$, the domain constraint allows at least n distinct values, then j is implied by $D \cup I$ if and only if j is implied by D.   □

We are now ready for the definition of our final normal form. We say that a constraint is *primitive* if it is either a key dependency or a domain constraint. The relation scheme $[R, C]$ is in *domain-key normal form (DKNF)* if every constraint in C is implied by the primitive constraints in C^+.

A characterization of DKNF can be given by means of a formalization of the notion of anomaly. A few preliminary definitions are required. Let r be a relation over a scheme $R(U)$, and t a tuple over U that is not contained in r. We say that t is *compatible* with r if

r	SSN	Age	Division	Manager
	564734327	35	CS	Brown
	467545763	37	EE	Smith

t	264901223	32	CS	Jones

Figure 5.16. An instance for Example 5.9

1. for every attribute $A \in U$, the value of t belongs to the corresponding domain: $t[A] \in dom(A)$;

2. for every key K of R and every tuple $t' \in r$, we have $t[K] \neq t'[K]$.

Essentially, t is compatible with r if $r \cup \{t\}$ does not violate key dependencies and domain constraints.

Then, we say that a relation scheme $[R, D]$ has an *insertion anomaly* if there exist (1) a consistent instance r of R, and (2) a tuple t compatible with R such that $r \cup \{t\}$ is not a consistent instance of R. Similarly, R has a *deletion anomaly* if there exist a consistent instance r of R and a tuple $t \in r$ such that $r - \{t\}$ is not a consistent instance of R.

Example 5.9   Consider the scheme

$$R \ (SSN, Age, Division, Manager)$$

with constraints

$$SSN \rightarrow Age, Division, Manager$$
$$Division \rightarrow Manager$$
$$dom \ (SSN) = \mathbf{string}(15)$$
$$dom \ (Age) = \mathbf{integer}$$
$$dom \ (Division) = \mathbf{string}(2)$$
$$dom(Manager) = \mathbf{string}(20)$$

Consider the relation r and the tuple t in Figure 5.16: t is compatible with r, but gives rise to an insertion anomaly, since $r \cup \{t\}$ violates the functional dependency $D \rightarrow M$.

THEOREM 5.12   A relation scheme is in DKNF if and only if it has no insertion and deletion anomalies.

PROOF

Only if. Assume that R is in DKNF, r is a consistent instance of R, and t is a tuple compatible with r. Then $r \cup \{t\}$ satisfies all the constraints in R because, by definition of compatibility, it satisfies key and domain constraints, and by definition of DKNF, these constraints imply all other constraints. The situation is similar for deletions.

If. We show that a scheme not in DKNF suffers from anomalies. If R is not in DKNF, then it has at least one constraint c that is not logically implied by the primitive constraints. This means that an instance r exists where the primitive constraints hold, and c does not hold. At the same time, since we assume our sets of constraints to be coherent, there is at least one consistent instance r_*. Suppose now that we build r from r_* by first deleting one at the time the tuples in r_* (this is possible since there are no dynamic constraints and our relations are finite; see Section 1.2) and then adding all the tuples in r. Now, since r_* is consistent and r is not, there must exist two instances r' and r'' such that (1) r' is consistent, (2) r'' is not consistent, and (3) $r'' = r' \cup \{t\}$ or $r'' = r' - \{t\}$. Let us consider the two cases separately:

- $r'' = r' - \{t\}$. In this case $r' \subset r_*$, and so r' is consistent. Since r'' is not consistent, there is a deletion anomaly.

- $r'' = r' \cup \{t\}$. In this case, $r' \subset r$, and so, since r satisfies the primitive constraints, we have that t is compatible with r'. Then, since r'' is not consistent, we have an insertion anomaly.   □

Considering again the scheme **R** in Example 5.9, we can see that it is not in DKNF, since the FD *Division* → *Manager* is not implied by the primitive constraints. Similarly, the scheme **R** used in Section 5.1 to discuss horizontal decompositions is not in DKNF: whichever reasonable domain constraints we introduce, we have that constraint c_1 is not implied by the primitive constraints.

DKNF has several interesting properties with respect to other normal forms:

- It can be expressed in terms of primitive properties.

- It is based on a formal notion of anomaly.

- It is stronger than all other normal forms.

This last property holds under very general hypotheses, stated in the next theorems.

THEOREM 5.13   Let $[R, D]$ be a relation scheme such that the domain constraints allow at least k distinct values, where k is the number of components in the JD with the largest number of components of a set of JDs J that is a cover of the JDs in D^+. If $[R, D]$ is in DKNF, then it is in PJNF.

PROOF   Let $d \in D^+$ be a JD. Since R is in DKNF, we have that every JD $j \in J$ is implied by the primitive constraints in D^+. By Lemma 5.8, each j is then implied by the key dependencies in D^+. Then, by the definition of cover, d is implied by J, and therefore by the key dependencies; thus R is in PJNF.   □

THEOREM 5.14   Let $[R, D]$ be a relation scheme such that the domain constraints allow at least two distinct values for each attribute. If $[R, D]$ is in DKNF, then it is in 4NF and in (3,3)NF.

PROOF   The proof is similar to the proof of Theorem 5.13.   □

Figure 5.17 presents a synopsis of the normal forms we have seen in this chapter, plus two others, 2NF and EKNF, which are defined in Exercises 5.6 and 5.7, respectively.

Exercises

5.1 Consider a database scheme $\mathbf{R}$ with a single relation scheme $[R, F]$, where F is a set of FDs, and a scheme $\mathbf{S}$ whose constraints are embedded FDs. Prove that if $\mathbf{S}$ is a β-adequate decomposition of $\mathbf{R}$ and if for each FD $X \to A \in F^+$, there is at most one relation scheme $R_i(U_i)$ such that $XA \subseteq U_i$, then it is the case that $\mathbf{S}$ is a γ-adequate decomposition of $\mathbf{R}$.

5.2 Prove Lemma 5.1.

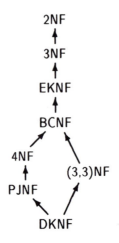

Figure 5.17. Comparison of normal forms

5.3 Consider the following definition: **S** is a *J-adequate vertical decomposition* of **R** if

- for every $\mathbf{s} \in H(\mathbf{S})$, $\mathbf{s} \in L(\mathbf{S})$ if and only if $\bowtie_{\mathbf{S}}(\mathbf{s}) \in L(\mathbf{R})$, and
- **S** is a lossless decomposition of **R**.

Show the relationships between *J*-adequacy and the other notions of adequacy, both in general and with respect to FDs.

5.4 Prove Lemma 5.5 and Theorem 5.7.

5.5 Prove the correctness of Algorithm 5.1.

5.6 A relation scheme $[R, F]$ is in *second normal form (2NF)* if F^+ does not contain any partial dependency $K \to A$ where K is a key and A is a nonprime attribute (where a *partial dependency* $X \to A$ is an FD in F^+ such that, for some $X' \subset X$, it is the case that $X' \to A$ is also in F^+). Prove that 2NF is strictly weaker than 3NF.

5.7 A relation scheme $[R, F]$ satisfies *elementary-key normal form (EKNF)* if for every nontrivial $X \to A \in F$, it is the case that X is an elementary key or A is part of an elementary key (where a key is *elementary* if there is at least an attribute $A \in U$ such that for no $K' \subset K$ is it the case that $K' \to A \in F^+$). Prove that EKNF is strictly weaker than BCNF and strictly stronger than 3NF.

5.8 Characterize the uniqueness of 3NF γ–adequate decompositions.

5.9 Prove Theorem 5.10, and show that it would not hold if the definition of 4NF referred only to the MVDs in D and not to those in the closure D^+.

5.10 Prove that each scheme obtained by a synthesis algorithm for FDs (5.1 or 5.2) could be obtained by means of an analysis approach based on binary projections that preserve the target notion of adequacy at each step.

5.11 Implement a program ("CASE Tool") able to perform all the normalization algorithms described in this chapter. Use a procedural language, say Pascal or C.

5.12 Develop the tool in the previous exercise using a logic programming language like Prolog. (See Ceri and Gottlob [63].)

5.13 Prove that a scheme is in BCNF (4NF) if for every FD (MVD) d in the given set of dependencies, there is *one* key dependency that implies d. Show that a similar result does not hold for JDs and PJNF.

5.14 Complete the proof of Lemma 5.7, considering also MVDs.

5.15 Show that without the hypothesis that domains contain at least two values, Lemma 5.7 would not hold.

5.16 Prove Lemma 5.8.

Comments and References

The seminal work on normalization, with the definition of 3NF and the basic ideas on the analysis approach, was carried out by Codd [78]. The notions of adequate and equivalent decomposition presented in Section 5.2 have been originally conceived for this book, and derive from many different contributions, which include Delobel and Casey [91], Rissanen and Delobel [186], Rissanen [184], Arora and Carlson [21], Beeri and Rissanen [46], and two papers that present a systematization of the various approaches, Beeri et al. [41] and Maier et al. [163]. The main differences between these approaches and ours is that most of them are heavily based on the so-called *universal relation assumption*, which requires the decomposed database to be a projection of a single relation. This assumption and a number of its variations are discussed by Beeri et al. [41], Bernstein and Goodman [50], Ullman [214,215], Atzeni and Parker [30], Fagin et al. [102], and Kent [135,136].

All the above approaches refer only to adequacy of vertical decompositions, and therefore compare the information embodied in the decomposed scheme with that of a single relation scheme. More general points of view were later taken by Beeri et al. [45] and Rissanen [185], who generalized the concept of the equivalent decomposition to the concept of equivalent transformation, where both the starting schema and the resulting schema are made of an arbitrary number of relational schemas. Possible transformations are compositions of join and projection. More general transformations, possibly including horizontal decompositions, were then studied by Kandzia and Klein [132], Ausiello et al. [33], and Atzeni et al. [22]. In these papers the concept of the equivalence of database instances is interpreted to mean that they have the same ability to respond to queries. Existing results on vertical decompositions are rephrased in the model, while horizontal decompositions are characterized in terms of properties of tuple constraints. Horizontal decompositions were also considered by Fagin [99], Smith and Smith [201,202], Armstrong and Delobel [20], and deeply studied by DeBra and Paredaens [89,90]; a duality between properties that characterize horizontal and vertical decompositions is discussed by Maier and Ullman [166]. A comprehensive approach to the problems of adequacy and equivalence was studied by Hull [123], who considered general mappings. The general definitions we gave at the beginning of Section 5.2 follow Hull's proposal.

The notion of constraint representation (also called *preservation*), with reference to FDs, was conceived by Bernstein [49], together with the proposal of the synthesis approach. Beeri and Honeyman [43] give an algorithm for the efficient test of FD preservation, which can allow the computation of the embedded FDs, if the test is successful. (As we saw, this result is fundamental for the analysis approach, but less important for the synthesis approach).

3NF and BCNF were originally proposed by Codd [78,80], 4NF, PJNF, and DKNF by Fagin [98,99,100], and (3,3)NF by Smith [201]. EKNF (Exercise 5.7), which is strictly weaker than BCNF and strictly stronger than 3NF, was proposed by Zaniolo [234] and tries to push a little further the border of existence of γ-adequate decompositions.

Formal studies of anomalies are due to LeDoux and Parker [150], Bernstein and Goodman [50], and Chan [67]. NP-completeness of the test for 3NF was shown by Jou and Fischer [130].

The various algorithms for normalization proposed in the literature are summarized in the table in Figure 5.18, with reference to the following:

- The strategy

- The normal form guaranteed

- The constraints considered

- The relationship between the original and the decomposed scheme (*LD* stands for lossless decomposition, and *CR* for constraint representation)

- The complexity

It should be noted that most analysis algorithms have an exponential complexity because they require the computation of the embedded cover, and because it is inherently exponential to check for some normal forms. On tho other hand, synthesis algorithms are suited for FDs and not for MVDs.

Author(s)	Strategy	NF	Const'ts	Rel'ship	Compl.
Bernstein [49]	Synthesis	3NF	FD	CR	Poly
Fagin [98]	Analysis	4NF	FD+MVD	LD	Exp
Biskup et al. [53]	Synthesis	3NF	FD	LD+CR	Poly
Ullman [213]	Analysis	4NF	FD+MVD	LD	Exp
Tsou and Fischer [211]	Analysis	4NF	FD+MVD	LD	Poly
Zaniolo and Melkanoff [237]	Analysis	3NF	FD+MVD	LD+CR	Exp

Figure 5.18. Algorithms for normalization

More recently, Beeri and Kifer [44] proposed a novel approach to the design of database schemes, whose goal is still the generation of normalized schemes, but with the possibility of modifying the given scheme and dependencies. An early proposal for adding attributes in order to improve schemes was formulated by Sciore [199].

A final comment about normalization is important. In practical database design, the modeling step is the crucial phase, as it requires the designer to formalize the informal requirements of the application into a database scheme. For this reason, the design of a database scheme is usually carried out [38,206,210] by using first a *conceptual model* (for example the *entity-relationship model* [74]), which allows an easier representation of the data from the real-world point of view. This representation, called the *conceptual scheme* of the application, is then used as a basis to produce, by means of a sort of translation process, the relational (or network or hierarchical) database scheme. If the process is carried out carefully, this often presents a sufficient degree of normalization. In this framework, normalization does not provide a theory of automated design, as was claimed for a while, but it can still play a useful role as a formal tool for quality checking.

Chapter 6

The Theory of Null Values

The relational model requires a rather rigid structure for the data to be handled: only pieces of information corresponding to tuples can be represented, and each tuple has to conform to the template imposed by a relation scheme. In most cases the available information about the application (or even the actual information meaningful for the application) does not fit the template. Some values may be missing, or just partially known; in other cases, there may be uncertainty about whole tuples (there may be alternatives between tuples). In all these cases, we say that there is a need to handle *incomplete information*.

In this chapter we focus our attention on the simplest way of representing incomplete information: the use of special values, called *null values*, as values of tuples on specific attributes, that is, as placeholders for unavailable values.

The topic has been widely studied in the last few years, without producing definitive answers. For this reason, in Chapters 2–5, we almost always assumed our relations to be null-free. The three sections of this chapter are devoted to the main issues about null values tackled in the literature. Section 6.1 studies the interpretation of the null values, that is, the meaning attached to tuples that contain nulls. Section 6.2 discusses the semantics of the query operations when relations contain null values. Section 6.3 considers integrity constraints on relations with null values, with specific reference to generalizations of functional dependencies.

More sophisticated forms of incomplete information can be handled in deductive databases, which we will consider in Chapter 9.

yalta	FirstName	MiddleName	LastName
	Franklin	Delano	Roosevelt
	Winston	ϕ	Churchill
	Charles	ϕ	DeGaulle
	Joseph	ϕ	Stalin

Figure 6.1. A relation with the basic types of null values

6.1   Types of Null Values

The Basic Types

There are many situations where values from the domains (in the following we will call these values *specified* values, to distinguish them from *null* values) cannot be used, so null values are needed. Consider for example the relation in Figure 6.1, which contains first names, middle names, and last names for the four participants in the Yalta Conference. Considering the values for the attribute *MiddleName*, we note that the only specified value is for Roosevelt, while null values have been used for the others. However, there is a different motivation for each of them. DeGaulle was French, and would not use a middle name. Churchill was a British Lord, so he definitely had a middle name, and we assume that we do not know it. Stalin was Russian (actually, Georgian), so he probably had a patronymic as middle name, but might have abandoned it together with his original last name (Dzhugashvili).

Thus, the three null values in this relation represent three different cases. If we analyzed critically more complex situations, we could come up with more cases, all different from one another: a report published by the American National Standards Institute [17] lists fourteen different types of null values that can appear in relations or in answers to queries. In that list, most of the distinctions depend on application or implementation considerations, which are not relevant from a theoretical point of view. With respect to our interest, the fourteen types can definitely be reduced to the three in Figure 6.1, which can be described as follows.

The tuple referring to DeGaulle contains a value *nonexistent* or *attribute inapplicable*: there does not exist a meaningful, specified value. Consider a relation scheme *COURSES (Student, Course, Grade)*, used to represent the registration of students in courses and, when they are available, the final grades obtained. Here, this type of null could be used as the value for the attribute *Grade* in tuples referring to courses where a final grade is not yet available. In a sense, this value represents complete information—the inapplicability of a property—so it can be considered as a special value of the domain of the attribute.

Churchill's tuple contains an *unknown* value: in the application, there is a value associated with the tuple and the attribute, but it is not currently known to our database. In the *COURSES* relation scheme, it could be used in tuples referring to exams that have been passed, with the grade not yet known to the database.

Stalin's tuple contains a *no-information* value: nothing is known with respect to the value of the attribute for the tuple; it may exist or not, and if it exists nothing is known about its value. Intuitively, this value can be considered as the logical disjunction of the other two (this claim will be formalized shortly). In the *COURSES* relation scheme, it may be associated with the attribute *Grade* in tuples where a student was enrolled in the course, but we do not know whether he took the exam. This kind of null may also be useful in database management systems that allow the modification of the relation schemes without interrupting the operation of the system. Considering again the same example, suppose we add to the relation scheme the attribute *Student#*. If the numbers are not available when the scheme is modified, null values must be used in their places; moreover, if there may exist students without student numbers, the value to be used is the no-information null value.

Null Values and First-Order Logic

It is interesting to try to give a formalization of null values based on first-order logic. To avoid heavy notation, we argue by means of examples, omitting general definitions. With a relation scheme $R(A_1, A_2, \ldots, A_n)$, we can associate an n-ary predicate R, and with each tuple t in the corresponding relation r, the sentence $R(t[A_1], t[A_2], \ldots, t[A_n])$.

Then the three types of null values can be handled as follows (for the sake of simplicity, we present the basic cases where each tuple contains only one null value).

An unknown value represents a value that exists, but is presently unknown, and so it can be treated by means of an existential quantifier. So, a tuple t with a null for the attribute A_k can be represented by means of the sentence

$$\exists x (R(\dots, t[A_{k-1}], x, t[A_{k+1}], \dots))$$

In the *yalta* example, we would have

$$\exists x (YALTA(\text{Winston}, x, \text{Churchill}))$$

With respect to the nonexistent null, reasoning as above, we obtain the negative sentence

$$\neg \exists x (R(\dots, t[A_{k-1}], x, t[A_{k+1}], \dots))$$

which somehow hides the positive information embedded in the $n-1$ specified values, so it has to be coupled with a positive sentence on an $(n-1)$-ary predicate, with places corresponding to all the attributes except A_k:

$$R_{-k}(\dots, t[A_{k-1}], t[A_{k+1}], \dots)$$

In the example, we would have the following two sentences:

$$\neg \exists x (YALTA(\text{Charles}, x, \text{DeGaulle}))$$

$$YALTA_{-2}(\text{Charles}, \text{DeGaulle})$$

Finally, the best way to express the complete lack of information about an attribute is to use a predicate that does not mention it. So, a tuple t with a no-information null for the attribute A_k, could be represented by the sentence:

$$R_{-k}(\dots, t[A_{k-1}], t[A_{k+1}], \dots)$$

In the example, we would have

$$YALTA_{-2}(\text{Joseph}, \text{Stalin})$$

The need for the positive tuple for the case of nonexistent nulls suggests that more positive information is embedded in our tuples than is expressed by just the single sentences based on the predicate R: in fact, each tuple expresses not only the information about the whole set of attributes X in the scheme $R(X)$, but also information about the subsets of X. The formalization of this argument requires the introduction of more predicate symbols, associated with all the subsets of X. Then we can associate (with the whole database) general quantified formulas that state the implication between each m-ary predicate (corresponding, say, to the set of attributes Y), and all the $(m-1)$-ary predicates corresponding to the subsets of Y with cardinality $m-1$. So we have universally quantified formulas such as the following:

$$\forall a_1(\ldots \forall a_n(R(a_1,\ldots,a_n) \rightarrow R_{-k}(a_1,\ldots,a_{k-1},a_{k+1},\ldots,a_n))\ldots)$$

At this point, it is possible to formalize the intuition, mentioned above, that the no-information null is the logical disjunction of the unknown and nonexistent values. We leave as an exercise the proof that the sentence corresponding to the no-information null

$$R_{-k}(\ldots,t[A_{k-1}],t[A_{k+1}],\ldots)$$

is equivalent to the disjunction of the sentences corresponding to the other two types of null values:

$$\exists x(R(\ldots,t[A_{k-1}],x,t[A_{k+1}],\ldots)) \vee$$
$$(\neg \exists x(R(\ldots,t[A_{k-1}],x,t[A_{k+1}],\ldots)) \wedge R_{-k}(\ldots,t[A_{k-1}],t[A_{k+1}],\ldots))$$

Hierarchies of Null Values

The values above can be generalized in various ways. Let us say that a type of null value N_1 is the *generalization* of another type N_2 if N_1 allows the representation of more detailed information than N_2, thus keeping the possibility of reducing to N_2 as a special case.

The unknown value, as we saw, allows one to represent the fact that a value exists, but is not currently known. Then it must be one of the values of the domain of the attribute. The value does not specify, as is reasonable in many cases, any preference among such values. In some cases, however, it is possible to know that the value belongs to a subset of the domain. In our running example, assuming that grades are recorded as percentages (1 to 100), it may happen that for some student the actual mark is not known, but the letter grade is available: for example an *A* may mean that the mark is between 80 and 90. Situations of this kind can be represented by means of the *partially specified* value, which indicates the nonempty subset *S* of the domain to which the actual value belongs. By means of partially specified values, it is possible to represent the unknown value (with the set *S* equal to the domain *D*), the completely specified value (with a singleton set *S*), and all the intermediate possibilities. If we want to handle the nonexistent value in the same framework, we have two possibilities: (1) drop the restriction requiring *S* to be nonempty; (2) add the nonexistent value to the domain. Solution 2 is probably more interesting, since it allows us to represent a larger variety of situations. In fact, the nonexistent value can be handled by both (Solution 1 would have an empty *S*, and Solution 2 a singleton *S* containing only the nonexistent value), but only the second technique allows us to distinguish between the case where the value exists and belongs to a certain subset *S* and the case where the value may exist and belong to *S*, or not exist. Moreover, Solution 2 allows us to represent also the no-information value by means of a set *S* composed of the domain plus the nonexistent value. In this way, the partially specified value is a generalization of the specified value and of all three types of null values above described. The relation *courses* in Figure 6.2 demonstrates its various uses (in the figure, the symbol "−" represents the nonexistent value, considered as a special value of the domain). The six tuples in Figure 6.2 represent, respectively, the following pieces of information:

t_1 – specified value: Smith has passed the exam for Calculus I with 90% mark.

t_2 – unknown value: Robinson has taken the exam for Geometry, but the grade is not known.

t_3 – nonexistent value: Jones has not taken the exam for Geometry.

t_4 – no-information value: it is not known whether Smith has taken the exam for Physics I, and if so, the grade is unknown.

courses	Student	Course	Grade
t_1	Smith	Calculus I	90
t_2	Robinson	Geometry	1,2,...,100
t_3	Jones	Geometry	–
t_4	Smith	Physics	–,1,2,...,100
t_5	Robinson	Calculus I	80,...,90
t_6	Black	Calculus II	–,80,...,90

Figure 6.2. A relation with partially specified values

t_5 – existent, partially specified value: Robinson has passed the exam
for Calculus I, with a mark between 80% and 90%.

t_6 – partially specified value: if Black has taken the exam for Calculus
II, then the grade is between 80% and 90%; however, it is not
known whether he or she has taken the exam. (This is clearly
a quite unrealistic case, but we mention it here for the sake of
generality).

It is possible to generalize the partially specified value by associating an "importance," or better, a "probability," with each of the values
in the set S. Actually we can even get rid of the set S by associating
a probability with each value in the domain D, with a probability
zero for the values in $(D - S)$. To consider the nonexistent value,
we have again two possibilities: (1) associate a probability with the
nonexistent value, as well as with the values in D; (2) allow the sum
s of the probabilities to be strictly smaller than 1, thus attributing
the complement $1 - s$ to the nonexistent value. In this case the two
possibilities have the same expressive power. This model generalizes
most of those presented above, as follows (we adopt Solution 2 above
for the representation of the nonexistent value):

• A specified value can be represented by assigning probability 1
  to it and 0 to all the other values in the domain.

• The nonexistent value can be represented by assigning probability 0 to all the elements of the domain.

- The unknown value can be represented by assigning the same probability $1/n$ to all the elements of the domain (where n is the cardinality of the domain, assumed finite; if it were infinite, we would have to refer to distributions).[1]

- The partially specified value, composed of a set of k values from the domain, can be represented by assigning probability $1/k$ to each of them and probability 0 to all the other values in the domain.

This kind of value does not generalize the no-information value, because by assigning a probability to the various elements of the domain and, more important, to the nonexistent value, we assume the availability of some information on the value of the attribute, in contrast with what happens for the no-information value.

In Figure 6.3 we present a hierarchy of the various models presented so far, based on their generality. The model without null values is at the bottom of the hierarchy, because it is generalized by all the others. Figure 6.4 presents a hierarchy of the various types of nulls based on the quantity of information provided by each of them. The no-information value is at the bottom of the hierarchy because it does not provide any information about the attribute, while the nonexistent value is at the top, together with the specified value, because it does provide complete information with respect to the attribute: its nonexistence.

Marked Nulls

Another technique for the enrichment of the information content of null values is to associate subscripts with their various occurrences, in order to distinguish one from another. For unknown values, this technique can be used to indicate that certain values, though unknown, are equal. In Figure 6.5 we show an instance of the *courses* relation, enlarged to include student numbers, where the names of the students are unknown, but it is known that some of the values coincide. The use of nulls with subscripts (called *marked nulls*) is useful in various

---

[1] We assume that we can represent the lack of further information about the elements in the domain by means of the equality of the respective probabilities.

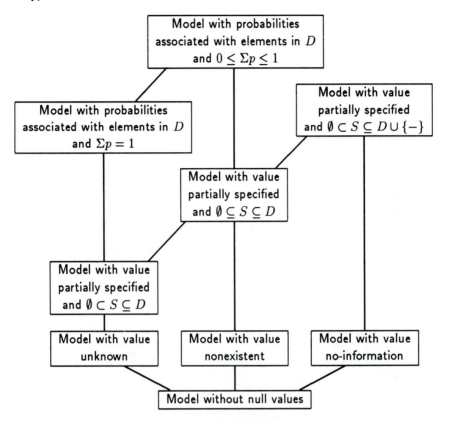

Figure 6.3. The hierarchy of the relational models with null values

situations: we have already encountered a variant of them when dealing with weak and representative instances in Chapter 4. Moreover, this technique can be useful when, in decomposing relations with null values, it is important to keep track of the original tuples in the decomposed relations. We do not elaborate more on the subject, but just show an example. If we want to decompose the *courses* relation in Figure 6.6 into two relations on the attributes *Student#, Student,* and *Student#, Course, Grade*, respectively, we obtain the two relations c_1 and c_2 in the same figure, from which it is impossible to obtain the original relation again. If instead we use marked nulls in the *Student#* attribute (Figure 6.7), we obtain decomposed relations from which the original relation can be reconstructed.

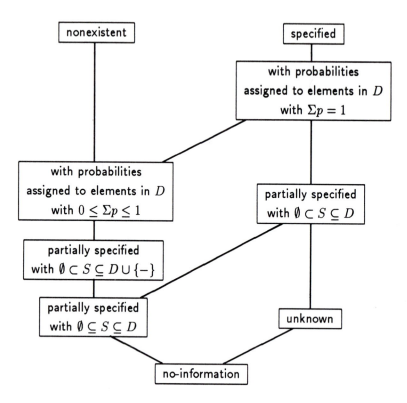

Figure 6.4. The hierarchy of null values, based on the information content

courses	Student#	Student	Course	Grade
	26654	ϕ_1	Calculus	90
	26654	ϕ_1	Geometry	85
	43345	ϕ_2	Physics	75
	65432	ϕ_3	Geometry	80

Figure 6.5. A relation with marked nulls

courses

Student#	Student	Course	Grade
ϕ	Smith	Calculus	90
ϕ	Smith	Geometry	85
ϕ	Jones	Physics	75
ϕ	Jones	Geometry	80

c_1

Student#	Course	Grade
ϕ	Calculus	90
ϕ	Geometry	85
ϕ	Physics	75
ϕ	Geometry	80

c_2

Student#	Student
ϕ	Smith
ϕ	Jones

Figure 6.6. An unsatisfactory decomposition with unmarked nulls

courses

Student#	Student	Course	Grade
ϕ_1	Smith	Calculus	90
ϕ_1	Smith	Geometry	85
ϕ_2	Jones	Physics	75
ϕ_2	Jones	Geometry	80

c_1

Student#	Course	Grade
ϕ_1	Calculus	90
ϕ_1	Geometry	85
ϕ_2	Physics	75
ϕ_2	Geometry	80

c_2

Student#	Student
ϕ_1	Smith
ϕ_2	Jones

Figure 6.7. A decomposition with marked nulls

courses	Student	Course	Grade
	Smith	Calculus I	90
	Jones	Geometry	ϕ
	Smith	Physics	64

Figure 6.8. A relation for Example 6.1

6.2   Query Languages and Null Values

If relations are allowed to contain null values, the definition of the semantics of relational algebra and relational calculus expressions is not always straightforward. The problem arises, possibly with variants, with respect to all types of nulls.

> **Example 6.1**   Consider the relation in Figure 6.8 and the following, equivalent expressions:
>
> $$\sigma_{Grade > 70}(courses)$$
> $$\{x_1.* \, |x_1(COURSES)|x_1.Grade > 70\}$$
>
> What is the result of these expressions? Clearly, it should include the first tuple of the relation, and should not include the third; but how about the second? If the null is unknown, it stands for an actual value, but we do not know it, and therefore we do not know whether it is larger than 70 or not. If it is nonexistent, then the result should probably contain only the first tuple. However, the following expressions are intuitively equivalent to those above, and it is not clear whether the second tuple should appear in the result.
>
> $$\sigma_{\neg(Grade \leq 70)}(courses)$$
> $$\{x_1.* \, |x_1(COURSES)|\neg(x_1.Grade \leq 70)\}$$

Let us concentrate on unknown nulls first. We show that an approach that at first could appear reasonable often exhibits an undesirable behavior.

Example 6.1 suggests that the ordinary two-valued logic is not capable of assigning a reasonable truth value to Boolean expressions involving null values, which would be needed in order to decide whether a tuple belongs to a result.

The extension of relational query languages to a model allowing relations to contain null values of the unknown type can be based on a three-valued logic and the *null substitution principle*. We first present the approach informally, showing also some of the problems that arise, and then formalize it, in order to investigate the origins of the problems and consider how they can be overcome.

The crucial point of the approach is the use, together with *true* and *false*, of a third truth value, *unknown*, representing uncertainty.[2] Intuitively, for every expression, two versions are defined: the *true*-version, for the tuples that are certainly selected by the condition, regardless of the values represented by the nulls, and the *maybe*-version, for the tuples that may or may not represent tuples satisfying the conditions. For the expressions in Example 6.1, the first tuple appears in the *true*-result and the second in the *maybe*-result.

With respect to relational algebra, the approach suggests a double version for the selection operator, and a syntactic treatment of the null value for the other operators.[3] The definition of selection extends to the three-valued logic the two-valued definition given in Section 1.4, which we repeat here for convenience:

$$\sigma_F(r) = \{t \in r | F(t) = true\}$$

If null values are allowed, condition F can assume any of the three truth values; as a consequence, two versions are defined for the selection operator: the *true*-version and the *maybe*-version, whose results respectively contain the tuples upon which F evaluates to *true* and those upon which it evaluates to *unknown*. For the sake of simplicity, let us assume that F is an elementary condition of the form $A\theta B$; then the *maybe*-version can be denoted by putting the symbol ϕ beside the comparison operator.

In this approach, the union, intersection, selection, Cartesian product, and renaming operators maintain the usual definitions, with the symbol ϕ treated analogously to the ordinary values.

---

[2] The term *unknown* is used both for the null value and for the third truth value, since their respective meanings are identical.

[3] We do not consider the join operator, assuming that it is expressed by renamings, Cartesian products, selections, and projections.

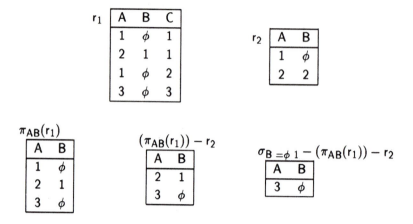

Figure 6.9. Operations in the three-valued relational algebra

Complex relational algebra expressions are evaluated by means of repeated applications of the various operators, according to the respective definitions (see the example in Figure 6.9).

Unfortunately, this approach presents some undesirable properties. For example, the expressions

$$\sigma_{Grade > 70}(courses) \cup \sigma_{Grade \leq 70}(courses) \tag{6.1}$$

$$\{x_1.* \mid x_1(COURSES) \mid (x_1.Grade > 70) \lor (x_1.Grade \leq 70)\} \tag{6.2}$$

which are equivalent with respect to null-free relations, do not necessarily have the same *true*-result; the result of expression (6.2) always equals the relation *courses*, whereas the result of (6.1) does not include the tuples having a null for the attribute *Grade*, as they are not selected by either subexpression.

In order to explain the reasons for this undesirable behavior, we formalize the definition of the null substitution principle and of the associated three-valued logic in a simpler framework. The results on relational expressions will be extensions thereof.

Let us start with simple propositional expressions containing only constant terms, *true*, *false*, and *unknown*. Then an expression (possibly) containing the value *unknown* assumes a truth-value according to the following rules:

- *True*, if all two-valued logic expressions obtained by substituting the occurrences of *unknown* with *true* and *false* in all the possible ways assume the logical value *true*

- *False*, if all the above expressions assume the value *false*

- *Unknown*, otherwise, that is, if some of the expressions assume the value *true*, and the others assume the value *false*.

Example 6.2 Let us evaluate a few expressions.

1. $(true \lor unknown) \lor \neg unknown$
   - If we replace both occurrences of *unknown* with *true*, we obtain $(true \lor true) \lor \neg true$, whose value is *true*.
   - If we replace the first occurrence with *true* and the second with *false*, we obtain $(true \lor true) \lor \neg false$, whose value is *true*.
   - If we replace the first occurrence with *false* and the second with *true*, we obtain $(true \lor false) \lor \neg true$, whose value is *true*.
   - Finally, if we replace both occurrences of *unknown* with *false*, we obtain $(true \lor false) \lor \neg false$, whose value is again *true*.

   Since all substitutions produce expressions whose value is *true*, we have that our original three-valued logic expression assumes the value *true*.

2. $(true \land unknown) \land \neg(true \lor unknown)$
   Here, if we enumerated all the substitutions, as above, we would find that all of them generate ordinary two-valued expressions that assume the value *false*; hence, the three-valued expression assumes the value *false*.

3. $(true \land unknown) \lor false$
   - If we replace *unknown* with *true*, we obtain $(true \land true) \lor false$, whose value is *true*.
   - If we replace *unknown* with *false*, we obtain $(true \land false) \lor false$, whose value is *false*.

   Hence, the expression assumes the value *unknown*.

From the above examples it is clear that the application of the null substitution principle is quite laborious, since the number of substitutions to be performed grows exponentially with the number of

X	¬(X)
true	false
false	true
unknown	unknown

∧	true	false	unknown
true	true	false	unknown
false	false	false	false
unknown	unknown	false	unknown

∨	true	false	unknown
true	true	true	true
false	true	false	unknown
unknown	true	unknown	unknown

Figure 6.10. Truth tables for three-valued logic

occurrences of the null value. Fortunately, it is not always the case that we have to apply the principle in a case-by-case analysis. The following theorem gives a method for the evaluation of three-valued expressions by means of truth tables that are extensions of the ordinary two-valued logic truth tables.

THEOREM 6.1 For every three-valued logic expression on constant terms (*true, false, unknown*), the evaluation based on the null substitution principle is equivalent to the evaluation based on the accumulative application of the truth tables in Figure 6.10.

PROOF   Consider a generic expression e. We proceed by induction on the number of operators in it.
Basis: no operators. Trivial.
Induction: $n > 0$ operators, assuming the claim is valid for expressions with $m < n$ operators. Clearly, e has one of the following forms:

$$e = \neg(e_1)$$
$$e = e_1 \vee e_2$$
$$e = e_1 \wedge e_2$$

Now the proof can be completed by means of a case analysis, using the fact that by the induction hypothesis, the claim holds for expressions e_1 and e_2.   □

Example 6.3   Let us evaluate by means of the truth tables the expressions we evaluated in Example 6.2 by means of the null substitution principle: clearly, we obtain the same values.

1. $(true \lor unknown) \lor \neg unknown = true \lor unknown = true$

2. $(true \land unknown) \land \neg(true \lor unknown) = unknown \land \neg(true) = unknown \land false = false$

3. $(true \land unknown) \lor false = unknown \lor false = unknown$

Up to now, we have considered only expressions with logical constants. With respect to expressions whose terms have the form $a\theta b$, where a and b are constants from a domain or the null value ϕ, and θ is a comparison operator, we can prove a result similar to Theorem 6.1 by assigning the truth value $unknown$ to every term involving the null value ϕ.

Finally, if we consider expressions whose terms have the form $x\theta y$, where θ is again a comparison operator, and x, y are constants from a domain, null values, or variables ranging over constants and nulls, it is no longer the case that we can extend Theorem 6.1 with full generality. Consider as an example the expression

$$(x = 1) \lor (x \neq 1)$$

assuming that the current value of the variable x is the null value ϕ. If we use the null substitution principle, we find that the value of the expression is $true$:

- If the null value is replaced by 1, then the first term and therefore the expression evaluate to $true$.

- Otherwise (that is, if the null value is replaced by any value other than 1), the second term evaluates to $true$, and the expression again evaluates to $true$.

On the other hand, if we use truth tables, we evaluate both terms to $unknown$, thus evaluating the whole expression to $unknown$. Intuitively, the reason for this undesirable behavior is the presence of a variable with two occurrences and a current value equal to ϕ: this prevents substitutions for the null from being made independently of one another, forcing the value to be the same for both occurrences. In this case, the most we can do is to state the following restricted theorem.

THEOREM 6.2 Let e be a three-valued logic expression whose terms have the form $x\theta y$, where each of x, y, is a constant from a domain D, or a null value ϕ, or a variable ranging over $D \cup \{\phi\}$. Then, given an assignment of values to the variables, if no variable whose current value is ϕ appears more than once in e, then the evaluation of e based on the null substitution principle is equivalent to the evaluation based on the accumulative application of the truth tables in Figure 6.10, being the atomic terms evaluated to *unknown* if they contain null values, and as in ordinary two-valued logic otherwise.

PROOF   Since no variable whose value is ϕ appears twice or more, all the substitutions of ϕ can be performed independently, and so we can proceed by induction, as in the proof of Theorem 6.1.   □

Let us now translate these properties to the context of relational calculus and relational algebra. The result of relational calculus expressions has been defined by applying the null substitution principle in a global manner, in the same way as we have done for the three-valued logic expressions. On the other hand, the semantics of relational algebra expressions has been defined in terms of the semantics of the individual operators, in a way similar to the evaluation of expressions by means of truth tables. Thus, it is clear that the undesirable nonequivalence of expressions (6.1) and (6.2) could be explained by means of a result similar to Theorem 6.2: in simple words, we have an operand that contains nulls and that appears twice in the expression, and in relational algebra the substitutions of the nulls are made independently, while in relational calculus they are performed in a coordinated way.

Summarizing, we can say that the use of the null substitution principle as seen so far is unsatisfactory, despite its intuitive appeal. It is sound only with respect to relational calculus, but the evaluation of queries cannot rely directly on it, because the number of different substitutions to be performed would make it impractical. It would be meaningful only if there were the possibility of translating global expressions into elementary steps, each of which could be performed easily (more or less as happens for null-free relations, where queries are usually expressed in some version or variant of relational calculus, and their evaluation is implemented in terms of the corresponding, equivalent algebraic expressions).

Let us show another way of seeing that the algebraic approach based on the null substitution principle does not work. A relation with unknown null values can be seen as "representing" a set of relations, that is, those that can be obtained by replacing the nulls with specified values.[4] Then, the operators should be extended to relations with nulls in such a way that their application to the "representing" relations (with nulls) produce relations (with nulls) that represent the relations (without nulls) that would be obtained by applying the classical operators to the "represented" relations (without nulls). Unfortunately, the basic extensions we have seen do not preserve this notion of representation.

An extension that guarantees a better behavior is based on the use of additional information in relations with nulls, namely, conditions on the values possibly represented by nulls that therefore constrain the possible substitutions. We refer to the literature (Imielinski and Lipski [127], Abiteboul et al. [7], Grahne [116]) for complete presentations, limiting our attention to how this approach would solve the problem with expressions (6.1) and (6.2). A *table* is similar to a relation with marked nulls, except that there is a condition on nulls associated with each tuple. A substitution for the various nulls generates a relation that contains the tuples that (1) are obtained, by means of the substitution, from the tuples of the table, and (2) are associated with conditions satisfied by the substitution. The operators in relational algebra can be extended to tables in a rather natural way. Let us now consider expression (6.1) and the relation *courses* in Figure 6.8. A relation can be seen as a table whose conditions are all identically *true*—we show such a table at the beginning of Figure 6.11. The figure also shows the results of the two subexpressions and the

---

[4]A number of details must be considered here that would result in different definitions; we present only the general idea.

courses

Student	Course	Grade	
Smith	Calculus I	90	true
Jones	Geometry	ϕ_1	true
Smith	Physics	64	true

$\sigma_{\text{Grade} > 70}(\text{courses})$

Student	Course	Grade	
Smith	Calculus I	90	true
Jones	Geometry	ϕ_1	$\phi_1 > 70$

$\sigma_{\text{Grade} \leq 70}(\text{courses})$

Student	Course	Grade	
Jones	Geometry	ϕ_1	$\phi_1 \leq 70$
Smith	Physics	64	true

$\sigma_{\text{Grade} > 70}(\text{courses}) \cup \sigma_{\text{Grade} \leq 70}(\text{courses})$

Student	Course	Grade	
Smith	Calculus I	90	true
Jones	Geometry	ϕ_1	$\phi_1 > 70$
Jones	Geometry	ϕ_1	$\phi_1 \leq 70$
Smith	Physics	64	true

$\sigma_{\text{Grade} > 70}(\text{courses}) \cup \sigma_{\text{Grade} \leq 70}(\text{courses})$

Student	Course	Grade	
Smith	Calculus I	90	true
Jones	Geometry	ϕ_1	$\phi_1 > 70 \vee \phi_1 \leq 70$
Smith	Physics	64	true

Figure 6.11. Tables with conditions

final result, which contains two equal rows with different conditions and can therefore be transformed into the last table in the same figure. Since the condition associated with the second tuple is a tautology, we have that the final table represents the same relations as the original table, thus implementing the expression in the desired manner.

It should be noted that the method based on tables, though sound and interesting from the theoretical point of view, may become inconvenient from the practical point of view, as conditions may grow complex, and their management may be difficult (for example, in some cases it would be necessary to detect tautological conditions, and this is computationally intractable, in general).

The best practical method for avoiding the undesirable behavior of expressions such as (6.1) and (6.2) renounces the concept of substitution, and treats nulls from the syntactic point of view. A special atomic unary predicate is introduced, in both calculus and algebra, to test whether a given value is specified or null: the atom *NULL(A)*, for a tuple t and an attribute A, evaluates to *true* if $t[A]$ is a null value and to *false* if it is specified. Then the null values are considered as special symbols that do not satisfy any elementary condition. So, the meaning of $A\theta B$ is "$t[A]$ *and* $t[B]$ *are specified, and* $t[A]$ *stands in relation* θ *with* $t[B]$." This means that the negation of an atom such as $A = B$ is

$$A \neq B \ \vee \ NULL(A) \ \vee \ NULL(B)$$

Then it is clear that the meaning we wanted to give to expressions (6.1) and (6.2) can be achieved by means of the following expressions, which can be easily shown to be equivalent:

$$\sigma_{G > 70}(courses) \cup \sigma_{G \leq 70}(courses) \cup \sigma_{NULL(G)}(courses) \qquad (6.3)$$

$$\{x_1.* \mid x_1(COURSES) \mid$$
$$(x_1.G > 70) \vee (x_1.G \leq 70) \vee NULL(G)\} \qquad (6.4)$$

The advantage of this approach is also that the third truth value is eliminated, thus avoiding the quite inconvenient *maybe*-versions of the operators, which, though semantically meaningful, are not very practical. Also, this approach is meaningful for all basic types of null values: unknown, nonexistent, and no-information. It is interesting to note that this is the way SQL systems handle null values.

6.3   Integrity Constraints and Null Values

The main issues about integrity constraints on relations with nulls concern (1) the extensions of "classical" constraints to the more complex framework, and (2) the study of new constraints that specifically arise when relations may contain nulls. With respect to the former issue, we consider only functional dependencies, and consider the unknown null separately from the inapplicable and no-information ones.

A simple notion that will be used throughout the section is the following: A tuple t of a relation $r(X)$ is *A-total* for some $A \in X$ if $t[A]$ is a specified value; it is Y-total for $Y \subseteq X$ if it is A-total for every $A \in Y$; if it is X-total, then we also say that it is *total*.

FDs and Unknown Values

If the interpretation of interest for the null value is unknown, we can handle functional dependencies by means of a three-valued logic and the null substitution principle. This is motivated by the fact that FDs, as well as any other kind of constraints, are predicates defined on relations.

Thus, we can say that an FD f assumes, on a relation r,

- the truth value *true* if all possible substitutions of the null values in r generate null-free relations that satisfy f according to the standard definition;

- the truth value *false* if all substitutions generate relations that violate f;

- the truth value *unknown* otherwise; that is, if some of the relations obtained by substitution satisfy f and some others do not.

Then f is said to be

- *strongly satisfied* by r if f assumes the truth value *true* on r;

- *weakly satisfied* by r if it assumes the value *true* or the value *unknown*;

- not satisfied (or violated) if it assumes the value *false*.

Clearly, strong satisfaction is a strictly stronger concept than weak satisfaction, thus justifying the respective names.

r_1

A	B	C
1	1	1
2	1	ϕ
1	ϕ	1

r_2

A	B	C
1	1	ϕ
1	1	1

r_3

A	B	C
1	1	1
1	1	2
ϕ	2	ϕ

Figure 6.12. Relations for Example 6.4

Example 6.4   Let us consider the relations in Figure 6.12: the FD $f : AB \rightarrow C$ is strongly satisfied by r_1, because all substitutions of null values generate null-free relations that satisfy f. At the same time, f is weakly satisfied by r_2, because if the null value is replaced by 1, then f is satisfied, while f is violated if the null is replaced by any other value. Finally, r_3 violates f, because of its first two tuples, which are invariant with respect to any substitution.

If the domains are infinite, then the two forms of satisfaction can be characterized as follows.

LEMMA 6.1   A relation $r(XYZ)$ strongly satisfies an FD $X \rightarrow Y$ if and only if for every pair of tuples $t_1, t_2 \in r$, one of the following conditions holds:

- for some attribute $A \in X$, t_1 and t_2 are A-total and not equal; or
- for every attribute $A \in Y$, t_1 and t_2 are A-total and equal.   □

LEMMA 6.2   A relation $r(XYZ)$ weakly satisfies an FD $X \rightarrow Y$ if and only if for every pair of tuples $t_1, t_2 \in r$, one of the following conditions holds:

- for some attribute $A \in X$, t_1 and t_2 are not A-total or not equal; or
- for every attribute $A \in Y$, t_1 and t_2 are equal or one of them is not A-total.   □

The following interesting result holds for the implication problem of functional dependencies, under strong satisfaction.

THEOREM 6.3 Let F and f be, respectively, a set of FDs and an FD over a relation scheme $R(U)$. Then the following are equivalent:

1. F implies f with respect to the ordinary notion of satisfaction in null-free relations.

2. F implies f with respect to the notion of strong satisfaction in relations with null values.

PROOF   Let us first show that (1) implies (2). We proceed by showing that if (2) is false then (1) is also false; that is, if F does not imply f with respect to strong satisfaction, then F does not imply f with respect to null-free satisfaction. If F does not imply f with respect to strong satisfaction, then there is a relation r (possibly with null values) that strongly satisfies F and does not strongly satisfy f. Then there must be some null-free relation r', obtained by substitution from r, that satisfies F and does not satisfy f. But this means that F does not imply f with respect to null-free satisfaction.
To show that (2) implies (1), assume that condition (2) holds. Let r be a null-free relation over $R(U)$ satisfying F; if we consider it as a relation (possibly) with nulls, it strongly satisfies F, and so, by (2), it strongly satisfies f. Clearly, this means that it satisfies f.   □

We invite the reader to note that the above proof does not use any concept specific to FDs, and so, for any constraint for which we defined a notion of strong satisfaction, we could derive the analogous result.

Theorem 6.3 has the important consequence that all the results we proved in Chapter 3 about FDs in null-free relations also hold for relations with null values, if we are interested in strong satisfaction.

With respect to weak satisfaction, a simple counterexample shows that the analogue of Theorem 6.3 does not hold. Consider the relation in Figure 6.13, which weakly satisfies the FDs $A \to B$ and $B \to C$, but violates $A \to C$. Essentially, this is due to the fact that any null-free relation obtained from r by substitution satisfies $A \to B$ if and only if it violates $B \to C$.

The example also shows that weak satisfaction presents a property that we have never encountered before: two FDs, considered separately, are weakly satisfied, but there is no null-free relation obtained

r	A	B	C
	1	ϕ	1
	1	ϕ	2

Figure 6.13. A counterexample for the transitivity rule for weak satisfaction

by substitution that satisfies both of them. The two FDs, considered together, are not weakly satisfied. Let us say that a notion of satisfaction is *additive* for a class of constraints if satisfaction (according to that notion) of two sets of constraints C_1 and C_2 implies satisfaction of the joint set $C_1 \cup C_2$. Then ordinary satisfaction of all the classes of constraints over null-free relations we saw in Chapters 3 and 4 is additive, whereas weak satisfaction of FDs (and of other constraints) is not. Therefore, before even studying the implication of weak satisfaction, it is meaningful to study a problem connected with weak satisfaction: Given a relation r and a set F of FDs, each of which is weakly satisfied by r, does r weakly satisfy the whole set F? That is, does there exist a null-free relation r', obtained from r by substitution, that satisfies all FDs in F?

If the domains are assumed to be infinite, then the above problem can be solved by using tableaux and the chase algorithm. Given a relation with null values r and a set of FDs F, we build a tableau T_r obtained from r by replacing each null with a distinct ndv. Then the characterization of weak satisfaction is based on the result of the application of the chase to T_r, as stated by the following theorem.

THEOREM 6.4 A relation r weakly satisfies a set of FDs F if and only if the tableau $CHASE_F(T_r)$ satisfies F.

PROOF
If. Let $CHASE_F(T_r)$ satisfy F. Then, by replacing each variable in it by means of a distinct constant (and this is possible because the domains are infinite), we obtain a null-free relation that satisfies F.
Only if. If r weakly satisfies F, then there is a null-free relation r_s, obtained from r by substitution, that satisfies F. Since all the

variables in T_r are distinct, there is a containment mapping ψ from T_r to r_s, and so, by Lemma 4.2, we have that $CHASE_F(T_r)$ satisfies F.

$\square$

With respect to the implication problem, the relation in Figure 6.13 shows that rule FD3 (extended transitivity) is not sound; conversely, rules FD1 (reflexivity) and FD2 (decomposition), are sound, as is the following rule:

FD4 *(Extended) union*: **if** $XZ \rightarrow Y$, $X \rightarrow W$, **then** $XZ \rightarrow YW$

The next theorem guarantees their completeness. Its proof is left as an exercise.

THEOREM 6.5 The set of inference rules {FD1, FD2, FD4} is sound and complete with respect to the implication of FDs with respect to weak satisfaction.

$\square$

As we did in Section 3.3 for classic FDs, we could devise efficient algorithms for the implication problem. We just say that we can proceed exactly in the same way, with an algorithm to compute the closure of a set of attributes with respect to a set of FDs (somehow different from Algorithm 3.1; we leave as an exercise its complete specification), and to be used in the test for implication.

FDs and Nonexistent and No-Information Values

When dealing with nonexistent or no-information values, the notion of null substitution is not meaningful.

To handle FDs in these frameworks and define their satisfaction, we can argue as follows. Let us consider a relation $r(U)$, an FD $X \rightarrow Y$ with $XY \subseteq U$, and two tuples $t_1, t_2 \in r$.

- We want our definition to be an extension of that referring to null-free relations, and therefore r must violate $X \rightarrow Y$ if t_1 and t_2 are both XY-total, agree on X, and disagree on Y (that is, $t_1[X] = t_2[X]$ and $t_1[Y] \neq t_2[Y]$).

r_2	Course	Section	Instructor
	CS101	ϕ	White
	CS101	ϕ	Jones
	CS201	A	ϕ
	CS201	B	ϕ

r_1	Employee	Child	Telephone
	Smith	Mike	332-2341
	Smith	Paul	ϕ

Figure 6.14. Relations for the examples on NFDs

- If $t_1[X] = t_2[X]$, but with some null value involved, it does not seem necessary to require $t_1[Y] = t_2[Y]$.

- If $t_1[X] = t_2[X]$ without nulls, and for some A in Y, $t_1[A]$ is null and $t_2[A]$ is specified (or vice versa), then the FD must be violated (because different information is available with respect to A in the two tuples, as opposed to the intuitive definition of FD as a functional relationship).

- If $t_1[X] = t_2[X]$ without nulls, and $t_1[A]$ and $t_2[A]$ are both nulls, then it is reasonable to say that there is no violation (because the same information is available about $t_1[A]$ and $t_2[A]$).

Synthesizing, we can say that a *functional dependency with null values (NFD)* is satisfied by a relation r (possibly containing null values) if for every pair of tuples t_1, t_2 in r without null values on X and such that $t_1[X] = t_2[X]$, we have $t_1[Y] = t_2[Y]$.

As an example, consider the two relations in Figure 6.14: r_1 does not satisfy the NFD $E(mployee) \rightarrow T(elephone)$, because the two tuples have the same E-value and different T-values, one of them being null. On the other hand, relation r_2 satisfies the NFD $C(ourse)$ $S(ection) \rightarrow I(nstructor)$, because there is no pair of tuples with the same nonnull CS-values (the first two tuples have the same CS-values, but with a null).

Considering now the implication problem for NFDs, we can see that, again, it is different from the implication problem for FDs. The counterexample is the same used for weak satisfaction: relation r in

A	B	C	D
1	ϕ	1	ϕ
1	ϕ	ϕ	2

Figure 6.15. A counterexample that proves nonequivalence of NFDs and weak satisfaction of FDs

Figure 6.13 satisfies the NFDs $A \to B$, $B \to C$, whereas it violates the NFD $A \to C$, thus showing that the inference rule of transitivity is not sound for NFDs. On the other hand, it is evident that rules FD1 (extended reflexivity), FD2 (decomposition), and FD4 (extended union) are sound. The next theorem (whose proof is again left as an exercise) guarantees their completeness. Let us note that this result does not follow directly from Theorem 6.5, because the two notions of weak satisfaction for FDs with unknown nulls and satisfaction of FDs for no-information nulls are not equivalent from the syntactic point of view, as the relation in Figure 6.15 shows, with respect to the FD $A \to C$.

THEOREM 6.6 The set of inference rules {FD1, FD2, FD4} is sound and complete with respect to the implication of NFDs. □

Clearly, since the inference rules are the same, the algorithms for NFDs are the same as those for FDs with respect to weak satisfaction.

Before concluding the section, we present two lemmas that will be referred to in the next chapter; their proofs are left as exercises.

LEMMA 6.3 Let F and G be equivalent sets of NFDs. Then, for every $Y \to A \in F$, there is an NFD $Z \to A \in G$ such that $Z \subseteq Y$. □

LEMMA 6.4 For every set F of NFDs there is one and only one nonredundant cover H. Also, it is the case that $H \subseteq F$. □

r_1	Employee#	Salary	Telephone
	543276	25000	332-2341
	756321	35000	654-7643
	335271	55000	ϕ

Figure 6.16. A relation without nulls in the key

Constraints on Null Values: Existence Constraints

In the previous subsections, we have studied FDs (and said something about other dependencies) on relations with null values; thus, we have tried to extend to relations with null values notions already defined for null-free relations. In this final subsection, we want to mention that there also exist classes of constraints that explicitly refer to relations with null values and are trivial or not meaningful in null-free relations.

In many situations it is reasonable to control the presence of null values in the tuples of our relations. For example, as we said in Section 1.3, it is common to require the primary key of every relation to be null-free. In the relation in Figure 6.16, it would be very unreasonable to have null values for the attribute *Employee#*, which is the primary key of the relation.

In other situations, the presence or absence of null values for some attributes may be related to their presence or absence for some other attributes. For example, in the relation in Figure 6.17, it is reasonable to require a first name to be present only if the corresponding last name is present.

A constraint that allows us to handle situations of this kind is the *existence constraint*, defined as follows. Consider a relation scheme $R(U)$, and let $XY \subseteq U$. A relation r over R satisfies the *existence constraint (EC)* $e : X \vdash Y$, if each X-total tuple $t \in r$ is also Y-total. If Y is the empty set, then the EC is assumed satisfied. If X is empty, then the constraint requires all tuples to have specified values on all the attributes in Y.

Thus, the example in Figure 6.16 can be handled by the EC $\emptyset \vdash$

Department	HeadFirstName	HeadLastName
CS	Mike	Smith
EE	ϕ	Robinson
IE	ϕ	ϕ

Figure 6.17. An example for the definition of ECs

Employee#, and the one in Figure 6.17 by the EC *HeadFirstName* ⊢ *HeadLastName*.

With respect to implication, we have the following theorem, which shows the interesting property that existence constraints have essentially the same inference rules as FDs in null-free relations. The proof, similar to that of Theorem 3.1, is left as an exercise.

THEOREM 6.7 The inference rules obtained from FD1–FD3 by replacing the symbol "→" of FD with the symbol " ⊢" of EC, form a sound and complete set of inference rules for the derivation of ECs. □

Theorem 6.7 has the important consequence that most of the theory developed for FDs (including closure and implication algorithms) can be extended to ECs with no further effort.

Exercises

6.1 Show how the first-order logic formalizations for the nulls can handle situations where nulls of different sorts are present.

6.2 Prove the equivalence of the first-order logic formalization of the no-information value and the logical disjunction of the unknown and nonexistent values.

6.3 Show why the number of substitutions required to apply the null substitution principle grows exponentially with the number of occurrences of the null value ϕ.

6.4 Prove Lemmas 6.1 and 6.2, explaining why the hypothesis on nonfiniteness of the domains is essential.

6.5 Give a complete explanation of the basis part of the induction proof of Theorem 6.1.

6.6 Complete the induction step of the proof of Theorem 6.1.

6.7 State and prove the analogue of Theorem 6.1 when the terms have the form $x\theta y$, where x, y are constants from a domain or null values, and θ is a comparison operator.

6.8 Give the notions of strong and weak satisfaction for inclusion dependencies in databases with null values, and prove the analogue of Theorem 6.3.

6.9 Prove the following claim: Given a set F of FDs, weakly satisfied by a relation r, if there exists a null-free relation r', obtained from r by means of substitutions, that satisfies F, then r' satisfies all FDs implied by F with respect to null-free implication.

6.10 Show the soundness of the inference rules for FDs under weak satisfaction.

6.11 Show the analogue of Algorithm 3.1 for FDs under weak satisfaction; that is, an algorithm that computes the closure of a set of attributes with respect to a set of FDs under weak satisfaction.

6.12 Show the soundness of the inference rules for NFDs.

6.13 Study the implication for the joint class of NFDs and ECs.

Comments and References

The unknown null value, with the extension of relational algebra by means of three-valued logic and the null substitution principle, is extensively discussed by Codd [81]; some of the problems presented by the approach are shown by Grant [117]. The whole idea is extended and further discussed by Biskup [51,52]. In a formal context based on denotational semantics, Vassiliou [224,226] considers at the same time the unknown and nonexistent values. The nonexistent value is also studied by Lien [152] and Lerat and Lipski [151], whereas the no-information value is studied by Zaniolo [233,235], Keller [134], Atzeni and Morfuni [29,28], and, in a different context, by Atzeni and De Bernardis [26].

With respect to the generalizations of null values, the partially specified value is deeply studied by Lipski [155,156], while the approach based on probabilities is due to Wong [230].

The use of indices to distinguish nulls from each other was proposed, in different contexts, by Korth and Ullman [145], Maier [160], Sagiv [191], and Imielinski and Lipski [125].

A number of algebraic operators have been proposed that are significant only for relations with null values. They include *augmentation*, a unary operator that produces a relation on the attributes of the operand plus some others, and whose tuples are the tuples of the operand extended by means of nulls; *outer (natural) join* [148], a generalization of the natural join whose result receives contributions from all tuples in the operands; *total projection* [191], a projection followed by the elimination of the tuples that contain nulls (we will see this operator again in the context of the weak instance model in Chapter 7). It is easy to show that these operators can be expressed by means of expressions involving classical operators and constant relations (involving nulls).

The study of FDs for unknown nulls is essentially due to Vassiliou [225]; his results are closely related to the results on the satisfaction of FDs as interrelational constraints, obtained by Honeyman [120], which we discussed in Chapter 4. Another approach to dependencies (of any kind) is presented by Imielinski and Lipski [126]. With respect to the no-information value, FDs are treated by Lien [153] and Atzeni and Morfuni [28,29], who also consider the interaction of FDs with constraints on null values. Existence constraints are from Maier [160]. Other constraints on null values are the *objects* proposed by Sciore [198], and the *disjunctive existence constraints* studied by Maier [160], Goldstein [113], and Atzeni and Morfuni [29].

Chapter 7

The Weak Instance Approach

We have seen in Chapter 5 that it is common during the design of a database to decompose, for the sake of normalization, a relation scheme R into two or more relation schemes $R_1, \ldots, R_n$ that adequately represent R. However, the relation scheme R is the result of the modeling activity, and therefore it may represent the application requirements more closely than the normalized schemes. Also, the new database scheme may be more complex (at least because it includes more relation schemes), and queries would usually involve longer expressions, often based on the same sequences of joins. Therefore, in some cases it may be undesirable for users to have to know details of the decomposition: it would be useful to allow queries based on the relation scheme R (which does not really exist), thus liberating users from the need to know about the decomposition. Similarly, it may be reasonable to perform updates by inserting or deleting tuples (possibly defined on a proper subset of the attributes) without referring to the decomposition. The *weak instance approach*, based on the notions of weak and representative instances introduced in Chapter 4, provides a framework that allows the user to refer to the original relation scheme and maps the external requests for queries or updates to the actual decomposed scheme. As often happens, the basic idea is quite natural, but some development is required to obtain a general and consistent framework.

This chapter is devoted to the presentation of the approach and to the characterization of the main properties. It is organized as follows. In Section 7.1 we present the weak instance approach to query answering, with a definition and a characterization. In Section 7.2 we demonstrate how the information content of a database instance can be represented by the set of its weak instances, and discuss a notion of equivalence and a lattice on the partition induced by this equivalence. These notions are important for two reasons: (1) they clarify the semantics of the query-answering mechanism, and (2) they give the basis for subsequent notions related to decompositions and to updates. In Section 7.3 a notion of the adequacy of decompositions based on the weak instance approach is introduced, and its relationships with the notions introduced in Chapter 4 are shown. In Section 7.4 the weak instance approach to updates is presented, with its main properties. In Section 7.5 a formulation of the weak instance approach based on logical theories is shown that gives a good insight into its foundations; specifically, it confirms that each tuple in each relation should be considered as existentially quantified with respect to the attributes in the universe and not in its scheme. In Section 7.6, we argue that this fact is undesirable, and another formulation of the weak instance approach, which preserves its main properties, is described.

7.1   Query Answering with Weak Instances

We introduce the approach by discussing an example.[1] Consider a database scheme $\mathbf{R} = \{[R(U), F]\}$ in which $U = EDCMSP$ (the attributes *Employee, Department, Category, Manager, Salary,* and *Project* are abbreviated with the respective initials), and F contains the FDs $E \rightarrow CDM$, $D \rightarrow M$, $M \rightarrow D$, $C \rightarrow S$. A decomposed, normalized scheme $\mathbf{S}$ contains four relation schemes:

$$[R_0(EP), \{\}]$$
$$[R_1(ECD), \{E \rightarrow CD\}]$$
$$[R_2(CS), \{C \rightarrow S\}]$$
$$[R_3(DM), \{D \rightarrow M, M \rightarrow D\}]$$

[1] For the sake of simplicity, we assume that the original database scheme contains only one relation scheme. In general it contains more, and each of them can be decomposed, but the extension is straightforward.

r_0	Employee	Project		r_1	Employee	Category	Dept
	Smith	A			Smith	1	CS
	Smith	B			Adams	3	EE
	Jones	B			White	5	EE

S

r_2	Category	Salary
	1	20K
	2	25K
	3	30K
	4	35K

r_3	Department	Manager
	CS	Black
	IE	Brown

Figure 7.1. An instance for a decomposed scheme

$\bowtie_S (s)$

Employee	Proj	Dept	Mgr	Category	Salary
Smith	A	CS	Black	1	20K
Smith	B	CS	Black	1	20K

Figure 7.2. The join of the instance in Figure 7.1

In fact, S is in BCNF and is a δ-adequate representation of R since (1) it represents the FDs in F; (2) it is independent; and (3) it is a lossless decomposition of R.

Consider the instance s of S shown in Figure 7.1. It is legal and so globally consistent. Clearly, there is no instance of R that represents exactly the same information: the instance r obtained as $\bowtie_S (s)$ (shown in Figure 7.2) does not embody the information represented by the dangling tuples. However, if a query involves a proper subset of the given set of attributes U, then it is often reasonable to return also information that cannot be derived from the join of all the relations in the current instance. For example, if the query is about employees and their departments and salaries, for example, "List names and departments of the employees that earn more than 22K," then it is reasonable to consider all the employees whose salary and department are known (Figure 7.3) and then select those that satisfy the condition

Employee	Dept	Salary
Smith	CS	20K
Adams	EE	30K

Figure 7.3. An intermediate result for a query

Employee	Dept
Adams	EE

Figure 7.4. The result of a query

(Figure 7.4). Clearly, the result in Figure 7.4 cannot be obtained from the join of the relations in the database instance (Figure 7.2): it is the intermediate result in Figure 7.3 that allows us to include the tuple about Adams in the result.

The idea shown in the example is indeed general: more information is available if for each query we consider only the attributes actually involved and all the available tuples over them. The approach can be structured by saying that the answer to each query that virtually refers to the original relation can be generated by means of a two-step procedure:

1. *Binding*, which produces a relation x over the set of attributes X actually involved in the query; x is often called the *window* over X and is indicated with $[X](\mathbf{s})$. If the database instance is clear from the context, then we just write $[X]$.

2. *Evaluation*, which performs the specific operations involved in the query (often just a selection followed by a projection).

In the example, the relation in Figure 7.3 is the window $[EDS]$ over EDS, and the final result is obtained as $\pi_{ED}(\sigma_{S>22K}([EDS]))$.

Clearly, the evaluation step, though specific for each query, can be implemented by means of ordinary relational algebra (or calculus) expressions. In contrast, the binding step is typical of this approach, and is independent of the specific evaluation step, in the sense that it depends only on the involved attributes. Therefore, the crucial point is the definition of the window $[X]$ for any given set of attributes X. We can argue as follows. The decomposed database scheme $\mathbf{S}$ is an adequate decomposition of the original scheme $\mathbf{R}$, and therefore its instances should somehow correspond to instances of $\mathbf{R}$. Now, for each join-consistent instance $\mathbf{s}$ of $\mathbf{S}$, that is, $\mathbf{s} \in U(\mathbf{S})$, there is (by definition) an instance $\mathbf{r} \in L(\mathbf{R})$ such that $\mathbf{s} = \pi_{\mathbf{S}}(\mathbf{r})$. For these instances, it is therefore reasonable to consider $[X]$ to be defined as $\pi_X(r)$ (where $\mathbf{r} = \{r\}$). However, for each instance $\mathbf{s} \in L(\mathbf{S}) - U(\mathbf{S})$, there is no such r, but in most interesting cases, there is something similar: if $\mathbf{s}$ is globally consistent, then there is a weak instance for $\mathbf{s}$ (usually many more, and infinitely many if the domains are infinite). The argument does not apply for the instances that satisfy the local constraints but are not globally consistent. We believe that this is not a problem, since $\mathbf{S}$ is the decomposition of a database scheme with a single relation scheme, and so it is reasonable to consider the information embodied in its instances as a whole; also, if $\mathbf{S}$ is independent, then no instance falls in this category. As we know, if a database instance $\mathbf{s}$ is globally consistent, then there are many weak instances for it. Each of them embodies the information in $\mathbf{s}$, plus some more. In a sense, we may assume that the information in a database instance is represented by the set of all its weak instances.

Let us formalize this concept. Unless otherwise specified, we refer to a database scheme $\mathbf{S}$, with n relation schemes, $[R_i(X_i), F_i]$, for $i = 1, ..., n$, where F_i is a set of FDs over X_i. Also, $F = \cup_{i=1}^{n} F_i$, $U = \cup_{i=1}^{n} X_i$ (U is called the *universe*), and $W(\mathbf{S})$ is the set of globally consistent instances of $\mathbf{S}$, that is, the set of instances of $\mathbf{S}$ that have a weak instance with respect to F. Finally, for every instance $\mathbf{s} \in W(\mathbf{S})$, $WEAK(\mathbf{s})$ indicates the set of weak instances of $\mathbf{s}$, $T_{\mathbf{s}}$ the state tableau of $\mathbf{s}$, and $RI(\mathbf{s})$ the representative instance of $\mathbf{s}$, that is, the tableau obtained by chasing the state tableau: $RI(\mathbf{s}) = CHASE_F(T_{\mathbf{s}})$.

Then we can define the *window* $[X](\mathbf{s})$ over a set of attributes X, for a consistent instance $\mathbf{s}$ of $\mathbf{S}$, as the set of tuples on X that belong to every weak instance of $\mathbf{s}$:

$$[X] = \bigcap_{w \in WEAK(\mathbf{s})} (\pi_X(w))$$

Employee	Proj	Dept	Mgr	Category	Salary
Smith	A	CS	Black	1	20K
Smith	B	CS	Black	1	20K
Jones	B	ϕ_1	ϕ_2	ϕ_3	ϕ_4
Smith	ϕ_5	CS	Black	1	20K
Adams	ϕ_6	EE	ϕ_7	3	30K
White	ϕ_8	EE	ϕ_7	5	ϕ_9
ϕ_{10}	ϕ_{11}	ϕ_{12}	ϕ_{13}	1	20K
ϕ_{14}	ϕ_{15}	ϕ_{16}	ϕ_{17}	2	25K
ϕ_{18}	ϕ_{19}	ϕ_{20}	ϕ_{21}	3	30K
ϕ_{22}	ϕ_{23}	ϕ_{24}	ϕ_{25}	4	35K
ϕ_{26}	ϕ_{27}	CS	Black	ϕ_{28}	ϕ_{29}
ϕ_{30}	ϕ_{31}	IE	Brown	ϕ_{32}	ϕ_{33}

Figure 7.5. The representative instance of the database in Figure 7.1

It can be seen that the relation in Figure 7.3 is actually the set of tuples over EDS that belong to every weak instance of the database in Figure 7.1. At the same time, if we compute the representative instance $RI(\mathbf{s})$ of the database $\mathbf{s}$ in Figure 7.1, we obtain the tableau in Figure 7.5; we see that the EDS-total tuples it contains correspond to the tuples in the relation on EDS in Figure 7.3. This is not a coincidence. In fact, it is always the case that the window over a set of attributes equals the *total projection* of the representative instance over those attributes, where the total projection $\pi^\downarrow_X(T)$ of a tableau T over a set of attributes X is defined as the set of total tuples in the projection of T on X:

$$\pi^\downarrow_X(T) = \{t \mid t \in \pi_X(T) \text{ and } t \text{ is total}\}$$

The following theorem states and proves this claim.

THEOREM 7.1   For every $\mathbf{s} \in W(\mathbf{S})$, for every $X \subseteq U$, it is the case that

$$\bigcap_{w \in WEAK(\mathbf{s})} (\pi_X(w)) = \pi^\downarrow_X(RI(\mathbf{s}))$$

PROOF   We prove containment in the two directions.

- *If $t \in \pi_X(w)$ for every $w \in \text{WEAK}(\mathbf{s})$, then $t \in \pi^\downarrow_X(\text{RI}(\mathbf{s}))$.* As we said in the proof of Theorem 4.5, the relations obtained by replacing each variable in $\text{RI}(\mathbf{s})$ with a distinct constant are weak instances. If t belongs to the X-projection of each of them, then it belongs to the portion that is common to all of them, that is, the X-total projection of $\text{RI}(\mathbf{s})$.

- *If $t \in \pi^\downarrow_X(\text{RI}(\mathbf{s}))$, then $t \in \pi_X(w)$ for every $w \in \text{WEAK}(\mathbf{s})$.* Let $w \in \text{WEAK}(\mathbf{s})$; by Lemma 4.3, there is a containment mapping ψ from the state tableau $T_\mathbf{s}$ of $\mathbf{s}$ to w. Then, by Lemma 4.2, ψ is also a containment mapping from $\text{RI}(\mathbf{s})$ to w. Now, if $t \in \pi^\downarrow_X(\text{RI}(\mathbf{s}))$, then there is an X-total tuple $t' \in \text{RI}(\mathbf{s})$ such that $t'[X] = t$. By definition of containment mapping, $\psi(t') \in w$, and $\psi(t')[X] = t'[X] = t$, and so $t \in \pi_X(w)$. $\qquad\square$

Theorem 7.1 establishes another relationship between weak and representative instances and confirms the robustness of the definition of the window.

7.2 Equivalence and Completeness of Database Instances

In this section we formalize and elaborate on the claim made in the previous section that the information in a database instance can be considered as represented by the set of its weak instances. A first observation to be made is that there may be database instances of the same scheme that have exactly the same weak instances; an example is given by the two instances $\mathbf{s}_1$ and $\mathbf{s}_2$ in Figure 7.6, which refer to a scheme $\mathbf{S}$ with two relation schemes, $[R_1(CSI), \{C \to I\}]$ and $[R_2(CSP), \{S \to P\}]$. We say that two database instances $\mathbf{s}_1$, $\mathbf{s}_2$ are *equivalent* (in symbols, $\mathbf{s}_1 \sim \mathbf{s}_2$) if they have the same set of weak instances; the property is clearly reflexive, symmetric, and transitive, and so it is actually an equivalence relation. Similarly, we say that $\mathbf{s}_1$ is *weaker* than $\mathbf{s}_2$ ($\mathbf{s}_1 \preceq \mathbf{s}_2$) if each weak instance of $\mathbf{s}_2$ is also a weak instance of $\mathbf{s}_1$. The following lemma and the subsequent theorem confirm the robustness of these two notions, as they show their respective equivalence to other meaningful conditions.

r_1	Course	Student	Instr
	CS101	Smith	White
	MA101	Jones	Black

r_2	Course	Student	Program
	CS101	Jones	CS
	MA101	Smith	EE

s_1

r_1	Course	Student	Instr
	CS101	Jones	White
	MA101	Smith	Black

r_2	Course	Student	Program
	CS101	Smith	EE
	MA101	Jones	CS

s_2

Figure 7.6. A pair of equivalent database instances

LEMMA 7.1 If s_1 and s_2 are globally consistent instances of **S**, then the following conditions are equivalent:

1. $s_1 \preceq s_2$

2. There is a containment mapping from $RI(s_1)$ to $RI(s_2)$

3. $[X](s_1) \subseteq [X](s_2)$, for every $X \subseteq U$

PROOF We show the following chain of implications: $(1) \Rightarrow (3) \Rightarrow (2) \Rightarrow (1)$.

- *(1) ⇒ (3).* Assume that $WEAK(s_2) \subseteq WEAK(s_1)$, and let $t \in [X](s_1)$; we show that $t \in [X](s_2)$. In fact, it suffices to show that $t \in \pi_X(w)$ for every $w \in WEAK(s_2)$. Consider the generic $w \in WEAK(s_2)$. By (1), we have $w \in WEAK(s_1)$, and so, since $t \in [X](s_1) = \cap_{w \in WEAK(s_1)}(\pi_X(w))$, we have $t \in \pi_X(w)$.

- *(3) ⇒ (2).* We show that if $[X](s_1) \subseteq [X](s_2)$ for every $X \subseteq U$, then there is a containment mapping from $RI(s_1)$ to $RI(s_2)$. By Theorem 7.1, if for every $X \subseteq U$, $[X](s_1) \subseteq [X](s_2)$, we have that for every $X \subseteq U$, $\pi^{\downarrow}_X(RI(s_1)) \subseteq \pi^{\downarrow}_X(RI(s_2))$. Now, consider the state tableau T_{s_1} of s_1. We have that for every $X \subseteq U$, $\pi^{\downarrow}_X(T_{s_1}) \subseteq \pi^{\downarrow}_X(RI(s_1))$, and so $\pi^{\downarrow}_X(T_{s_1}) \subseteq \pi^{\downarrow}_X(RI(s_2))$. We claim that as a consequence, there is a containment mapping from T_{s_1} to $RI(s_2)$. Since all variables in T_{s_1} are distinct, it suffices to show that for every tuple $t \in T_{s_1}$ originating from $r_{1,i} \in s_1$, there is a tuple $t' \in RI(s_2)$ such that $t[X_i] = t'[X_i]$;

but this follows from the fact that $\pi^{\downarrow}{}_X(T_{\mathbf{s}_1}) \subseteq \pi^{\downarrow}{}_X(RI(\mathbf{s}_2))$, for every $X \subseteq U$. Then the existence of the containment mapping from $RI(\mathbf{s}_1)$ to $RI(\mathbf{s}_2)$ follows, by Lemma 4.2, from the existence of the containment mapping from $T_{\mathbf{s}_1}$ to $RI(\mathbf{s}_2)$ and the fact that $RI(\mathbf{s}_1) = CHASE_F(T_{\mathbf{s}_1})$.

- *(2) ⇒ (1).* We show that if there is a containment mapping from $RI(\mathbf{s}_1)$ to $RI(\mathbf{s}_2)$, then every weak instance of $\mathbf{s}_2$ is also a weak instance of $\mathbf{s}_1$. By Lemma 4.3, if w is a weak instance of $\mathbf{s}_2$, then there is a containment mapping from $T_{\mathbf{s}_2}$ to w. Then, by Lemma 4.2, there is a containment mapping from $RI(\mathbf{s}_2)$ to w. Thus, by transitivity of containment mappings, there is also a containment mapping from $RI(\mathbf{s}_1)$ to w. Finally, by Lemma 4.4, from this condition and the fact that w satisfies F (since it is a weak instance for $\mathbf{s}_2$), we have that w is a weak instance of $\mathbf{s}_1$.

$\square$

A couple of definitions are useful here. Two database instances are *query-equivalent* (in the weak instance approach) if for every $X \subseteq U$, their windows over X are equal. Two tableaux T_1 and T_2 are *tableau-equivalent* (or simply *equivalent*) if there exist both a containment mapping from T_1 to T_2 and a containment mapping from T_2 to T_1.

THEOREM 7.2 If $\mathbf{s}_1$ and $\mathbf{s}_2$ are globally consistent instances of $\mathbf{S}$, then the following conditions are equivalent:

1. $\mathbf{s}_1$ and $\mathbf{s}_2$ are equivalent

2. $RI(\mathbf{s}_1)$ and $RI(\mathbf{s}_2)$ are tableau-equivalent

3. $\mathbf{s}_1$ and $\mathbf{s}_2$ are query-equivalent

PROOF   The proof follows from Lemma 7.1 and the above definitions.

$\square$

The two instances in Figure 7.6 have exactly the same representative instance, shown in Figure 7.7. This is a coincidence, due to the fact that in this case all variables are promoted to constants. It is interesting to note that if we perform the total projections of this representative instance on the relation schemes in $\mathbf{S}$ (by extending the

Course	Student	Instr	Program
CS101	Smith	White	EE
MA101	Jones	Black	CS
CS101	Jones	White	CS
MA101	Smith	Black	EE

Figure 7.7. The representative instance for the database instances in Figure 7.6

	r_1	Course	Student	Instr	r_2	Course	Student	Program
s		CS101	Smith	White		CS101	Smith	EE
		MA101	Jones	Black		MA101	Jones	CS
		CS101	Jones	White		CS101	Jones	CS
		MA101	Smith	Black		MA101	Smith	EE

Figure 7.8. The total projection of the representative instance in Figure 7.7 on the database scheme

notation π_S used in Chapter 4, we indicate it with $\pi^{\downarrow}s$, and call it the *total projection on the database scheme*), we obtain the database instance **s** in Figure 7.8, whose relations are supersets of the corresponding relations in both s_1 and s_2. The instance **s** is equivalent to s_1 and s_2, and so its representative instance is the tableau in Figure 7.7. Therefore, **s** equals the total projection of its own representative instance on the database scheme. This property, which is not enjoyed by s_1 nor by s_2, is rather interesting, because it corresponds to the fact that each relation embodies all the relevant information: if a database instance does not satisfy it, then there is information corresponding to some relation scheme that can be derived from information in other relations. Therefore, we say that a database instance **s** is *complete* if $\mathbf{s} = \pi^{\downarrow}s(RI(\mathbf{s}))$. It turns out that for each instance $\mathbf{s} \in W(\mathbf{S})$, there is one and only one complete equivalent instance $\mathbf{s}^*$, which can be obtained as $\mathbf{s}^* = \pi^{\downarrow}s(RI(\mathbf{s}))$. Another interesting property, whose proof is also left as an exercise, is stated in the next lemma, which adds another condition to Lemma 7.1, and so to Theorem 7.2.

LEMMA 7.2 Let $s_1 = \{r_{1,1}, \ldots, r_{1,n}\}$ and $s_2 = \{r_{2,1}, \ldots, r_{2,n}\}$ be globally consistent, complete instances of S. Then the following conditions are equivalent:

1. $s_1 \preceq s_2$

2. There is a containment mapping from $RI(s_1)$ to $RI(s_2)$

3. $[X](s_1) \subseteq [X](s_2)$, for every $X \subseteq U$

4. $r_{1,i} \subseteq r_{2,i}$, for $i = 1, \ldots, n$ $\square$

It is interesting to note that the relation $\preceq$ is not a partial order on the set of all consistent instances, because it is not antisymmetric. However, on the set of the complete instances, it is a partial order, as it is reflexive, antisymmetric, and transitive. With a technical modification, $\preceq$ can become a *complete lattice* on the set of complete instances. Let us first recall a few definitions from lattice theory. Given a set $\mathcal{D}$, with a partial order $\leq$, a *lower bound* of two elements d_1 and d_2 is an element d such that $d \leq d_1$ and $d \leq d_2$. The *greatest lower bound (glb)* of d_1 and d_2 is a lower bound d of d_1 and d_2 such that for every other lower bound d' of d_1 and d_2 it is the case that $d' \leq d$. It follows that if there is a glb, it is unique. The *least upper bound (lub)* of d_1 and d_2 is defined dually: d is an *upper bound* of d_1 and d_2 if $d_1 \leq d$ and $d_2 \leq d$; d is the lub if it is an upper bound and for every other upper bound d', it is the case that $d \leq d'$. A known property of lattices is the associativity of both the glb and lub operations; therefore, we can speak of the glb and lub of finite sets of instances. A lattice over a domain $\mathcal{D}$ is *complete* if each (finite or infinite) subset of $\mathcal{D}$ has both a glb and a lub.

In order to show the lattice on the set of complete instances, we need to introduce a fictitious instance, needed for technical reasons. We assume that all instances that do not globally satisfy the given FDs are equivalent (and this is coherent with the definition of equivalence, as the empty set is the set of weak instances of each of them), and that there is one *complete inconsistent instance*, indicated with s_∞. Also, we assume that they all have the same representative instance, which is called the *inconsistent tableau* T_∞, and we assume that there is a containment mapping from every tableau to the inconsistent tableau.

Also, we define the total projection of the inconsistent tableau on a set of attributes X as *the inconsistent relation* over X, and we assume that the complete inconsistent instance contains inconsistent relations; clearly, it is the instance obtained by totally projecting the inconsistent tableau on the database scheme. If we assume that the inconsistent relation over X is a superset of every other relation on X, that every instance is weaker than $\mathbf{s}_\infty$, and that every inconsistent instance is equivalent to $\mathbf{s}_\infty$, we can extend Lemma 7.2 to inconsistent instances. We also assume that for every X, every tuple on X belongs to the X-total projection of the inconsistent tableau.

The next two lemmas show the existence of the glb and lub, with respect to the partial order $\preceq$, on the set of complete instances extended with the complete inconsistent instance.

LEMMA 7.3   For each set $\mathcal{R}$ of complete instances there is a glb, which is equivalent to the instance obtained as the relationwise intersection of the instances in $\mathcal{R}$.

PROOF   For every $1 \leq j \leq n$, let r_j be the relation obtained by intersecting all the relations on the scheme R_j of the instances in $\mathcal{R}$. The instance $\mathbf{s} = \{r_1, r_2, \ldots, r_n\}$ is consistent (because each weak instance for any instance in $\mathcal{R}$ is also a weak instance for it) and weaker than each of the instances in $\mathcal{R}$. For each instance $\mathbf{s}' \in \mathcal{R}$ there is a containment mapping from $T_\mathbf{s}$ to $T_{\mathbf{s}'}$, and so, by Lemma 4.2 and an observation made before it, there is a containment mapping from $RI(\mathbf{s})$ to $RI(\mathbf{s}')$; thus, the claim follows by the equivalence of properties (1) and (2) in Lemma 7.2. The instance $\mathbf{s}$ need not be complete, but the projection $\mathbf{s}_g$ of its representative instance on the database scheme is equivalent to it and complete; therefore, $\mathbf{s}_g$ is a lower bound of $\mathcal{R}$. Let $\mathbf{s}'$ be any other lower bound. Since it is complete, by the equivalence of (1) and (4) in Lemma 7.2, it follows that each of its relations is a subset of the intersection of the respective relations of the instances in $\mathcal{R}$; therefore, by the equivalence of (1) and (4) in Lemma 7.2, it is weaker than $\mathbf{s}_g$.   □

LEMMA 7.4   For each set $\mathcal{R}$ of complete instances there is a lub, which is equivalent to the instance obtained as the relationwise union of the instances in $\mathcal{R}$ or to the inconsistent instance.

PROOF   The argument is dual than that in the proof of Lemma 7.3. Instead of the intersection, we use the union: if the instance s contains infinite relations or is inconsistent, then the lub is the complete inconsistent instance s_∞; otherwise, the lub is the complete instance equivalent to s.   □

7.3   Weak Instances and Adequacy of Decompositions

In this section we show how we can define a notion of the adequacy of decompositions within the weak instance approach, based on the notion of equivalence of database instances, and closely related to the notions presented in Chapter 5.

The notion of equivalence of instances defined and studied in Section 7.2 can be extended to instances of different database schemes. Given $\mathbf{R}$ and $\mathbf{S}$, an instance $\mathbf{r} \in W(\mathbf{R})$ is equivalent to an instance $\mathbf{s} \in W(\mathbf{S})$ if every weak instance of $\mathbf{r}$ is also a weak instance of $\mathbf{s}$ and vice versa. Clearly, a necessary condition for equivalence of instances is that the two database schemes have the same universe.

Let us restrict our attention to vertical decompositions, as we did in Chapter 5, and consider a database scheme $\mathbf{R}$ with a single relation scheme $[R(U), F]$ and a database scheme $\mathbf{S} = {}^t[R_i(X_i), G_i] \mid i = 1, \ldots, n}$, with $X_1 \ldots X_n = U$. Let $G = \cup_{i=1}^n G_i$. We say that $\mathbf{S}$ is a *WI-adequate decomposition* of $\mathbf{R}$ if for every $\mathbf{r} \in W(\mathbf{R})$, there is $\mathbf{s} \in W(\mathbf{S})$ such that $\mathbf{r} \sim \mathbf{s}$.

The next theorem shows that WI-adequacy is indeed equivalent to β-adequacy. We show two useful lemmas first; their proofs are left as exercises.

LEMMA 7.5   Let $\mathbf{s} = {r_1, \ldots, r_n} \in I(\mathbf{S})$ and t be a tuple in a tableau obtained as an intermediate or final result of the chase of the state tableau T_s of $\mathbf{s}$. If t is X-total, then it originates from a tuple t' in a relation $r_i \in \mathbf{s}$ such that $X_i \to X \in G^+$.   □

LEMMA 7.6   Let $\mathbf{s} = {r_1, \ldots, r_n} \in W(\mathbf{S})$. If t is a tuple over U, and $t[X_i] \in r_i$ for $1 \leq i \leq n$, then $RI(\mathbf{s})$ contains, for $1 \leq i \leq n$, a tuple t_i

such that $t_i[X_i^+] = t[X_i^+]$ (where X_i^+ is the closure of X_i with respect to G). $\square$

THEOREM 7.3 **S** is a WI-adequate decomposition of **R** if and only if (1) $F^+ = G^+$ and (2) **S** is a lossless decomposition of **R**.

PROOF

If. For every $\mathbf{r} = \{r\} \in W(\mathbf{R})$, let $\mathbf{s} = \{r_1, \ldots, r_n\}$, with $r_i = \pi_{X_i}(r)$ for $1 \le i \le n$. We claim that $\mathbf{s} \in W(\mathbf{S})$ and $\mathbf{r} \sim \mathbf{s}$. The first statement is easy, as r is a weak instance for $\mathbf{s}$ (it satisfies F, which is equivalent to G, and its projections on the relation schemes are equal to the respective relations in $\mathbf{s}$). Equivalence of $\mathbf{r}$ and $\mathbf{s}$ is proved by showing that $\mathbf{r} \preceq \mathbf{s}$ and $\mathbf{s} \preceq \mathbf{r}$.

- $\mathbf{s} \preceq \mathbf{r}$: If w is a weak instance for $\mathbf{r}$, then it satisfies F and $w \supseteq r$; we claim that w is also a weak instance for $\mathbf{s}$:

  - w satisfies G, since it satisfies F, and F is equivalent to G; and

  - for every $1 \le i \le n$, $\pi_{X_i}(w) \supseteq r_i$, since $w \supseteq r$ and $r_i = \pi_{X_i}(r)$.

- $\mathbf{r} \preceq \mathbf{s}$: We show that, for every $X \subseteq U$, $\pi^{\downarrow}_X(RI(\mathbf{s})) \supseteq \pi^{\downarrow}_X(RI(\mathbf{r}))$; then the claim follows by the equivalence of properties (1) and (3) in Lemma 7.1. If $t \in \pi^{\downarrow}_X(RI(\mathbf{r}))$, then, since $r = RI(\mathbf{r})$, there is a tuple $t_U \in r$ such that $t_U[X] = t$. Then, since **S** is a lossless decomposition of **R**, there is, by Lemma 5.2, a relation scheme $R_i(X_i)$ in **S** such that $X_i \to U \in G^+ = F^+$. Thus, by Lemma 7.6, $t_U \in \pi^{\downarrow}_U(RI(\mathbf{s}))$, and so $t \in \pi^{\downarrow}_X(RI(\mathbf{s}))$.

Only if.

1. We show that $G^+ = F^+$ by showing the two containments in turn.

   - $G^+ \supseteq F^+$: Assume by way of contradiction that there is a relation w over U that satisfies G and violates F. By removing all guilty tuples, we can obtain a relation $w' \subset w$ that satisfies both F and G. Then consider the instance $\mathbf{r} = \{w'\}$, which belongs to $W(\mathbf{S})$, since w' satisfies F. We claim that there is no instance $\mathbf{s} \in W(\mathbf{S})$ that is equivalent to

$\mathbf{r}$: if there were such an $\mathbf{s}$, then w' would be a weak instance for $\mathbf{s}$. As a consequence, w would also be a weak instance for $\mathbf{s}$, since it satisfies G and is a superset of w'. But w is not a weak instance for $\mathbf{r}$, since it does not satisfy F, and so $\mathbf{s}$ and $\mathbf{r}$ do not have the same weak instances, which is a contradiction.

- $F^+ \supseteq G^+$: Again, by contradiction, assume that there is a relation w that satisfies F and violates G. Then for $\mathbf{r} = \{w\}$, which belongs to $W(\mathbf{R})$, since w satisfies F, there is no equivalent $\mathbf{s} \in W(\mathbf{S})$, because w violates G and so it cannot be a weak instance for any $\mathbf{s} \in W(\mathbf{S})$.

2. If $\mathbf{S}$ is not lossless, then by Lemmas 5.2 and 7.5, there is no instance $\mathbf{s} \in W(\mathbf{S})$, for which the representative instance can have U-total tuples. Then, since for every $\mathbf{r} = \{r\} \in W(\mathbf{R})$ the representative instance $RI(\mathbf{r})$ equals r, for no $\mathbf{r} \in W(\mathbf{R})$ is there an equivalent instance $\mathbf{s} \in W(\mathbf{S})$ (because by Lemma 7.1, two instances are equivalent if and only if their representative instances are tableau-equivalent). □

It should be clear that WI-adequacy does not require independence because it refers only to globally consistent instances; the other instances are considered as illegal. At the same time, efficient maintenance of constraints can be obtained with independent schemes, and so it is reasonable to require the decomposed scheme to be independent. The following corollary (which follows immediately from the definitions of β- and δ-adequacy and by Theorem 7.3) shows that these requirements, taken together, are equivalent to δ-adequacy.

COROLLARY 7.1

1. $\mathbf{S}$ is a β-adequate decomposition of $\mathbf{R}$ if and only if $\mathbf{S}$ is a WI-adequate decomposition of $\mathbf{R}$.

2. $\mathbf{S}$ is a δ-adequate decomposition of $\mathbf{R}$ if and only if $\mathbf{S}$ is a WI-adequate decomposition of $\mathbf{R}$ and $\mathbf{S}$ is independent. □

7.4   Updates Through Weak Instances

In this section we show how it is possible to update decomposed databases without referring to the individual relation schemes, but only to (a subset of) the universe. We consider insertions and deletions of tuples, defined over any subset of the universe, in the same way that queries can be defined on any subset of the universe. The general idea is that the result of an insertion (a dual approach can be taken for deletions) of a tuple in a consistent instance is a consistent instance that contains (1) the information in the original instance and (2) the information embodied in the new tuple. Part (1) can be formalized by requiring the original instance to be weaker than the result; part (2), by requiring the new tuple to appear in the appropriate total projection of the representative instance of the result.

> **Example 7.1**   If we want to insert in the instance in Figure 7.1 a tuple defined on EM, with values $Adams$ for E and $Green$ for M, we can consistently add a tuple to relation r_3, with values EE for D and $Green$ for M. Because of the dependency $D \to M$, the chase would combine the tuple $< Adams, 3, EE >$, already in r_1, with this tuple, thus generating a tuple in the representative instance with values $Adams$ for E and $Green$ for M.

In general, there are many *potential results*, with different modifications with respect to the original instance. For example, other tuples may be added to the relations besides those strictly needed to generate the new tuple as a result of queries.

> **Example 7.2**   In the insertion discussed in Example 7.1, the suggested update does not introduce any further information besides the old and the newly added. On the other hand, if we want to insert into the same instance another tuple defined on EM, but with values $Cook$ for E and $Moore$ for M, we obtain a potential result only if we add a tuple $< Cook, c, d >$ to r_1, and a tuple $< d, Moore >$ to r_3, whatever the values c and d may be (provided that the constraints are not violated). In this case, some further pieces of information (i.e., the category c and the name of the department d) have to be added, and there are several possible choices.

It makes sense to say that if there is a *minimum* potential result (that is, a result that precedes, in the partial order, all the others), then it is an "ideal" result, because it includes only information that is strictly needed. Unfortunately, the minimum result need not exist, as sometimes there may be several, incomparable "minimal" results. Therefore, we distinguish between *deterministic* and *nondeterministic* insertions, depending on the existence of the minimum result.

There are also cases where it is not possible to obtain a consistent result, because of inconsistency between the original instance and the new tuple or because of intrinsic weaknesses of the database scheme.

> **Example 7.3**   If the tuple to be inserted in Example 7.1 had values *Smith* for E and *Mason* for M, we could not find any consistent instance that would contain both the information in the original instance and that in the new tuple because, given the functional dependencies, they contradict each other, assigning two distinct managers to an employee.

> **Example 7.4**   Given the universe *Professor, Student, Course,* and the database with the relation schemes $R_1(PC)$, $R_2(SC)$, with the empty set of constraints, no total tuple over the universe can belong to the representative instance of any instance, and therefore no result can be found for any insertion of a tuple over the three attributes.

Let us formalize these concepts. We refer to our usual database scheme $\mathbf{S} = \{R_1(X_1), \ldots, R_n(X_n)\}$, with $U = X_1 X_2 \ldots X_k$, and consider an instance $\mathbf{s} \in W(\mathbf{S})$ and a tuple t over a set of attributes $X \subseteq U$, such that $t \notin [X](\mathbf{s})$. We consider the *insertion* of t into $\mathbf{s}$. An instance $\mathbf{s}_p \in I(\mathbf{S})$ is a *potential result* for the insertion of t into $\mathbf{s}$ if $\mathbf{s} \preceq \mathbf{s}_p$ and $t \in [X](\mathbf{s}_p)$.

For each instance and each tuple, there is a potential result; for example, the inconsistent instance is always a potential result. It is also possible that the inconsistent instance is the only potential result. As shown in the examples above, this may occur for very different reasons. In Example 7.4, the reason for the nonexistence of a consistent potential result is that the dependencies cannot generate any X-total tuple in the representative instance. In Example 7.3, the reason is a violation of the constraints. This gives rise to the following definitions: (1) The insertion of a tuple t in an instance $\mathbf{s}$ is *possible* if there is a consistent instance $\mathbf{s}'$ such that $t \in [X](\mathbf{s}')$. (2) A possible insertion is *consistent* if it has a consistent potential result. So, the insertion in Example 7.4 is impossible, whereas that in Example 7.3 is inconsistent.

The definition of *potential result* only requires the instance to contain the information in the original instance and that in the new tuple; any other piece of information may be included. It is interesting to consider the information that is common to all potential results: in the lattice framework described in Section 7.2, this is the glb of the potential results. It should be noted that this instance need not be a potential result. The glb of the potential results of the insertion of the tuple $<$ *Cook, Moore* $>$ in Example 7.2 is the original instance itself, which does not include the new tuple in its *ED* window. If the glb of the potential results is not a potential result, there are various minimal potential results (that is, potential results such that there is no properly weaker potential result), each of which represents a way to insert the new tuple by altering the instance as little as possible. Since each of them would have the same right to be considered as "the result" for the insertion, it is reasonable to talk of nondeterminism. We say that a possible and consistent insertion is *deterministic* if the glb of the potential results is a potential result.

Now, we give necessary and sufficient conditions for possibility, consistency, and determinism. We refer to our usual database scheme **S**, and consider a tuple t defined over a subset X of the universe U.

THEOREM 7.4 For every instance $\mathbf{s} \in W(\mathbf{S})$, the insertion of t in $\mathbf{s}$ is possible if and only if there is a relation scheme $R_i(X_i) \in \mathbf{R}$ such that F implies the FD $X_i \to X$.

PROOF
Only if. If the insertion is possible, then, by definition, there is an instance $\mathbf{s}' \in W(\mathbf{S})$ such that $t \in [X](\mathbf{s}') = \pi^\downarrow_X(RI(\mathbf{s}'))$. Then the claim follows by Lemma 7.5.
If. Let t' be any tuple obtained by extending t by means of constants to the universe U, and let $\mathbf{s}'$ be the instance obtained by projecting it on the various relation schemes. Then, since $X_i \to X$, we have, by Lemma 7.6, that $t \in [X](\mathbf{s}')$, and so the insertion is possible.   □

From Theorem 7.4 and Lemma 4.2 we have the following corollary, which confirms the importance of lossless decomposition.

COROLLARY 7.2 For every instance $s \in W(S)$, there are possible insertions over every subset X of U if and only if the database scheme $\mathbf{R}$ is a lossless decomposition of the database scheme
$$\mathbf{R}_0 = \{[R_0(U), \cup_{i=1}^n F_i]\} \qquad \square$$

We now turn our attention to consistency, assuming that the insertion is possible. Let $RI(s)$ be the representative instance of s, and $T_{s,t}$ be the tableau obtained by adding to $RI(s)$ a tuple t_e obtained by extending t to the universe U by means of unique variables.

LEMMA 7.7 For every potential result s_p, it is the case that there are a containment mapping from $T_{s,t}$ to $CHASE_F(T_{s,t})$ and a containment mapping from $CHASE_F(T_{s,t})$ to $RI(s_p)$.

PROOF We prove that there is a containment mapping from $T_{s,t}$ to $RI(s_p)$. Then the two containment mappings in the claim will follow from Lemma 4.2.
If s_p is an inconsistent instance, then its representative instance $RI(s_p)$ is the inconsistent tableau, and by definition, there is a containment mapping from $T_{s,t}$ to $RI(s_p)$. Therefore, assume s_p to be a consistent potential result for the insertion of t into s. Then by definition, we have $s \preceq s_p$, and $t \in [X](s_p)$; therefore, by Lemma 7.2, there is a containment mapping from $RI(s)$ to $RI(s_p)$, and $t \in \pi^{\downarrow}_X(RI(s_p))$. Thus, since all the variables in t_e are unique and $T_{s,t} = RI(s) \cup \{t_e\}$, there is a containment mapping from $T_{s,t}$ to $RI(s_p)$. $\qquad \square$

THEOREM 7.5 Let the insertion of t in s be possible. It is consistent if and only if $CHASE_F(T_{s,t}) \neq T_\infty$.

PROOF
Only if. Let the insertion be possible and consistent: there is a potential result s_p such that $RI(s_p) \neq T_\infty$. By Lemma 7.7, there is a containment mapping from $CHASE_F(T_{s,t})$ to $RI(s_p)$, and so, by Lemma 4.2, $CHASE_F(T_{s,t}) \neq T_\infty$.
If. Assume that the insertion is possible and that $CHASE_F(T_{s,t}) \neq T_\infty$. Consider the tableau T' obtained by changing all the variables in $CHASE_F(T_{s,t})$ to distinct constants not appearing in s nor in t, and the instance s_p obtained by projecting T' onto the various relation

schemes. By construction, $t \in \pi^{\downarrow}{}_X(T')$. Then, since the insertion is possible, by Theorem 7.4, there is a relation scheme $R_i(X_i) \in \mathbf{S}$ such that F implies the FD $X_i \to X$, and so t can be reconstructed by the chase from the projections on the database scheme of a U-total tuple that contains it. Therefore, $t \in \pi^{\downarrow}{}_X(RI(\mathbf{s}_p))$. Also, there is a containment mapping from $T_{\mathbf{s},t}$ to T', and so $\pi^{\downarrow}{}_\mathbf{S}(T_{\mathbf{s},t}) \preceq \pi^{\downarrow}{}_\mathbf{S}(T')$. Since $\mathbf{s} \preceq \pi^{\downarrow}{}_\mathbf{S}(T_{\mathbf{s},t})$ (by construction of $T_{\mathbf{s},t}$), and $\mathbf{s}_p = \pi^{\downarrow}{}_\mathbf{S}(T')$ (by definition of $\mathbf{s}_p$), it follows that $\mathbf{s} \preceq \mathbf{s}_p$, and therefore $\mathbf{s}_p$ is a consistent potential result. $\square$

We now turn our attention to the characterization of deterministic insertions. Let $\mathbf{s}_+$ be the instance obtained by (totally) projecting $CHASE_F(T_{\mathbf{s},t})$ on the database scheme: $\mathbf{s}_+ = \pi^{\downarrow}{}_\mathbf{S}(CHASE_F(T_{\mathbf{s},t}))$.

LEMMA 7.8 Let the insertion of t in $\mathbf{s}$ be possible and consistent. Then $\mathbf{s}_+$ is the glb of the potential results.

PROOF   Let us first prove that $\mathbf{s}_+$ is a lower bound of the potential results. It suffices to prove that if $\mathbf{s}_p$ is a potential result, then $\mathbf{s}_+$ is weaker than $\mathbf{s}_p$. We have that there are containment mappings from $CHASE_F(T_{\mathbf{s},t})$ to $RI(\mathbf{s}_p)$ (by Lemma 7.7) and from $RI(\mathbf{s}_+)$ to $CHASE_F(T_{\mathbf{s},t})$ (by Lemma 4.2, since, by construction, there are containment mappings from $T_{\mathbf{s}_+}$ to $CHASE_F(T_{\mathbf{s},t})$), and consequently from $RI(\mathbf{s}_+)$ to $RI(\mathbf{s}_p)$.

Now let $\mathbf{s}_g$ be the glb of the potential results; we will complete the proof by showing that $\mathbf{s}_g \preceq \mathbf{s}_+$. Consider $CHASE_F(T_{\mathbf{s},t})$ and two injective functions ψ_1, ψ_2 that map all the variables in $CHASE_F(T_{\mathbf{s},t})$ to constants that do not appear in $CHASE_F(T_{\mathbf{s},t})$. Also, let the set of new constants of each mapping be disjoint from the set of the other. Let $T_1 = \psi_1(CHASE_F(T_{\mathbf{s},t}))$ and $T_2 = \psi_2(CHASE_F(T_{\mathbf{s},t}))$, and let $\mathbf{s}_1 = \pi^{\downarrow}{}_\mathbf{S}(T_1)$ and $\mathbf{s}_2 = \pi^{\downarrow}{}_\mathbf{S}(T_2)$. Since the insertion is possible, by Theorem 7.4, there is a relation scheme R_i such that F implies $X_i \to X$. As a consequence, the chase can reconstruct t from the projections of total tuples that contain it, and therefore, since T_1 and T_2 contain only total tuples, t belongs to the window on X of both $\mathbf{s}_1$ and $\mathbf{s}_2$. Since, by construction, $\mathbf{s} \preceq \mathbf{s}_1$ and $\mathbf{s} \preceq \mathbf{s}_2$, it follows that both $\mathbf{s}_1$ and $\mathbf{s}_2$ are potential results. Since all constants in each of $\mathbf{s}_1$ and $\mathbf{s}_2$ are either new constants (not appearing in the other instance nor in $CHASE_F(T_{s,t})$) or constants in $CHASE_F(T_{s,t})$, it follows that s_+ is the relationwise intersection of s_1 and s_2. Therefore, by Lemma 7.3, s_+ is the glb of s_1 and s_2. Now, s_g is the glb of the set of the potential results, a set of instances that includes s_1 and s_2, and therefore it is weaker than the lower bound of s_1 and s_2. That is, s_g is weaker than s_+, and therefore, since we already established the converse $(s_+ \preceq s_g)$, we have $s_+ \sim s_g$. Thus, since s_+ is complete (being constructed as the projection of a chased tableau), it is the glb of the potential results.

$\square$

THEOREM 7.6 Let the insertion of t in s be possible and consistent. It is deterministic if and only if $CHASE_F(T_{s,t}) \equiv RI(s_+)$.

PROOF   Since the insertion is possible and consistent, then by Theorem 7.5, we have that $CHASE_F(T_{s,t}) \neq T_\infty$.
If.   It suffices to show that if $CHASE_F(T_{s,t}) \equiv RI(s_+) \neq T_\infty$, then s_+ is a potential result.

1. $t \in [X](s_+)$: By construction of $T_{s,t}$, we have that t belongs to $\pi^{\downarrow}_X(CHASE_F(T_{s,t}))$. Then since $CHASE_F(T_{s,t}) \equiv RI(s_+)$, it follows that $t \in \pi^{\downarrow}_X(RI(s_+))$.

2. $s \preceq s_+$: By construction of $T_{s,t}$, again, there is a containment mapping from $RI(s)$ to $CHASE_F(T_{s,t})$. Then since, by hypothesis, $CHASE_F(T_{s,t}) \equiv RI(s_+)$, we have a containment mapping from $RI(s)$ to $RI(s_+)$, and so $s \preceq s_+$.

Only if.   If the insertion of t into s is deterministic, then by definition, the glb of the potential results is a potential result itself. As a consequence, by Lemma 7.8, s_+ is a potential result, and so, by Lemma 7.7, there is a containment mapping from $CHASE_F(T_{s,t})$ to $RI(s_+)$. Since, by construction of s_+, we also have a containment mapping from $RI(s_+)$ to $CHASE_F(T_{s,t})$, it follows $CHASE_F(T_{s,t}) \equiv RI(s_+)$.

$\square$

COROLLARY 7.3 Let the insertion of t in s be possible and consistent. It is deterministic if and only if $t \in \pi^{\downarrow}_X(RI(s_+))$.

PROOF
If.   If the insertion is possible and consistent, then by Theorem 7.5,

$RI(\mathbf{s_+})$ is a consistent tableau, and there is a containment mapping from $RI(\mathbf{s})$ to $RI(\mathbf{s_+})$. If $t \in \pi^\downarrow_X(RI(\mathbf{s_+}))$, then there is also a containment mapping from $T_{\mathbf{s},t}$ to $RI(\mathbf{s_+})$, and so, by Lemma 4.2, we have that there is also a containment mapping from $CHASE_F(T_{\mathbf{s},t})$ to $RI(\mathbf{s_+})$. Then by Lemma 7.8, we also have a containment mapping from $RI(\mathbf{s_+})$ to $CHASE_F(T_{\mathbf{s},t})$, and so $RI(\mathbf{s_+}) \equiv CHASE_F(T_{\mathbf{s},t})$. Therefore, by Theorem 7.6, the insertion is deterministic.

Only if. If the insertion is possible, consistent, and deterministic, then by Theorem 7.6, $RI(\mathbf{s_+}) \equiv CHASE_F(T_{\mathbf{s},t})$. Thus, since, by construction of $T_{\mathbf{s},t}$, t belongs to $\pi^\downarrow CHASE_F(T_{\mathbf{s},t})$, we have that it also belongs to $\pi^\downarrow_X(RI(\mathbf{s_+}))$.   □

Corollary 7.3 gives an effective characterization of insertibility: Given $\mathbf{s}$ and t, we can build $T_{\mathbf{s},t}$, chase it with respect to the given constraints, then generate $\mathbf{s_+}$ and compute its representative instance $RI(\mathbf{s_+})$, and finally check whether the total projection $\pi^\downarrow_X(RI(\mathbf{s_+}))$ contains t. It should be noted that this procedure is not necessarily efficient. We refer to the bibliography [32] for efficient algorithms for the implementation of this procedure for the class of independent schemes.

> **Example 7.5**   Consider again the insertion in Example 7.1. Following the definitions, we could build the tableau $T_{\mathbf{s},t}$, chase it, project the result on the database scheme, and thus obtain exactly the instance we suggested as a result.

Let us now consider deletions. The definitions will be somehow symmetric with respect to those concerning insertions. However, the case will be easier, because no problems will arise regarding consistency and possibility.

An instance $\mathbf{s}_p$ is a *potential result* for the deletion of a tuple t from an instance $\mathbf{s}$ if $\mathbf{s}_p \preceq \mathbf{s}$ and $t \notin [X](\mathbf{s}_p)$.

The empty instance is a consistent potential result for every deletion, and so there is no need to define the notions of possible and consistent results for deletions. However, as for insertions, there may be several, incomparable potential results.

> **Example 7.6**   If we want to delete the tuple $< Smith, Black >$ on EM from the database in Figure 7.1, then it suffices to eliminate either the tuple $< Smith, 1, CS >$ from r_1 or the tuple

$< CS, Black >$ from r_3. The two instances obtained in these
ways are incomparable and are both potential results and maxi-
mal among the potential results.

It is therefore reasonable to introduce a notion of deterministic
result, in a way that is dual with respect to that followed for insertions. A deletion is *deterministic* if the lub of the potential results is
a potential result. It turns out that deletions are deterministic only
in very restricted cases.

LEMMA 7.9   Let **s** be a consistent instance and t be a tuple on X
that belongs to the window of **s** on X. The deletion of t from **s**
is deterministic only if there is a relation scheme $R_i(X_i)$ such that
$X \subseteq X_i$.

PROOF   If there is no relation scheme X_i that contains X, then $t \in$
$[X](\mathbf{s})$ only if there is a set of tuples $\mathcal{T} = \{t_1 \in r_{i_1}, \ldots, t_h \in r_{i_h}\}$ that
allow the chase to generate a tuple $t' \in RI(\mathbf{s})$ such that $t[X] = t'[X]$.
In general, there may be several nonredundant sets of tuples with
this property: $\mathcal{T}_1 = \{t_{1,1}, \ldots, t_{1,H_1}\}$, $\ldots$, $\mathcal{T}_q = \{t_{q,1}, \ldots, t_{q,H_q}\}$. The
instances obtained by removing from the relations in **s** one tuple from
each of the $\mathcal{T}_j$'s are all potential results (since they are weaker than
s, and by the nonredundancy assumption, t does not belong to the
window on X of any of them). It is clear that the lub of this set of
instances is **s** itself, which is not a potential result, since $t \in [X](\mathbf{s})$.
□

The condition in Lemma 7.9 is not sufficient, in general, to guarantee determinism; a further condition on the instance is needed, similar
to the one we found for insertions.

Let $\mathbf{s}_-$ be the instance obtained by removing from each relation r_i
such that $X \subseteq X_i$ each tuple t' such that $t'[X] = t[X]$.

LEMMA 7.10   Let **s** be a consistent instance and t be a tuple that
belongs to the window of **s** on X. The deletion of t from **s** is deterministic only if t does not belong to the window of $\mathbf{s}_-$ on X.

PROOF   If $t \in [X](\mathbf{s}_-)$, then it is constructed by the chase from a
set of tuples neither of which coincides with t on X; therefore, we can
reason as in the proof of Lemma 7.9.
□

LEMMA 7.11 Let $\mathbf{s}$ be a consistent instance and t be a tuple that belongs to the window of $\mathbf{s}$ on X. If (1) there is a relation scheme $R_i(X_i)$ such that $X \subseteq X_i$ and (2) t does not belong to the window of $\mathbf{s}_-$ on X, then the deletion of t from $\mathbf{s}$ is deterministic.

PROOF   By construction, the instance $\mathbf{s}_-$ is weaker than $\mathbf{s}$. By hypothesis, we have $t \notin [X](\mathbf{s}_-)$; therefore, $\mathbf{s}_-$ is a potential result. At the same time, no potential result can contain any tuple that coincides with t on X. Thus, every potential result is weaker than $\mathbf{s}_-$, and therefore it is the lub of the potential results, and so the deletion is deterministic.   □

THEOREM 7.7 Let $\mathbf{s}$ be a consistent instance and t be a tuple on X that belongs to $[X](\mathbf{s})$. The deletion of t from $\mathbf{s}$ is deterministic if and only if (1) there is a relation scheme $R_i(X_i)$ such that $X \subseteq X_i$ and (2) t does not belong to $[X](\mathbf{s}_-)$.

PROOF   The proof follows from Lemmas 7.9, 7.10, and 7.11.   □

7.5   The Weak Instance Approach and First-Order Logic

There is an interesting way to look at the weak instance model, based on logical theories, which gives a good insight into its foundations.[2] Given a fixed scheme $\mathbf{S}$, there is a language that allows us to express predicates over all the possible sets of attributes, and for each instance $\mathbf{s}$ of $\mathbf{S}$, there is a theory that enjoys a number of interesting properties. The theory contains (1) sentences that depend on the instance $\mathbf{s}$, describing the tuples in the relations in $\mathbf{s}$, and (2) sentences that depend on the scheme, referring to both the structure and to the dependencies.[3] The sentences in the second category essentially describe the semantics of the weak instance approach, namely the fact that the various relations are considered in a common framework, and

---

[2] Although the necessary concepts are briefly defined, this section requires some knowledge of first-order theories. It can be better understood after reading Chapter 9.

[3] A *sentence* is a formula with no free variables.

that there is a virtual, although unknown, relation over the universe, from which the various relations are derived.

Let us now describe the logical theories in detail. In order to give examples, we refer to the database instance in Figure 7.1 and to its scheme.

Given a database scheme $\mathbf{S} = \{[R_i(X_i), F_i] \mid i = 1, \ldots, n\}$, with $U = \cup_{i=1}^n X_i$, and $F = \cup_{i=1}^n F_i$, a *first-order language* (that is, a language that allows us to define formulas in a way similar to that used in Section 2.5 for the relational calculus) is defined: its *constant symbols* are exactly the constants in the domain of the database, there are no *function symbols*, and there is a *predicate symbol* for each nonempty subset X of U. With some abuse of notation, we will often use shorthand for our formulas, indicating tuples of constants or variables, rather than just individual constants and variables; for example, we may use the formula $(\forall x)(\exists y)(XY(x, y))$, where $X = A_1 A_2 \ldots A_h$, $Y = B_1 B_2 \ldots B_k$, instead of

$$(\forall a_1)(\forall a_2) \ldots (\forall a_h)(\exists b_1)(\exists b_2) \ldots (\exists b_k)$$
$$(XY(a_1, a_2, \ldots, a_h, b_1, b_2, \ldots, b_k))$$

Also, we will have little regard for the order of the arguments in the predicates, but the meaning will always be understood from the context.

With every database instance $\mathbf{s} = \{r_1, r_2, \ldots, r_n\}$, a theory with five kinds of sentences is associated:

1. A set *DB* of atomic sentences describing the content of the relations in the database: for every relation $r_i \in \mathbf{s}$ defined on the relation scheme $R_i(X_i)$, and for every tuple $t \in r_i$, there is the sentence $X_i(t)$. For example, for the database instance in Figure 7.1, we have the twelve sentences in Figure 7.9.

2. A set *INC* of sentences saying that the relations in $\mathbf{s}$ are projections of the weak instance(s). These sentences are existentially quantified with respect to the attributes not appearing in the relation scheme: for every relation scheme R, if $Y = U - R$, there

EP(Smith,A)	CS(1,20K)
EP(Smith,B)	CS(2,25K)
EP(Jones,B)	CS(3,30K)
ECD(Smith,1,CS)	CS(4,35K)
ECD(Adams,3,EE)	
ECD(White,5,EE)	DM(CS,Black)
	DM(IE,Brown)

Figure 7.9. The DB sentences for the instance in Figure 7.1

$$(\forall e)(\forall p)(\exists d)(\exists m)(\exists c)(\exists s)\ (EP(e,p) \Rightarrow EPDMCS(e,p,d,m,c,s))$$
$$(\forall e)(\forall c)(\forall d)(\exists p)(\exists m)(\exists s)\ (ECD(e,p) \Rightarrow EPDMCS(e,p,d,m,c,s))$$
$$(\forall c)(\forall s)(\exists e)(\exists p)(\exists d)(\exists m)\ (EP(e,p) \Rightarrow EPDMCS(e,p,d,m,c,s))$$
$$(\forall d)(\forall m)(\exists e)(\exists p)(\exists c)(\exists s)\ (DM(d,m) \Rightarrow EPDMCS(e,p,d,m,c,s))$$

Figure 7.10. The INC sentences for the instance in Figure 7.1

is the sentence $(\forall t)(\exists y)(R(t) \Rightarrow U(t,y))$.[4] In the example, there
are the four sentences in Figure 7.10.

3. A set CON of sentences saying that for every tuple t over the
universe, all of its subtuples are meaningful pieces of information
over the involved attributes: for each $\emptyset \subset X \subset U$ there is the
sentence $(\forall t)(U(t) \Rightarrow X(t[X]))$. If U contains m attributes, then
CON includes $2^m - 2$ sentences. In the example above there are
sixty-two sentences; some of them are shown in Figure 7.11. For
example, the last sentence says that if the instance implies a tuple
over U with the six values, then e is an employee.

It is important to note that the sentences INC and CON,
together, imply that each sentence $X(t)$ implies, for every $Y \subset X$,
the sentence $Y(t[Y])$; in plain words, each tuple implies all its
subtuples, and the weak instances implement this implication.

---

[4] The connective $\Rightarrow$ is shorthand: $f_1 \Rightarrow f_2$ stands for $\neg(f_1) \vee f_2$; its intuitive meaning is "if f_1, then f_2."

$$(\forall e)(\forall p)(\forall d)(\forall m)(\forall c)(\forall s)\ (EPDMCS(e,p,d,m,c,s) \Rightarrow EPDMC(e,p,d,m,c))$$
$$(\forall e)(\forall p)(\forall d)(\forall m)(\forall c)(\forall s)\ (EPDMCS(e,p,d,m,c,s) \Rightarrow EPDMS(e,p,d,m,s))$$

$$\ldots$$

$$(\forall e)(\forall p)(\forall d)(\forall m)(\forall c)(\forall s)\ (EPDMCS(e,p,d,m,c,s) \Rightarrow E(e))$$

Figure 7.11. Some of the CON sentences for the instance in Figure 7.1

$$(\forall e)(\forall p_1)(\forall d_1)(\forall m_1)(\forall c_1)(\forall s_1)(\forall p_2)(\forall d_2)(\forall m_2)(\forall c_2)(\forall s_2)$$
$$((EPDMCS(e,p_1,d_1,m_1,c_1,s_1) \wedge EPDMCS(e,p_2,d_2,m_2,c_2,s_2)) \Rightarrow (c_1 = c_2))$$
$$(\forall e)(\forall p_1)(\forall d_1)(\forall m_1)(\forall c_1)(\forall s_1)(\forall p_2)(\forall d_2)(\forall m_2)(\forall c_2)(\forall s_2)$$
$$((EPDMCS(e,p_1,d_1,m_1,c_1,s_1) \wedge EPDMCS(e,p_2,d_2,m_2,c_2,s_2)) \Rightarrow (d_1 = d_2))$$
$$(\forall c)(\forall e_1)(\forall p_1)(\forall d_1)(\forall m_1)(\forall s_1)(\forall e_2)(\forall p_2)(\forall d_2)(\forall m_2)(\forall s_2)$$
$$((EPDMCS(e_1,p_1,d_1,m_1,c,s_1) \wedge EPDMCS(e_2,p_2,d_2,m_2,c,s_2)) \Rightarrow (s_1 = s_2))$$
$$(\forall d)(\forall e_1)(\forall p_1)(\forall m_1)(\forall c_1)(\forall s_1)(\forall e_2)(\forall p_2)(\forall m_2)(\forall c_2)(\forall s_2)$$
$$((EPDMCS(e_1,p_1,d,m_1,c_1,s_1) \wedge EPDMCS(e_2,p_2,d,m_2,c_2,s_2)) \Rightarrow (m_1 = m_2))$$
$$(\forall m)(\forall e_1)(\forall p_1)(\forall d_1)(\forall c_1)(\forall s_1)(\forall e_2)(\forall p_2)(\forall d_2)(\forall c_2)(\forall s_2)$$
$$((EPDMCS(e_1,p_1,d_1,m,c_1,s_1) \wedge EPDMCS(e_2,p_2,d_2,m,c_2,s_2)) \Rightarrow (d_1 = d_2))$$

Figure 7.12. The DEP sentences for the instance in Figure 7.1

4. A set *DIS* of sentences stating that all constants are distinct. This a technical set of sentences.

5. A set *DEP* of first-order sentences representing the dependencies in *F*. Since we refer to global consistency, it is convenient to write all of them with the predicate symbol associated with the universe *U*. The approach works for rather general constraints; as usual, we consider only FDs. In the example, there are five FDs (decomposed in order to have singleton rhs's), and so five sentences; they are shown in Figure 7.12.

There are two important results that can be shown with respect to these theories, which confirm their actual correspondence to the weak instance approach. A few definitions are needed. An *interpretation* for a theory is a function that associates with each predicate symbol a relation of the same degree.[5] Therefore, we assume that for every predicate symbol X, the interpretation contains a relation x over the attributes X. Then we can define the notion of *substitution* as we did in Section 2.5 for the formulas of the relational calculus, and the notion of the *value* of a sentence on a substitution with respect to the given interpretation.[6] Note that all the formulas in our theories are sentences, and therefore their final values are independent of the substitution. Then we say that an interpretation i *satisfies* a sentence f if f has the value *true* on i. An interpretation is a *model* for a theory if it satisfies all its sentences. A theory is *satisfiable* if it has a model. A sentence is *implied* by a theory if it is satisfied by every model of the theory.

THEOREM 7.8 Given $\mathbf{S}$ and F as above, a database instance $\mathbf{s}$ of $\mathbf{S}$ globally satisfies F if and only if the theory associated with $\mathbf{s}$ is satisfiable.

PROOF

If. If the theory associated with $\mathbf{s}$ is satisfiable, then there is a model of the theory. Let u be the relation over U in the model. We claim that u is a weak instance for $\mathbf{s}$. In fact, by the sentences in DEP, u satisfies F, and for every $R_i(X_i) \in \mathbf{S}$, we have, by the sentences in INC, that the relation x_i in the model is contained in the projection of u on X_i. Then, by the sentences in DB, the relation $r_i \in \mathbf{S}$ is contained in x_i; thus, by transitivity, $r_i \subseteq \pi_{X_i}(u)$.

Only if. If $\mathbf{s}$ is globally consistent, then there is a weak instance w for $\mathbf{s}$. We claim that the set of relations obtained by projecting w on all the nonempty subsets X of U is a model for the theory. Let

---

[5]Strictly speaking, the interpretation should also involve a mapping from constant symbols to constants; we assume that this mapping is the identity: constant symbols are mapped to themselves. The *DIS* sentences require that the mapping be injective, and so every mapping is isomorphic to the identity; therefore, we do not lose generality.

[6]In the relational calculus the notion of interpretation was implicit, as we always referred to the "current" database instance, which was in fact an interpretation.

$x = \pi_X(w)$ for every $\emptyset \subset X \subseteq U$. In fact, this interpretation satisfies all the sentences.

- The sentences in DB are satisfied because w is a weak instance; thus, for every $R_i \in \mathbf{S}$, $\pi_{X_i}(w) \supseteq r_i$, and therefore $x_i \supseteq r_i$.

- The sentences in INC and CON are satisfied because for every $X \subseteq U$, $x_i = \pi_X(w)$, and so $x_i = \pi_X(u)$ (containment in one direction guarantees satisfaction for INC and containment in the other guarantees it for CON).

- The sentences in DIS are satisfied because all constants are distinct.

- The sentences in DEP are satisfied because w is a weak instance, and so it satisfies F. $\qquad\square$

It should be noted that, from the sentences, and even more from the proof of Theorem 7.8, the weak instance approach postulates that there is a relation over the universe that need not be completely known, but does exist. In fact, the sentences in INC closely resemble the sentences we used in Section 6.1 to describe the semantics of the unknown null value.

The second result shows the close correspondence that exists between the weak instance approach to query answering and the logical theories associated with it; again, this confirms the robustness of the approach.

THEOREM 7.9   For every consistent instance $\mathbf{s} \in W(\mathbf{S})$, for every set X of attributes, the set of tuples t such that $X(t)$ is implied by the theory associated with $\mathbf{s}$ coincides with the window $[X](\mathbf{s})$ over X.

PROOF   We prove containment in the two directions.

- *If $t \in [X](\mathbf{s})$, then $X(t)$ is implied by the theory associated with $\mathbf{s}$.* If $t \in [X](\mathbf{s})$, then by definition, t belongs to the X-projection of each weak instance w; that is, for each $w \in WEAK(\mathbf{s})$, there is a tuple $t' \in w$ such that $t'[X] = t$. Then, since (by the proof of the previous theorem) each weak instance corresponds to a model, we have that in the relation u over U of each model there is a tuple $t'[X] = t$, and so, by the sentences in CON, t belongs to the relation x over X of each model. Thus, $X(t)$ is satisfied by every model; that is, it is implied by the theory.

- *If $X(t)$ is implied by the theory associated with* **s**, *then $t \in [X](\mathbf{s})$.* If $X(t)$ is implied by the theory associated with **s**, then in every model the relation x over X contains t, and so the relation u over U contains a tuple t' such that $t'[X] = t$. By the proof of the previous theorem, we have that each such u is a weak instance, and vice versa. Thus, for each $w \in WEAK(\mathbf{s})$, there is a tuple $t' \in w$ such that $t'[X] = t$, and this means precisely that $t \in [X](\mathbf{s})$. □

7.6   Interpretation of Nulls in the Weak Instance Approach

The logical theories that can be associated with database instances in the weak instance approach confirm, as we said in Section 7.5, that each tuple in each relation $r_i(X_i)$ is considered as a tuple over the universe whose values on the attributes in $U - X_i$ are not known, but do exist. In other words, the representative instance can be considered as the actual relation, and its variables are indeed marked unknown null values. In this section, we argue that this point of view is not completely desirable, and that it is possible to transform the weak instance model in a way that preserves most of the properties and does not present this shortcoming.

Let us present an example first. Consider again the instance in Figure 7.1 and its scheme. The logical theories in Section 7.5 say that because of the FDs, for every employee there exist exactly one category, one salary, one department, one manager, and at least one project. For the same reasons, the variables in its representative instance (Figure 7.5) stand for existing, although unknown, values. It would therefore be conceptually wrong to use this database to model an application where employees need not work on projects.

As a consequence, from a conceptual point of view, the weak instance approach considers only relations over the universe, and does not allow, at least in principle, the possibility of representing applications for which some of the tuples need not be extendible over the universe of attributes.

In this section we show how the definition of the weak instance approach can be modified in order to deal with applications where the missing values are not necessarily existent.

We will redefine some concepts, such as the weak instance, the chase process (and so the representative instance), and the logical theory associated with a database. In order to distinguish the two approaches, we will use the adjective *classic* for the definitions presented in the previous sections, and the adjective *new* for those we are going to introduce. We will find that the new definitions enjoy the main properties seen in the previous sections and also, for some meaningful classes of schemes, provide the same windows as the classic definitions.

The first difference is that the new weak instances may contain nonexistent nulls, which, as we saw in Chapter 6, represent the fact that there exist no ordinary values for the respective attributes. The notion of total projection, which we have used with reference to tableaux, constants and variables, can be easily extended to relations (with nulls), constants and nonexistent nulls: the *total projection* $\pi^{\downarrow}{}_X(r)$ of a relation r with nulls is the set of null-free tuples in the projection of r on X.

Then a *new weak instance* for a database instance is a relation w (with nulls) that satisfies the FDs (considered as NFDs, see Section 6.3) and contains the base relations in its projections. We stress the fact that we do not allow nonexistent values in the database, but only in the weak instance. Two possible weak instances for the database instance in Figure 7.1 are shown in Figure 7.13; note that the first one is a weak instance also according to the classic definition, whereas the second is not, since it contains nonexistent values.

Since each weak instance represents a "possible world" compatible with the data in the database, we can say that with the new definition, the possibility that Adams works for a project is open: he need not work for one.

In a similar way, we modify the definition of the representative

Employee	Proj	Dept	Mgr	Category	Salary
Smith	A	CS	Black	1	20K
Smith	B	CS	Black	1	20K
Jones	B	M	Cauchy	1	20K
Adams	C	EE	Ohm	3	30K
White	D	EE	Ohm	5	40K
Grey	F	P	Galilei	2	25K
Reds	F	P	Galilei	4	35K
Cook	E	IE	Brown	5	40K

Employee	Proj	Dept	Mgr	Category	Salary
Smith	A	CS	Black	1	20K
Smith	B	CS	Black	1	20K
Jones	B	ϕ	ϕ	ϕ	ϕ
Adams	ϕ	EE	ϕ	3	30K
White	ϕ	EE	ϕ	5	ϕ
ϕ	ϕ	ϕ	ϕ	2	25K
ϕ	ϕ	ϕ	ϕ	4	35K
ϕ	ϕ	IE	Brown	ϕ	ϕ

Figure 7.13. Two new weak instances for the instance in Figure 7.1

instance in order to give a different meaning to the variables used, taking into account the possibility that they represent nonexistent values. Essentially, the variables in the representative instance are now no-information nulls, since they represent the logical disjunction of the unknown and nonexistent values (see Chapter 6). The chase process is modified as follows: *when two tuples t_1, t_2 and a dependency $Y \to A$ are considered, their A values are equated if and only if (1) both tuples are Y-total, (2) they coincide on Y, and (3) exactly one is A-total.* Thus, as opposed to what happens with the classic definitions, variables are never equated, and equality of variables is not

A	B	C	D	E
a_1	b_1	v_1	v_2	e_1
v_3	b_1	c_1	v_4	v_5

Figure 7.14. A tableau for an application of the new chase

used to infer equality of other values.[7] As an example, in the tableau in Figure 7.14, where the v_i's are variables and the other values are constants with the dependencies $A \rightarrow B$, $B \rightarrow C$, $C \rightarrow D$, $D \rightarrow E$, the variable v_1 is equated to c_1, but the equality of the C-values is not used to infer equality of the two variables in the D-column; thus, v_5 is not equated to e_1, as happens in the classic approach.

Let us discuss the properties of the new chase. First of all, it is clear that its result does not depend on the order of application of the rules; arguments similar to those used for the classic chase (Theorem 4.1) can be used to prove this claim.

Second, the definition of the new chase parallels the definition of NFDs, and it is therefore coherent with the implication of NFDs (*N-implication* in the following), whereas it may be in contrast with the classic notion of implication (*C-implication*). For example, if the tableau above were chased with respect to the FDs $A \rightarrow B$, $B \rightarrow C$, $C \rightarrow D$, $D \rightarrow E$, $A \rightarrow E$, which form a set that is C-equivalent (but not N-equivalent) to the given one, then variable v_5 would indeed be equated to e_1, as opposed to what we had above. To confirm the coherence of the new chase with N-implication of FDs, we have the result in the following theorem.

THEOREM 7.10   Let T be a tableau and F and G be two N-equivalent sets of FDs, and let T_F and T_G be the tableaux obtained applying the new chase to T with respect to F and G, respectively. Then the two tableaux T_F and T_G are identical.

PROOF   We show that if H is a nonredundant N-cover of F, then $T_F = T_H$ (where T_F is as above, and T_H is the result of the new

---

[7] As a matter of fact, in the construction of the representative instance, the initial tableau has all distinct variables, and so the new chase never encounters equality of variables.

chase of T with respect to H). Then the claim would follow, as the
same would hold for G, and the nonredundant N-cover is unique by
Lemma 6.4.

Consider an execution of the new chase on T that uses F. We show
that the transformation generated in the generic step can also be
obtained by means of an FD in H. By an induction argument, this
can be shown to imply that the new chase with respect to H can
perform at least the same modifications as the new chase with respect
to F. Since the process is independent of the order of execution of the
steps, and, by Lemma 6.3, $H \subseteq F$, it follows that the modifications
are exactly the same.

Now, let the generic step involve the FD $Y \to A$ and two tuples t_1,
t_2 that agree and are total on Y, disagree on A, and at least $t_1[A]$ or
$t_2[A]$ is a constant. By Lemma 6.4, H contains an FD $Z \to A$ with
$Z \subseteq Y$. Clearly, t_1 and t_2 agree and are total on Z, and so the FD
$Z \to A$ can be applied and produces the same transformation.   □

We have the following two theorems, parallel to Theorems 4.5
and 7.1, respectively. Their proofs are left as exercises.

THEOREM 7.11   Given the new definition of satisfaction and the new
definition of the chase algorithm, a database instance satisfies the set
F of functional dependencies if and only if there is no FD $Y \to A$
violated by two (YA)-total tuples in its representative instance.   □

THEOREM 7.12   Assume the new definitions of weak instance and
representative instance. For every X, the set of total tuples that
appear in the projection on X of every weak instance is exactly the
X-total projection of the representative instance.   □

Theorem 7.12 allows us to define the new window over X as either
of the two identical sets of tuples, thus obtaining, as in the classic
model, a robust concept.

As we mentioned above, the new chase differs from the classic
chase, in general, and so the classic window and the new window
need not coincide. Also, since the new chase is C-cover-sensitive, the
new window is also C-cover-sensitive. However, it is interesting to
note that, for some classes of schemes, these differences do not arise.

In fact, the independent schemes[8] enjoy the following property (the *two-phase chase property*): The execution of the classic chase of every state tableau, with respect to every embedded C-cover of the given set of FDs, can be divided into two phases. In the first one all applications of FDs promote variables to constants. In the second one no variable is promoted; that is, only variables are equated to one another. Clearly, a chase performed in this way produces exactly the same total tuples as the new chase. Since this holds for every embedded C-cover, and the classic chase is C-cover-insensitive, we have that for independent schemes, the new window function coincides with the classic one and is C-cover-insensitive. Obviously, the same would hold for every other class of schemes satisfying the two-phase chase property. Considering again the example discussed at the beginning of the section, we can easily see that the new representative instance is exactly the same as the classic one (Figure 7.5). This is not a coincidence, but happens because the scheme is independent. However, as we have claimed while giving the definitions and will confirm shortly by means of logical theories, the variables in it need not stand for existing values.

The aspect of the theories described in Section 7.5 that did not satisfy us was the use of existential quantifiers in the sentences of the set *INC*. The new theories do not have sentences of this form because, given a tuple $t \in r$, we do not want to assume anything about the values for the attributes in $U - R$, not even their existence. This is similar to the formalization of the no-information nulls given in Section 6.1.

Since we get rid of the sentences in *INC*, we have to modify the sentences in *CON* in order to be able to specify that for every tuple t satisfying a predicate X, for every subset Y of X, the subtuple $t[Y]$ satisfies the predicate associated with Y. In the classic theories this was implied by the sentences in *CON* together with those in *INC*, which we do not have. More precisely, in *CON* we have, for every

---

[8] We refer to independence in the classic sense; that is, a scheme is independent if local satisfaction implies classic global satisfaction. It would be possible to give a new definition of independence based on new global satisfaction, but this would not add much to the discussion; here, we just want to show an interesting property of the schemes that are independent in the classic sense: they have, in the new approach, the same query-answering behavior as in the classic one.

subset X of U, and for every nonempty, proper subset Y of X, a sentence stating that if $X(t)$ holds, then $Y(t[Y])$ also holds. With the usual conventions,

$$(\forall y)(\forall z)(X(y, z) \Rightarrow Y(y))$$

With respect to dependencies, the new theory has to take into account the different meaning we attach to the values in the weak instances, as we have done in the definition of the chase process. Due to the lack of a universal tuple extending each tuple, we cannot use the universal predicate as is done in the classic approach, and so the definition is somewhat complex. We give the definition first, and then briefly explain it. The functional dependency $Y \rightarrow A$ (again, without lack of generality, we assume the right-hand side to be a singleton) is expressed by means of the following sentences:

1. A sentence stating that if there are two (YA)-total tuples whose Y values coincide, then their A values must also coincide:

$$(\forall y)(\forall a_1)(\forall a_2)((YA(y, a_1) \wedge YA(y, a_2)) \Rightarrow (a_1 = a_2))$$

2. For every nonempty set $Z \subseteq U - YA$, we have a sentence stating that if there exist a tuple t over YA and a tuple t' over YZ whose Y values are identical, then the second tuple must be the projection of a tuple defined at least on YAZ, with the same value as t on A:

$$(\forall y)(\forall a)(\forall z)((YA(y, a) \wedge YZ(y, z)) \Rightarrow YAZ(y, a, z))$$

For example, if $U = ABCDE$, we have four sentences for the FD $BC \rightarrow A$:

1. $(\forall a_1)(\forall a_2)(\forall b)(\forall c)((ABC(a_1, b, c) \wedge ABC(a_2, b, c)) \Rightarrow (a_1 = a_2))$

2a. $(\forall a)(\forall b)(\forall c)(\forall d)((ABC(a, b, c) \wedge BCD(b, c, d)) \Rightarrow ABCD(a, b, c, d))$

2b. $(\forall a)(\forall b)(\forall c)(\forall e)((ABC(a, b, c) \wedge BCE(b, c, e)) \Rightarrow ABCE(a, b, c, e))$

2c. $(\forall a)(\forall b)(\forall c)(\forall d)(\forall e)$
$\quad ((ABC(a, b, c) \wedge BCDE(b, c, d, e)) \Rightarrow ABCDE(a, b, c, d, e))$

Clearly, Sentence 1 enforces the dependencies with respect to nonnull values. Sentences 2a–2c formalize the requirement that if tuples t, t' assume the same values on Y and $t[A]$ is not null, then $t'[A]$ is not null either, and it is equal to $t[A]$.

Now we can finally say that the theory T we associate with a database instance contains four kinds of sentences:

1. *DB*, as in the classic theory

2. *CON*, as defined above

3. *DIS*, as in the classic theory

4. *DEP*, corresponding to the functional dependencies, as defined above

With respect to the example in Section 7.3, the theory associated with the database would have the same sentences in DB and DIS as in the classic theory, and the same sentences in CON as in the classic theory, plus many more involving proper subsets of U and their respective nonempty, proper subsets:

$$(\forall e)(\forall p)(\forall d)(\forall m)(\forall c)(EPDMC(e,p,d,m,c)\Rightarrow EPDM(e,p,d,m))$$
$$(\forall e)(\forall p)(\forall d)(\forall m)(\forall c)(EPDMC(e,p,d,m,c)\Rightarrow EPDC(e,p,d,c))$$
$$\cdots$$
$$(\forall c)(\forall s)(CS(c,s)\Rightarrow S(s))$$

It would also have five groups of sentences in DEP, one for each FD; for example, for the FD $E \rightarrow D$, there is the sentence

$$(\forall e)(\forall d_1)(\forall d_2)((ED(e,d_1) \wedge ED(e,d_2))\Rightarrow(c_1 = c_2))$$

and the sentences

$$(\forall e)(\forall p)(\forall d)((ED(e,d) \wedge EP(e,p))\Rightarrow EPD(e,p,d))$$
$$(\forall e)(\forall d)(\forall m)((ED(e,d) \wedge EM(e,m))\Rightarrow EPD(e,d,m))$$
$$\cdots$$
$$(\forall e)(\forall p)(\forall d)(\forall m)(\forall c)(\forall s)$$
$$((ED(e,d) \wedge EPMCS(e,p,m,c,s))\Rightarrow EPDMCS(e,p,d,m,c,s))$$

As opposed to what happens with the classic theory, the new theory does not imply the sentence $(\exists p)(EP(\text{Adams}, p))$, stating that Adams works on a project.

As we anticipated, the new theories enjoy the same properties as the classic theories (cf. Theorems 7.8 and 7.9); again, the proofs are left as exercises.

THEOREM 7.13   The database instance **s** satisfies the FDs in F, according to the new definition, if and only if the corresponding new theory is satisfiable.   □

THEOREM 7.14   Let **s** be a database instance and T be the associated new theory. For every set X of attributes, the set of tuples on X implied by the theory coincides with the new window over X.   □

Theorems 7.13 and 7.14 show that the new logical theories actually describe the new approach to the weak instance model, since they map the notion of consistency to that of satisfiability and query answering to logical implication, in the same way as the classic theories describe the classic weak instance model. Since in the new theories the missing values are not existentially quantified, these results confirm that the values we used in representative instances are indeed no-information values. Also, Theorem 7.14 shows that if the scheme satisfies the two-phase chase property, the missing values in the classic representative instance can be considered as no-information: if the total projections of the representative instance in the two approaches coincide, then each tuple is implied by the new theory if and only if it is implied by the classic theory.

Exercises

7.1 Prove that for each consistent database instance there is one and only one equivalent complete instance, and that it can be obtained as the projection of the representative instance on the database scheme.

7.2 Assume that null values are allowed in the instances of a database scheme, with the only restriction that each tuple is total on some key, and a weak instance is a null-free relation that satisfies the FDs and contains in its projections the total projections of the relations on the subsets of their schemes. Then consider two database schemes $\mathbf{R}$ (with one relation scheme) and $\mathbf{S}$, a WI-adequate decomposition of $\mathbf{R}$. We say that $\mathbf{S}$ is a *useless* decomposition of $\mathbf{R}$ if there is a one-to-one correspondence between the equivalence classes of instances in $W(\mathbf{R})$ and those in $W(\mathbf{S})$. Characterize useless decompositions.

7.3 A database scheme is *separable* if each locally consistent instance is globally consistent and complete. Characterize separable schemes.

7.4 Prove Lemma 7.2.

7.5 Prove Lemma 7.5.

7.6 Prove Lemma 7.6.

7.7 Formalize and prove the claim that for every tableau, the result of the new chase is independent of the order of application of the rules.

7.8 Analyze the relationship between the implication of NFDs and the new chase.

7.9 Prove Theorem 7.11.

7.10 Prove Theorem 7.12.

7.11 Prove Theorem 7.13.

7.12 Prove Theorem 7.14.

Comments and References

The weak instance approach to query answering was proposed by Sagiv [191,192] in terms of total projections of the representative instance. Theorem 7.1 was proved by Maier, Ullman, and Vardi [167]. The origin of the approach can be traced in a wider family of interfaces, known as *universal relation interfaces*, that allow the user to query the database as if it contained a single relation. The first ideas in this direction were formulated by Osborn [175]; subsequently, there have been many different proposals, surveyed by Maier et al. [165,167] and Vardi [223]. Most of the approaches to universal relation interfaces are based on heuristics and informal assumptions, and this gave rise to a strong debate on its foundations (see Kent [135], Atzeni and Parker [30], Ullman [214], Codd [82], Vardi [222]). Within the universal relation interfaces, the weak instance approach emerged as the most solid because of its foundations, demonstrated by Mendelzon [170] with the notions of equivalence and completeness of database instances (including Theorem 7.2) and the notion of WI-adequacy of decompositions (with Theorem 7.3). It should be noted that we used a different terminology than the original one. The notion of completeness was further investigated by Graham, Mendelzon, and Vardi [114] and by Chan and Mendelzon [69]; the latter studied the class of *separable* schemes (Exercise 7.3).

The class of *bounded* schemes, for which total projections can be computed by means of predefined relational algebra expressions, was defined by Maier, Ullman, and Vardi [167]. Boundedness of independent schemes and properties of the involved expressions were studied by Sagiv [191,192,193]; Chan [66]; Ito, Iwasaki, and Kasami [128]; and Atzeni and Chan [23,24,25]. Other classes of bounded schemes were studied by Chan and Hernández [68]. The related class of *constant-time maintainable* schemes has been studied by Wang and Graham [228] and Hernàndez and Chan [119].

The lattice on states was studied by Atzeni and Torlone [31], as a preliminary step towards the formulation of the weak instance approach to database updates, described in Section 7.4. The reformulation of the weak instance approach by means of logical theories was proposed by Maier, Ullman, and Vardi [167] with all the results in Section 7.5. The analysis of the interpretation of null values in the representative instance, and its alternative definition presented in Section 7.4 were presented by Atzeni and De Bernardis [26,27].

Chapter 8

Generalizing Relations

This chapter and the next are devoted to theoretical aspects related to database systems under development that are aimed at improving the capabilities of current systems. This chapter briefly discusses the main requirements of future database systems and presents some extensions of the relational model and other models based on a complex object structure. Chapter 9 describes the main features of the relationship between relational databases and first-order logic.

This chapter is organized as follows. Section 8.1 discusses the limitations of the relational model and the main directions of research related to future database systems. In Sections 8.2 and 8.3 we describe the *nested relational model*, which is the first extension of the relational model, both with respect to the time of proposal and in terms of conceptual "distance." The first section is devoted to the structural aspects and the second to the query languages. In Section 8.4 we present extensions to the nested relational model, which allow more complex models. Finally, in Section 8.5 we briefly describe models that are somehow different from the relational, as they are based on the notion of *object identity*. The presentation is mainly descriptive; several models are considered, since no consensus has been reached on any of them. The number of the more or less different proposals markedly contrasts with the literature on the relational model, in which a broad consensus was reached around Codd's original proposal [75]. That convergence was clearly allowed, even determined, by the structural simplicity of the model. In our present framework, the goal of the research is the individuation of the constructs that allow the best possible organization of complex structures, and the plurality of the proposals is a natural consequence.

8.1   Beyond the Relational Model

The relational model, in its practical versions, which are indeed very similar to the model presented in Chapter 1, represents a *de facto* standard in the current generation of database systems, and it is generally agreed that it provides a satisfactory response to the typical needs of business applications—those for which it was conceived, or better, for which the very idea of a database as a large collection of persistent data to be handled in an effective, efficient, and reliable manner was conceived.

The main feature of the relational model is the simplicity of the structures used to organize data: a relation is a set of tuples of *atomic* values (as we have seen in Section 1.5, this is the *first normal form* assumption). Moreover, no explicit connection exists between data in a relation or in different relations; relationships are implicitly represented by means of (equality of) values. For this reason it is often said that the relational model is *value-based*.

Business applications usually involve large amounts of data that have a relatively simple structure but many possible interrelations based on values that are not always known in advance. With respect to these needs, the relational model is satisfactory: the simplicity and the naturalness of the structures, the independence from the implementation aspects, and the possibility of specifying global operations (that is, on sets of tuples rather than on single tuples) justify the claim that the relational model has improved the productivity of software developers.

More recently, because of the increasing computing power available, the need for systems with database capabilities (management of large sets of persistent data in a shared, reliable, efficient, and effective manner) has emerged in other application areas, such as computer-aided design, computer-aided software engineering, and in knowledge-based, office, and multimedia systems. These areas have a number of common requirements that are not fulfilled by relational systems:

- The operations require an expressive power that is not provided by the traditional languages for relational database systems; for example, in many cases the availability of recursive operations, such as the transitive closure, is fundamental.

- The involved data often have complex structures that cannot be represented in a natural way in the relational model.

- The semantics of the data and their mutual relationships are crucial, and need to be expressed in a more explicit way than just by means of values.

In response to each of these needs, a research trend has been developed:

- Methods for the efficient and effective exploitation, with respect to databases, of concepts and techniques developed in the framework of artificial intelligence, specifically with respect to the use of first-order logic in *knowledge representation*. One important direction has been the integration of databases and logic programming languages, initially referring to the relational model and later to more general models.

- Models that generalize the relational one have been defined, relaxing the first normal form constraint. Values need not be atomic; they may be sets or tuples or combinations thereof.

- Models with richer semantics have been studied, based not only on values, but also on the notion of identity, which allows the representation of explicit relationships between objects, of isa hierarchies, and of object sharing. Starting points for this trend have been the semantic models, originally developed for use in the analysis and design phases of application development, and object-oriented languages.

These issues and many more have been considered in the last few years, as researchers study, propose, and experiment with *next-generation database systems*. This chapter and the next discuss the aspects that are most closely related to the subject of this book. Despite this restriction, the significant material is indeed wide, and there is not yet enough maturity in the field to single out and deeply study a few topics. For this reason, these chapters have a different style than the previous ones: rather than technical, detailed studies of the respective topics, they present tutorial introductions, with reference to the relevant literature; here, we will have more definitions, descriptions, and discussions, and fewer, if any, theorems and proofs than in the previous chapters.

Among the topics connected with future database systems, we are mainly interested in the modeling aspects and in those related to query formulation and answering. Moreover, since this book is devoted to relational databases, we will give specific attention to what can be considered as extensions of the relational model, or at least preserves the positive features of the relational model, that is, formalization, structural clarity, data independence, and the possibility of formulating set-theoretic operations. In this respect, any reference to the traditional, record-based models (hierarchical and network) is omitted because, although they allow the representation of complex structures, they are closely related to implementation structures, and their languages are based on a tuple-at-the-time strategy.

8.2   Nested Relations

Adopting a programming language terminology, we could say that a relational database is composed of a set of variables (the relations), each of which has a name and a type (the relation scheme). In a Pascal-like programming language, we would say that the type of each relation is obtained by applying the *relation* constructor to the atomic types that correspond to the domains, in the same way as the structured variables in Pascal are obtained by the (possibly repeated) application of the various constructors, *array*, *record*, *set*, and *file*. Let us consider the domains as elementary, predefined types (which is actually the case in relational database systems, as well as in programming languages). Then a relation scheme $R(A_1 : D_1, A_2 : D_2, \ldots, A_k : D_k)^1$ corresponds to the definition of a variable R, which could be expressed as follows in a pseudo-Pascal syntax:

var R: **relation** A_1: D_1 ; A_2: D_2 ; $\ldots$; A_k: D_k **end**;

So, a database with n relations would contain n relation variables, one for each relation scheme.

The easiest way to define a data model that allows for the representation of complex structures is a direct extension of the relational model, obtained by relaxing the *first normal form* assumption. As we saw in Section 1.5, a relation is in 1NF if its attributes are simple; that is, their respective domains contain only atomic values. First normal form was proposed by Codd [75] in his seminal paper on the relational model, where the notion of *relation* was introduced regardless of the nature of domains (simple or nonsimple), and first normal form was presented as a desirable property.[2] All relations were assumed to be in 1NF, or *flat*. Most of the subsequent literature referred only to the *flat relational model*, calling it simply the *relational model*.

In *nested* relations (also called *non–first normal form—NFNF* or *¬1NF*), values can be nested relations themselves, with unbounded depth.[3] Using the formalism introduced above, a *nested relation scheme* can be described as follows:

var R: **relation** $A_1 : T_1; \ldots; A_k : T_k$ **end**

where each of the T_j's, for $j = 1, \ldots, k$, is either

1. an atomic domain D_j, or

2. a nested relation scheme: **relation** $A_{j_1} : T_{j_1}; \ldots; A_{j_l} : T_{j_l}$ **end**.

---

[1]In order to lay the basis for a subsequent argument, we have indicated the corresponding domain together with each attribute name.

[2]In [75] 1NF is simply called *normal form*; the adjective *first* was introduced later (Codd [77]), when further normal forms were defined.

[3]In the following, if necessary to avoid ambiguity, the term *flat relation* will be used to indicate an ordinary relation, and the term *nested relation* will be used to indicate the more general case, namely a *possibly* nested relation: a flat relation is also a nested relation, whereas the converse is not necessarily true.

```
var Company: relation
              Dept: string;
              Projects: relation
                        P_Code: string;
                        Budget: integer;
                        Staff: relation
                               Employee: string;
                               Role: string
                               end
                        end;
              Manager: string
       end
```

Figure 8.1. A nested database scheme

We will also use a more compact notation with parentheses () instead of the keywords **relation** and **end,** and the atomic domains omitted, if they are irrelevant or understood.

The notion of a *nested relation* over a nested relation scheme is the natural extension of the notion of a flat relation. A *nested tuple* is a function that associates a value from the corresponding domain with each attribute in the scheme. The value is atomic if the attribute is simple, and it is a nested relation otherwise. A *nested relation* is a set of nested tuples over the corresponding scheme.[4] Figure 8.1 shows a nested relation scheme for an application referring to a company that is subdivided into departments, where teams of employees work on projects, each of which has a budget. In the compact notation, we would write it as follows:

$$Company:(Dept, Projects:(P\_Code,\ Budget, Staff:(Employee,\ Role)), Manager)$$

Figure 8.2 shows an instance of the nested relation *Company.*

---

[4]Some authors introduce the requirement that the values of nested attributes are *nonempty* sets. For most of the results, this distinction is irrelevant, and we will therefore ignore it, except when it is strictly necessary.

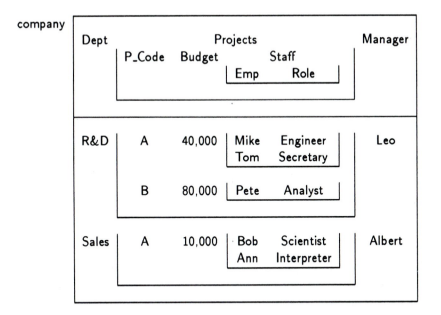

Figure 8.2. A nested relation

The main motivation for adopting flat relations (see Codd [75, p. 381]) was their simplicity: they are convenient from the implementation point of view (storage structures for them are very natural and potentially efficient), for the interchange of data between different systems, and for the formulation of queries. Also, Codd [75] argued that a nested relation whose primary key is composed of simple attributes can always be transformed into a collection of flat relations. Figure 8.3 shows the collection of relations corresponding to the nested relation in Figure 8.2.

However, it cannot be said that flat relations are more desirable from every point of view; in most cases (for example the one in Figures 8.2 and 8.3), the flat model requires several relations rather than a single one. Also, there are applications whose data have a naturally nested structure: they include office systems, which usually involve forms with repeated fields, computer-aided design, and text- and picture-processing systems. On the basis of these arguments, var-

company

Dept	Manager
R&D	Leo
Sales	Albert

projects

Dept	P_Code	Budget
R&D	A	40,000
R&D	B	80,000
Sales	A	10,000

staff

Dept	P_Code	Emp	Role
R&D	A	Mike	Engineer
R&D	A	Tom	Secretary
R&D	B	Pete	Analyst
Sales	A	Bob	Scientist
Sales	A	Ann	Interpreter

Figure 8.3. Flat relations corresponding to the nested relation in Figure 8.2

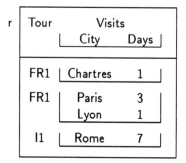

Figure 8.4. A nested relation with undesirable properties

ious authors, beginning with Makinouchi [168], proposed the use of nested relations.

A desirable form of nested relations can be obtained by restricting their definition on the basis of the following observation. Let us consider the relation r in Figure 8.4: it has clearly undesirable features. We could even say that it is "wrong." One of the motivations for introducing nested relations is that data often have a complex structure, and we need to group related information into sets. In the example, we have tours, with the visits included in each tour, with cities visited and number of days respectively spent. It would be reasonable to group together, in one tuple, all the visits included in each tour—and this does not happen for r. The notion of *partitioned normal form* characterizes the nested relations that are well behaved with respect to this point of view. It makes use of FDs, whose notion trivially extends to nested relations, since equality of tuples over a nested attribute is meaningful, being equality of sets of tuples.

Let $r(XY)$ be a nested relation, where the attributes in X are simple and those in Y nested. We say that r is in *partitioned normal form (PNF)* if

1. r satisfies the FD $X \rightarrow Y$, and

2. for each $A \in Y$ and for each $t \in r$, the relation $t[A]$ is in PNF.

Equivalently, a relation is in PNF if, at each level of nesting, the simple attributes form a key: the relation (and each of its subrelations) does not contain two distinct tuples that agree on the simple attributes. If a relation is flat, then the set of attributes Y is empty, and so $X \rightarrow Y$ is trivially satisfied. This guarantees a bound for the recursive definition.

The above definition refers to the *instance level* of nested relations. It can be formulated with reference to the scheme level on the basis of suitable definitions of FDs (or at least keys) with respect to the internal relation schemes.

8.3   Languages for Nested Relations

Query languages for the nested relational model can be defined by extending the various classic languages. Among the various possibilities, the easiest and most interesting extension is the algebraic one. When defining an algebra for a generalization of the relational model, two kinds of extensions may be considered: (1) extensions to existing operators that take into account the more general structures, and (2) new operators meaningful only in the more general framework. In case 1, the semantics of the operators should reduce to the classic one if the operators are flat relations.

This section is divided into three subsections. The first one is devoted to two operators that characterize most of the algebras for nested relations. The second and third are much shorter, and discuss the extensions of the traditional algebraic operators and the basic ideas of a relational calculus for nested relations, respectively.

Nesting and Unnesting

There are two new, important operators used to modify the structure of relations, called *nest* and *unnest*, respectively.

The *nest* operator, as its name suggests, produces nested relations from flatter ones (not necessarily flat). Given a relation and a subset of its attributes, it aggregates the tuples that agree on those attributes. In order to give the formal definition, we need some notation. Let r be a nested relation over the attributes (and domains) $(A_1 : T_1, \ldots, A_h : T_h, A_{h+1} : T_{h+1}, \ldots, A_k : T_k)$, with $0 < h < k$, and B an attribute name not appearing in $A_1, \ldots, A_k$. Then the nesting of r with respect to $A_{h+1} \ldots A_k$ aggregated into B (assuming that the subscripts of the attributes have been suitably rearranged) is denoted by $\nu_{B=(A_{h+1} \ldots A_k)}$, and it is a relation over the attributes

$$(A_1 : T_1, \ldots, A_h : T_h, B : (A_{h+1} : T_{h+1}, \ldots, A_k : T_k))$$

containing the tuples obtained from the tuples in r by aggregating the tuples that have equal values on $A_1 \ldots A_h$. More precisely, $\nu_{B=(A_{h+1} \ldots A_k)}$ contains a tuple t for each tuple $t' \in \pi_{A_1 \ldots A_h}(r)$, defined as follows:

- $t[A_1 \ldots A_h] = t'[A_1 \ldots A_h]$;

- $t[B] = \{t''[A_{h+1} \ldots A_k] \mid t'' \in r \text{ and } t''[A_1 \ldots A_h] = t'[A_1 \ldots A_h]\}$; that is, $t[B]$ is equal to the set of tuples obtained by projecting on $A_{h+1} \ldots A_k$ the tuples in r that are equal to t' on $A_1 \ldots A_h$ (note that B is a nested attribute and so $t[B]$ is a set of tuples over the domain of B, which consists of $A_{h+1} \ldots A_k$).

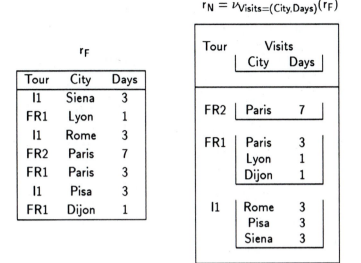

Figure 8.5. A flat relation and a nest operation

As an example, consider Figure 8.5: the nested relation r_N can be obtained by means of a nest operation from the flat relation r_F:

$$r_N = \nu_{Visits=(City,Days)}(r_F)$$

The *unnest* operator is a sort of inverse of nest. Given a nested relation, it disaggregates the tuples over a nested attribute, thus producing a flatter structure. Let r be a nested relation over the attributes $A_1, \ldots, A_h, B$, where B is a nested attribute over attributes $A_{h+1} \ldots A_k$ (with our notation, the type of r is $(A_1 : T_1, \ldots, A_h : T_h, B : (A_{h+1} : T_{h+1}, \ldots, A_k : T_k))$, where the T_i's are the types of the various attributes, which could be simple or nested). Then, the unnest of r with respect to B, denoted by $\mu_B(r)$, is a relation over the attributes and types $(A_1 : T_1, \ldots, A_h : T_h, A_{h+1} : T_{h+1}, \ldots, A_k : T_k)$ defined as follows:

$$\mu_B(r) = \{\, t \mid \text{ there is } t' \in r \text{ such that } t[A_1 \ldots A_h] = t'[A_1 \ldots A_h] \text{ and } t[A_{h+1} \ldots A_k] \in t'[B] \,\}$$

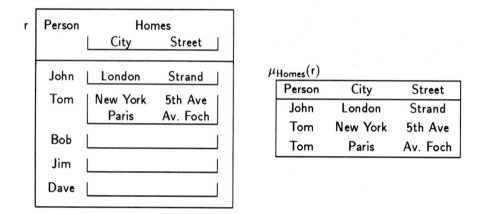

Figure 8.6. Unnesting relations with empty sets

$\mu_{Homes}(r)$ Person	City	Street
John	London	Strand
Tom	New York	5th Ave
Tom	Paris	Av. Foch
Bob	ϕ	ϕ
Jim	ϕ	ϕ
Dave	ϕ	ϕ

Figure 8.7. Unnesting the relation in Figure 8.6 with null values

Essentially, an unnest operation generates for each tuple in the operand relation as many tuples as there are in the relation that is the value of the attribute being unnested. If empty sets are allowed as values for nested attributes, then, following this definition, no tuple is generated (see Figure 8.6); an alternative definition could be adopted for this case, provided that null values are allowed for atomic attributes (see Figure 8.7).

Let us clarify the relationship between nest and unnest—in particular, whether one is the inverse of the other. Unnest is indeed the inverse of nest. For example, unnesting the nested relation r_N in Figure 8.5 on the attribute *Visits*, we obtain the original relation r_F: $r_F = \mu_{Visits}(\nu_{Visits=(City,Days)}(r_F))$. This is not coincidental: as proved in the next theorem, it is always the case that a nest followed by an unnest on the same attributes preserves the original operand.

THEOREM 8.1 For every nested relation $r(X)$ and for every $Y \subseteq X$ and $A \notin X$, it is the case that $r = \mu_A(\nu_{A=(Y)}(r))$.

PROOF We show that each tuple in r is also in $\mu_A(\nu_{A=(Y)}(r))$, and vice versa. Let t be a tuple in r; we show that $t \in \mu_A(\nu_{A=(Y)}(r))$. By definition of the nest operator, since $t \in r$, there is a tuple $t' \in nest_{A=(Y)}(r))$ such that $t'[X-Y] = t[X-Y]$ and $t[Y] \in t'[A]$. Then, by definition of the unnest operator, since $t' \in nest_{A=(Y)}(r)$, there is a tuple $t'' \in \mu_A(\nu_{A=(Y)}(r))$ for each element $t_A \in t'[A]$, with $t''[X-Y] = t'[X-Y]$ and $t''[Y] = t_A$. Therefore, since $t[Y] \in t'[A]$, there is a tuple $t'' \in \mu_A(\nu_{A=(Y)}(r))$ such that $t''[X-Y] = t'[X-Y]$ and $t''[Y] = t[Y]$. It follows that $t'' = t$, and so $t \in \mu_A(\nu_{A=(Y)}(r))$, which completes the first part of the proof.

With respect to the converse, let t be a tuple in $\mu_A(\nu_{A=(Y)}(r))$; we show that $t \in r$. If $t \in \mu_A(\nu_{A=(Y)}(r))$, then there is a tuple $t' \in \nu_{A=(Y)}(r)$ such that $t'[X-Y] = t[X-Y]$ and $t[Y] \in t'[A]$. Therefore, by definition of the nest operator, there is a tuple $t'' \in r$ such that $t''[X-Y] = t[X-Y]$ and $t''[Y] = t[Y]$. That is, $t'' = t$, and so $t \in r$. □

The dual property about unnests followed by nests does not hold in general; it holds in some cases. For example, given the relation r_N in Figure 8.5, we have that

$$r_N = \nu_{Visits=(City,Days)}(r_F) = \nu_{Visits=(City,Days)}(\mu_{Visits}(r_N))$$

whereas the same does not hold for the relation r in Figure 8.8.

Invariance of unnest-renest can be characterized by means of functional dependencies. We state a simple lemma first.

LEMMA 8.1 Let $r(XY)$ be a nested relation, where $A \notin XY$ and $X \cap Y$ is empty. Then $\nu_{A=(Y)}(r)$ satisfies the FD $X \to A$. □

r

Tour	Visits	
	City	Days
FR1	Chartres	1
FR1	Paris	3
	Lyon	1
I1	Rome	7

$\mu_{\text{Visits}}(r)$

Tour	City	Days
FR1	Chartres	1
FR1	Paris	3
FR1	Lyon	1
I1	Rome	7

$\nu_{\text{Visits}=(\text{City},\text{Days})}(\mu_{\text{Visits}}(r))$

Tour	Visits	
	City	Days
FR1	Chartres	1
	Paris	3
	Lyon	1
I1	Rome	7

Figure 8.8. An unnest followed by a nest

THEOREM 8.2 Let $r(XA)$ be a nested relation, where A is a nested attribute over the attributes Y (with $A \notin XY$). Then r equals $\nu_{A=(Y)}(\mu_A(r))$ if and only if r satisfies $X \to A$.

PROOF

If. Let r satisfy $X \to A$. Then, we show that $r = \nu_{A=(Y)}(\mu_A(r))$, by showing that (1) if $t \in r$, then $t \in \nu_{A=(Y)}(\mu_A(r))$, and (2) vice versa. In order to prove Claim 1, let $t \in r$. By definition of unnest and nest, there is a tuple $t' \in \nu_{A=(Y)}(\mu_A(r))$ such that $t'[X] = t[X]$. Now, since r satisfies the FD $X \to A$, there is no other tuple $t'' \in r$ that agrees with t on X, and therefore all the tuples in $\mu_A(r)$ that agree with t on X originate from t, and so the subsequent nest rebuilds t exactly as in the original relation. Let us now prove Claim 2. If $t \in \nu_{A=(Y)}(\mu_A(r))$, then for each $t' \in t[A]$ there is a tuple $t'' \in \mu_A(r)$ such that $t''[Y] = t'$

and $t''[X] = t'[X] = t[X]$. Now, let $t'_1, t'_2 \in t[A]$ and consider the corresponding $t''_1, t''_2 \in \mu_A(r)$; by definition of unnest, there are tuples $t_1, t_2 \in r$ from which they respectively originate. Since $t_1[X] = t_2[X]$ and r satisfies $X \to A$, we have that $t_1 = t_2$; that is, t''_1, t''_2 originate from the same tuple, and so we have that all tuples in $t[A]$ originate from the same tuple $t'' \in r$, which agrees with t on X. Therefore $t = t''$, and so $t \in r$.

Only if. By Lemma 8.1, $\nu_{A=(Y)}(\mu_A(r))$ satisfies $X \to A$; thus, if $\nu_{A=(Y)}(\mu_A(r))$ equals r, we also have that r satisfies $X \to A$. □

By definition of PNF, we have the following corollary, which confirms the desirability of PNF itself.

COROLLARY 8.1   If $r(XA)$ is a nested relation in PNF, where A is a nested attribute over the attributes Y (with $A \notin XY$ and $X \cap Y \neq \emptyset$), then $r = \nu_{A=(Y)}(\mu_A(r))$. □

Therefore, if we limit our attention to the world of PNF relations, nest and unnest are indeed each the inverse of the other.

As PNF is a nice property for nested relations, it is important to study whether it is preserved by the various operators. Given a PNF relation, does a nest or an unnest operation produce a PNF relation? What about the classic operators? We provide an answer to the first question here, and briefly discuss the second in the next subsection.

THEOREM 8.3   The class of PNF relations is closed under unnesting.

PROOF   Let $r(VA)$ be a PNF relation, where A is a nested attribute over the attributes Z, and $V = XW$, where the attributes in X are simple and those in W nested. We show that $\mu_A(r)$ is also in PNF. As the internal subrelations in $\mu_A(r)$ also appear in r, in order to prove that it is in PNF, it suffices to show that $\mu_A(r)$ satisfies the FD $XZ \to W$, or, equivalently, that it does not contain a pair of distinct tuples which agree on XZ (and disagree on W). Assume by way of contradiction that such tuples t_1, t_2 exist; by definition of unnest, they originate from a pair of tuples $t'_1, t'_2 \in r$, with $t'_1[XW] = t_1[XW]$, $t'_2[XW] = t_2[XW]$, and from two tuples in subrelations $t''_1 \in t'_1[A]$ and $t''_2 \in t'_2[A]$, with $t_1[Z] = t''_1$ and $t_2[Z] = t''_2$. Then, if $t_1[XZ] = t_2[XZ]$ and $t_1 \neq t_2$, we have that $t_1[W] \neq t_2[W]$. Thus

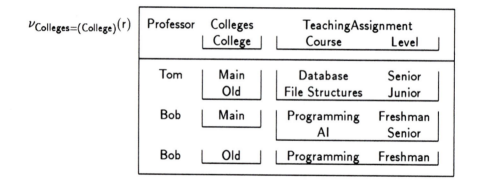

Figure 8.9. Nesting does not preserve PNF

(since $t_1[XZ] = t_2[XZ]$, $t_1'[XW] = t_1[XW]$, and $t_2'[XW] = t_2[XW]$), we have $t_1'[X] = t_2'[X]$, and (since $t_1[W] \neq t_2[W]$, $t_1'[XW] = t_1[XW]$, and $t_2'[XW] = t_2[XW]$) $t_1'[W] \neq t_2'[W]$. That is, t_1' and t_2' are distinct tuples in r that agree on X; since X is the set of the simple attributes of r, this contradicts the assumption that r is in PNF.   □

The analogous property does not hold in general for nesting, as shown by the counterexample in Figure 8.9. Again, a characterization of the property can be expressed in terms of FDs, as shown in the next theorem, whose proof is left as Exercise 8.2.

THEOREM 8.4 Let $r(XYZ)$, where the attributes in X are simple and those in Y are nested. Then $\nu_{A=(Z)}(r)$ is in PNF if and only if r satisfies the FD $X \to Y$.   □

Traditional Algebraic Operators over Nested Relations

Algebraic operators can be extended to nested relations by attempting to treat values regardless of whether they are atomic or nested. This requires some technicalities for selection, but it is immediate for the other operators.

If attention is restricted to PNF relations, problems arise. Let us refer to the set-theoretic operators first. Union, intersection, and difference do not preserve PNF (see Figures 8.10 and 8.11), or at least they produce unnatural results. For example, the intersection of the relations r_1 and r_2 in Figure 8.10 is empty, whereas it could be argued that it would be more reasonable to produce as a result the sets of *Dept*'s that appear in both r_1 and r_2 and, for each of them, the projects that appear in both relations, with the respective employees that appear in both (see Figure 8.12). In general, it would be desirable to have definitions for the set-theoretic operators that operate, according to their meaning (union, intersection, difference), by going down in the nested structure of the relations. The desirable results of extended versions of the set-theoretic operators on the relations in Figure 8.10 are shown in Figures 8.11 and 8.12 (assuming that empty-set values are not allowed). Note that the results all enjoy PNF. We leave as Exercise 8.9 the definitions of extended operators that satisfy these properties. Cartesian product, selection, and renaming can be easily shown to preserve PNF (Exercise 8.10). For projection, the same problems as for set-theoretic operations arise: the classical definition does not preserve PNF. An extended version consisting of a classical projection followed by a (recursive) merge of the tuples with identical values on the atomic attributes does preserve PNF (Exercise 8.11).

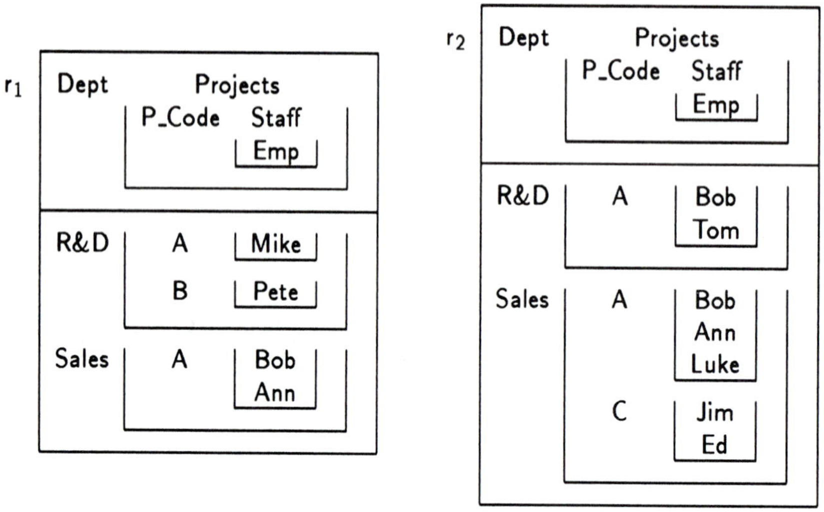

Figure 8.10. Operands for set-theoretic operations

A Relational Calculus for Nested Relations

A (tuple) calculus for nested relations can be defined as an extension to the TRC presented in Section 2.8. It involves two additional forms of atoms:

1. $x_1 \in x_2.A$, where x_1 and x_2 are variables defined over X_1 and X_2, respectively, and A is a nested attribute in X_2, internally defined on X_1; this asserts that x_1 is a tuple in the subrelation $x_2[A]$.

2. $x.A = e$, where x is a variable defined over X, A is a nested attribute in X, internally defined on a set Y, and e is an expression of the TRC defining a relation over Y.

Moreover, atoms of the form $x_1.A_1 \theta x_2.A_2$ or $x_1.A_1 \theta c$ may also involve set-valued attributes (although we may assume that in such a case the comparison operator is equality or inequality).

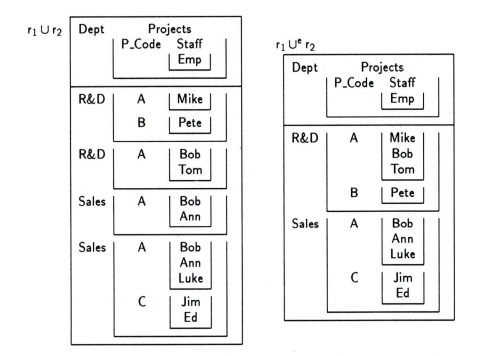

Figure 8.11. Union and extended union of the relations in Figure 8.10

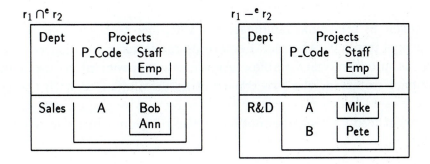

Figure 8.12. Extended intersection and difference on the relations in Figure 8.10

8.4   Extending Nested Relations

Let us consider again the definition of the nested relational model, as proposed at the beginning of Section 8.2. As a matter of fact, the relation constructor can be considered as the composition of two constructors, which correspond, in Pascal terms, to the record (with no variant part) and set constructors: as we know, a relation is a set of homogeneous tuples, and tuples are essentially records, with fields corresponding to attribute names and component types corresponding to domains. That is, a flat relation

$$\textbf{var } R\text{: } \textbf{relation } A_1\text{: } D_1 \text{ ; } A_2\text{: } D_2 \text{ ; } \dots \text{ ; } A_k\text{: } D_k \textbf{ end};$$

could be described as

$$\textbf{var } R\text{: } \textbf{set of record } A_1\text{: } D_1 \text{ ; } A_2\text{: } D_2 \text{ ; } \dots \text{ ; } A_k\text{: } D_k \textbf{ end};$$

We could even have said that the whole database is a variable that has a type with a top-level record constructor, a field for each relation scheme, and lower levels as above:

$$\textbf{var } D\text{: } \textbf{record}$$
$$R_1\text{: } \textbf{set of record } A_{1,1}\text{: } D_{1,1} \text{ ; } \dots \text{ ; } A_{1,k_1}\text{: } D_{1,k_1} \textbf{ end}$$
$$\vdots$$
$$R_n\text{: } \textbf{set of record } A_{n,1}\text{: } D_{n,1} \text{ ; } \dots \text{ ; } A_{n,k_n}\text{: } D_{n,k_n} \textbf{ end}$$
$$\textbf{end}$$

However, in relational languages the reference to the whole database is always implicit, whereas the various relations are indicated explicitly, as autonomous variables. Again, it is convenient to use a more compact notation: the two constructors are indicated with the symbols ⊛ (set) and ⊗ (record), with their respective arguments enclosed in parentheses. Using this notation, the relation scheme above is denoted by

$$\textbf{var } R\text{: } \circledast (\otimes(A_1\text{: } D_1 , A_2\text{: } D_2 , \dots , A_k\text{: } D_k))$$

or, if the domains are irrelevant or implicit, by

$$\textbf{var } R\text{: } \circledast (\otimes(A_1 , A_2 , \dots , A_k))$$

Then nested relation schemes have the following form:

$$\textbf{var } R\text{: } \textbf{set of record } A_1 : T_1; \ldots; A_k : T_k \textbf{ end}$$

where each of the T_j's, for $j = 1, \ldots, k$, is either

1. an atomic domain D_j, or

2. a nested relation scheme:

$$\textbf{set of record } A_{j_1} : T_{j_1}; \ldots; A_{j_l} : T_{j_l} \textbf{ end}$$

In the compact notation, the relation scheme in Figure 8.13 can be described as

$$\textbf{var } \textit{Company: } \circledast(\otimes(\textit{Dept, Projects:}\circledast(\otimes(\textit{Code, Budget,}$$
$$\textit{Staff:}\circledast(\otimes(\textit{Employee, Role}))))))$$

It is interesting to note that in nested relations, the set and record constructors always alternate. More precisely, (1) the top level has always a set constructor; (2) the argument of each set constructor is a record constructor; and (3) the arguments of each record constructor are set constructors or atomic domains. These properties are more apparent if a graphic notation is used: a scheme can be represented by means of a tree with three types of nodes that correspond respectively to the two constructors and to atomic domains. Each atomic or set node has a label, which is the relation name for the root and the corresponding attribute name for each of the others. Then (1) the root is always a set node; (2) each set node has one and only one child, which is a record node; (3) the children of each record node are set nodes or leaves; and (4) each leaf is an atomic node and vice versa. Figure 8.13 shows the tree corresponding to the nested relation scheme

$$R : \circledast(\otimes(A_1 : D_1, A_2 : \circledast(\otimes(A_{21} : \circledast(\otimes(A_{211} : D_1, A_{212} : D_2)),$$
$$A_{22} : D_2)), A_3 : D_3))$$

Now, a more general model can be obtained by relaxing the constraints that require (1) alternation between the two constructors, and (2) a set constructor at the top level. In this model, the components of a database should no longer be called *relations*, since the top-level set-of-record pattern need not be satisfied. We use the term *object*; therefore, an *object scheme* has one of the following forms:

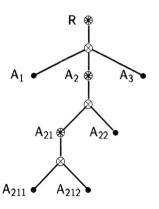

Figure 8.13. Graphic representation for a nested relation scheme

1. D, where D is an atomic domain;

2. $\circledast(O)$, where O is an object scheme;

3. $\otimes(A_1 : O_1, \ldots, A_n : O_n)$, where the A_i's are distinct symbols, and the O_i's are object schemes.

Object instances can be recursively defined following the definition of object scheme. Let O be an object scheme;

1. if O is an atomic domain D, then each element of D is an instance of O;

2. if O has the form $\circledast(O')$, then an instance of O is a finite set of instances of O';

3. if O has the form $\otimes(A_1 : O_1, \ldots, A_n : O_n)$, then an instance of O is a tuple t over $A_1, \ldots, A_n$ such that $t[A_i]$ is an instance of O_i, for $1 \leq i \leq n$.

Figure 8.14 shows the linguistic, compact, and graphic representations of an object scheme referring to a soccer tournament, with location, date (year and month) and teams, for which names and possible jersey colors are relevant. An instance of the object is shown in Figure 8.15.

tournament :   ⊗(location, date : ⊗(year, month),

teams : ⊛(⊗(name, colors : ⊛(⊛(string)))))

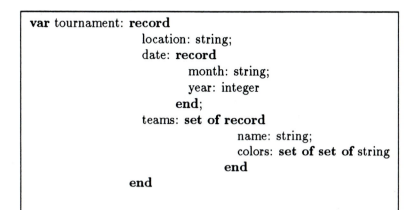

```
var tournament: record
              location: string;
              date: record
                      month: string;
                      year: integer
                    end;
              teams: set of record
                            name: string;
                            colors: set of set of string
                          end
        end
```

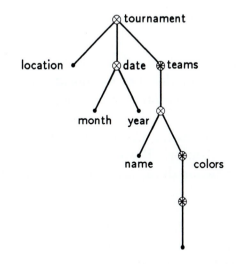

Figure 8.14. Three representations for an object scheme

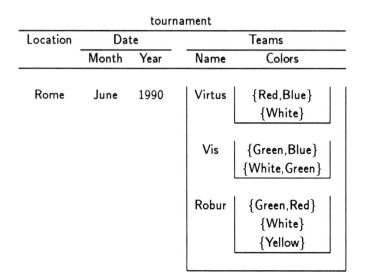

Figure 8.15. An instance of the object scheme in Figure 8.14

As a matter of fact, this model is only an apparent generalization of the nested relational model. Let us consider the restrictions on the nested schemes discussed before, which are relaxed here:

1. The possibility of having a record constructor at the top level is indeed a generalization. However, in databases we usually have *sets* of homogeneous data, so this feature is probably not very important.

2. If a set constructor has an argument that is not a record constructor, then we can always introduce an intermediate record constructor with a single field.

3. If a record constructor has another record constructor as one of its components, then we can collapse the two into a single record constructor (possibly changing some attribute names).

```
var tournament: relation
                location: string;
                month: string;
                year: integer;
                teams: relation
                       name: string;
                       jersey-colors: relation
                                      colors: relation
                                              color: string
                                      end
                               end
                       end
                end
```

Figure 8.16. A nested relation scheme for the object scheme in Figure 8.14

This transformation is always possible, and it can be shown (see Exercise 8.15) that the new object scheme has the same representative power as the original one. Thus, the new model is not really more expressive than the model with rigid alternation between sets and records. However, it may allow more natural representations for some applications. Figure 8.16 shows the linguistic representation of a nested relation scheme corresponding to the object scheme in Figure 8.14; a top-level set constructor has been added; and the **set of record** patterns have been compacted as **relation**.

Further constructs can be added to complex objects in order to allow for more refined representations of object systems. They include *multiset, sequence* (as in the ALGRES proposal [61,62]), or even *array* (useful for engineering or scientific applications). Although significant in practice, they would not add much to our discussion, and therefore we will not refer to them again.

A further extension can be obtained by introducing another constructor, which allows for more flexible structures in the objects. With respect to the relational model, we already have less rigidity, having relaxed the first normal form assumption and having allowed free composition of the set and record constructors. However, apart from the possibility of using null values, we still have for each tuple (or subtuple) a fixed relation, with exactly the same attributes and with exactly the same domain. Consider, for example, an application concerning publications. For each publication we have a title, but we may have author(s) if it is a monograph or an article, or editor(s) if it is a collection, a publisher and a city if it is a book, and so on. Now, with the nested relational model, or its extension just described, it is impossible to model this application unless we use many null values. A natural way to handle this kind of situation is by means of the *union* construct, which resembles the variant record construct of Pascal.

The definition of an *object scheme* is then extended with a fourth case:

4. $\oplus(O_1, \ldots, O_n)$, where $\oplus$ is the *union* construct and the O_i's are object schemes.

Similarly for the definition of an *object instance*:

4. o is an instance of $\oplus(O_1, \ldots, O_n)$, if and only if it is an instance of O_i, for some $1 \le i \le n$.

A variation of the union construct is the *marked union*, where labels are associated with the various alternatives; at the scheme level, we would thus have:

4. $\bigoplus(A_1 : O_1, \ldots, A_n : O_n)$, where $\bigoplus$ is the *marked union* construct, the A_i's are distinct symbols, and the O_i's are object schemes.

At the instance level, we would have

4. An instance of $\bigoplus(A_1 : O_1, \ldots, A : n : O_n)$ is a pair of the form $A_i : o_i$, where o_i is an instance of O_i, for some $1 \le i \le n$.

A scheme for the bibliographic application, using the marked union construct, is shown in Figure 8.17, and an instance is shown in Figure 8.18.

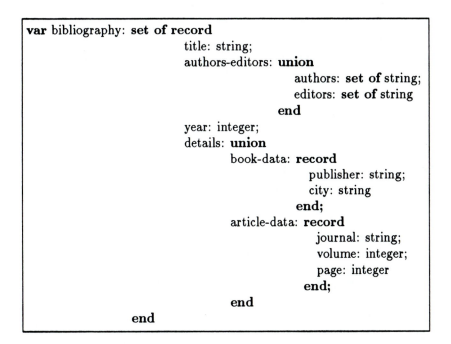

```
var bibliography: set of record
                    title: string;
                    authors-editors: union
                                    authors: set of string;
                                    editors: set of string
                                end
                    year: integer;
                    details: union
                        book-data: record
                                    publisher: string;
                                    city: string
                                end;
                        article-data: record
                                    journal: string;
                                    volume: integer;
                                    page: integer
                                end;
                    end
            end
```

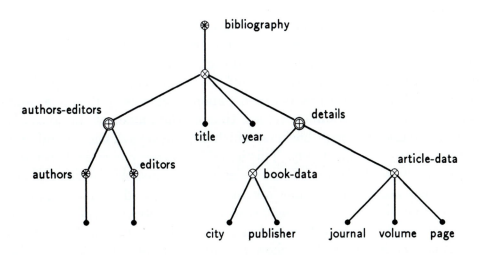

Figure 8.17. An object scheme with marked union

bibliography

Title	Authors-Editors		Year	Details			
	Authors			Book-data			
		Editors		Publisher		City	
						Article-data	
				Journal	Volume		Page
Summa Technica	{Jim, John}		1887	XYZ Publ. Co.		New Orleans	
A theorem on ...	{Dave}		1956	The Mag	87		764
Opera omnia	{Tom}		1920	AA Publishers	Chicago		
Results on ...	{Sam, Mike}		1934	Acta	132		137

Figure 8.18. An instance for the object scheme in Figure 8.17

8.5   Complex Objects with Identity

All the models we have seen in the previous sections, beginning with
the relational one, embed all the semantics of the object system in
the values of the domains.[5] If two related portions of the object system are represented by means of two relations, then the relationship
between them can only be represented by means of common values.
For this reason, the relational model and all its extensions we have
seen so far are said to be *value-based*. For example, in Figure 8.19 we
can establish connections between papers, journals, publishers, and
cities through the common values, that is, the names of the journals
and the names of the publishers, which are the keys of the second and
third relations, respectively. This is indeed rather convenient in most
cases, as it can be implemented by means of joins. At the same time,
some real-world entities may not have expressive identifiers, or their
values may be complex, either because they involve several attributes
or because the single attribute has a long value. As a matter of fact,
all relations in Figure 8.19 show this disadvantage in some way: for
both the relations *journals* and *publishers*, the key is composed of a

---

[5]To be more precise, the *structural*, or *static*, semantics; the *behavioral*, or *dynamic*, semantics is expressed by means of the programs.

papers

Author	Title	Journal	Vol.	Page	Year
Tom	Category ...	J. of Algebra & Geometry	27	331	1965
Tim	Relaxation	J. of Algebra & Geometry	29	132	1967
Mike	A result on ...	Ann. Society of Sc.	79	231	1967
Tim	A theorem on ...	Int. J. of Calculus	80	34	1967

journals

Name	Publisher
J. of Algebra & Geometry	Mathematics Press
Ann. Society of Sc.	The Society of Scientists
Int. J. of Calculus	Mathematics Press

publishers

Name	City
Mathematics Press	London
The Society of Scientists	New York

Figure 8.19. Relationships represented by common values

single attribute, but its value is always long, which wastes space, creates more possibilities for mistakes, and wastes time when values are inserted. For the relation *papers*, it would actually be difficult to say which attributes form a key, as papers usually but not always have different titles, and so on. In most practical situations, new, user-defined (or somehow computed, but visible to the user) identifiers are introduced. Many codes or numbers in business or organization applications have been introduced in order to provide short, unique identifiers for the various objects. Social security numbers, student numbers, file numbers, and so forth, originate from this need. Following this technique, the relations in Figure 8.19 could be modified by introducing one attribute for each relation, whose values uniquely identify the respective tuples and are used to establish connections (Figure 8.20).

papers

Code	Author	Title	Journal	Vol.	Page	Year
To65	Tom	Category ...	JAG	27	331	1965
Ti67	Tim	Relaxation	JAG	29	132	1967
Mi67	Mike	A result on ...	ASS	79	231	1967
Ti67a	Tim	A theorem on ...	IJC	80	34	1967

journals

Code	Name	Publisher
JAG	J. of Algebra & Geometry	MP
ASS	Ann. Society of Sc.	SS
IJC	Int. J. of Calculus	MP

publishers

Code	Name	City
MP	Mathematics Press	London
SS	The Society of Scientists	New York

Figure 8.20. Relationships represented by user-defined identifiers

Value-based models have a number of advantages. Since all information is retained in the values, all semantic relationships, though somehow implicit, can be detected. For the same reason, interchange of data between different systems is simplified, as nothing is hidden—exchanging the values is sufficient. They also have some disadvantages, some of which have been shown in the previous example. If an object does not have a natural identifier, an artificial one may be useful or needed. Also, semantic relationships are not really explicit, being hidden in values. It is also difficult to represent taxonomic hierarchies among classes of objects. Assume, for example, that we want to represent data about publications of various types, say journal papers, monographs, edited volumes, and articles in collections. It is clear that the relevant properties depend on the type of the publication: each publication has a title; edited volumes have editors; other publications have authors; monographs have publishers; and so on. If a single relation is used to represent all these data, then it contains many null values. Otherwise, it would not be easy to decide how to decompose and then to relate data in the various relations.

These shortcomings can be overcome by introducing the notion of *object identity*: each object in the database has a unique identifier (the *object identifier*, or *oid*), which is managed by the system and not visible to the user. Models with object identity are no longer value-based, as there is other information than that represented by means of values. They are usually called *identity-based* or *object-based*. Let us describe a simplified identity-based model. A *database scheme* contains a set of *class schemes*, each having a name and a type. The types have the following forms, which extend the possible forms for object schemes discussed in the previous section:

1. D, where D is an atomic domain

2. $\circledast(T)$, where T is a type

3. $\otimes(A_1 : T_1, \ldots, A_n : T_n)$, where the A_i's are distinct symbols, and the T_i's are types

4. C, where C is a class name

Given a class C, we indicate with $\text{TYP}(C)$ the associated type. We assume that, for each class C, the type $\text{TYP}(C)$ has a set constructor at the top level and a record constructor at the second level. At the lower levels, the constructors can be freely combined.

At the instance level, we introduce for each class name C an additional domain $\text{OID}(C)$, whose values are the oids for the corresponding class. We assume that distinct classes have disjoint sets of oids. Then a *database* is a set of *class extensions*. The *extension* c of a class C is a subset of $\text{OID}(C)$. With each element of c there is an associated *object* with type $\text{TYP}(C)$, where the possible objects are defined as follows for a type T:

1. If T is a domain D, then the objects with type T are the elements of D.

2. If $T = \circledast(T')$, then the objects with type T are the finite subsets of the objects with type T'.

3. If $T = \otimes(A_1 : T_1, \ldots, A_n : T_n)$, then the objects with type T are tuples over $A_1, \ldots, A_n$, whose values on each A_i are objects with type T_i.

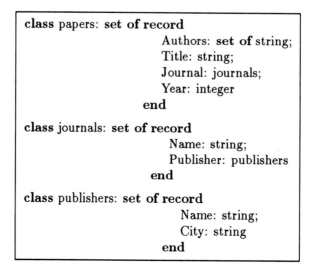

Figure 8.21. A database scheme for an object-based model

4. If T is a class name C, then the objects with type T are the oids in $\text{OID}(C)$.

Essentially, the oids are used to make references between objects in different classes—as conceptual, but hidden, pointers. A scheme and an instance for an application similar to that in Figure 8.20 are shown in Figures 8.21 and 8.22 respectively.

It is interesting to note that object identity makes it possible to define recursive objects or, more generally, cyclic structures—something that is not allowed in value-based models, because it would lead to the definition of unbounded objects. Figure 8.23 shows an example of a recursive class referring to persons, with various properties, including spouse. In the graphic notation already used in this chapter, we could represent references to classes, thus obtaining structures that possibly contain cycles, as shown in Figures 8.24 and 8.25 for the schemes in Figures 8.21 and 8.23.

The models based on identity first emerged in the framework of semantic models, which are data models used in the analysis and design of database applications in order to describe the semantics of

papers

	Authors	Title	Journal	Year
p1	{Tom,Bob}	Category ...	j1	1965
p2	{Tim}	Relaxation	j1	1967
p3	{Mike,Jim}	A result on ...	j2	1967
p4	{Tim,Sam}	A theorem on ...	j3	1967

journals

	Name	Publisher
j1	J. of Algebra & Geometry	pu1
j2	Ann. Society of Sc.	pu2
j3	Int. J. of Calculus	pu1

publishers

	Name	City
pu1	Mathematics Press	London
pu2	The Society of Scientists	New York

Figure 8.22. An instance of the database scheme in Figure 8.21

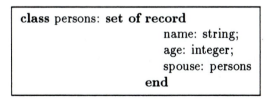

Figure 8.23. A scheme with a recursive class

the object system as accurately as possible (see Hull and King [124] and Tsichritzis and Lochovski [210] for discussions and surveys). A fundamental component of these models is the notion of *isa relationships*, an interesting form of semantic relationship between classes, which allow the representation of hierarchies or taxonomies. We omit a detailed description of how isa relationships could fit in the simple model described above, limiting the presentation to an example. The scheme in Figure 8.26 refers to a bibliography application (similar to that described by means of the complex object scheme in Figure 8.17),

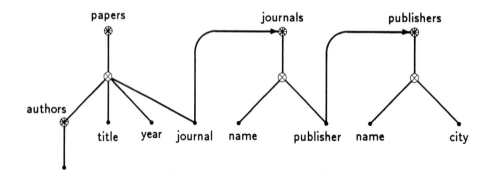

Figure 8.24. Graphic representation for the scheme in Figure 8.21

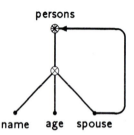

Figure 8.25. Graphic representation for a recursive scheme

with various types of publications. Each class has an associated type with a top level that has a **set of record** structure; the keyword **attributes** is used instead of **set of record** because each class inherits the attributes of the classes that appear in its **isa** clause. For example, the type of *authored-publication* is a **set of record** with the fields *authors*, explicitly mentioned, and *title* and *year* inherited from publication, and so forth. At the instance level there are a few subtle points that can be solved in different ways; they are left as exercises.

Query languages for identity-based models can take advantage of oids to implement connections. The "dot notation" used in relational languages to denote attribute values can be extended by allowing references to objects related to one another by means of oids. For ex-

```
class publication: attributes
                        title: string;
                        year: integer
                  end
class authored-publication isa publication: attributes
                                               authors: set of string
                                            end
class edited-publication isa publication: attributes
                                            editors: set of string
                                         end
class book isa publication: attributes
                              publisher: string;
                           end
class monograph isa book, authored-publication
class collection isa book, edited-publication
class journal-article isa authored-publication: attributes
                                                  journal: string;
                                               end
class paper-in-collection isa authored-publication: attributes
                                                       in: collection;
                                                    end
```

Figure 8.26. A scheme with isa relationships

ample, consider the following query in tuple relational calculus, which
refers to the database in Figure 8.20 and requests the triples with paper titles, journal names, and publisher's city for all the papers in the
database:

$$\{t_1.Title, t_2.Name, t_3.City \mid$$
$$papers(t_1) \wedge journals(t_2) \wedge publishers(t_3) \wedge$$
$$t_1.Journal = t_2.Code \wedge t_2.Publisher = t_3.Code\}$$

In a calculus for an identity-based model, this could be expressed in
a more synthetic way, as follows:

$$\{ t.Title, t.Journal.Name, t.Journal.Publisher.City \mid papers(t)\}$$

Exercises

8.1 Prove that if a nested relation is completely flattened and then renested, following a sequence of nests that parallels the unnests, then the result is a PNF relation over the same scheme as the original relation.

8.2 Prove Theorem 8.4.

8.3 Show whether nesting is commutative. That is, show whether it is the case that $\nu_{A=(Y)}(\nu_{B=(Z)}(r))$ equals $\nu_{B=(Z)}(\nu_{A=(Y)}(r))$ for every nested relation $r(XYZ)$, with X, Y, Z pairwise disjoint, $A \neq B$, and A, B not in XYZ. If the answer is negative, give a characterization of commutativity.

8.4 Let $\Omega(r)$ be an expression obtained by repeated (correct) applications of nest and unnest: $\Omega(r) = \Omega_n(\Omega_{n-1}(\ldots(\Omega_2(\Omega_1(r)))\ldots))$, where Ω_j is either $\nu_{A_j=(X_j)}$, with A_j not appearing among the attributes of $\Omega_{j-1}(\ldots(\Omega_1(r))\ldots)$, or μ_{A_j}, with A_j a nested attribute of $\Omega_{j-1}(\ldots(\Omega_1(r))\ldots)$. Given a flat relation r, give a characterization of the following equality: $\Omega(r) = r$.

8.5 Let $\Omega(r)$ be as in the previous exercise, and r be a flat relation. Prove that $\mu^*(\Omega(r)) = r$.

8.6 Show whether nest is distributive with respect to union, that is, whether it is the case that $\nu_{A=(Y)}(r_1 \cup r_2) = \nu_{A=(Y)}(r_1) \cup \nu_{A=(Y)}(r_2)$. Study the same property for unnest.

8.7 Show whether nest and unnest are distributive with respect to intersection.

8.8 Show whether nest and unnest are distributive with respect to difference.

8.9 Give definitions for extensions of the union, intersection, and difference operators with the behavior described in the text (and exemplified in Figure 8.12). Verify that the new operators preserve PNF, and discuss whether nest and unnest satisfy the distributive property with respect to them.

8.10 Show that Cartesian product, selection, and renaming preserve PNF.

8.11 Show that projection does not preserve PNF, and define an extension of it that does preserve PNF. Show that a possible definition of it would be equivalent, in the domain of PNF relations, to a classical projection followed by a (complete) unnest and by a symmetric renest.

8.12 Consider the implications of the assumption of nonnull set values for nested attributes, and that of allowing null values for atomic attributes. Also, discuss how the two are related.

8.13 Present a complete definition of the tuple relational calculus for nested relations sketched in the text.

8.14 Define a range-restricted version of the TRC for nested relations.

8.15 Formalize, with a suitable notion of equivalent representation, the claim that for each complex object scheme with the set and record constructors freely combined, there is an equivalent nested relation scheme.

8.16 Give a formal definition for a model with object identity and isa relationships.

Comments and References

Various papers exist on the recent trends in the evolution of database systems, including those by Kim [141], Silberhatz et al. [200], and Stonebraker [204]. Experimental systems have been implemented, including Starburst (Lohman et al. [158]), Postgres (Stonebraker and Kemnitz [205]), O_2 (Deux et al. [93]), Gemstone (Butterworth et al. [57]), ORION (Kim et al. [142]), IRIS (Wilkinson et al. [229]), and ObjectStore (Lamb et al. [149]).

General papers on the subject of this chapter, from which we have taken ideas and notions, were published by Abiteboul and Grumbach [4], Beeri [39], and Hull [121].

Makinouchi [168] was the first to advocate the use of nested relations. Other work related to the early development of this topic was published by Furtado and Kerchsberg [106] and by Kambayashy et al. [131]. It was probably with the work of Jaeschke and Schek [129] that the main trend of research on nested relations actually started, although they considered a restricted version of the model that allowed only nesting of single attributes, with unbounded depth. The nested relational model as we have presented it here was proposed by Fischer and Thomas [104,208].

PNF was introduced by Roth et al. [189]. The same notion in a slightly different framework (where nested attributes have no global names) was adopted as the definition of nested relations by Abiteboul and Bidoit [3]. PNF is a basic normalization goal for nested relations. A further normal form was later defined by Ozsoyoglu and Yuan [176].

Other work on nested relations was published by Arisawa et al. [18], Roth et al. [187,188,189], Fischer et al. [103,105], and Schek and Scholl [197]. Some experimental systems based on the nested relational model have been implemented: they include VERSO [37,227] (which adopts PNF relations), DASDBS [194,195,196], and AIM [83].

The first published work on algebra for nested relations was by Jaeschke and Schek [129], who introduced nest and unnest and proved a number of results about them, including a special case of Theorem 8.1 (where the nest operator can nest single attributes rather than sets thereof). Further results on these operators were later published by Fischer and Thomas [104,208], who proved the general version of Theorem 8.1. They showed other results on sequences of nests and unnests (see Exercise 8.4), which led them to introduce a new operator (the *complete unnest*,[6] denoted with μ^*) that, given a nested relation, generates a flat relation. Fischer and Thomas [104,208] also noted that FDs could be naturally extended to nested relations, and proved Theorem 8.2. Commutativity of single-attribute nesting (see Exercise 8.3) was also studied by Jaeschke and Schek [129] by means of the notion of *weak multivalued dependency*, which was later extended by Thomas and Fischer [207,208] and further studied by Fischer and Van Gucht [105]. Extensions to the classic relational algebra operators

---

[6] Fischer and Thomas [104,208] indicate it with *UNNEST**, without a name.

were proposed by Thomas and Fischer [208], with the explicit goal of attempting to treat values regardless of whether they are atomic or nested. The interaction of nest and unnest with the binary operators (for example, about distributivity) results in positive and negative properties (see Exercises 8.6, 8.7, and 8.8).

Abiteboul and Bidoit [3] and Roth et al. [189] proposed algebras for PNF relations (with preservation of PNF). Slight differences exist between the two proposals; Abiteboul and Bidoit [3] allow empty sets in nested attributes, whereas Roth et al. [189] do not.

A tuple calculus for nested relations was proposed by Roth et al. [189]. Domain independence is again relevant. Roth et al. [189] follow Ullman [212] in using safety as a remedy, and so define a safe version of the calculus with syntactic restrictions, which include a condition to avoid the uncontrolled generation of powersets. Within this framework, they proved equivalence of algebra and calculus with reference to PNF relations only. This final hypothesis is not marginal, as it allows us to unnest and renest whenever needed, in such a way that the equivalence proof is rather similar to the proof for flat relations.

Abiteboul and Beeri [2] defined powerful query languages for a complex objects model (with set and record constructors). The algebra includes operators to manipulate sets of sets: *set-collapse*, to flatten sets of sets into sets, and *powerset*, to build sets of sets. The calculus is the natural extension of the classical tuple relational calculus, with no restrictions (as opposed to what happens for the calculus proposed by Roth et al. [189]). Thus, it includes the possibility of expressing powersets, and its domain-independent subset turns out to be equivalent to algebra. For example, given an object scheme $O : \circledast(A)$ with a top-level set constructor, the powerset of an object over O can be defined as

$$\{x \mid \forall y(\neg(y \in x) \vee (O(y)))\}$$

An important point is that transitive closures can be expressed by means of powersets (and so by means of calculus expressions). Therefore, these languages are strictly more expressive than the languages for the flat relational model.

Hull and King [124] and Tsichritzis and Lochovski [210] present detailed discussions and surveys concerning semantic models. For-

Chapter 9

Logic and Databases

This chapter focuses on the influence of first-order logic on the database field. The main motivations for the study of this interaction are related to the opportunity to provide future information systems with more and more powerful mechanisms for data representation and computation. Most of the effort has been devoted to the definition of richer database systems, capable of representing *knowledge* rather than just raw *data*. There has been a convergence between research and practice in database systems and in knowledge-based systems, as proposed in the field of artificial intelligence.

The aim of this chapter is to provide an overview of the main topics concerning the relationships between logic and databases. Section 9.1 introduces the main issues. Section 9.2 is devoted to a short review of mathematical logic. Section 9.3 presents two logical approaches to databases: the proof-theoretic approach and the model-theoretic approach. In Section 9.4 we give a definition of deductive databases, and in Section 9.5 we present Datalog as a database language that allows the integration of deductive capabilities with data management.

9.1 Databases and Knowledge Bases

The field of artificial intelligence (AI) is aimed at studying techniques for the definition and construction of intelligent systems able to simulate the behavior of an observed world.

In these systems, knowledge bases containing information about the world play essentially the same role played by databases in traditional information systems. Many researchers have addressed the problem of understanding the relationship between databases and knowledge bases. The point can be summarized as follows.

- In a knowledge-based system, the contained information is formal knowledge about a specific world. It consists of observed facts, integrity constraints that hold in the considered world, and rules for inferring new knowledge from existing knowledge. A fundamental requirement for knowledge-based systems is the availability of a rich semantic theory for interpreting the information they contain in a way that is correct with respect to the world they refer to.

- In a database system, the contained information is an integrated collection of data, shared by many users, to be properly used and updated. Therefore, the availability of an effective computational theory for an efficient, reliable, and secure information management in a multiuser environment is mandatory.

Given this characterization and taking into account the requirements of the emerging applications that call for integrated systems at the confluence between the database and AI approaches, it is widely recognized that a strict interaction between these approaches, in the next years, can give rise to profitable research results. Specifically, the prevalent interest is devoted to the development of *knowledge base management systems* (*KBMS*s) capable of treating information as knowledge and of providing suitable reasoning techniques associated with the efficiency and reliability features typical of current database management systems (DBMSs).

One of the major contributions in this direction derives from logic, which is a candidate formalism for knowledge representation (having the capability, in general, to represent incomplete, negative, and recursive knowledge and to infer new knowledge from existing knowledge) with a well-defined semantics and associated with a sound proof system. Relevant in this framework is the theoretical reformulation of the relational model as a first-order theory, as we shall see in the following sections. According to this reformulation, the foundation for the development of the relational model in order to represent "more" knowledge are defined.

Here we briefly discuss which kind of knowledge can be represented. The knowledge represented in a database has the following features:

- It is positive (by means of schemes and instances, we assert general and factual properties of data).

- It is not deductive: no information can be inferred from the stored data.[1]

Furthermore, there are three implicit assumptions that govern query evaluation and integrity-constraint management in a database:

1. *Closed world:* facts that are not known to be true (that is, they are not present in the database) are assumed to be false.

2. *Closed domains:* there are no other individuals than those stored in the database.

3. *Unique names:* individuals with different names are distinct.

In order to extend the power of database systems we would like to represent more knowledge, specifically, of the following kinds:

- *Incomplete knowledge*

    - To state that something has a certain property without specifying actual values (for example, to say *Smith has a wife*)
    - To state that each individual of a class has a certain property without enumerating the individuals (for example, to say *All people having an account are customers of a bank*)
    - To state that one of two sentences is true without saying which one (for example, to say *Smith has an account number 13427 or 13428*)

---

[1]The only exception, not considered in this text, but actually available in all systems, is the possibility of defining *views*, that is, relations that are not actually stored but are defined by means of queries on the stored relations.

  - To state or to leave in doubt the fact that two different ex-
    pressions refer to the same individual (for example, to say
    Jane Smith and *Smith's wife*).

- *Negative knowledge*

  - To state explicitly that something is false (for example, to
    say *Smith has no wife*).

Furthermore, we would like to create database systems that are
able to reason, to extract and use implicit information, and to make
conclusions.

Given these requirements, mathematical logic is the favorite candidate formalism to model databases, and KBMSs will have to combine
inference mechanisms from logic with the secure management of large
volumes of information from DBMSs.

Specifically, a single declarative language will play the role of both
the data manipulation language (DML), which in traditional DBMSs
allows efficient access to the database, and the host language, which
is a general-purpose procedural language embedding the DML. Note
that the distinction between DML and host language, typical of current DBMSs, meets the requirements of the classical database applications, that is, business applications. In fact, such applications are
characterized by large data volumes with complex interrelationships
but simple manipulation operations. For this reason, the DML is a
declarative language with a limited expressive power, and it is exactly
this limitation that permits query optimization.

Newer database applications, knowledge bases and the others discussed in Section 8.1 require models and languages with high expressive power in order to represent knowledge of interest in adequate
way and to express operations that can be complex. For this reason,
the DML/host-language distinction is now considered a real handicap,
and the related "impedance mismatch" that is due to the combination
of a declarative DML with a procedural host language is unacceptable.

In the following, we focus on the logical approach to the development of knowledge base management systems. Looking at the general research and development strategies in this framework, we see
that most of the current contributions can be framed in a strategy

of evolution of the existing technologies (loose or tight coupling of relational database systems and logic-programming systems). The trend, however, is towards the complete integration of database systems and logic-programming systems. That means the development of new data structures and algorithms specifically designed for using logic programming as a database language. There are several problems to be solved. With respect to the full utilization of knowledge bases in real applications, the main critical aspects are those related to the decidability and efficiency of the operations performed by a KBMS to answer questions against a given knowledge base. In fact, the declarative nature of the approach makes the system more powerful but requires it to have sound optimization algorithms to find efficient execution strategies.

9.2   Mathematical Logic

Mathematical logic underlies several aspects of the theoretical research on databases discussed in the previous chapters. To mention just the two major aspects, it gives a clear basis to (1) relational calculus in its various versions and to (2) dependency theory, with the notions of satisfaction and implication. In most cases, in the previous chapters, we have used notions from mathematical logic without discussing their common origin and their mutual relationships. In this section, we briefly introduce *first-order predicate calculus*, a framework that allows the clarification of these issues. We first give the definition of the syntax of predicate calculus formulas, then discuss their semantics, and finally introduce the notion of a proof system.

First-Order Languages

The formulas of a first-order predicate calculus form a *first-order language*. The symbols of such a language are (1) variables, constants, and function and predicate symbols; (2) logical connectives: negation ($\neg$), conjunction ($\wedge$), disjunction ($\vee$), and possibly conditional ($\Rightarrow$) and biconditional ($\Leftrightarrow$); (3) quantifiers: universal ($\forall$) and existential ($\exists$); and (4) parentheses. In the context of databases, it is usually assumed that there are no function symbols and that the predicate names coincide with relation names plus a set of "standard" predicates (usually called *built-in* predicates), such as equality and other comparison operators.

In this framework, a *term* is either a constant or a variable.[2]

An *atom* has the form $p(t_1, \ldots, t_n)$ where p is an n-ary predicate symbol, and $t_1, \ldots, t_n$ are terms. In our database context, as we saw in relational calculus, it is convenient to distinguish between two forms of atoms:

1. $R(t_1, \ldots, t_p)$, also written as $R(A_1 : t_1, \ldots, A_p : t_p)$, with a non-positional notation, where $R(A_1 \ldots A_p)$ is a relation scheme, and the t_i's are terms (that is, constants or variables).

2. $t_1 \theta t_2$, where t_1, t_2 are terms, and θ is a comparison operator (that is, a built-in predicate).

Formulas are defined recursively as follows, together with the notion of *free* and *bound* (occurrences of) variables. Nothing else is a formula.

1. An atom is a formula; all occurrences of variables in it are free.

2. If f_1 and f_2 are formulas, then $(f_1) \wedge (f_2)$, $(f_1) \vee (f_2)$, and $\neg(f_1)$ are formulas (parentheses may be omitted when no ambiguity may arise); each occurrence of a variable in them is free (bound) if it is free (bound) in the subformula where it appears. Conditional and biconditional are used as shorthand: $f_1 \Rightarrow f_2$ stands for $(\neg f_1) \vee f_2$, and $f_1 \Leftrightarrow f_2$ stands for $(f_1 \Rightarrow f_2) \wedge (f_2 \Rightarrow f_1)$.

3. If f is a formula and x a variable, then $\exists x(f)$ and $\forall x(f)$ are formulas. The occurrences of x in f (if any) are bound in $\exists x(f)$ and $\forall x(f)$; each occurrence of any other variable is free (bound) if it is free (bound) in f.

---

[2]In more general languages with function symbols, terms may be recursively defined: if f is an n-ary function and $t_1, \ldots, t_n$ are terms, then $f(t_1, \ldots, t_n)$ is a term.

A formula is *open* if it has free variables; otherwise it is *closed*. Closed formulas are often called *sentences*. A *theory* is a set of sentences.[3]

There are some classes of formulas that are especially meaningful. A formula is in *prenex normal form* if all quantifiers appear at an outer level relative to all connectives. Thus, a formula in prenex normal form can be written as $Q_{j_1} x_1(Q_{j_2} x_2(\ldots Q_{j_k} x_k(f) \ldots))$, where each of the Q_{j_i}'s is a quantifier, and f is a quantifier-free formula. A formula is in *Skolem normal form (SNF)* if it is in prenex normal form and it involves only universal quantifiers.

A *literal* is an atom (*positive* literal) or has the form $\neg(A)$, where A is an atom (*negative* literal). A *clause* is an SNF formula

$$\forall x_1(\forall x_2(\ldots \forall x_k(f)\ldots))$$

where f is a disjunction of literals: $L_1 \lor L_2 \lor \ldots \lor L_h$. Since all variables in a clause are quantified by means of a universal quantifier, clauses are often written by omitting the quantifiers and indicating only the internal, quantifier-free subformula. A *Horn clause* is a clause with at most one positive literal. A formula is in *conjunctive normal form (CNF)* if it is in SNF and its quantifier-free subformula f has the form $C_1 \land C_2 \land \ldots \land C_h$, where each C_j is a disjunction of literals.

A clause (a literal) is *ground* if it contains no variables.

In the next subsection, after the definition of the semantics of first-order languages, we will sketch the importance of formulas of these classes.

Semantics of First-Order Languages

An *interpretation* for a first-order language consists of the specification of a nonempty domain D, and an assignment of values to each (1) constant, (2) function, and (3) predicate symbol. Each constant is assigned an element in D. Each n-ary function symbol is assigned

---

[3]The term *theory* is used with (at least) two different meanings in logic frameworks. In proof systems (as defined later in this section), a sequence of formulas that form a derivation is often called a *theory*. However, we will not use the term to refer to this notion.

a function from D^n to D. Each n-ary predicate is assigned a (mathematical) relation on D^n. In our database context, (1) D is the domain of values for the relations and each constant is assigned to itself; (2) there are no functions; (3a) each predicate corresponding to a relation name in the database scheme is assigned a (database) relation over that scheme; (3b) each built-in predicate (equality, greater than, and so on) is assigned the relation with the pairs of values that satisfy the corresponding definition. A close correspondence therefore exists between interpretations and database instances.

Given an interpretation (in our specific framework, a database instance), it is possible to define the truth values of formulas. In general, free variables may be involved, so the truth value of a formula depends on the values associated with the free variables. Therefore, each closed formula is just *true* or *false* in the interpretation, whereas each open formula is *true* with respect to certain substitutions for the variables and *false* with respect to the others. Let us formalize these notions.[4] We need a preliminary definition: a *substitution* is a total function s that associates a constant with each variable. Now we recursively define the value of formulas on substitutions, given an interpretation.

1. Atoms: $P(x_1, \ldots, x_p)$ is *true* for a substitution s, if the relation that the interpretation assigns to P contains a p-tuple $(s(x_1), \ldots, s(x_p))$. In the database context:

   - The value of $R(A_1 : x_1, \ldots, A_p : x_p)$ on a substitution s is *true* if the relation r over R contains a tuple t such that $t[A_i] = s(x_i)$, for $1 \leq i \leq p$, and *false* otherwise.
   - For atoms of the form $t_1 \theta t_2$, there are various cases, depending on whether t_1 and t_2 are constants or variables. As they are similar, let us consider just two of them.
     a. They are both variables; $t_1 = x_1$ and $t_2 = x_2$. Then $x_1 \theta x_2$ is *true* for s if $s(x_1)$ stands in relation θ with $s(x_2)$.
     b. The term t_1 is a variable x_1, and t_2 is a constant c. Then $x_1 \theta c$ is *true* for s if $s(x_1)$ stands in relation θ with c.

---

[4] The definition of the truth value of a formula is essentially the same as defined in Section 2.5 for relational calculus. We repeat it here for the sake of completeness.

2. The values of $f_1 \wedge f_2$, $f_1 \vee f_2$, and $\neg f_1$ over a substitution s are defined according to the semantics of the Boolean connectives on the values of f_1 and f_2 on s.

3. The value of $\exists x(f)$ on a substitution s is *true* if there is a substitution s' on which f is *true* that differs from s at most on x; otherwise it is *false*. Symmetrically, the value of $\forall x(f)$ on a substitution s is *true* if f is *true* for every substitution s' that differs from s at most on x; otherwise it is *false*.

Let us give a few more definitions. Consider a fixed database scheme **R**, so that interpretations correspond to instances of **R**. A *model* of a set of closed formulas F is an interpretation in which all formulas in F are true. If I_1 and I_2 are interpretations, and $\mathbf{r}_1$ and $\mathbf{r}_2$ are the corresponding databases, we say that $I_1 \subseteq I_2$ if each relation in $\mathbf{r}_1$ is a subset of the corresponding relation in $\mathbf{r}_2$. A model M_0 of F is *minimal* if there is no other model M of F such that $M \subseteq M_0$.

Two (sets of) closed formulas are *equivalent* if they have the same models.

A formula f is a *logical consequence* of (or *is implied* by) a set of formulas F (in symbols, $F \models f$) if and only if f is true in all models of F (or, equivalently, every model of F is a model of $F \cup \{f\}$).

> **Example 9.1**   Consider a domain $D = \{John, Mary, Paul, Ann\}$ and the interpretation that associates constants with themselves; the pairs *(John,Paul)*, *(Mary,Paul)*, and *(Paul,Ann)* with the predicate *parent*; the pairs *(John,Ann)* and *(Mary,Ann)* with the predicate *grandparent*; the 1-tuples *(John)* and *(Paul)* with the predicate *male*; and the 1-tuples *(Mary)* and *(Ann)* with the predicate *female*.
>
> The following closed formulas are *true*:
> - *parent(John,Paul)*
> - *parent(Mary,Paul)*
> - *¬parent(Paul,Paul)*
> - $\forall x(\forall y(\forall z \ (parent(x,y) \wedge parent(y,z) \Rightarrow grandparent(x,z))))$
> - $\forall \ x \ (male(x) \vee female \ (x))$
>
> The open formula $\forall \ x \ (grandparent(x,y) \Rightarrow female(y))$ is true for all substitutions (that is, for every value of D substituted to x)
>
> The open formula $\exists \ y \ (parent(x,y) \wedge female(x))$ is true for the substitutions that map x to *Mary* and *false* on the others.

The closed formula *(∀x (∃y (grandparent(x,y))))* is false.

The interpretation above is a model of the set composed of the following formulas:

- *∀x(∀y(∀z (parent(x,y) ∧ parent(y,z) ⇒ grandparent(x,z))))*
- *∀x (male(x) ∨ female (x))*

The interpretation is a minimal model for the set composed of the following formulas:

- *parent(John,Paul)*
- *parent(Mary,Paul)*
- *parent(Paul,Ann)*
- *grandparent(John,Ann)*
- *grandparent(Mary,Ann)*
- *male(John) ∧ male(Paul)*
- *female(Ann) ∧ female(Mary)*
- *(¬ (Ann = Mary)) ∧ (¬ (Ann = Paul)) ∧ (¬ (Ann = John))*
- *(¬ (Paul = Mary)) ∧ (¬ (Paul = John)) ∧ (¬ (Mary = John))*

Let us recall the two major applications of first-order predicate calculus seen in the previous chapters.

- Relational calculus was defined in Section 2.5 by means of open formulas. The semantics of calculus queries considers the database instance as an interpretation and associates with a formula the tuples of values corresponding to the substitutions on which the formula is true.

- Integrity constraints (Section 3.1) can be expressed by means of closed formulas. An integrity constraint is satisfied by the database instances that correspond to interpretations on which the formula is true. Also, the notion of logical consequence (also called *implication*) of first-order formulas coincides with the notion of implication of constraints.

Let us now comment on the special classes of formulas we introduced at the end of the previous subsection. Given a formula, it is always possible to find an equivalent formula in prenex normal form: the transformation is straightforward, apart from the possible need for renaming variables. Transformation in SNF is not always possible, as it often involves the introduction of function symbols. However, the class of SNF formulas is rather general.

Let us now consider a closed SNF formula:

$$\forall x_1(\forall x_2(\ldots \forall x_k(f)\ldots))$$

Then f is a formula involving only atoms and connectives. Therefore (by application of De Morgan's laws) it can always be transformed into an equivalent formula in conjunctive normal form: $f = C_1 \wedge C_2 \wedge \ldots \wedge C_K$, where each C_i is the disjunction of literals. Then it is the case that for every CNF formula, there is an equivalent set of clauses.

Proof Systems

The implication of first-order formulas can be studied by means of techniques that, given a set of formulas, allow the derivation of other formulas. We have already seen an application of this method in Section 3.2, when we studied the implication of FDs by means of inference rules. These techniques are known as *formal systems* or *proof systems*. Their fundamental component is a set of *logical axioms*, which correspond to formulas that are true in every interpretation, and a set of *inference rules*, which allow the derivation of formulas that are implied by the axioms and by the given set of formulas. We write $F \vdash f$ if f can be derived from F by means of the inference rules.

Various proof systems have been defined for first-order predicate calculus. Here we just mention a rather general one that considers only clauses and involves only one inference rule, the so-called Robinson Resolution Principle. Let us describe the rule by means of an example.

Let us consider the clauses (with quantifiers omitted) $\neg r(a, b) \vee q(c, d)$ and $r(x, y) \vee p(x, y)$, where a, b, c, d are constants, and x, y are variables. From these clauses, it is possible to derive the clause $q(c, d) \vee p(a, b)$. This clause is derived by finding two literals in the two clauses with the same predicate name, but of opposite sign (that is, one is positive and the other negative). In our case we find the literals with the predicate name r. We then determine if the two literals can be made identical (*unified*) by replacing the variables with other variables or constants. We can substitute a for x and b for y. Then we generate a clause (the *resolvent*) that is the disjunction of all the literals in the two original clauses except the unified literals, and apply to it the unifying substitution. Note that the substitution may change variables in both clauses, and some variables in the two clauses may remain unchanged.

Resolution is a *refutation* process: in order to prove $F \models f$, one tries to show that F and $\neg f$ are contradictory; that is, there is no model for $F \cup \{\neg f\}$. In other words, the refutation process derives a contradiction from the negation of the desired result. Contradiction is detected when the empty clause is generated, because the empty clause has no model.

Now we can state two relevant properties of a proof system: *soundness* and *completeness*. A proof system is *sound* if for all F and f, whenever $F \vdash f$, it is the case that $F \models f$ (in other words, whenever f can be derived from F using the rules, f is true in all models of F). It is *complete* if for all F and f, whenever $F \models f$, it is the case that $F \vdash f$ (in other words, whenever f is a logical consequence of F, f can be derived from F using the rules).

Resolution refutation is sound and complete for first-order formulas. The empty clause is derived if and only if the clause to be proven is a logical consequence of the given set of formulas. However, there is an element of undecidability; specifically, if the clause to be proved is not a logical consequence, the inference process need not terminate. The process always terminates if all the clauses are Horn clauses.

9.3   Logical Approaches to Databases

A database can be considered from the viewpoint of logic in two different ways: either as a *model* of a theory or as a *theory*. Following the terminology introduced by Reiter [181], the two approaches are called *model-theoretic* and *proof-theoretic*, respectively. The former can be used to describe conventional databases, and the latter corresponds to deductive databases.

In both cases, the predicate symbols of a (first-order) language include the relation names of a database scheme. Let **R** be a database scheme and $\mathcal{L}$ be the language.

Model-Theoretic Approach

The basic principle of the model-theoretic approach is the fact that the database instances are the *models* of a theory. As we said, there is a first-order language $\mathcal{L}$ associated with the database scheme **R**. The integrity constraints associated with the scheme are described by a theory T. Then the interpretations of the theory correspond to the (consistent or inconsistent) instances of **R**, and the models correspond to the consistent instances.

A query is an open[5] formula of $\mathcal{L}$ that is evaluated with respect to the model of the theory that corresponds to the current database instance d. As we saw in Section 2.5, which defined the semantics of relational calculus, the answer to the query is the set of tuples generated by the substitutions on which the formula is *true*.

It is useful to comment on the unique name, closed world, and domain closure assumptions. The unique name assumption is enforced by means of the fact that we only consider interpretations that interpret each constant as itself. The domain closure assumption is in general not enforced, but it is satisfied by domain-independent queries, which form the set of meaningful queries, as we argued in Section 2.6. The closed world assumption is enforced via the semantics of relational calculus: an atom is *true* if it denotes a tuple in the corresponding relation, and *false* otherwise.

Figure 9.1 shows a model-theoretic database. More precisely, it shows the relations in the interpretation and the integrity constraints. The constraints are satisfied by the relations; that is, the database is a model of the integrity constraints.

Proof-Theoretic Approach

As in the model-theoretic approach, a first-order language $\mathcal{L}$ is associated with the database scheme. Then database instances are described by theories, that is, sets of sentences of $\mathcal{L}$. In this approach, query evaluation and integrity-constraint satisfaction are defined by

---

[5] Closed formulas could be used to express queries whose answers are Boolean values. We omit them for the sake of simplicity.

INTEGRITY CONSTRAINTS

supplies(x,y) $\Rightarrow$ supplier(x), product(y)
uses(x,y) $\Rightarrow$ department(x), product(y)
$\forall x$ (product(x) $\Rightarrow$ $\exists y$ (supplies(y,x)))
$\forall y$ (supplier(y) $\Rightarrow$ $\exists x$ (supplies(y,x)))

A MODEL

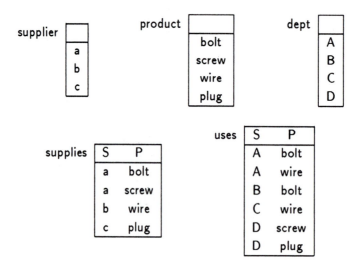

Figure 9.1. A model-theoretic database

means of implication. Let T be the theory that corresponds to the database.

- The answer to a query formulated as $Q(x_1, \ldots, x_p)$, where $x_1, \ldots, x_p$ are the free variables in the formula Q, consists of those tuples $(c_1, \ldots, c_p)$ such that $Q(c_1, \ldots, c_p)$ is implied by T.

- A constraint c is satisfied if and only if T implies c.

Because the only way to verify implication is based on proof systems, this approach is meaningful only if associated with a proof system—in fact this argument justifies the name given to the approach itself. For technical reasons, axioms are needed to describe the closed world, domain closure, and unique name assumptions.

Therefore, in this approach a theory contains the following axioms:

1. *Factual axioms.* For each relation r over a relation scheme R in the database, and for each tuple $(c_1, \ldots, c_n)$ in r, there is an axiom $R(c_1, \ldots, c_n)$. These axioms are often called *facts* and describe the actual content of the database.

2. *Particularization axioms.* These axioms explicitly state the database assumptions that govern query evaluation:

   a. *Completion axioms.* For each relation scheme R there is a completion axiom that states that r has only the tuples described by the factual axioms.

   b. *The domain closure axiom.* If $c_1, \ldots, c_q$ are all the constants in the database instance, it states that $\forall x((x = c_1) \lor (x = c_2) \lor \ldots \lor (x = c_q))$.

   c. *The unique name axioms.* If $c_1, \ldots, c_q$ are all the constants in the database instance, the unique name axioms are $(c_1 \neq c_2), \ldots, (c_1 \neq c_q), \ldots, (c_{q-1} \neq c_q)$.

3. *Equality axioms.* These axioms are needed to force equality to be interpreted in the standard way. They specify the usual properties of equality:

   - *Reflexivity:* $\forall x(x = x)$
   - *Commutativity:* $\forall x \forall y((x = y) \Rightarrow (y = x))$
   - *Transitivity:* $\forall x \forall y \forall z((x = y) \land (y = z) \Rightarrow (x = z))$
   - Leibnitz's *principle of substitution* of equal terms:

   $$\forall x_1 \ldots \forall y_N(p(x_1, \ldots, x_N) \land (x_1 = y_1) \land \ldots \land (x_N = y_N) \Rightarrow p(y_1, \ldots, y_N))$$

Figure 9.2 shows the proof-theoretic database corresponding to the model-theoretic database in Figure 9.1.

There are two important properties for proof-theoretic databases:

Factual axioms

supplier(a)

supplier(b)

supplier(c)

product(bolt)

product(screw)

product(wire)

product(plug)

dept(A)

dept(B)

dept(C)

dept(D)

supplies(a,bolt)

supplies(a,screw)

supplies(b,wire)

supplies(c,plug)

uses(A,bolt)

uses(A,wire)

uses(B,bolt)

uses(C,wire)

uses(D,screw)

uses(D,plug)

Particularization axioms

(A) Completion axioms

$supplier(X) \Rightarrow (X = a) \lor (X = b) \lor (X = c)$

. . .

(B) The domain closure axiom

$(x = a) \lor (x = b) \lor \dots \lor (x = D)$

(C) The unique name axioms

$\neg(a = b)$

$\neg(a = c)$

$\neg(a = bolt)$

. . .

Integrity constraints

$supplies(x,y) \Rightarrow supplier(x), product(y)$

$uses(x,y) \Rightarrow department(x), product(y)$

$\forall x \, (product(x) \Rightarrow \exists y \, (supplies(y,x)))$

$\forall y \, (supplier(y) \Rightarrow \exists x \, (supplies \, (y,x)))$

Figure 9.2. A proof-theoretic database

1. If T is a theory of L, as in the definition of proof-theoretic databases, then T has a unique minimal model.

2. If **r** is a relational database, then there is a theory T that has a minimal model that corresponds to **r**.

It is important to note that, although according to this view query evaluation calls for proof techniques, the database remains a conventional (i.e., nondeductive) database. No other positive facts than those explicitly stated in the factual axioms can be derived from T.

9.4   Deductive Databases

In this section we provide the formal definition of deductive databases and a general overview of the related implementation issues. These issues are explored in more detail in the next section, when we introduce the Datalog language as an effective means to handle deductive databases. Informally, deductive databases are a generalization of proof-theoretic databases, as defined in the previous section. Besides facts, the theory contains sentences that describe *intensional* knowledge that can be used to deduce additional information from the facts.

Both facts and intensional knowledge can be described by means of clauses. We saw in Section 9.2 that a clause is a formula

$$\forall x_1 (\forall x_2 (\ldots \forall x_k (f) \ldots))$$

where f is a disjunction of literals: $L_1 \vee L_2 \vee \ldots \vee L_h$. Also, we have said that clauses are often written by omitting the quantifiers and indicating only the internal, quantifier-free subformula. With this convention, a clause has the form

$$\neg p_1 \vee \neg p_2 \vee \ldots \vee \neg p_n \vee r_1 \vee \ldots \vee r_m$$

By De Morgan's laws and the definition of the conditional $\Rightarrow$, such a clause can be written in the equivalent form

$$(p_1 \wedge p_2 \wedge \ldots \wedge p_n) \Rightarrow (r_1 \vee \ldots \vee r_m)$$

which suggests the deductive use that can be made of clauses: "From $p_1 \wedge p_2 \wedge \ldots \wedge p_n$, derive $r_1 \vee \ldots \vee r_m$." The conjunction of the p_i's is referred to as the *left-hand side* of the clause, and the disjunction of the r_j's as the *right-hand side*. Terms that are arguments of the p_i's and r_j's are either constants or variables. A clause is said to be *range-restricted* whenever each variable that occurs in the right-hand side of a clause also occurs in its left-hand side. We can classify the clauses depending on the respective values of n and m.

1. $n = 0$, $m = 1$. Clauses have the form $\Rightarrow r(t_1, ..., t_k)$.

   a. If the t_i's are constants, then the clause is a *ground* clause and represents a *fact* in the database. The set of all such ground clauses for the predicate r corresponds to a relation R in a relational database.

   b. When some or all of the t_i's are variables, then the clause corresponds to a general statement in the database. For example $\Rightarrow loves(God,X)$ states that God loves all individuals in the database. These are *non-range-restricted* clauses and assume that all the individuals in the database are of same type.

2. $n = 1$, $m = 0$. Clauses have the form $p(t_1, ..., t_k) \Rightarrow$.

   a. If the t_i's are constants, then the clause represents a *negative fact*. For example, $loves(Paul, Mary) \Rightarrow$ states that *Paul* does not love *Mary*.

   b. If some of the t_i's are variables, this may represent either an integrity constraint (see below) or the nonexistent null values. The clause $loves(Paul,x) \Rightarrow$ states that *Paul* loves nobody.

3. $n > 1$, $m = 0$. Clauses have the form $p_1 \wedge ... \wedge p_k \Rightarrow$ and can be used to express integrity constraints. For example, $married(x) \wedge unmarried(x) \Rightarrow$ states that no individual can be both married and unmarried.

4. $n \geq 1$, $m = 1$. A clause in this class has the form $p_1 \wedge ... \wedge p_k \Rightarrow r_1$. It is a Horn clause, and may be considered either as an integrity constraint or as a definition of the predicate r_1 in terms of the predicates $p_1, ..., p_k$ (that is, it is a deductive law). The clause $parent(x,y) \wedge parent(Y,Z) \Rightarrow grandparent(X,Z)$ is an example of a Horn clause.

5. $n = 0$, $m > 1$. Clauses have the form $\Rightarrow r_1 \vee ... \vee r_k$ and represent disjunctive statements: one or more of the r_i's is true, but we do not know which ones.

6. $n \geq 1$, $m > 1$. Clauses have the form $p_1 \wedge ... \wedge p_k \Rightarrow r_1 \vee ... \vee r_h$ and may be interpreted as either integrity constraints or as the definition of indefinite data.

7. A clause where $n = 0$, $m = 0$ (the *empty clause*) denotes falsity and should not be part of a database.

Note that in conventional databases there are only facts and integrity constraints, while in a deductive database clauses may be treated as deductive laws. According to the types of allowed clauses, two classes of deductive databases can be distinguished: *definite* deductive databases, in which no clauses of either Type 5 or Type 6 appear, and *indefinite* deductive databases, in which such clauses do appear. We consider only definite databases in the following, because indefinite databases present problems of domain dependence, of nonexistence of answers composed of facts, and of nontermination of proof systems.

Definite Deductive Databases

A *definite* deductive database is defined as a first-order theory whose proper axioms are characterized by the presence of particular deductive laws, with an associated set of integrity constraints. More precisely, a definite deductive database consists of the following:

1. A theory T whose proper axioms are

   - Axioms 1 (the elementary facts): a set of ground atomic formulas. These axioms define a regular relational database state.

   - Axioms 2 (the particularization axioms): the completion axioms, the domain closure axiom, and the unique name axioms. The completion axioms are more complex here than in the proof-theoretic definition of conventional databases, as tuples in relations can be facts (Axioms 1), or they can be derived by means of the deductive laws (Axioms 4).

   - Axioms 3: the equality axioms.

- Axioms 4 (the deductive laws): a set of Horn clauses. These axioms define new relations from existing relations.

2. A set of integrity constraints C.

In a deductive database, queries and integrity constraints are treated exactly as in a conventional database viewed from the proof-theoretic perspective. The answer to a query formulated as $Q(x_1, \ldots, x_p)$ is the set of tuples $(c_1, \ldots, c_p)$ such that $q(c_1, \ldots, c_p)$ is implied by T. Similarly, a deductive database *satisfies* the integrity constraints in C if and only if for every formula (constraint) c in C, $T \models c$. Deductive laws (Horn clauses in Axioms 4) that imply a relation R provide an intensional definition for R. The tuples $(d_1, ..., d_m)$ that satisfy R are the tuples such that $r(d_1, ..., d_m)$ is a fact in Axioms 1, and the tuples such that $r(d_1, ..., d_m)$ is derivable through the deductive laws. Such relations are called *derived relations*, and constitute a generalization of relations defined as views in a conventional database.

Implementation Issues for Deductive Databases

In the definition, a deductive database has been introduced as a first-order theory in which query evaluation and integrity-constraint satisfaction are treated in terms of implication (or, if there is a sound and complete proof system, derivability). A possible way to implement a deductive database could then be by means of a standard theorem prover based on the theory's axioms. However, particularization axioms present such combinatorial complexity that their explicit handling would highly reduce the efficiency of the system. For this reason, it is convenient to adopt the same attitude as for conventional databases, that is, to treat them implicitly.

First of all, it is possible to eliminate the need for the domain closure axiom if the formulas are required to be range-restricted. An intuitive justification for this claim can be based on the same arguments that led to the versions of relational calculus with range declarations: range-restricted formulas generate only ground formulas from the database.

The other two sets of particularization axioms (unique name and completion) can be eliminated if negation is interpreted as *finite failure*: for any positive literal p, we can infer $\neg p$ if and only if we cannot infer p by means of a finite derivation. Note that this technique corresponds to the closed world assumption (CWA) defined for conventional databases. The requirement of finite failure states that all proofs terminate. As a side effect of the elimination of the particularization axioms, it is possible to eliminate also the equality axioms (they were needed because of the presence of equality in the particularization axioms). According to this reformulation, query evaluation and integrity-constraint satisfaction remain defined as for the proof-theoretic approach, except that *derivable* must now be interpreted as "derivable under negation as finite failure." This operational definition of a definite deductive database is not strictly equivalent to the formal definition. In fact, the formal definition is stated in first-order logic, which is monotonic, whereas the use of negation as failure in the operational definition leads to a nonmonotonic logic. A logic is said to be *monotonic* if, given a theory T in which a formula f can be proved, the addition to T of an axiom f_1 still allows us to prove f; that is, $(T \cup \{f_1\}) \vdash f$. According to negation as failure, $\neg p(a)$ can be inferred from $\{p(b), q(c)\}$ but not from $\{p(b), q(c)\} \cup \{p(a)\}$; thus we have a nonmonotonic logic.

9.5   Datalog

We have introduced deductive databases as an evolution of conventional databases by exploiting the capabilities of logic for representing knowledge and expressing deductions, in order to achieve the future objective of knowledge base management systems. In this light, we need a programming language that is based on logic and can also be used as a database language. This language has to be rule-based, nonprocedural, and set-oriented, with no function symbols; it must also be suitable for applications that use a large number of facts stored in a relational database. A candidate language to meet these requirements is Datalog, a logic-programming language specifically designed for an efficient integration of logic programming with relational databases.

Datalog: Syntax and Semantics

In Datalog, clauses are written in the logic-programming notation: $q \leftarrow p_1, ..., p_n$ stands for $\neg p_1 \vee ... \vee \neg p_n \vee q$ (or, equivalently, $p_1 \wedge ... \wedge p_n \Rightarrow q$). For such a clause, q is the *head*, and the set of the p_i's is the *body*. A *Datalog database* is a finite set of Horn clauses, each of which is either

- a ground *fact*, q, or

- a range-restricted *rule*, $q \leftarrow p_1, ..., p_n$, with $n > 0$,

with the condition that the predicates are partitioned into two sets:

1. *Extensional (EDB) predicates*, which appear in facts and bodies of rules, but not in heads of rules

2. *Intensional (IDB) predicates*, which appear in heads and bodies of rules, but not in the facts

EDB predicates correspond to physically stored relations (the *extensional database, EDB*), whereas IDB predicates correspond to derived relations, defined by means of rules.

An interesting property of Datalog is that its semantics can be defined in three equivalent ways:

1. *Model-theoretic semantics.* Each Datalog program has in general many possible models, but it admits a unique minimal model that defines the canonical semantics of the program.

2. *Proof-theoretic semantics.* A Datalog program represents a collection of axioms to be used in a proof, and the canonical semantics of the program is the set of predicate instances that contain the tuples of the database (the facts) and all the tuples that can be inferred from the facts using the rules.

3. The *fixpoint semantics*, which is sketched in the next subsection.

Datalog as a Database Language

A Datalog program can be seen as a query against the EDB, producing a relation as answer. This section shows that Datalog can truly be considered as a language able to provide access to data stored in database. In fact, each rule of a Datalog program can be translated, by a syntax-directed translation algorithm, into an inclusion relationship (disequation) of relational algebra. In the clause, each IDB predicate of the Datalog program corresponds to a variable relation; each EDB predicate corresponds to a constant relation. The rationale of the translation is that for each clause, body literals with common variables give rise to natural joins, while the head literal determines the projection. As an example, if relation p is defined on attribute A and r is defined on BC, with the natural correspondence between positional and nonpositional notation, a rule of the form $p(x) \leftarrow p(y), r(x,y)$ is translated into the inequality $\rho_{A \leftarrow B}(\pi_B(p \bowtie_{A=C} r)) \subseteq p)$.

In general, for a given clause

$$p(x_1, ..., x_n) \leftarrow q_1(y_1, ..., y_m), ..., q_m(z_j, ..., z_h)$$

the translation associates with the clause an inclusion relationship $E(Q_1, ..., Q_m) \subseteq P$ among the relations $P, Q_1, ..., Q_m$ that correspond to predicates $p, q_1, \ldots, q_m$. Note that some of the q_i's might be p itself, thus yielding to a recursive rule. For each IDB predicate p, we then collect all the inclusion relationships of the form $E(Q_1, \ldots, Q_m) \subseteq P$, and generate an algebraic equation having P as left-hand side, and as right-hand side the union of all the left-hand sides of the inclusion relationships:

$$P = E_1(Q_1, ..., Q_m) \cup E_2(Q_1, ..., Q_m) \cup ... \cup E_k(Q_1, ..., Q_m)$$

Determining a solution of the system corresponds to determining the value of the variable relations that satisfy the system of equations. Note that the transformation of several disequations into one equation expresses the fact that we are only interested in those ground facts that are consequences of our program.

As an example, consider the program with the following rules:

$p(x) \leftarrow p(y), r(x,y)$
$p(x) \leftarrow s(y,x)$
$q(x,y) \leftarrow p(x), r(x,z), s(y,z)$

The rules can be translated in the following disequations (assuming suitable attribute names):

$$\rho_{A \leftarrow B}(\pi_B(P \bowtie_{A=C} R)) \subseteq P$$
$$\rho_{A \leftarrow E}(\pi_E(S)) \subseteq P$$
$$\rho_{FG \leftarrow AD}((P \bowtie_{A=B} R) \bowtie_{C=E} S) \subseteq Q$$

In turn, they can be translated into the equations:

$$P = \rho_{A \leftarrow B}(\pi_B(P \bowtie_{A=C} R)) \cup \rho_{A \leftarrow E}(\pi_E(S))$$
$$Q = \rho_{FG \leftarrow AD}((P \bowtie_{A=B} R) \bowtie_{C=E} S)$$

Therefore, we have a system of algebraic equations where P and Q are variable relations, while R and S are constant relations. To solve the system, we can evaluate one of the equations and then substitute its value in the other. To solve equations with variables in the right-hand side, we have to look for the *least fixpoint* of the equation, which is the smallest relation over P that satisfies the equation. It can be shown that the equations obtained from Datalog rules always have a fixpoint. We show this concept by means of the "ancestor program," which contains the following rules:

$$ancestor(x,y) \leftarrow parent(x,y)$$
$$ancestor(x,y) \leftarrow parent(x,z),\ ancestor(z,y)$$

Let the corresponding relations be $N(AD)$ (for aNcestor, Ancestor, and Descendant) and $P(RC)$ (for Parent, paRent, Child). Then we have the disequations

$$\rho_{AD \leftarrow RC}(P) \subseteq N$$

$$\rho_{A \leftarrow R}(P \bowtie_{C=A} N) \subseteq N$$

and the equation

$$N = \rho_{AD \leftarrow RC}(P) \cup \rho_{A \leftarrow R}(P \bowtie_{C=A} N)$$

and therefore the value of the ancestor relation is the least fixpoint of the equation, which can be obtained as follows: let N_0 be the empty set, P the *parent* relation, and

$$N_i = \rho_{AD \leftarrow RC}(P) \cup \rho_{A \leftarrow R}(P \bowtie_{C=A} N_{i-1})$$

for every $i > 0$. Then the least fixpoint equals the first N_i in the sequence $N_0, N_1, \ldots$ such that $N_i = N_{i+1}$. For example, if the *parent* relation is as in Figure 9.3, then N_0 is the empty set of tuples, N_1 contains the first seven tuples in the *ancestor* relation also in Figure 9.3

Parent	Child
Henry	John
Henry	Arthur
John	Charles
Charles	Anthony
Arthur	Tom
Tom	George
Tom	James

parent

ancestor

Parent	Child
Henry	John
Henry	Arthur
John	Charles
Charles	Anthony
Arthur	Tom
Tom	George
Tom	James
Henry	Charles
Henry	Tom
John	Anthony
Arthur	George
Arthur	James
Henry	Anthony
Henry	George
Henry	James

Figure 9.3. The *parent* relation and the computation of the *ancestor* relation

(and so equals the *parent* relation), N_2 contains the first twelve, and N_3 and all N_i's for $i > 3$ contain all the tuples; therefore, the *ancestor* relation in Figure 9.3 is the least fixpoint of the equation.

The Expressive Power of Datalog

No expression E of relational algebra obtained by translating Datalog clauses involves the difference operator. Since, among the basic relational algebra operators, the difference operator is the only non-monotonic operator, we can say that E is written in *monotonic relational algebra*: RA_M. It can be easily shown that each expression of RA_M can also be translated into a Datalog program. This means that Datalog is at least as expressive as RA_M. However, Datalog is strictly more expressive than RA_M, because in Datalog it is possible to express recursive queries, which are not expressible in RA_M. On the other hand, full relational algebra and Datalog are incomparable,

since there are expressions that make use of the difference operator
that cannot be expressed by Datalog programs.

The Datalog syntax we have been considering so far corresponds
to a very restricted subset of first-order logic and is often referred to as
pure Datalog. Several extensions have been proposed in the literature
or are currently under investigation. In the following we limit our
presentation to the most important of these extensions concerning
built-in predicates and negation.

Built-in Predicates

Built-in predicates correspond to the comparison operators $>$, $\geq$, and
so on, and can occur in the right-hand side of a Datalog rule. They
can be treated as special EDB predicates: they have no correspon-
dent relation stored in the EDB, but are implemented as procedures
that are evaluated during the execution of a Datalog program. In
most cases they yield infinite relations. For example, $x > y$ represents the relation of all pairs (x, y) such that x is greater than y. This
endangers the safety of programs. *Safety* means that the intensional
relations defined by a Datalog program must be finite. Safety can be
guaranteed by requiring that each variable occurring as an argument
of a built-in predicate in a rule body also occurs in an ordinary (EDB
or IDB) predicate of the same rule body, or must be bound by an
equality (or a sequence of equalities) to a variable of such an ordinary
predicate or to a constant. When Datalog rules are transformed into
algebraic equations, built-in predicates are expressed through selection conditions. For example, $p(x, y) \leftarrow q(x, y), x = a$, is transformed
into the expression $P = \sigma_{X=a}(Q(X, Y))$.

Negation

In pure Datalog we can adopt the closed world assumption (CWA),
which allows us to infer negative facts from a set of pure Datalog
clauses. In the context of Datalog the CWA can be formulated, by the
negation-as-failure convention, as follows: "If a fact cannot be derived
from a set of Datalog clauses, then we conclude that the negation of
that fact is true." Therefore, according to the CWA, we can deduce

negative facts from a set of clauses, but we cannot use these negative facts in order to deduce some further facts. In fact, since pure Datalog is concerned with Horn clauses, negated literals are not allowed to appear in a rule. In order to extend pure Datalog by allowing explicit negations, we define Datalog¬ as the language whose syntax is that of Datalog except that negated literals are allowed in rule bodies. Therefore, a Datalog¬ clause is either a positive (ground) fact or a rule with negative literals in the body. To guarantee safety, we require that each variable occurring in a negative literal of a rule body must also occur in a positive literal of the same rule body. The following is a Datalog¬ rule:

$$associateprofessor(X) \leftarrow professor(X), \neg fullprofessor(X)$$

The relational algebra expression corresponding to this rule consists of the application of the difference operator to the relations corresponding to the involved predicates. Thus, we obtain $ASSOC = PROF - FULL$. The incorporation of the negation into Datalog produces several problems of both semantic and computational nature. Let P be a Datalog¬ program. We require that the set of all positive facts derivable from P be a minimal model of P. However, P may have several minimal models.

The rule above with the fact $professor(Smith)$ has two minimal models, both of which include the fact $professor(Smith)$. Then one includes the fact $associateprofessor(Smith)$ and the other the fact $fullprofessor(Smith)$.

In the presence of several minimal models, which of the different minimal models should be chosen? Furthermore, the model minimality requirement is inconsistent with the CWA. In the example, both facts $\neg associateprofessor(Smith)$ and $\neg fullprofessor(Smith)$ can be deduced by the CWA, and thus neither of the models is consistent with the CWA. There is a method that permits us to select a distinguished minimal model by approximating the CWA. However, this method does not apply to all Datalog¬ programs, but only to a particular subclass, the so-called stratified programs. The underlying idea is simple: When evaluating a rule with negative literals in the body, first evaluate the predicates corresponding to these negative literals. Then the CWA is locally applied to these predicates. In the

above example, we first evaluate the predicate *fullprofessor*. In the
program there are no rules and facts allowing us to deduce any fact of
the form *fullprofessor(...)*, so that the set of positive answers to this
predicate is empty. This means that *fullprofessor(Smith)* cannot be
derived, and by applying the CWA locally to the predicate of interest,
we can derive the negated fact ¬*fullprofessor(Smith)*. Now, by evaluating the unique rule of the example, we obtain the model with the
fact *associateprofessor(Smith)*. In general, in any Datalog¬ program
with several rules, it is required that before evaluating a predicate
in a rule head, it must always be possible to completely evaluate all
the predicates that occur negatively in the rule body or in the bodies
of some subsequent rules and all those predicates that are needed in
order to evaluate these negative predicates. If a program fulfills this
condition, it is called *stratified*. Any stratified program P can be partitioned into disjoint sets of clauses $P = S_1 \cup \ldots \cup S_n$, called *strata*,
such that the following hold:

- Each IDB predicate of P has its defining clauses within one stratum.

- S_1 contains only clauses with either no negative literals or negative literals corresponding to EDB predicates.

- Each stratum S_i contains only clauses whose negative literals correspond to predicates defined in strata included in $S_1, \ldots, S_{i-1}$.

The partition of P is called a *stratification* of P. Note that a stratified program has, in general, several different stratifications. However, it can be shown that all stratifications are equivalent; that is, the
result of the evaluation of a stratified Datalog¬ program is independent of the stratification used. Given a program P with stratification
$S_1...S_n$, the evaluation is done stratum by stratum using the CWA
at each level. To decide whether a program P is stratified, we can
construct a graph (the *extended dependency graph*) $G(P)$ of P. The
nodes of the graph consist of the IDB predicate symbols occurring in
P. There is a directed edge (p, q) if and only if the predicate symbol
q occurs positively or negatively in a body of a rule whose head predicate is p. The edge is marked with a ¬ sign if and only if there exists
at least one rule R with head predicate p such that q occurs negatively

in the body of R. A Datalog¬ program P is stratified if and only if $G(P)$ does not contain any cycle involving an edge labeled with ¬. In other words, negation cannot cross a recursion; that is, there cannot exist a predicate p defined from ¬q if q itself is defined from p. It can be shown that the stratum-by-stratum evaluation of a stratified program P on the base of an underlying extensional database E always produces a minimal model of $P \cup E$.

Exercises

Suppose we have the following relations:

- *EMP(name,dept,job)*
- *PRODUCES(dept,product)*
- *SUPPLIES(company,product,dept)*
- *SUBPRODUCT(product1,product2)* (describing the subproducts of composite products)
- *PART(product,part)* (describing the parts that form a product)
- *MANAGER(name)*
- *BOSS(name1,name2)*
- *WORKSON(name,product)*
- *USES(product,part)* (describing the parts involved in a product, directly or through a subproduct)

9.1 Which of the relations above can be defined in terms of the others; that is, which should be EDB and which IDB?

9.2 For each IDB relation identified in Exercise 9.1, write a clause to define that relation.

9.3 For each nonrecursive IDB relation above, write a relational database expression that represents that relation.

9.4 Write a Datalog program for the IDB relations.

9.5 Show how to compute the semantics of the Datalog program produced in Exercise 9.4.

9.6 Write formulas for the following constraints:
- No employee works in more than one department.
- Everyone in the Headquarters department is a manager.
- No employee earns more than his/her boss.

9.7 Classify as safe or nonsafe each of the following Datalog rules:
$$p(x,y) \leftarrow x > y$$
$$p(x,y) \leftarrow p(x)$$
$$p(x,y) \leftarrow q(x,z), w = a, y = w$$

9.8 Consider the EDB relations *BORROWED (Book)* and *BORROW (Student, Book)*, and define, using safe rules, the IDB predicate *can-borrow(S,B)*, which is *true* if a student asks for a book that is not borrowed.

9.9 Write relational algebra expressions for the rules written in answer to Exercise 9.8.

9.10 Show that it is possible to express universal quantification by use of negation in rule bodies. Assume that p and q are unary EDB predicates, and show that one can write a Datalog¬ program such that the fact $r(a)$ is true if and only if the formula $\forall X(p(X) \Rightarrow q(X))$ is true.

Comments and References

Many general textbooks on mathematical logic exist, such as those by Enderton [96] or Mendelson [169].

Since the very beginning of the existence of the relational database theory, strict connections to mathematical logic have been established through the definition of the relational query languages [78]. However, it is only since 1978, when the first Logic and Databases conference was organized by Gallaire and Minker, that the relationships between logic programming and databases have been systematically investigated, and deductive databases have been defined. Basic results in this area are documented in the proceedings [107,108,109]. Gallaire, Minker, and Nicolas [110] have provided a good synthesis of the results achieved before 1984, whereas a more recent collection was edited by Minker [171]. A standard textbook on the theory of logic programming is Lloyd's [157]. Grant and Minker [118] have recently discussed the impact of logic programming on databases. Recent international workshops and conferences have presented sessions and panels on logic programming and databases; specifically, a growing interest has been shown in the evolution of database systems and their relationship with knowledge-based systems [54,55,56,182]. Relevant work on the theoretical reformulation of the relational model as a first-order theory has been done by Reiter [181], who also introduced the closed world assumption in the context of databases [180]. Parallel interest in expert database systems has been presented through the series of Expert Database Systems conferences organized by Kerschberg [137,138,139,140]. A comparison of research projects for integrating logic and databases is provided by a collection of papers edited by Zaniolo [236].

The appearence of Datalog is marked by the paper of Ullman [216]; see also the other early publications on Datalog listed in the References [35,36]. Datalog is extensively described in recent textbooks by Ullman [217,218], Ceri, Gottlob, and Tanca [64], and Gardarin and Valduriez [111], which can satisfy the reader looking for a more detailed description. Specifically, in [64] the reader can find a formal definition of the syntax and semantics of Datalog, the description of query optimization techniques for Datalog, discussions on several possible extensions, and an overview of the main projects for integrating logic programming and databases. Naqvi and Tsur [173] and Chimenti et al. [74] describe the Logic Data Language (LDL), which extends pure Datalog with sets, negation, and updates.

Abiteboul and Kanellakis [6] have proposed a Datalog extension for a model with complex objects with identity. Further proposals have been formulated by Ceri et al. [58] and Hull and Yoshikawa [122]. In their full versions these languages can be as powerful as CH-complete languages (see Section 2.9).

Bibliography

1. S. Abiteboul. Updates, a new frontier. In *ICDT'88 (Second International Conference on Data Base Theory), Bruges, Lecture Notes in Computer Science 326*. Berlin: Springer-Verlag, 1988, 1–18.

2. S. Abiteboul and C. Beeri. On the power of languages for the manipulation of complex objects. Technical Report 846. INRIA, 1988.

3. S. Abiteboul and N. Bidoit. Nonfirst normal form relations: An algebra allowing data restructuring. *Journal of Comp. and System Sc.* 33(1):361–393. 1986.

4. S. Abiteboul and S. Grumbach. Base de donnés et objets structurés. *Technique et Science Informatiques* 6(5):383–404. 1987.

5. S. Abiteboul and R. Hull. IFO: A formal semantics database model. *ACM Trans. on Database Syst.* 12(4):297–314. 1987.

6. S. Abiteboul and P. Kanellakis. Object identity as a query language primitive. In *ACM SIGMOD International Conf. on Management of Data*, 1989:159–173.

7. S. Abiteboul, P. Kanellakis, and G. Grahne. On the representation and querying of possible worlds. In *ACM SIGMOD International Conf. on Management of Data*, 1987:34–48.

8. S. Abiteboul and V. Vianu. Equivalence and optimization of relational transactions. *Journal of the ACM* 35(1):70–120. 1988.

9. S. Abiteboul and V. Vianu. Procedural and declarative database update languages. In *Seventh ACM SIGACT SIGMOD SIGART Symp. on Principles of Database Systems*, 1988:240–250.

10. S. Abiteboul and V. Vianu. A transaction-based approach to relational database specification. *Journal of the ACM* 36(4):758–789. 1989.

11. S. Abiteboul and V. Vianu. Procedural languages for database queries and updates. *Journal of Comp. and Syst. Sc.* 41(2):181–229. 1990.

12. S. Abiteboul and V. Vianu. Datalog extensions for database queries and updates. *Journal of Comp. and System Sc.* 43(1):62–124. 1991.

13. A. V. Aho, C. Beeri, and J. D. Ullman. The theory of joins in relational databases. *ACM Trans. on Database Syst.* 4(3):297–314. 1979.

14. A. V. Aho, Y. Sagiv, and J. D. Ullman. Efficient optimization of a class of relational expressions. *ACM Trans. on Database Syst.* 4(4):435–454. 1979.

15. A. V. Aho, Y. Sagiv, and J. D. Ullman. Equivalence of relational expressions. *SIAM Journal on Computing* 8(2):218–246. 1979.

16. A. V. Aho and J. D. Ullman. Universality of data retrieval languages. In *Sixth ACM Symp. on Principles of Programming Languages*, 1979:110–117.

17. ANSI/X3/SPARC Study Group on Database Management Systems. Interim Report 75-02-08. *FDT-Bulletin ACM SIGMOD* 7(2). 1975.

18. H. Arisawa, K. Moriya, and T. Miura. Operations and the properties of non-

first-normal-form databases. In *Ninth International Conf. on Very Large Data Bases, Florence*, 1983:197–204.

19. W. W. Armstrong. Dependency structure of database relationships. In *IFIP Congress*, 1974:580–583.

20. W. W. Armstrong and C. Delobel. Decompositions and functional dependencies in relations. *ACM Trans. on Database Syst.* 5(4):404–430. 1980.

21. A. K. Arora and C. R. Carlson. The information preserving properties of certain relational database transformations. In *Fourth International Conf. on Very Large Data Bases, Berlin*, 1978:352–359.

22. P. Atzeni, G. Ausiello, C. Batini, and M. Moscarini. Inclusion and equivalence between relational database schemata. *Theoretical Computer Science* 19(2):267–285. 1982.

23. P. Atzeni and E. P. F. Chan. Efficient query answering in the representative instance approach. In *Fourth ACM SIGACT SIGMOD Symp. on Principles of Database Systems*, 1985:181–188.

24. P. Atzeni and E. P. F. Chan. Efficient optimization of simple chase join expressions. *ACM Trans. on Database Syst.* 14(2):212–230. 1989.

25. P. Atzeni and E. P. F. Chan. Efficient and optimal query answering on independent schemes. *Theoretical Computer Science* 77(3):291–308. 1990.

26. P. Atzeni and M. C. De Bernardis. A new basis for the weak instance model. In *Sixth ACM SIGACT SIGMOD SIGART Symp. on Principles of Database Systems*, 1987:79–86.

27. P. Atzeni and M. C. De Bernardis. A new interpretation for null values in the weak instance model. *Journal of Comp. and System Sc.* 41(1):25–43. 1990.

28. P. Atzeni and N. M. Morfuni. Functional dependencies in relations with null values. *Information Processing Letters* 18(4):233–238. 1984.

29. P. Atzeni and N. M. Morfuni. Functional dependencies and constraints on null values in database relations. *Information and Control* 70(1):1–31. 1986.

30. P. Atzeni and D. S. Parker Jr. Assumptions in relational database theory. In *ACM SIGACT SIGMOD Symposium on Principles of Database Systems*, 1982:1–9.

31. P. Atzeni and R. Torlone. Updating databases in the weak instance model. In *Eighth ACM SIGACT SIGMOD SIGART Symposium on Principles of Database Systems*, 1989:101–109.

32. P. Atzeni and R. Torlone. Efficient updates to independent database schemes in the weak instance model. In *ACM SIGMOD International Conf. on Management of Data*, 1990:84–93.

33. G. Ausiello, C. Batini, and M. Moscarini. On the equivalence among database schemata. In *Proc. International Conference on Databases*. Aberdeen, 1980.

34. F. Bancilhon. On the completeness of query languages for relational databases. *Mathematical Foundations of Computer Science, LNCS 64*. Berlin: Springer-Verlag, 1978, 112–124.

35. F. Bancilhon, D. Maier, Y. Sagiv, and J. D. Ullman. Magic sets and other strange ways to implement logic programs. In *Fifth ACM SIGACT SIGMOD Symp. on Principles of Database Systems*, 1986:1–15.

36. F. Bancilhon and R. Ramakrishnan. An amateur's introduction to recursive query processing strategies. In *ACM SIGMOD International Conf. on Management of Data*, 1986:16–52.

37. F. Bancilhon, P. Richard, and M. Scholl. VERSO: A relational back end database machine. In D. K. Hsiao, editor, *Advanced Database Machine Architecture*. Englewood Cliffs, N.J.: Prentice-Hall, 1983, 1–18.

38. C. Batini, S. Ceri, and S. B. Navathe. *Database Design with the Entity-Relationship Model*. Menlo Park, Calif.: Benjamin/Cummings, 1991.

39. C. Beeri. Data models and languages for databases. In *ICDT'88 (Second International Conference on Data Base Theory), Bruges, Lecture Notes in Computer Science 326*. Berlin: Springer-Verlag, 1988, 19–37.

40. C. Beeri and P. A. Bernstein. Computational problems related to the design of normal form relational schemas. *ACM Trans. on Database Syst.* 4(1):30–59. 1979.

41. C. Beeri, P. A. Bernstein, and N. Goodman. A sophisticate's introduction to database normalization theory. In *Fourth International Conf. on Very Large Data Bases, Berlin*, 1978:113–124.

42. C. Beeri, R. Fagin, and J. H. Howard. A complete axiomatization for functional and multivalued dependencies. In *ACM SIGMOD International Conf. on Management of Data*, 1978:47–61.

43. C. Beeri and P. Honeyman. Preserving functional dependencies. *SIAM Journal on Computing* 10(3):647–656. 1981.

44. C. Beeri and M. Kifer. An integrated approach to logical design of relational database schemes. *ACM Trans. on Database Syst.* 11(2):134–158. 1986.

45. C. Beeri, A. O. Mendelzon, Y. Sagiv, and J. D. Ullman. Equivalence of relational database schemas. *SIAM Journal on Computing* 10(2):352–370. 1981.

46. C. Beeri and J. Rissanen. Faithful representation of relational database schemata. Report RJ 2722. IBM Research. San Jose, 1980.

47. C. Beeri and M. Y. Vardi. Formal systems for tuple and equality-generating dependencies. *SIAM Journal on Computing* 13(1):76–98. 1984.

48. C. Beeri and M. Y. Vardi. A proof procedure for data dependencies. *Journal of the ACM* 31(4):718–741. 1984.

49. P. A. Bernstein. Synthesizing third normal form relations from functional dependencies. *ACM Trans. on Database Syst.* 1(4): 277–298. 1976.

50. P. A. Bernstein and N. Goodman. What does Boyce-Codd normal form do? In *Sixth International Conf. on Very Large Data Bases, Montreal*, 1980:245–259.

51. J. Biskup. A formal approach to null values in database relations. In H. Gallaire, J. Minker, and J.-M. Nicolas, editors, *Advances in Database Theory*. New York: Plenum, 1981, 299–341.

52. J. Biskup. A foundation of Codd's relational maybe-operations. *ACM Trans. on Database Syst.* 8(4):608–636. 1983.

53. J. Biskup, U. Dayal, and P. A. Bernstein. Synthesizing independent database schemes. In *ACM SIGMOD International Conf. on Management of Data*, 1979:143–151.

54. M. L. Brodie and J. Mylopoulos. Knowledge bases and databases: Semantic vs computational theories of information. In G. Ariav and J. Clifford, editors, *New Directions for Database Systems*. New York: Ablex, 1986.

55. M. L. Brodie and J. Mylopoulos, editors. *On Knowledge Base Management Systems*. Berlin: Springer-Verlag, 1986.

56. M. L. Brodie, J. Mylopoulos, and J. Schmidt, editors. *On Conceptual Modeling*. Berlin: Springer-Verlag, 1984.

57. P. Butterworth, A. Otis, and J. Stein. The Gemstone object database management system. *Comm. of the ACM* 34(10):64–77. 1991.

58. F. Cacace, S. Ceri, S. Crespi-Reghizzi, L. Tanca, and R. Zicari. Integrating object-oriented data modelling with a rule-based programming paradigm. In *ACM SIGMOD International Conf. on Management of Data*, 1990:225–236.

59. M. A. Casanova. The theory of functional and subset dependencies over relational expressions. Technical Report 3/81. Rio de Janeiro: Dept. de Informatica, Pontificia Unversidade Catolica. 1981.

60. M. A. Casanova, R. Fagin, and C. H. Papadimitriou. Inclusion dependencies and their interaction with functional dependencies. *Journal of Comp. and System Sc.* 28(1):29–59. 1984.

61. S. Ceri, S. Crespi-Reghizzi, A. Di Maio, and L. A. Lavazza. ALGRES. *IEEE Trans. on Software Eng.* SE-14(11). 1988.

62. S. Ceri, S. Crespi-Reghizzi, G. Lamperti, L. A. Lavazza, and R. Zicari. ALGRES: An advanced database system for complex applications. *IEEE Software* 7(4):68–78. 1990.

63. S. Ceri and G. Gottlob. Normalization of relations and Prolog. *Communications of the ACM* 29(6):524–544. 1986.

64. S. Ceri, G. Gottlob, and L. Tanca. *Logic Programming and Data Bases*. Berlin: Springer-Verlag, 1989.

65. D. D. Chamberlin et al. A history and evaluation of System R. *Communications of the ACM* 24(10). 1981.

66. E. P. F. Chan. Optimal computation of total projections with unions of simple chase join expressions. In *ACM SIGMOD International Conf. on Management of Data*, 1984:149–163.

67. E. P. F. Chan. A design theory for solving the anomalies problem. *SIAM Journal on Computing* 18(3):429–448. 1989.

68. E. P. F. Chan and H. Hernández. On the desirability of γ-acyclic BCNF database schemes. *Theoretical Computer Science* 62(1–2). 1988.

69. E. P. F. Chan and A. O. Mendelzon. Independent and separable database

schemes. *SIAM Journal on Computing* 16(5):841–851. 1987.

70. A. K. Chandra. Theory of database queries. In *Seventh ACM SIGACT SIG-MOD SIGART Symp. on Principles of Database Systems*, 1988:1–9.

71. A. K. Chandra and D. Harel. Computable queries for relational databases. *Journal of Comp. and System Sc.* 21:333–347. 1980.

72. A. K. Chandra, H. R. Lewis, and J. A. Makowsky. Embedded implicational dependencies and their inference problem. In *Thirteenth ACM SIGACT Symp. on Theory of Computing*, 1981:342–354.

73. A. K. Chandra and M. Y. Vardi. The implication problem for functional and inclusion dependencies is undecidable. *SIAM J. on Computing* 14(3):671–677. 1985.

74. P. P. Chen. The entity-relationship model: Toward a unified view of data. *ACM Trans. on Database Syst.* 1(1):9–36. 1976.

75. D. Chimenti, R. Gamboa, R. Krishnamurti, S. Naqvi, S. Tsur, and C. Zaniolo. The LDL system prototype. *IEEE Trans. on Knowledge and Data Eng.* 2(1):76–90. 1990.

76. E. F. Codd. A relational model for large shared data banks. *Communications of the ACM* 13(6):377–387. 1970.

77. E. F. Codd. A database sublanguage founded on the relational calculus. In *ACM SIGFIDET Workshop on Data Description, Access and Control*, 1971:35–61.

78. E. F. Codd. Further normalization of the data base relational model. In R. Rustin, editor, *Data Base Systems*. Englewood Cliffs, N.J.: Prentice-Hall, 1972, 33–64.

79. E. F. Codd. Relational completeness of data base sublanguages. In R. Rustin, editor, *Data Base Systems*. Englewood Cliffs, N.J.: Prentice-Hall, 1972, 65–98.

80. E. F. Codd. Recent investigations into relational database systems. In *IFIP Congress*, 1974:1017–1021.

81. E. F. Codd. Extending the database relational model to capture more meaning. *ACM Trans. on Database Syst.* 4(4):397–434. 1979.

82. E. F. Codd. 'Universal' relation fails to replace relational model. Letter to the editor. *IEEE Software* 5(4):4–6. 1988.

83. S. Cosmadakis, P. C. Kanellakis, and M. Vardi. Polynomial-time implication problems for unary inclusion dependencies. *Journal of the ACM* 37(1):15–46. 1990.

84. P. Dadam et al. A DBMS prototype to support extended NF^2 relations: An integrated view of flat tables and hierarchies. In *ACM SIGMOD International Conf. on Management of Data*, 1986:356–367.

85. C. J. Date. *An Introduction to Database Systems*. Volume 2. Reading, Mass.: Addison Wesley, 1983.

86. C. J. Date. *A Guide to DB2*. Reading, Mass.: Addison Wesley, 1984.

87. C. J. Date. *An Introduction to Database Systems*. 4th ed. Volume 1. Reading,

Mass.: Addison Wesley, 1986.

88. C. J. Date. *A Guide to INGRES*. Reading, Mass.: Addison Wesley, 1987.

89. P. DeBra and J. Paredaens. An algorithm for horizontal decompositions. *Information Processing Letters* 17(2):91–95. 1983.

90. P. DeBra and J. Paredaens. Horizontal decompositions for handling exceptions to functional dependencies. In H. Gallaire, J. Minker, and J.-M. Nicolas, editors, *Advances in Database Theory*. Volume 2. New York: Plenum, 1984, 123–144.

91. C. Delobel and R. C. Casey. Decomposition of a database and the theory of Boolean switching functions. *IBM Journal of Research and Development* 17(5):370–386. 1972.

92. R. Demolombe. Syntactical characterization of a subset of domain independent formulas. Report. Toulouse: ONERA-CERT, 1982.

93. O. Deux et al. The O_2 system. *Communications of the ACM* 34(10):34–49. 1991.

94. R. Di Paola. The recursive unsolvability of the decision problem for the class of definite formulas. *Journal of the ACM* 16(2):324–327. 1969.

95. R. A. ElMasri and S. B. Navathe. *Fundamentals of Database Systems*. Menlo Park, Calif.: Benjamin/Cummings, 1988.

96. H. B. Enderton. *A Mathematical Introduction to Logic*. New York: Academic Press, 1972.

97. R. Fagin. The decomposition versus the synthetic approach to relational database design. In *Third International Conf. on Very Large Data Bases, Tokyo*, 1977:441–446.

98. R. Fagin. Multivalued dependencies and a new normal form for relational databases. *ACM Trans. on Database Syst.* 2(3):262–278. 1977.

99. R. Fagin. Normal forms and relational database operators. In *ACM SIGMOD International Conf. on Management of Data*, 1979:123–134.

100. R. Fagin. A normal form for relational databases that is based on domains and keys. *ACM Trans. on Database Syst.* 6(3):310–319. 1981.

101. R. Fagin. Horn clauses and database dependencies. *Journal of the ACM* 29(4): 952–983. 1982.

102. R. Fagin, A. O. Mendelzon, and J. D. Ullman. A simplified universal relation assumption and its properties. *ACM Trans. on Database Syst.* 7(3):343–360. 1982.

103. P. C. Fischer, L. V. Saxton, S. J. Thomas, and D. Van Gucht. Interactions between dependencies and nested relational structures. *Journal of Comp. and System Sc.* 31(2):343–354. 1985.

104. P. C. Fischer and S. J. Thomas. Operators for non-first-normal-form relations. In *Proc. of IEEE Computer Software Applications*, 1983:464–475.

105. P. C. Fischer and D. Van Gucht. Weak multivalued dependencies. In *Third ACM Symposium on Principles of Database Systems*, 1984:266–274.

106. A. L. Furtado and L. Kerschberg. An algebra of quotient relations. In *ACM SIGMOD International Conf. on Management of Data*, 1977:1–8.

107. H. Gallaire and J. Minker, editors. *Logic and Databases*. New York: Plenum, 1978.

108. H. Gallaire, J. Minker, and J. M. Nicolas, editors. *Advances in Database Theory*. Volume 1. New York: Plenum, 1981.

109. H. Gallaire, J. Minker, and J. M. Nicolas, editors. *Advances in Database Theory*. Volume 2. New York: Plenum, 1984.

110. H. Gallaire, J. Minker, and J. M. Nicolas. Logic and databases: A deductive approach. *ACM Computing Surveys* 16(2):153–185. 1984.

111. G. Gardarin and P. Valduriez. *Relational Databases and Knowledge Bases*. Reading, Mass.: Addison Wesley, 1990.

112. M. R. Garey and D. S. Johnson. *Computers and Intractability*. San Francisco: W. H. Freeman and Company, 1979.

113. B. S. Goldstein. Contraints on null values in relational databases. In *Seventh Int'l Conf. on Very Large Data Bases*, 1981:101–111.

114. M. Graham, A. O. Mendelzon, and M. Y. Vardi. Notions of dependency satisfaction. *Journal of the ACM* 33(1):105–129. 1986.

115. M. Graham and M. Yannakakis. Independent database schemas. *Journal of Comp. and System Sc.* 28(1):121–141. 1984.

116. G. Grahne. Horn tables—an efficient tool for handling incomplete information in databases. In *Eighth ACM SIGACT SIGMOD SIGART Symposium on Principles of Database Systems*, 1989:75–82.

117. J. Grant. Null values in a relational database. *Information Processing Letters* 6(5):156–159. 1977.

118. J. Grant and J. Minker. The impact of logic programming on databases. *Communications of the ACM* 35(3):66–81. 1992.

119. H. Hernández and E. P. F. Chan. Constant-time-maintainable BCNF database schemes. *ACM Trans. on Database Syst.* 16(4): 571–599. 1991.

120. P. Honeyman. Testing satisfaction of functional dependencies. *Journal of the ACM* 29(3):668–677. 1982.

121. R. Hull. A survey of theoretical research on typed complex database objects. In J. Paredaens, editor, *Databases*. New York: Academic Press, 1988, 193–256.

122. R. Hull and M. Yoshikawa. ILOG: Declarative creation and manipulation of object identifiers. In *Sixteenth International Conference on Very Large Data Bases, Brisbane*, 1990:455–468.

123. R. B. Hull. Relative information capacity of simple relational schemata. *SIAM Journal on Computing* 15(3):856–886. 1986.

124. R. B. Hull and R. King. Semantic database modelling: Survey, applications and research issues. *ACM Comp. Surveys* 19(3):201–260. 1987.

125. T. Imielinski and W. Lipski. On representing incomplete information in relational databases. In *Seventh International Conf. on Very Large Data Bases*,

Cannes, 1981:388–397.

126. T. Imielinski and W. Lipski. Incomplete information and dependencies in relational databases. In *ACM SIGMOD International Conf. on Management of Data*, 1983:178–184.

127. T. Imielinski and W. Lipski. Incomplete information in relational databases. *Journal of the ACM* 31(4):761–791. 1984.

128. M. Ito, M. Iwasaki, and T. Kasami. Some results on the representative instance in relational databases. *SIAM Journal on Computing* 14(2):334–354. 1985.

129. G. Jaeschke and H.-J. Schek. Remarks on the algebra for non first normal form relations. In *ACM SIGACT SIGMOD Symp. on Principles of Database Systems*, 1982:124–138.

130. J. H. Jou and P. C. Fischer. The complexity of recognizing 3NF relation schemes. *Information Processing Letters* 14(4):187–190. 1983.

131. Y. Kambayashi, K. Tanaka, and K. Takeda. Synthesis of unnormalized relations incorporating more meaning. *Inf. Sci.* 29:201–247. 1983.

132. P. Kandzia and H. Klein. On equivalence of relational databases in connection with normalization. In *Workshop on Formal Bases for Databases*. Toulouse: ONERA-CERT, 1979.

133. P. C. Kanellakis, S. Cosmadakis, and M. Vardi. Unary inclusion dependencies have polynomial-time inference problems. In *Fifteeenth ACM SIGACT Symp. on Theory of Computing*, 1983:, 264–277.

134. A. M. Keller. Set-theoretic problems of null completion in relational databases. *Information Processing Letters* 22(5):261–265. 1986.

135. W. Kent. Consequences of assuming a universal relation. *ACM Trans. on Database Syst.* 6(4):539–556. 1981.

136. W. Kent. The universal relation revisited. *ACM Trans. on Database Syst.* 8(4):644–648. 1983.

137. L. Kerschberg, editor. *Proc. First Workshop on Expert Database Systems*. Menlo Park, Calif.: Benjamin/Cummings, 1986.

138. L. Kerschberg, editor. *Proc. First Conf. on Expert Database Systems*. Menlo Park, Calif.: Benjamin/Cummings, 1987.

139. L. Kerschberg, editor. *Proc. Second Conf. on Expert Database Systems*. Menlo Park, Calif.: Benjamin/Cummings, 1988.

140. L. Kerschberg, editor. *Proc. Third Conf. on Expert Database Systems*. Menlo Park, Calif.: Benjamin/Cummings, 1990.

141. W. Kim. Object-oriented databases: Definition and research directions. *IEEE Trans. on Knowledge and Data Eng.* 2(3):327–341. 1990.

142. W. Kim, J. F. Garza, N. Ballou, and D. Woelk. Architecture of the ORION next-generation database system. *IEEE Trans. on Knowledge and Data Eng.* 2(1):109–124. 1990.

143. A. Klug. Equivalence of relational algebra and relational calculus query languages having aggregate functions. *Journal of the ACM* 29(3):699–717. 1982.

144. H. F. Korth and A. Silberschatz. *Database Systems Concepts*. New York: McGraw-Hill, 1986.

145. H. F. Korth and J. D. Ullman. System/U: A system based on the universal relation assumption. XP1 Workshop on Relational Database Theory, State University of New York, Stonybrook, N. Y. 1980.

146. G. M. Kuper. *The Logical Data Model: A New Approach to Database Logic*. Ph.D. diss. Stanford University, 1985.

147. G. M. Kuper and M. Y. Vardi. A new approach to database logic. In *Third ACM SIGACT SIGMOD Symp. on Principles of Database Systems*, 1984:86–96.

148. M. Lacroix and A. Pirotte. Generalized joins. *ACM SIGMOD Record* 8(3):14–15. 1976.

149. C. Lamb, G. Landis, J. Orenstein, and D. Weinreb. The ObjectStore database system. *Communications of the ACM* 34(10):50–63. 1991.

150. C. H. LeDoux and D. S. Parker. Reflections on Boyce-Codd normal form. In *Eighth International Conf. on Very Large Data Bases, Mexico City*, 1982:131–141.

151. N. Lerat and W. Lipski, Jr. Nonapplicable nulls. *Theoretical Computer Science* 46(1):67–82. 1986.

152. Y. E. Lien. Multivalued dependencies with null values in relational databases. In *Fifth International Conf. on Very Large Data Bases*, 1979:61–66.

153. Y. E. Lien. On the equivalence of database models. *Journal of the ACM* 29(2):333–362. 1982.

154. W. Lipski, Jr. Two NP-complete problems related to information retrieval. In *Fundamentals of Computation Theory, Lecture Notes in Computer Science 56*. Berlin: Springer-Verlag, 1977, 452–458.

155. W. Lipski, Jr. On semantic issues connected with incomplete information databases. *ACM Trans. on Database Syst.* 4(3):262–296. 1979.

156. W. Lipski, Jr. On databases with incomplete information. *Journal of the ACM* 28(1):41–70. 1981.

157. J. W. Lloyd. *Foundations of Logic Programming*. 2nd ed. Berlin: Springer-Verlag, 1987.

158. G. M. Lohman, B. Lindsay, H. Pirahesh, and K. B. Schiefer. Extensions to Starburst: Objects, types, functions, rules. *Communications of the ACM* 34(10):94–109. 1991.

159. C. L. Lucchesi and S. L. Osborn. Candidate keys for relations. *Journal of Comp. and System Sc.* 17(2):270–279. 1978.

160. D. Maier. Discarding the universal relation assumption: Preliminary report. XP1 Workshop on Relational Database Theory, State University of New York, Stonybrook, N. Y. 1980.

161. D. Maier. Minimum covers in the relational database model. *Journal of the ACM* 27(4):664–674. 1980.

162. D. Maier. *The Theory of Relational Databases*. Potomac, Md.: Computer Science Press, 1983.

163. D. Maier, A. O. Mendelzon, F. Sadri, and J. D. Ullman. Adequacy of decompositions in relational databases. *Journal of Computer and System Sc.* 21(3):368–379. 1980.

164. D. Maier, A. O. Mendelzon, and Y. Sagiv. Testing implications of data dependencies. *ACM Trans. on Database Syst.* 4(4):455–468. 1979.

165. D. Maier, D. Rozenshtein, and D. S. Warren. Window functions. In P. C. Kanellakis and F. P. Preparata, editors, *Advances in Computing Research*. Volume 3. Greenwich, Ct.: JAI Press, 1986, 213–246.

166. D. Maier and J. D. Ullman. Fragments of relations: First hack. XP2 Workshop on Relational Database Theory, Penn State University, State College, Pennsylvania, 1981.

167. D. Maier, J. D. Ullman, and M. Vardi. On the foundations of the universal relation model. *ACM Trans. on Database Syst.* 9(2):283–308. 1984.

168. A. Makinouchi. A consideration on normal form of not necessarily normalized relations. In *Third International Conf. on Very Large Data Bases, Tokyo,* 1977:447–453.

169. E. Mendelson. *Introduction to Mathematical Logic*. New York: Van Nostrand-Rehinold, 1978.

170. A. O. Mendelzon. Database states and their tableaux. *ACM Trans. on Database Syst.* 9(2):264–282. 1984.

171. J. Minker, editor. *Foundations of Deductive Databases and Logic Programming*. Los Altos, Calif.: Morgan Kauffman, 1988.

172. J. C. Mitchell. The implication problem for functional and inclusion dependencies. *Information and Control* 56(1):154–173. 1983.

173. S. Naqvi and S. Tsur. *A Logical Language for Data and Knowledge Bases*. Potomac, Md.: Computer Science Press, 1989.

174. J.-M. Nicolas. Logic for improving integrity checking in relational databases. *Acta Informatica* 18(3):227–253. 1982.

175. S. L. Osborn. Towards a universal relation interface. In *Fifth International Conf. on Very Large Data Bases, Rio de Janeiro,* 1979:52–60.

176. Z. M. Ozsoyoglu and L. Y. Yuan. A new normal form for nested relations. *ACM Trans. on Database Syst.* 12(1):111–136. 1987.

177. J. Paredaens. About functional dependencies in a database structure and their coverings. Report 342. Philips MBLE Lab. 1977.

178. J. Paredaens. On the expressive power of the relational algebra. *Information Processing Letters* 7(2):107–111. 1978.

179. A. Pirotte. High-level database languages. In H. Gallaire and J. Minker, editors, *Logic and Databases*. New York: Plenum, 1978, 409–435.

180. R. Reiter. On closed world databases. In H. Gallaire and J. Minker, editors, *Logic and Databases*. New York: Plenum, 1978, 55–76.

181. R. Reiter. Towards a logical reconstruction of relational database theory. In M. L. Brodie, J. Mylopoulos, and J. W. Schmidt, editors, *On Conceptual Modelling*. Berlin: Springer-Verlag, 1984.

182. R. Reiter. Foundations for knowledge-based systems. In *IFIP Congress*, 1986.

183. J. Rissanen. Theory of joins for relational databases — a tutorial survey. In *Mathematical Foundations of Computer Science, Lecture Notes in Computer Science 64*. Berlin: Springer-Verlag, 1979, 537–551.

184. J. Rissanen. Independent components of relations. *ACM Trans. on Database Syst.* 2(4):317–325. 1982.

185. J. Rissanen. On equivalence of database schemes. In *ACM SIGACT SIGMOD Symp. on Principles of Database Systems*, 1982:23–26.

186. J. Rissanen and C. Delobel. Decomposition of files, a basis for data storage and retrieval. Report RJ 1220. IBM Research, San Jose, 1973.

187. M. A. Roth and H. F. Korth. The design of ¬1NF relational databases into nested normal form. In *ACM SIGMOD International Conf. on Management of Data*, 1987:143–159.

188. M. A. Roth, H. F. Korth, and D. S. Batory. SQL/NF: A query language for ¬1NF relational databases. *Information Systems* 12(1):99–114. 1987.

189. M. A. Roth, H. F. Korth, and A. Silberschatz. Extended algebra and calculus for ¬1NF relational databases. *ACM Trans. on Database Syst.* 13(4):389–417. 1988.

190. F. Sadri and J. D. Ullman. Template dependencies: A large class of dependencies in the relational model and its complete axiomatization. *Journal of the ACM* 29(2):363–372. 1982.

191. Y. Sagiv. Can we use the universal instance assumption without using nulls? In *ACM SIGMOD International Conf. on Management of Data*, 1981:108–120.

192. Y. Sagiv. A characterization of globally consistent databases and their correct access paths. *ACM Trans. on Database Systems* 8(2):266–286. 1983.

193. Y. Sagiv. Evaluation of queries in independent database schemes. *Journal of the ACM* 38(1):120–161. 1991.

194. H.-J. Schek. Towards a basic relational NF2 algebra processor. In *Eleventh International Conference on Very Large Data Bases, Stockholm*, 1985:173–182.

195. H.-J. Schek, H. B. Paul, M. H. Scholl, and G. Weikum. The DASDBS project: Objectives, experiences, and future prospects. *IEEE Trans. on Knowledge and Data Eng.* 2(1):25–43. 1990.

196. H.-J. Schek and P. Pistor. Data structures for an integrated database management and information retrieval system. *Eighth International Conf. on Very Large Data Bases, Mexico City*, 1982.

197. H.-J. Schek and M. H. Scholl. The relational model with relation-valued attributes. *Information Systems*, 11(2). 1986.

198. E. Sciore. *The Universal Instance and Database Design*. Ph.D. diss. Princeton University (Dept. of EECS), 1980.

199. E. Sciore. A complete axiomatization of full join dependencies. *Journal of the ACM* 29(2):373–393. 1982.

200. A. Silberschatz, M. Stonebraker, and J.D. Ullman. Database systems: Achievements and opportunities. *Communications of the ACM* 34(10):110–120. 1991.

201. J. M. Smith. A normal form for abstract syntax. In *Fourth International Conf. on Very Large Data Bases, Berlin,* 1978:156–162.

202. J. M. Smith and D. C. P. Smith. Database abstractions: Aggregation and generalization. *ACM Trans. on Database Syst.* 2(2):105–133. 1977.

203. M. Stonebraker, editor. *The INGRES Papers.* Reading, Mass.: Addison Wesley, 1986.

204. M. Stonebraker. Future trends in database systems. *IEEE Trans. on Knowledge and Data Eng.* 1(1):33–44. 1989.

205. M. Stonebraker and G. Kemnitz. The Postgres next-generation database management system. *Comm. of the ACM* 34(10):78–93. 1991.

206. T. J. Teorey and J. P. Fry. *Database Design.* Englewood Cliffs, N.J.: Prentice-Hall, 1982.

207. S. J. Thomas. *A non-first-normal-form relational database model.* Ph.D. diss. Vanderbilt University, Nashville, Tenn. 1983.

208. S. J. Thomas and P. C. Fischer. Nested relational structures. In P. C. Kanellakis and F. P. Preparata, editors, *Advances in Computing Research.* Volume 3. Greenwich, Ct.: JAI Press, 1986, 269–307.

209. R. Topor. Domain-independent formulas and databases. *Theoretical Computer Science* 52:281–306. 1986.

210. D. Tsichritzis and F. H. Lochovski. *Data Models.* Englewood Cliffs, N.J.: Prentice-Hall, 1982.

211. D.-M. Tsou and P. C. Fischer. Decomposition of a relation scheme into Boyce-Codd normal form. *SIGACT News* 14(3):23–29. 1982.

212. J. D. Ullman. *Principles of Database Systems.* 2nd ed. Potomac, Md.: Computer Science Press, 1982.

213. J. D. Ullman. *Principles of Database Systems.* Potomac, Md.: Computer Science Press, 1982.

214. J. D. Ullman. The U. R. strikes back. In *ACM SIGACT SIGMOD Symp. on Principles of Database Systems,* 1982:10–22.

215. J. D. Ullman. On Kent's 'Consequences of assuming a universal relation'. *ACM Trans. on Database Syst.* 8(4):637–643. 1983.

216. J. D. Ullman. Implementation of logical query languages for databases. *ACM Trans. on Database Syst.* 10(3):289–321. 1985.

217. J. D. Ullman. *Principles of Database and Knowledge Base Systems.* Volume 1. Potomac, Md.: Computer Science Press, 1988.

218. J. D. Ullman. *Principles of Database and Knowledge Base Systems.* Volume 2. Potomac, Md.: Computer Science Press, 1989.

219. P. Valduriez and G. Gardarin. *Analysis and Comparison of Relational Database*

Systems. Reading, Mass.: Addison Wesley, 1989.

220. M. Y. Vardi. The decision problem for database dependencies. *Information Processing Letters* 12(5):251–254. 1981.

221. M. Y. Vardi. The implication and finite implication problems for typed template dependencies. *Journal of Comp. and System Sc.* 28(1):3–28. 1984.

222. M. Y. Vardi. Response to a letter to the editor. *IEEE Software* 5(4):4–6. 1988.

223. M. Y. Vardi. The universal relation data model for logical independence. *IEEE Software* 5(2):80–85. 1988.

224. Y. Vassiliou. Null values in database management: A denotational semantics approach. *ACM SIGMOD International Conf. on Management of Data,* 1979:162–169.

225. Y. Vassiliou. *A Formal Treatment of Imperfection in Database Management.* Ph.D. diss. University of Toronto, 1980.

226. Y. Vassiliou. Functional dependencies and incomplete information. In *Sixth International Conf. on Very Large Data Bases, Montreal,* 1980:260–269.

227. Verso, J. (pen name for the Verso team). Verso: A database machine based on non-1NF relations. Technical Report 523. INRIA, 1986.

228. K. Wang and M. H. Graham. Constant-time maintainability: A generalization of independence. *ACM Trans. on Database Syst.* 17(2):201–246. 1992.

229. K. Wilkinson, P. Lyngbaek, and W. Hasan. The IRIS architecture and implementation. *IEEE Trans. on Knowledge and Data Eng.* 2(1):63–75. 1990.

230. E. Wong. A statistical approach to incomplete information in database systems. *ACM Trans. on Database Syst.* 7(3):470–488. 1982.

231. M. Yannakakis and C. Papadimitriou. Algebraic dependencies. *Journal of Comp. and System Sc.* 21(1):2–41. 1982.

232. C. Zaniolo. *Analysis and Design of Relational Schemata for Database Systems.* Ph.D. diss. UCLA, 1976.

233. C. Zaniolo. Relational views in a database system; support for queries. In *IEEE Int. Conference on Computer Software and Applications,* 1977:267–275.

234. C. Zaniolo. A new normal form for the design of relational database schemas. *ACM Trans. on Database Syst.* 7(3):489–499. 1982.

235. C. Zaniolo. Database relations with null values. *Journal of Comp. and System Sc.* 28(1):142–166. 1984.

236. C. Zaniolo, editor. Special Issue on Databases and Logic. *Data Engineering,* 10(4). IEEE Computer Society, 1987.

237. C. Zaniolo and M. A. Melkanoff. On the design of relational database schemata. *ACM Trans. on Database Syst.* 6(1):1–47. 1981.

238. M. M. Zloof. Query-by-Example: A database language. *IBM Systems Journal* 16(4):324–343. 1977.

Index